Crete

Jeanne Oliver

D1535616

LONELY PLANET PUBLICATIONS
Melbourne • Oakland • London • Paris

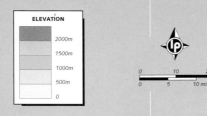

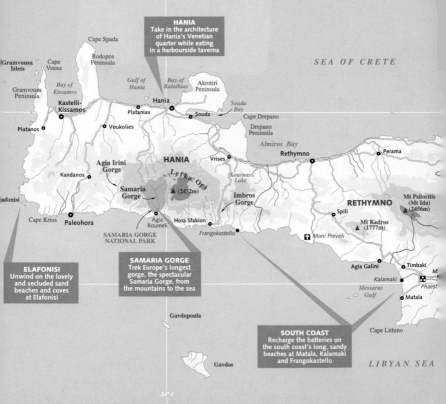

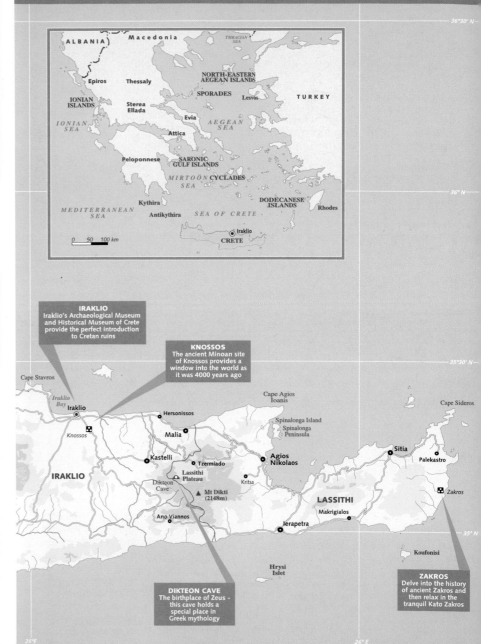

CRETE

IRAKLIO
Iraklio's Archaeological Museum
and Historical Museum of Crete
provide the perfect introduction
to Cretan ruins

KNOSSOS
The ancient Minoan site
of Knossos provides a
window into the world as
it was 4000 years ago

DIKTEON CAVE
The birthplace of Zeus –
this cave holds a
special place in
Greek mythology

ZAKROS
Delve into the history
of ancient Zakros and
then relax in the
tranquil Kato Zakros

Crete
1st edition – April 2000

Published by
Lonely Planet Publications Pty Ltd A.C.N. 005 607 983
192 Burwood Rd, Hawthorn, Victoria 3122, Australia

Lonely Planet Offices
Australia PO Box 617, Hawthorn, Victoria 3122
USA 150 Linden St, Oakland, CA 94607
UK 10a Spring Place, London NW5 3BH
France 1 rue du Dahomey, 75011 Paris

Photographs
Many of the images in this guide are available for licensing from
Lonely Planet Images.
email: lpi@lonelyplanet.com.au

Front cover photograph
Shapes and shadows of the early morning outside a cafe in Loutro
(Trevor Creighton)

ISBN 1 86450 074 3

text & maps © Lonely Planet 2000
photos © photographers as indicated 2000

Printed by Colorcraft Ltd, Hong Kong

Although the authors
and Lonely Planet try
to make the informa-
tion as accurate as
possible, we accept
no responsibility for
any loss, injury or
inconvenience sus-
tained by anyone
using this book.

Contents – Text

THE AUTHOR

THIS BOOK

FOREWORD

INTRODUCTION

FACTS ABOUT CRETE

FACTS FOR THE VISITOR 51

GETTING THERE & AWAY 86

GETTING AROUND 99

HANIA 106

INDEX   252

MAP LEGEND   back page

METRIC CONVERSION   inside back cover

Contents – Maps

CRETE MAP INDEX

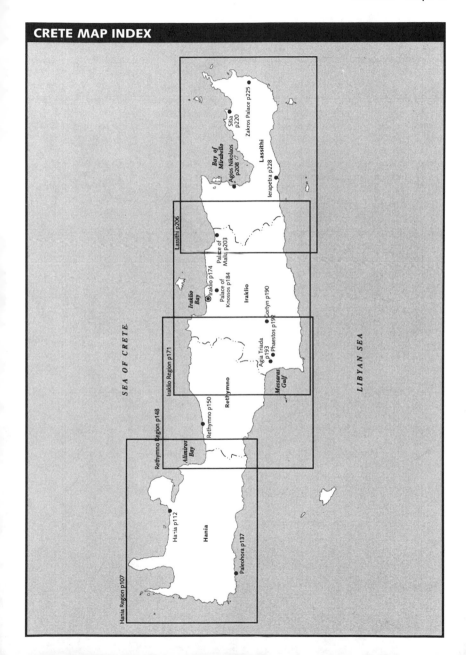

The Author

Jeanne Oliver

Born in New Jersey, USA, Jeanne spent her childhood mulling over the New York Times travel section and plotting her future voyages. She received a BA in English and then a law degree but her legal practice was interrupted by ever-more-frequent trips to Central and South America, Europe, the Middle East, Africa and Asia. She finally settled in France to work as a travel writer. Jeanne has contributed to Lonely Planet's *Mediterranean Europe* and *Eastern Europe* guides and wrote the 1st edition of *Croatia*. She can be found in cyberspace at j-oliver@worldnet.fr.

FROM THE AUTHOR

I would like to thank Toula Chryssanthopoulou of the Greek National Tourism Office (EOT) in Athens for her valuable assistance. Haris Kakoulakis of the EOT office in Iraklion provided an extraordinary amount of advice and assistance that greatly aided the research of this book. In Iraklion, Motor Club and Prince Travel helped with my transportation arrangements. Nikos Petrakis and Georgia Stavrakaki of Sitia went out of their way to show me the Lassithi region; Apostolis Kimalis and Antonia Karandinou made me feel at home in Sitia. Rony Oren and Dimitri Petridis were wonderful hosts in Bali as was Eftihis Konstadinitis in Hania and Manos Dermitzakis in Ierapetra. A warm thanks to Johanne Gaudreau for her introduction to Argiroupolis.

In Nice I would like to thank Jeanette Macdonald and Jennifer Jones for their help and especially Frederic Tiglio for his unstinting support. Thanks also to my patient editors at Lonely Planet Katie Cody and Darren O'Connell.

This Book

From the Publisher

The 1st edition of *Crete* was produced in the Melbourne office and was coordinated by Darren O'Connell (editorial) and Heath Comrie (mapping and design). Susannah Farfor, Fiona Meiers, Ada Cheung and Tony Davidson assisted with editing and proofing, and Yvonne Bischofberger, Ann Jeffree, Shahara Ahmed, Joelene Kowalski, Celia Wood and Verity Campbell assisted with mapping. Rachel Imeson, Anna Judd and Maree Styles assisted with layout. Thanks also to Tim Uden and Paul Dawson for Quark support.

Illustrations were supplied by Matt King, Quentin Frayne prepared the Language section, and the cover was designed by Jamieson Gross. Photographs were supplied by Fiona Croyden at Lonely Planet Images. Special thanks to Rachel Imeson, Katie Cody, Tony Davidson and Verity Campbell for their guidance.

Foreword

ABOUT LONELY PLANET GUIDEBOOKS

The story begins with a classic travel adventure: Tony and Maureen Wheeler's 1972 journey across Europe and Asia to Australia. Useful information about the overland trail did not exist at that time, so Tony and Maureen published the first Lonely Planet guidebook to meet a growing need.

From a kitchen table, then from a tiny office in Melbourne (Australia), Lonely Planet has become the largest independent travel publisher in the world, an international company with offices in Melbourne, Oakland (USA), London (UK) and Paris (France).

Today Lonely Planet guidebooks cover the globe. There is an ever-growing list of books and there's information in a variety of forms and media. Some things haven't changed. The main aim is still to help make it possible for adventurous travellers to get out there – to explore and better understand the world.

At Lonely Planet we believe travellers can make a positive contribution to the countries they visit – if they respect their host communities and spend their money wisely. Since 1986 a percentage of the income from each book has been donated to aid projects and human rights campaigns.

Updates Lonely Planet thoroughly updates each guidebook as often as possible. This usually means there are around two years between editions, although for more unusual or more stable destinations the gap can be longer. Check the imprint page (following the colour map at the beginning of the book) for publication dates.

Between editions up-to-date information is available in two free newsletters – the paper *Planet Talk* and email *Comet* (to subscribe, contact any Lonely Planet office) – and on our Web site at www.lonelyplanet.com. The *Upgrades* section of the Web site covers a number of important and volatile destinations and is regularly updated by Lonely Planet authors. *Scoop* covers news and current affairs relevant to travellers. And, lastly, the *Thorn Tree* bulletin board and *Postcards* section of the site carry unverified, but fascinating, reports from travellers.

Correspondence The process of creating new editions begins with the letters, postcards and emails received from travellers. This correspondence often includes suggestions, criticisms and comments about the current editions. Interesting excerpts are immediately passed on via newsletters and the Web site, and everything goes to our authors to be verified when they're researching on the road. We're keen to get more feedback from organisations or individuals who represent communities visited by travellers.

Lonely Planet gathers information for everyone who's curious about the planet – and especially for those who explore it first-hand. Through guidebooks, phrasebooks, activity guides, maps, literature, newsletters, image library, TV series and Web site we act as an information exchange for a worldwide community of travellers.

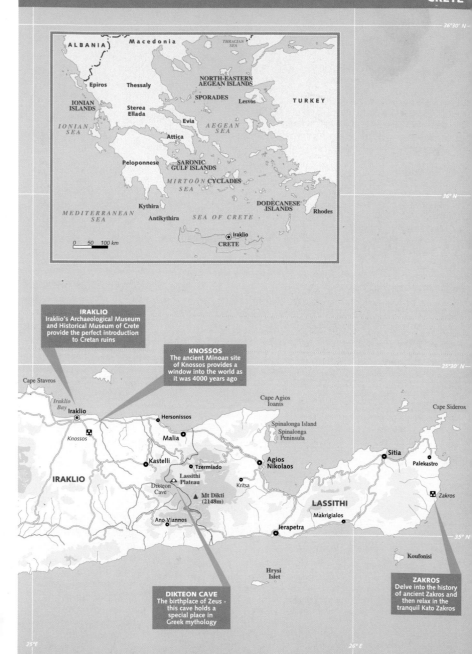

IRAKLIO
Iraklio's Archaeological Museum and Historical Museum of Crete provide the perfect introduction to Cretan ruins

KNOSSOS
The ancient Minoan site of Knossos provides a window into the world as it was 4000 years ago

DIKTEON CAVE
The birthplace of Zeus - this cave holds a special place in Greek mythology

ZAKROS
Delve into the history of ancient Zakros and then relax in the tranquil Kato Zakros

ALBANIA
Macedonia
THRACIAN SEA
Epiros
Thessaly
NORTH-EASTERN AEGEAN ISLANDS
SPORADES
Lesvos
TURKEY
IONIAN ISLANDS
Sterea Ellada
IONIAN SEA
Evia
AEGEAN SEA
Attica
Peloponnese
SARONIC GULF ISLANDS
MIRTOÖN SEA
CYCLADES
MEDITERRANEAN SEA
Kythira
DODECANESE ISLANDS
Rhodes
Antikythira
SEA OF CRETE
Iraklio
CRETE

0   50 100 km

36°30' N
36° N
25°30' N
35° N

Cape Stavros
Iraklio Bay
Iraklio
Knossos
Hersonissos
Malia
Kastelli
IRAKLIO
Tzermiado
Lassithi Plateau
Dikteon Cave
Mt Dikti (2148m)
Ano Viannos
Cape Agios Ioanis
Spinalonga Island
Spinalonga Peninsula
Agios Nikolaos
Kritsa
LASSITHI
Makrigialos
Ierapetra
Cape Sideros
Sitia
Palekastro
Zakros
Koufonisi
Hrysi Islet

25° E
26° E

Crete
Ist edition – April 2000

Published by
Lonely Planet Publications Pty Ltd A.C.N. 005 607 983
192 Burwood Rd, Hawthorn, Victoria 3122, Australia

Lonely Planet Offices
Australia PO Box 617, Hawthorn, Victoria 3122
USA 150 Linden St, Oakland, CA 94607
UK 10a Spring Place, London NW5 3BH
France 1 rue du Dahomey, 75011 Paris

Photographs
Many of the images in this guide are available for licensing from
Lonely Planet Images.
email: lpi@lonelyplanet.com.au

Front cover photograph
Shapes and shadows of the early morning outside a cafe in Loutro
(Trevor Creighton)

ISBN 1 86450 074 3

text & maps © Lonely Planet 2000
photos © photographers as indicated 2000

Printed by Colorcraft Ltd, Hong Kong

Contents – Text

2 Contents – Text

RETHYMNO   147

IRAKLIO   170

LASSITHI   205

LANGUAGE   231

GLOSSARY   237

INDEX 252

MAP LEGEND back page

METRIC CONVERSION inside back cover

Contents – Maps

CRETE MAP INDEX

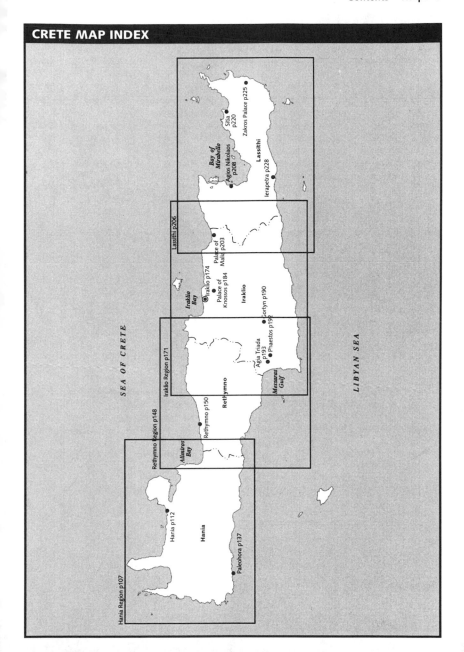

SEA OF CRETE

LIBYAN SEA

Sitia p220
Zakros Palace p225
Lassithi p228
Bay of Mirabello
Agios Nikolaos p208
Ierapetra

Lassithi p206
Palace of Malia p203
Iraklio p174
Iraklio Bay
Palace of Knossos p184
Iraklio
Gortyn p190
Phaestos p192
Iraklio Region p171
Agia Triada p193
Messaras Gulf
Rethymno p150
Rethymno
Rethymno Region p148
Almiros Bay
Hania p112
Hania
Paleohora p137
Hania Region p107

The Author

Jeanne Oliver

Born in New Jersey, USA, Jeanne spent her childhood mulling over the New York Times travel section and plotting her future voyages. She received a BA in English and then a law degree but her legal practice was interrupted by ever-more-frequent trips to Central and South America, Europe, the Middle East, Africa and Asia. She finally settled in France to work as a travel writer. Jeanne has contributed to Lonely Planet's *Mediterranean Europe* and *Eastern Europe* guides and wrote the 1st edition of *Croatia*. She can be found in cyberspace at j-oliver@worldnet.fr.

FROM THE AUTHOR

I would like to thank Toula Chryssanthopoulou of the Greek National Tourism Office (EOT) in Athens for her valuable assistance. Haris Kakoulakis of the EOT office in Iraklion provided an extraordinary amount of advice and assistance that greatly aided the research of this book. In Iraklion, Motor Club and Prince Travel helped with my transportation arrangements. Nikos Petrakis and Georgia Stavrakaki of Sitia went out of their way to show me the Lassithi region; Apostolis Kimalis and Antonia Karandinou made me feel at home in Sitia. Rony Oren and Dimitri Petridis were wonderful hosts in Bali as was Eftihis Konstadinitis in Hania and Manos Dermitzakis in Ierapetra. A warm thanks to Johanne Gaudreau for her introduction to Argiroupolis.

In Nice I would like to thank Jeanette Macdonald and Jennifer Jones for their help and especially Frederic Tiglio for his unstinting support. Thanks also to my patient editors at Lonely Planet Katie Cody and Darren O'Connell.

Research Authors aim to gather sufficient practical information to enable travellers to make informed choices and to make the mechanics of a journey run smoothly. They also research historical and cultural background to help enrich the travel experience and allow travellers to understand and respond appropriately to cultural and environmental issues.

Authors don't stay in every hotel because that would mean spending a couple of months in each medium-sized city and, no, they don't eat at every restaurant because that would mean stretching belts beyond capacity. They do visit hotels and restaurants to check standards and prices, but feedback based on readers' direct experiences can be very helpful.

Many of our authors work undercover, others aren't so secretive. None of them accept freebies in exchange for positive write-ups. And none of our guidebooks contain any advertising.

Production Authors submit their raw manuscripts and maps to offices in Australia, USA, UK or France. Editors and cartographers – all experienced travellers themselves – then begin the process of assembling the pieces. When the book finally hits the shops, some things are already out of date, we start getting feedback from readers and the process begins again ...

WARNING & REQUEST

Things change – prices go up, schedules change, good places go bad and bad places go bankrupt – nothing stays the same. So, if you find things better or worse, recently opened or long since closed, please tell us and help make the next edition even more accurate and useful. We genuinely value all the feedback we receive. Julie Young coordinates a well travelled team that reads and acknowledges every letter, postcard and email and ensures that every morsel of information finds its way to the appropriate authors, editors and cartographers for verification.

Everyone who writes to us will find their name in the next edition of the appropriate guidebook. They will also receive the latest issue of *Planet Talk*, our quarterly printed newsletter, or *Comet*, our monthly email newsletter. Subscriptions to both newsletters are free. The very best contributions will be rewarded with a free guidebook.

Excerpts from your correspondence may appear in new editions of Lonely Planet guidebooks, the Lonely Planet Web site, *Planet Talk* or *Comet*, so please let us know if you *don't* want your letter published or your name acknowledged.

Send all correspondence to the Lonely Planet office closest to you:

Australia: PO Box 617, Hawthorn, Victoria 3122
USA: 150 Linden St, Oakland, CA 94607
UK: 10A Spring Place, London NW5 3BH
France: 1 rue du Dahomey, 75011 Paris

Or email us at: talk2us@lonelyplanet.com.au

For news, views and updates see our Web site: www.lonelyplanet.com

HOW TO USE A LONELY PLANET GUIDEBOOK

The best way to use a Lonely Planet guidebook is any way you choose. At Lonely Planet we believe the most memorable travel experiences are often those that are unexpected, and the finest discoveries are those you make yourself. Guidebooks are not intended to be used as if they provide a detailed set of infallible instructions!

Contents All Lonely Planet guidebooks follow roughly the same format. The Facts about the Destination chapters or sections give background information ranging from history to weather. Facts for the Visitor gives practical information on issues like visas and health. Getting There & Away gives a brief starting point for re-searching travel to and from the destination. Getting Around gives an overview of the transport options when you arrive.

The peculiar demands of each destination determine how sub-sequent chapters are broken up, but some things remain constant. We always start with background, then proceed to sights, places to stay, places to eat, entertainment, getting there and away, and getting around information – in that order.

Heading Hierarchy Lonely Planet headings are used in a strict hierarchical structure that can be visualised as a set of Russian dolls. Each heading (and its following text) is encompassed by any preceding heading that is higher on the hierarchical ladder.

Entry Points We do not assume guidebooks will be read from beginning to end, but that people will dip into them. The tradi-tional entry points are the list of contents and the index. In addition, however, some books have a complete list of maps and an index map illustrating map coverage.

There may also be a colour map that shows highlights. These highlights are dealt with in greater detail in the Facts for the Visitor chapter, along with planning questions and suggested itin-eraries. Each chapter covering a geographical region usually begins with a locator map and another list of highlights. Once you find something of interest in a list of highlights, turn to the index.

Maps Maps play a crucial role in Lonely Planet guidebooks and include a huge amount of information. A legend is printed on the back page. We seek to have complete consistency between maps and text, and to have every important place in the text captured on a map. Map key numbers usually start in the top left corner.

Although inclusion in a guidebook usually implies a recommen-dation we cannot list every good place. Exclusion does not necessarily imply criticism. In fact there are a number of reasons why we might exclude a place – sometimes it is simply inappropriate to encourage an influx of travellers.

Introduction

Cretans say that visitors to their island cry twice – first when they come and then when they leave. Overdevelopment along the northern coast can make a poor first impression but it doesn't take long to fall under the spell of Greece's largest and most southerly island. The sun-drenched south coast is a paradise of long sandy beaches and isolated coves. Major urban centres such as Iraklio, Rethymno, and Hania are within easy reach of crowded beaches, but tranquillity is not hard to find. In the east, Vai Beach contains Europe's only palm forest; Elafonisi Islet in the west is nearly undeveloped, Frango-kastello Beach in the south sees few visitors. In the island's rugged interior, the salty air and barren coastal cliffs give way to bracing mountain breezes and steep gorges blanketed with flowers and aromatic herbs. The famous Samaria Gorge is Europe's longest, and an enduring attraction for hikers. However, there are many kilometres of remote mountain trails used only by goats, shepherds and donkeys.

Crete's stunning natural beauty is equalled only by the richness of a culture that spans millenniums. For the ancient Greeks, Crete was the foundation of their elaborate mythology. Legend holds that the God Zeus was born and raised within the island's caves. Myths of the Minotaur, Daedalus and the Labyrinth emerged from Crete, perhaps inspired by the glorious Minoan civilisation that once ruled the Aegean. Knossos is the best known archaeological site but a profusion of evocative ruins scattered throughout the island conjure up this mysterious civilisation that vanished over 3000 years ago.

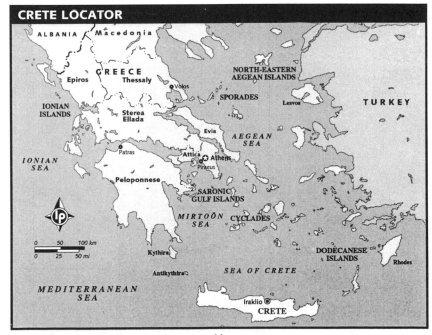

11

Yet the past and present coexist easily in Crete. Only kilometres away from ancient temples and palaces, coastal cities entertain several million tourists each year with luxurious resorts and sizzling nightlife.

Stroll through the old towns of Hania and Rethymno where 17th-century Venetian mansions have been turned into elegant hotels and restaurants. Drive into the country and you'll share the road with tractors, BMWs, pickup trucks and mules. In the urban centres, stylish Cretans run shops and businesses while, in the interior, the back-breaking work of shepherding, olive growing, and farming continues as it has for centuries.

Cretans have a unique ability to reconcile tradition with modernity. Their ferocious struggles for independence from foreign occupiers – Romans, Venetians, Turks and Germans – have left them with a profound attachment to the songs, dances and cuisine that forged their identity. As a practical people, Cretans have no trouble serving up international dance music in the discos and international food in the tourist restaurants, but their own tastes lie elsewhere. At traditional feasts and weddings, Cretans still sing *mantinades*, their age-old songs of love and betrayal, and stamp their feet to a vigorous, leaping folk dance accompanied by a lyre.

Crete is unique in the sheer variety of experiences packed into a relatively small space. Laze on the beach, hike through a gorge, poke around an archaeological site, take a harbourside walk at sunset, spend an evening listening to Cretan songs in a taverna. Maybe you won't cry when you leave; you'll be too busy planning your next trip back.

Facts about Crete

HISTORY

From ancient Minoan palaces and Roman cities to spectacular Byzantine churches and Venetian fortresses, the legacy of Crete's long and colourful history is everywhere.

Stone Age

Although the island may have been inhabited since the Palaeolithic period, the oldest evidence of human habitation was found at Knossos, and dates to what is known as the pre-pottery period (6100-5700 BC).

Little is known about these early inhabitants of Crete except that they survived by hunting and fishing and engaged in ancestor worship. Evidence is also sketchy about the people who inhabited Crete during the Neolithic period (5700-2800 BC). The earliest Neolithic people lived in caves or rough stone, mud or wood houses and worshipped female fertility goddesses. They were hunter-gatherers who also farmed, raised livestock and made primitive pottery.

In the late Neolithic period, trade routes developed between Crete and the Cyclades, Egypt and the Near East.

The Minoans

Around 3000 BC, Indo-European migrants introduced the processing of bronze (an alloy of copper and tin) into Greece. So began three remarkable civilisations: the Cycladic, Minoan and Mycenaean. Yet, it was the Minoans who assumed the starring role in prehistoric Crete. The Minoan civilisation (named after King Minos) was the first advanced civilisation to emerge in Europe, drawing its inspiration from two great Middle Eastern civilisations: the Mesopotamian and Egyptian. Archaeologists divide the Minoan civilisation into three phases: Early (3400-2100 BC), Middle (2100-1580 BC) and Late (1580-1200 BC).

Many aspects of Neolithic life endured during the Early period, but the advent of bronze, which was imported from Cyprus, allowed the Minoans to build better boats and thus expand their trade opportunities. The population increased and vibrant commercial centres emerged in the eastern part of the island, well placed to trade with the eastern Mediterranean. Pottery and goldworking became more sophisticated foreshadowing the subsequent great achievements of Minoan art. The island prospered from trade, olive-growing, livestock-rearing, imported silver from the Cyclades, gold from the North Aegean, and ivory and tin from the Near East.

The Minoan civilisation reached its peak during the Middle period, also called the Old Palace or Protopalatial period. Around 2000 BC the large palace complexes of Knossos, Phaestos, Malia, and Zakros were built, marking a sharp break with Neolithic village life. Crete is believed to have been governed by local rulers with power and wealth concentrated at Knossos. Society was organised on hierarchical lines and contained a large population of slaves.

The architectural advances were accompanied by great strides in pottery making. Kamares vases, named after the Kamares Cave where they were first produced, manifested highly advanced artisanship. The intricate red or white spirals on a black background were extraordinarily elegant and the thin walls of the 'eggshell-ware' were remarkably durable. The vases were used for barter as well as home and ceremonial use.

The first Cretan script also emerged during this period. At first highly pictorial, the writing gradually transformed from the representations of natural objects to more abstract figures that resembled Egyptian hieroglyphics. The most famous example is the Phaestos Disc dated to around 1700 BC.

Somewhat later, a syllable-based script emerged consisting of 70 linear signs which became known as Linear A. Like the earlier hieroglyphics, it has not yet been deciphered, but archaeologists believe that it was used to document trade transactions and the contents of royal storerooms, rather than to express abstract concepts.

Chronology of Major Events

6000 BC	**Neolithic age** Migration from the coast of Asia Minor and settlement of Crete by cave-dwellers
3000 BC	**Pre-palatial period** Another migration from the coast of Asia Minor and development of crafts and jewellery
2000 BC	**Proto-palatial period** First palaces built in Knossos, Phaestos, Malia and Zakros
1700 BC	**Neo-palatial period** Old Minoan palaces destroyed in earthquake; new palaces built
1450 BC	Minoan palaces destroyed
1100 BC	**Post-palatial period** Dorian colonists replace Mycenaeans as Crete's new masters
67 BC	**Roman Rule** Romans conquer Crete making Gortyn new capital
395 AD	Roman Empire splits with Crete ruled by Byzantium
1204	**Byzantine Empire** Byzantine prince Alexios sells Crete to Venice
1363	**Venetian Empire** St Titus revolution challenges Venetian rule
1669	Iraklio falls to the Turks leaving Crete under Ottoman rule
1821	**Ottoman Empire** Greek War of Independence spreads to Crete
1830	Crete given to Egypt
1866	Explosion at Arkadiou Monastery
1898	**Independence** Turkish rule ends; Crete ruled by Prince George
1913	Greece and Crete officially united
1941	Battle of Crete results in German occupation
1945	Liberation

The Middle period came to an end with the sudden destruction of the Minoan palaces of Knossos, Phaestos, Malia and Zakros in 1700 BC. Although there is some disagreement, most archaeologists believe that the destruction was caused by the eruption of a volcano on nearby Santorini which caused a massive earthquake. The Minoans rebuilt the palaces to a more complex design with multiple storeys, sumptuous royal apartments, reception halls, storerooms, workshops, living quarters for staff and an advanced drainage system. The complex design of the palaces later gave rise to the myth of the Cretan Labyrinth.

The excavation of Knossos begun by Sir Arthur Evans in 1900 (see boxed text) uncovered many remnants of Minoan society. Brightly coloured frescoes (now on view in the Archaeological Museum of Iraklio) depict white-skinned women with elaborately coiffured glossy black locks. Proud, graceful and uninhibited, these women had hourglass figures and were dressed in stylish gowns that revealed perfectly shaped breasts. The bronze-skinned men were tall, with tiny waists, narrow hips, broad shoulders and muscular thighs and biceps; the children were slim and lithe.

The Minoans also seemed to know how to enjoy themselves. They played board games, boxed and wrestled, played leapfrog over bulls and over one another, and performed bold acrobatic feats. The Minoan dancing portrayed in the frescoes was famous throughout ancient Greece.

Minoans had good reason to be happy. Their state had become a powerful thalassocracy or sea-based power. Trade with the eastern Mediterranean was booming helped by Minoan colonies in the Aegean and in Asia Minor. Minoan pottery, textiles and agricultural produce found ready markets throughout the Cyclades as well as in Egypt, Syria and possibly Sicily. According to ancient Greek historians, King Minos was the head of this powerful naval empire and promoted the expansion of Minoan interests. Historians now believe that the name Minos was a royal title that probably applied to all Minoan rulers.

Discovering the Minoans

Sir Arthur Evans was an archaeologist, journalist and adventurer who began a dig at Knossos upon a hunch; he soon uncovered the remains of an immense palace dating from 1700 BC. Evans named the civilisation Minoan after King Minos, the legendary leader of a great naval power whose capital was Knossos. Although criticised for an overly imaginative renovation of the site, Evans' rebuilt columns and supports undoubtedly make the palace more visitor-friendly. Sir Walter Evans spent about a quarter million pounds of his personal fortune over 30 years to unearth the jewellery, pottery, religious objects and frescoes that depict Minoan society. Most of the treasured objects are on display in the Archaeological Museum in Iraklio.

The Minoans were not given to building colossal temples or religious statuary. Historians have concluded that their spiritual life was organised around the worship of a Mother Goddess – often represented with snakes or lions, the Mother Goddess was the deity-in-chief with male gods clearly subordinate. The double-axe symbol that appears in frescoes and on the palace walls of Knossos was a sacred symbol for the Minoans. Called 'labrys', it was the origin of the word labyrinth, which later Greeks associated with Knossos. Other religious symbols that frequently appear in Minoan art include the mythical griffin bird, and figures with a human body and an animal head. It is also assumed that the Minoans worshipped the dead and believed in some form of after-life.

Whether or not related to the worship of a Mother Goddess, women apparently enjoyed a high degree of freedom and autonomy in Minoan society. Although the evidence for a matriarchal society is scanty, Minoan art shows women participating in games, hunting, and all public and religious festivals. It was not until the later invasions by the Dorians that women were condemned to a subordinate role.

Minoan culture came to an abrupt halt around 1450 BC in a mystery that has not yet been fully unravelled. In a great cataclysm around 1400 BC the palaces (except Knossos) and numerous smaller settlements were smashed to bits and burned.

This, too, may have been caused by the eruption of a volcano in nearby Santorini, one vulcanologists believe was more cataclysmic than any on record. They theorise that the fall-out of volcanic ash from the blast may have caused a succession of crop failures – with resulting social unrest. Other archaeologists believe that the damage was caused by the invading Mycenaeans eager to grab the Minoans' maritime commerce. Whether the Mycenaeans caused the catastrophe or merely profited from it, it is clear that their presence on the island closely coincided with the destruction of the palaces.

Mycenaean Civilisation

The Mycenaean civilisation (1900-1100 BC), which reached its peak between 1500 and 1200 BC, was the first great civilisation on the Greek mainland. Named after the ancient city of Mycenae, where the German archaeologist Heinrich Schliemann made his celebrated finds in 1876, it is also known as the Achaean civilisation after the Indo-European branch of migrants who had settled on mainland Greece and absorbed many aspects of Minoan culture.

Unlike Minoan society, where the lack of city walls seems to indicate relative peace under some form of central authority, Mycenaean civilisation was characterised by independent city-states such as Corinth, Pylos, Tiryns and, the most powerful of them all, Mycenae. These were ruled by kings who inhabited palaces enclosed within massive walls on easily defensible hilltops.

The Mycenaeans' most impressive legacy is magnificent gold jewellery and ornaments, the best of which can be seen in the National Archaeological Museum in Athens. The Mycenaeans wrote in what is called Linear B (an early form of Greek unrelated to the Linear A of Crete). Clay tablets inscribed with the script have been found at the palace of Knossos providing strong evidence of Mycenaean occupation of the island. Their colonisation of Crete lasted from 1400-1100 BC and became known as the Postpalatial or Mycenaean period. Although Knossos probably retained its position as capital of the island, its rulers were now subject to the house of Atreus in the Peloponnese. The Minoan Cretans either left the island or hid in the interior while the Mycenaeans founded new cities such as Lappa (Argiroupolis), Kydonia (Hania), and Polyrrinia.

The economy of the island stayed more or less the same, still based upon the export of local products, but the fine arts fell into decline. Only the manufacture of weapons flourished, reflecting the new militaristic spirit that the Mycenaeans brought to Crete. The Mycenaeans also replaced worship of the Mother Goddess with new Greek gods such as Zeus, Hera, and Athena.

Mycenaean influence stretched further than Crete: the city-states banded together to defeat Troy (Ilium) around the 12th century BC in order to protect their trade routes to the Black Sea. According to Homer, Cretan troops participated in the conquest of Troy under their leader Idomeneos. The Trojan War marked the high point of Mycenaean power; weakened by internal strife they were no match for the warlike Dorians who overran their cities.

Dorian Crete

The origins of the Dorians remain uncertain. They are generally thought to have come from Epiros or northern Macedonia, but some historians argue that although they arrived from there, they had been driven out of Doris, in central Greece, by the Mycenaeans.

The Dorians settled first in the Peloponnese, but soon fanned out over much of the mainland, razing the city-states and enslaving the inhabitants. Despite fierce resistance, they conquered Crete around 1100 BC causing many of the inhabitants to flee to Asia Minor. Others, known as Eteo-Cretans or true Cretans retreated to the hills and thus preserved their culture.

The Dorians brought a traumatic break with the past; the next 400 years are often referred to as Greece's 'dark age'. It would be unfair to dismiss the Dorians completely; they brought iron with them and developed a new style of pottery, decorated with striking geometrical designs – although art historians still disagree as to whether the Dorians merely copied the designs perfected by Ionians in Attica. The Dorians worshipped male gods instead of fertility goddesses and adopted the Mycenaean gods of Poseidon, Zeus and Apollo, paving the way for the later Greek religious pantheon.

The Dorians reorganised the political system of Crete and divided the society into three classes: free citizens who owned property and enjoyed political liberty; *perioeci*, which included land-holding peasants, merchants and seamen; and slaves. The monarchical system of government was replaced by a rudimentary democracy. Ruling committees called *kosmoi* were elected by free citizens and set policy. They were guided by a Council of Elders and answered to an Assembly of free citizens.

By about 800 BC, local agriculture and animal husbandry had become productive enough to trigger a resumption of maritime trading. New Greek colonies were established in north Africa, Italy, Sicily, southern France and southern Spain. The new emphasis on maritime trading and colonial expansion favoured Crete which took a prominent role in the new Greek Empire.

The people of the various city-states were unified by the development of a Greek alphabet (of Phoenician origin, though the Greeks introduced vowels), the verses of Homer (which created a sense of a shared Mycenaean past), the establishment of the Olympic Games (which brought all the city-states together). The setting up of central sanctuaries such as Delphi (a neutral meeting ground for lively negotiations), gave Cretans, for the first time, a sense of national identity as Greeks.

Most city-states were built to a similar plan, with a fortified acropolis (high city) at the highest point. The acropolis contained the cities' temples and treasury and also served as a refuge during invasions. Outside the acropolis was the agora (market), a bustling commercial quarter, and beyond it the residential areas. Rethymno, Polyrrinia, Kydonia (Hania), Falassarna, Gortyn, Phaestos and Lato were built according to the new defensive style but Knossos was never fortified.

The 6th-century-BC Laws of Gortyn, found at the end of the 19th century AD at the Gortyn archaeological site, opens a window onto the societal structure of Dorian Crete. Inscribed on 12 large stone tablets, the laws covered civil and criminal matters with clear distinctions drawn among the classes of free citizens and between citizens and slaves. Criminal offences, no matter how serious, were usually punished by fines; there is no mention of imprisonment or execution. Laws on inheritance, adoption and divorce were remarkably level-headed. Divisions of property upon divorce closely resemble today's 'community property' legal theories. Wives retained the property they brought into the marriage, plus half of whatever they had 'woven within' the marriage. If the husband caused the divorce he had to pay a fine but, if he denied it, the case went before a judge.

The Classical Age

As the rest of Greece entered its golden age from the 6th to 4th centuries BC, Crete remained a backwater. Suffering from the constant warfare between large commercial centres and smaller traditional communities, the island became increasingly impoverished and isolated from mainland Greece. Although Crete did not participate in the Persian wars or the Peloponnesian War their economic circumstances forced many Cretans to sign up as mercenaries in foreign armies or turn to piracy.

At the same time, Crete's role as the birthplace of Greek culture drew the attention of philosophers such as Plato and Aristotle who wrote extensively about Crete's political institutions.

The century preceding the Roman conquest of Crete was marked by continued turmoil on the island as Knossos, Gortyn, Lyttos and Kydonia (Hania) vied for supremacy. Egypt, Rhodes and the powerful

city-state of Sparta involved themselves in Cretan squabbles and piracy flourished. Meanwhile Rome was emerging as a great power.

Roman Rule

While Alexander the Great was forging his vast empire in the East, the Romans had been expanding theirs to the west and now also began making inroads into Greece. They found willing allies in Pergamum and Rhodes, who feared Syrian and Macedonian expansionism. The Romans defeated the Seleucid king, Antiochus III, in a three-year campaign and in 189 BC gave all of Asia Minor to Pergamum. Several wars were needed to subjugate Macedon, but in 168 BC Macedon lost the decisive Battle of Pydnaa.

The Achaean League was defeated in 146 BC; the Roman consul Mummius made an example of the rebellious Corinthians by completely destroying their beautiful city, massacring the men and selling the women and children into slavery. Attalos III, king of Pergamum, died without an heir in 133 BC, donating Asia Minor to Rome in his will.

In 86 BC, Athens joined in a rebellion against the Romans in Asia Minor staged by the king of the Black Sea region, Mithridates VI. In return, the Roman statesman Sulla invaded Athens, destroyed its walls and took off with its most valuable sculptures.

The Romans had various interests in Crete which included reducing piracy and exerting control over important sea routes. A Roman presence in Crete dated back to the 3rd century BC but it wasn't until the second Mithridatic War (74-64 BC) that they found a pretext for intervention. Using piracy as an excuse Marcus Antonius, father of Mark Antony, undertook a naval campaign against Crete which failed. The Cretans tried to negotiate and send envoys to Rome but they were rebuffed. Expecting a Roman invasion, the island united and assembled an army of 26,000 men. The Roman campaign began in 69 BC under the Roman consul Metellus near Kydonia, then spread throughout the island. Although the Cretans fought valiantly the Romans succeeded in subjugating the island two years later.

Greece then became a battleground as Roman generals fought for supremacy. In a decisive naval battle off Cape Actium (31 BC), Octavian was victorious over Mark Antony and Cleopatra and consequently became Rome's first emperor, assuming the title Augustus, the Grand One.

For the next 300 years Greece, as the Roman province of Achaea, experienced an unprecedented period of peace, the Pax Romana. The Romans had always venerated Greek art, literature and philosophy, and aristocratic Romans sent their offspring to the many schools in Athens. Indeed, the Romans adopted most aspects of Hellenistic culture, spreading its unifying traditions throughout their empire.

Although Crete lost power and influence under the Romans it did usher in a new era of peace, bringing to an end Crete's internal wars. Crete did not mount a major challenge to Roman rule although they became embroiled in the later rivalry between Antony and Octavian. When Antony ruled he punished the cities that supported Octavian and when Octavian triumphed he punished the cities that supported Antony.

In the early years of Roman rule, parts of Crete were given as favours to various Roman allies. In 27 BC Crete was united with Libya to form the Roman province of Cyrene. Gortyn became the capital and most powerful city of Crete. The Romans built an amphitheatre, temples and public baths and the population increased. Knossos appeared to fall into disuse but Kydonia (Hania) in the west became an important centre. Roman towns were linked by a network of roads, bridges and aqueducts, parts of which can still be seen. Under the Romans, the Cretans continued to worship Zeus in the Dikteon and Ideon Caves and also incorporated Roman and Egyptian deities into their religious rituals.

Christianity & the Byzantine Empire

Christianity arrived early in Crete with St Paul's visit in 63 AD. He left it to his disciple, Titus, to convert the island. Little is known about the early years of Christianity

in Crete but by the 3rd century persecution of Christians began in earnest.

The first Christian martyrs in Crete were the so-called Ten Saints (Aghi Deka) killed in the village of the same name in 250 AD.

At the same time, the Pax Romana began to crumble when the Goths invaded Greece, the first of a succession of invaders spurred on by the 'great migrations', which included the Visigoths in 395, the Vandals in 465, the Ostrogoths in 480, the Bulgars in 500, the Huns in 540 and the Slavs after 600.

Christianity, meantime, had emerged as the country's new religion. The definitive boost to the spread of Christianity in this part of the world came with the conversion of the Roman emperors and the rise of the Byzantine Empire, which blended Hellenistic culture with Christianity.

In 324 Emperor Constantine I (also known as Constantine the Great), a Christian convert, transferred the capital of the empire from Rome to Byzantium, a city on the western shore of the Bosphorus, which was renamed Constantinople (present-day Istanbul). This was as much due to insecurity in Italy itself as to the growing importance of the wealthy eastern regions of the empire. By the end of the 4th century, the Roman Empire was formally divided into a western and eastern section; Crete, along with the rest of Greece, found itself in the eastern half. While Rome went into terminal decline, the eastern capital grew in wealth and strength, long outliving its western counterpart (the Byzantine Empire lasted until the capture of Constantinople by the Turks in 1453).

Crete was a self governing province in the Byzantine Empire with Gortyn as its administrative and religious centre. Piracy decreased and trade flourished leaving the island wealthy enough to build scores of churches – the largest of which is the three aisled Basilica in Panormos that dates from the 5th century. Crete's attachment to the worship of icons provoked a revolt in 727 when Emperor Leo III banned their worship as part of the iconoclastic movement. The uprising was smashed and the

Byzantine emperors unleashed a fierce wave of retribution.

In the early 7th century Crete was attacked by Slavs but the more serious threat was posed by the Arabs in the mid-7th century. Naval attacks by the Arabs were unremitting and they finally conquered Crete around 824. It's unclear to what extent the Cretans resisted the Arab conquest or even whether the Arabs succeeded in securing control of the entire island. The Arabs established a fortress called Chandax in what is now Iraklio. Its main function was to store the treasure they amassed by piracy. Crete was an ideal base for Arab ships to launch attacks throughout the Aegean and Adriatic Seas; as the island's criminal reputation grew its economy dwindled and its cultural life ground to a halt.

The Byzantines were in no position to help Crete despite its strategic importance. The island was far away from Constantinople and the Byzantines had enough problems defending territories closer to home. Nevertheless, they made repeated attempts to recover the island, which ended disastrously. Not until the Byzantine general Nikiforas Fokas attacked Chandax in a bitter siege in 960 did the Arabs finally yield.

The Byzantines lost no time in fortifying the Cretan coast and consolidating their power. Chandax emerged as the island's new capital and the seat of the Cretan archdiocese while Gortyn faded away. Cretan tradition holds that the Byzantines established 12 aristocratic families known as *archontopoula* on the island who eventually became powerful voices of rebellion against Venetian rule. A powerful land holding class had emerged on the island by the late 11th century, but historians are uncertain whether a native Cretan aristocratic class dates back to the 10th century.

The Crusades

It is one of the ironies of history that the demise of the Byzantine Empire was accelerated not by invasions of infidels from the east, nor barbarians from the north, but by fellow Christians from the west – the Frankish crusaders.

The stated mission of the crusades was to liberate the Holy Land from the Muslims, but in reality they were driven as much by greed as by religious fervour. Constantinople was sacked in 1204 in the 4th Crusade and the crusaders installed Baldwin of Flanders as head of the short-lived Latin Empire of Constantinople. Meanwhile, in an effort to secure the throne, the Byzantine Prince Alexios promised Crete to Boniface of Montferrat. After the sack of Constantinople Boniface sold Crete to Venice.

Venetian Rule

Despite Crete's importance to Venetian control of the Mediterranean, Venice was slow to assert mastery over the island. Their archrivals for naval supremacy, the Genoese, moved in on the island but after a series of campaigns the Venetians finally prevailed in 1217. Genoa made periodic and futile efforts to recapture the island which remained under Venetian rule until 1669.

In order to solidify its authority, Venice rapidly colonised Crete with noble and military families, many of whom settled in Iraklio (Candia). During the first century of Venetian rule about 10,000 settlers came to Crete. In order to induce Venetians to settle on Crete the authorities seized the island's best and most fertile land and gave it to the newcomers. The former Cretan owners now worked as serfs for their new Venetian masters. Not only were the major landholders Venetian but political control was also firmly in Venetian hands. All government posts were held by Venetians who answered directly to Venice.

Cretan peasants were ruthlessly exploited under Venetian rule. Particularly onerous was the Venetian requirement that young men serve in the Venetian galleys. The work was exceptionally brutal and many young men did not survive the experience. Oppressive taxation added to the peasants' woes.

Religious life also suffered under the Venetians. Although not particularly religious themselves, the Venetians viewed the church as a symbol of national identity for the Cretans. The Orthodox Church was dismantled and replaced with the Catholic

Church, but despite the relentless persecution, Orthodox monasteries remained hotbeds of resistance and kept the spirit of national unity alive.

Cretans rebelled regularly against Venetian rule. Spearheaded by the now landless Cretan aristocracy, the rebellions followed a predictable pattern of Cretan uprising followed by brutal Venetian reprisals. The most serious challenge to Venetian rule was posed by the St Titus rebellion of 1363. Venetian feudal lords and the native Cretan aristocracy joined together to oppose the oppressive new taxes. Once again the rebellion was suppressed but eventually the incessant rebellions forced concessions from La Serenissima. By the 15th century the Cretan and Venetian communities reached an uneasy compromise that allowed Cretan cultural and economic life to flourish.

The Ottoman Empire

Venice was soon facing a much greater threat from the east. The Seljuk Turks, a tribe from Central Asia, had first appeared on the eastern fringes of the Byzantine Empire in the middle of the 11th century. They established themselves on the Anatolian plain by defeating a Byzantine army at Manzikert in 1071. The threat looked to have been contained, especially when the Seljuks were themselves overrun by the Mongols. By the time Mongol power began to wane, the Seljuks had been supplanted as the dominant Turkish tribe by the Ottomans – the followers of Osman, who ruled from 1289 to 1326. The Muslim Ottomans rapidly expanded the areas under their control and by the mid-15th century were harassing the Byzantine Empire on all sides. Western Europe was too embroiled in the Hundred Years' War to come to the rescue, and in 1453 Constantinople fell to the Turks under Mohammed II (the Conqueror).

The fall of Constantinople left Crete as the last remaining bastion of Hellenism. Byzantine scholars and intellectuals fled the dying empire and settled in Crete, establishing schools, libraries and printing presses. The cross pollination between Byzantine traditions and the flourishing

Italian Renaissance that was imported into Crete sparked a major cultural revival. Poetry and drama flourished and a 'Cretan School' of icon painting developed in the 16th and 17th centuries that combined Byzantine and Venetian elements. In the midst of this artistic ferment, the painter Domeniko Theotokopoulos was born in Iraklio in 1541. He studied in Italy under Titian and later moved to Spain where he became known as El Greco.

With the fall of Cyprus to the Turks in 1570 it seemed that Crete would be next on the Ottoman agenda but the Turkish defeats at the Battle of Lepanto in 1571 crimped Ottoman plans for further western expansion. By the early 17th century the Ottomans were on the move again while Venice was under severe economic pressure from the rise of Spanish, English and Dutch shipping. As a resource-rich and strategically well-located island, Crete was obviously attractive to the Ottomans. The island's defences had previously been strengthened against piracy but Venice was slow to rearrange their defences in the face of the looming Ottoman threat.

The Turks were looking for a pretext to invade the island and in 1644 they found one when pirates attacked a Turkish ship off the Cretan coast. The Turks amassed a huge force that landed in Hania in the early summer of 1645. Although the fortress was bravely defended it fell within two months and the Turks established their first foothold on the island. Rethymno was the next town to suffer siege, bombardment and defeat. With the western part of the island secured the Turks turned their attention to Iraklio (Candia). The siege began in May 1648 but the massive walls of the city kept the enemy at bay for 21 years. Both sides threw everything they had into the struggle. Venice appealed to other European powers for support arguing that the fate of Christianity hung in the balance. European mercenaries arrived but were in no position to match the overwhelming Turkish forces. Candia fell in 1669 leaving the entire island except for Spinalonga and Souda (which fell in 1715) in Turkish hands.

El Greco

One of the geniuses of the Renaissance, El Greco (meaning 'The Greek' in Spanish; his real name was Domeniko Theotokopoulos) was born and educated on Crete but had to travel to Spain to earn recognition.

El Greco was born in the Cretan capital of Candia (present-day Iraklio) in 1541 during a time of great artistic activity in the city. Many of the artists, writers and philosophers who fled Constantinople after it was conquered by the Turks in 1453 had settled on Crete, leading to the emergence of the Cretan school of icon painters. The painters had a formative influence upon the young El Greco, giving him the early grounding in the traditions of late Byzantine fresco painting that was to give such a powerful spiritual element to his later paintings.

Because Candia was a Venetian city it was a logical step for El Greco to head to Venice to further his studies, and he set off when he was in his early 20s to join the studio of Titian. It was not, however, until he moved to Spain in 1577 that he really came into his own as a painter. His highly emotional style struck a chord with the Spanish, and the city of Toledo was to become his home until his death in 1614. To view the most famous of his works, like his masterpiece *The Burial of Count Orgaz* (1586), you will have to travel to Toledo. The only El Greco work on display in Crete is *View of Mt Sinai and the Monastery of St Catherine* (1570), painted during his time in Venice. It hangs in Iraklio's Historical Museum of Crete.

A white marble bust of the painter stands in the city's Plateia El Greco, and there are streets named after him throughout the island.

Much has been made of the horrors of the Turkish occupation in Crete. However, in the early years at any rate, Cretans probably marginally preferred Ottoman to Venetian rule. Life was not easy under the Turks although they did allow the Orthodox Church to re-establish itself on the island. Nevertheless, there were tremendous political and economic advantages to embracing Islam. Mass conversions were common; sometimes entire villages changed their faith.

There were Turko-Cretans who wholly identified with the Turks and the crypto-Christians who secretly maintained their faith. Naturally, each hated the other.

Economically, the Cretans were no better off under Ottoman rule than they were under the Venetians. Rather than manipu-late trade for their own benefit, as the Venetians did, the Ottomans devised highly imaginative taxes in order to wring every last drop of wealth out of the island. In the early years of Ottoman rule the economy degenerated to a subsistence level, but trade activity picked up around the beginning of the 18th century and living standards improved. Crete exported grain and the abundance of olive oil launched a soap industry.

One of the most hated practices of the Turks was the Janissary system. In the Ottoman Empire, the Sultan impressed one out of five Christian boys from their subject populations into service. They were converted to Islam, given special training and made part of the Ottoman army elite. Known as Janissaries, they functioned as the Sultan's administrative representatives throughout the Ottoman Empire. Forbidden to marry, the Janissaries were granted special privileges in return for unquestioning loyalty and their rule began to spin out of control. Christian families on Crete who had initially thought the Ottoman Janissary system an honour for their sons were horrified to discover that the Janissaries on their island were more like hoodlums. They answered to no law but their own and ruthlessly terrorised the population with extortionate taxes, random attacks and even murder.

Under such oppression rebellion was inevitable. Many Cretans fled to the mountains and harassed the Turks with sporadic attacks and raids. In 1770 a more serious challenge to Turkish rule arose. The Turks never succeeded in fully subjugating the mountainous Sfakian region and, under their leader Daskalogiannis, 2000 Sfakians mounted an assault upon the Turks in western Crete. Although Daskalogiannis had received assurances of support from Russia, the aid never materialised and the rebellion was viciously suppressed. Daskalogiannis was skinned alive in the central square of Iraklio.

Sfakia was once again the nucleus of rebellion when the Greek War of Independence spread to Crete in 1821. With bitter memories of the 1770 fiasco, the Sfakian rebels fired the first shots in the struggle that soon spread throughout the island. Unfortunately the revolutionaries were hampered by poor organisation and constant infighting. The Turks swiftly retaliated and launched a wave of massacres primarily directed at the clergy.

Bogged down fighting rebels in the Peloponnese and mainland Greece, the Turks were forced to turn to Mehmet Ali of Egypt for help in dealing with the Cretans. Chronically short of arms and undisciplined, the Cretans fought furiously but were outnumbered by the Turkish-Egyptian forces.

With the rest of Greece torn by war, Crete was left on its own; the revolutionary movement flickered out in 1824. Fighting continued for a few more years provoking fearsome massacres of Cretan civilians but it was only a matter of time until the Turks prevailed. When a Greek state was finally established in 1830, Crete was not part of it and instead was given to Egypt.

Egyptian rule initially brought improvements. A general amnesty was issued which asked Cretans to lay down their arms. Muslims and Christians were to be treated equally, schools were organised and the authorities began rebuilding the island's infrastructure. Nevertheless, taxes remained high and soon new protests were underway. Meanwhile Mehmet Ali was defeated by the Turks in Syria and the Great Powers decided to give Crete back to the Ottomans in 1840. Another rebellion broke out in 1841 but was squashed.

Upon the restoration of Ottoman rule, Crete won important new privileges in the writ of Hatti Humayun allowing more religious freedom and the right to own property. A further decree granted Cretans more civil rights but the Sultan's repeated violations of these new laws sparked yet another uprising and a demand for *enosis*, or union with free Greece. Although Russia was partial to the Cretan position, Great Britain and France wished to maintain the status quo and refused any military or economic help. Rallying around the slogan 'Union Or Death', fighting broke out in western Crete. Once again the Turks joined forces with the Egyptians and attacked the civilian population in their mountain villages. About 900 rebels and their families took refuge in Moni Arkadiou. When 2000 Turkish soldiers staged an attack on the building, rather than surrender, the Cretans set light to a store of gun powder. The explosion killed almost everyone, Turks included, except one small girl. This sole survivor lived to a ripe old age in a village nearby. A bust of this woman, and the abbot who lit the gun powder, stand outside the monastery.

With the heroic stand at Moni Arkadiou, the Cretan cause gained worldwide attention. Although demonstrations erupted throughout Europe in support of the rebels, Great Britain and France maintained a pro-Turkish stance. The Great Powers forbade Greece from aiding the Cretan rebels and the revolution petered out.

The Russo-Turkish War of 1877 prompted another uprising in Crete. Sensing that Turkey might be defeated the Greek government decided to support Crete. Although the rebels seized major north coast cities, the Berlin conference of 1878 resolving the Russo-Turkish War firmly rejected Cretan union with Greece. Turkey made new concessions in the Haleppa Charter of 1878 turning Crete into a semi-autonomous province, sanctioning Greek as the official language and granting a general amnesty.

In 1889, fierce political infighting within the Cretan parliament inflamed passions and prompted a new rebellion against Turkish rule, prompting Turkey to revoke the Haleppa Charter and return to the iron-fisted policies of the past. A new figure of resistance emerged from Sfakia. Manoussos Koundouros headed a secret fraternity with the goal of securing autonomy for the island believing that it would eventually lead to unification with Greece. The rebels laid siege to the Turkish garrison at Vamos which led to violent reprisals by the Turks and an eventual intervention by the Great Powers. The Turks were forced to agree to a new constitution for Crete.

When violence erupted again in 1896, the Greek government sent a small force to the island and declared unification between Crete and Greece. The Great Powers rejected the idea and blockaded the coast, refusing to allow either the Turks or the Greeks to reinforce their position. Greece became embroiled in a war with Turkey and recalled its forces. The Great Powers appointed Prince George, son of King George of Greece, as High Commissioner.

In 1898, a detachment of British soldiers was implementing the transfer of power in Iraklio when an enraged mob of Turks stormed through the city slaughtering hundreds of Christian civilians and 17 British soldiers as well as the British Consul to the island. The British swiftly rounded up 17 Turkish troublemakers, hanged them and sent a squadron of ships steaming into the Iraklio Harbour. The Turks were ordered out of all their island fortresses, ending Ottoman rule over Crete forever.

Independence

Crete was placed under international administration, but union with its cultural brethren in Greece remained an unquenchable desire. A new movement coalesced around Eleftherios Venizelos. Born near Hania, this charismatic figure was Prince George's Minister of Justice and a member of the Cretan Assembly. In the face of Prince George's stubborn refusal to consider unification, Eleftherios Venizelos convened a revolutionary assembly in Theriso in 1905 which raised the Greek flag and declared unity with Greece. Venizelos then set up a rival government to administer the island. The rebellion spread, forcing the Great Powers to concede that Prince George had lost all support. They mediated a solution, allowing King George of Greece to appoint a new governor of Crete, which brought the island another step closer to union.

Although a new governor was appointed, the populace continued to agitate for unification. In 1908 the Cretan assembly issued a proclamation declaring unity with Greece but the Greek government refused to allow Cretan deputies to sit in the Greek Parliament. Even though Eleftherios Venizelos had become Prime Minister, Greece remained fearful of antagonising Turkey and the Great Powers who were adamantly opposed to the plan. Not until Greece, Serbia and Bulgaria declared war on the Ottoman Empire over Macedonia in the first Balkan War (1912) were Cretans finally allowed into the Greek Parliament. The 1913 Treaty of Bucharest ended the war and formally recognised Crete as part of the Greek state.

WWI & Smyrna

King Constantine, who was married to the sister of the German emperor, insisted that Greece remain neutral when WWI broke out in August 1914. As the war dragged on, the Allies (Britain, France and Russia) put increasing pressure on Greece to join forces with them against Germany and Turkey. They made promises which they couldn't hope to fulfil, including land in Asia Minor. Venizelos favoured the Allied cause, placing him at loggerheads with the king. Tensions between the two came to a head in 1916, and Venizelos set up a rebel government, first in Crete and then in Thessaloniki, while the pressure from the Allies eventually persuaded Constantine to leave Greece in June 1917. He was replaced by his more amenable second son, Alexander.

Greek troops served with distinction on the Allied side, but when the war ended in 1918 the promised land in Asia Minor was not forthcoming. Venizelos took matters into his own hands and, with Allied acquiescence, landed troops in Smyrna (present-day Izmir) in May 1919 under the guise of protecting the half a million Greeks living in that city (just under half its population). With a firm foothold in Asia Minor, Venizelos now planned to push home his advantage against a war-depleted Ottoman Empire. He ordered his troops to attack in October 1920 (just weeks before he was voted out of office). By September 1921, the Greeks had advanced as far as Ankara.

The Turkish forces were commanded by Mustafa Kemal (later to become Ataturk), a young general who also belonged to the Young Turks, a group of army officers pressing for Western-style political reforms. Kemal first halted the Greek advance outside Ankara in September 1921 and then routed them with a massive offensive the following spring. The Greeks were driven out of Smyrna and many of the Greek inhabitants were massacred.

The outcome of the failed Greek invasion and the revolution in Turkey was the Treaty of Lausanne of July 1923. This gave eastern Thrace and the islands of Imvros and Tenedos to Turkey, while the Italians kept the Dodecanese.

The treaty also called for a population exchange between Greece and Turkey to prevent any future disputes. Almost 1.5 million Greeks left Turkey and almost 400,000 Turks left Greece. On Crete, the entire Turkish population of about 30,000 people was ordered off the island, abandoning their homes to the incoming Greek refugees.

The Republic of 1924-35
The arrival of the refugees coincided with, and compounded, a period of political in-

stability unprecedented even by Greek standards. In October 1920, King Alexander had died from a monkey bite, resulting in the restoration of his father, King Constantine. Constantine identified himself too closely with the war against Turkey, and abdicated after the fall of Smyrna. He was replaced by his first son, George II, but George was no match for the group of army officers who seized power after the war. A republic was proclaimed in March 1924 amid a series of coups and counter-coups.

A measure of stability was attained with Venizelos' return to power in 1928. He pursued a policy of economic and educational reforms, but progress was inhibited by the Great Depression. His anti-royalist Liberal Party began to face a growing challenge from the monarchist Popular Party, culminating in defeat at the polls in March 1933. The new government was preparing for the restoration of the monarchy when Venizelos and his supporters staged an unsuccessful coup in March 1935.

Venizelos was exiled to Paris, where he died a year later. In November 1935, King George II was restored to the throne by a rigged plebiscite, and he installed the right-wing General Ioannis Metaxas as prime minister. Nine months later, Metaxas assumed dictatorial powers with the king's consent under the pretext of preventing a communist-inspired republic-an coup.

WWII
Metaxas' grandiose vision was to create a Third Greek Civilisation based on its glorious ancient and Byzantine past, but what he actually created was more like a Greek version of the Third Reich. He exiled or imprisoned opponents, banned trade unions and the KKE (Kommunistiko Komma Ellados, the Greek Communist Party), imposed press censorship, and created a secret police force and a fascist-style youth movement.

Metaxas is best known, however, for his reply of *ohi* (no) to Mussolini's request to allow the Italian forces to traverse Greece at the beginning of WWII, thus maintaining Greece's policy of strict neutrality. The

Italians invaded Greece, but were driven back into Albania.

A prerequisite of Hitler's plan to invade the Soviet Union was a secure southern flank in the Balkans. The British, realising this, asked Metaxas if they could land troops in Greece. He gave the same reply he had given the Italians, but died suddenly in January 1941. The king replaced him with the more timid Alexandros Koryzis, who agreed to British forces landing in Greece and then committed suicide when German troops marched through Yugoslavia and invaded Greece on 6 April 1941. The country was rapidly overrun and on 23 April the leader of the Greek government, Emmanuel Tsouderos, set up a government in exile in his native Crete.

Battle of Crete

With all available Greek and Cretan troops fighting the Italians in Albania, Greece asked Britain to defend Crete. Churchill was more than willing to oblige as he was determined to block Germany's advance through south-eastern Europe. British, Australian and New Zealand troops poured on to the last remaining part of free Greece.

The Allies were in a poor position to defend the island, since commitments in the Middle East were already draining military resources. The island's defences had been seriously neglected, particularly its defence against an air assault. There were few fighter planes and military preparation was hampered by six changes of command on the island in the first six months of 1941. The terrain was also a problem. The only viable ports were on Crete's exposed north coast; inadequate roads precluded the use of the more protected ports on the southern coast to resupply the army.

Meanwhile Hitler was determined to seize the island and use it as an air base to attack British forces in the eastern Mediterranean. In a stunning disregard for Crete's rebellious history, Hitler actually believed that German forces would be welcomed by the native population. They were not.

After a week-long aerial bombardment, an airborne invasion began on 20 May. Aiming to capture the airport at Maleme, thousands of parachutists floated down over Hania, Rethymno and Iraklio.

Old men, women and children grabbed rifles, old shotguns, sickles and whatever else they could find to defend their homeland. German casualties were appalling but they managed to capture the Maleme airfield. Although the Allies probably could have recaptured the airfield before the Germans had time to secure it, confusion and a lack of wireless sets prevented the Allies from redeploying their troops around the vital air base. Although the fighting continued until 30 May, once Maleme was in German hands at the end of the first day, the battle was effectively lost.

With Hania, Rethymno, and Iraklio under German control Allied soldiers were forced to retreat to the southern port of Hora Sfakion. About 12,000 men made their way over the eastern flank of the Lefka Ori (White Mountains) under attack by German soldiers all the way.

About three quarters of them were evacuated by ship from Hora Sfakion. Meanwhile King George and Emmanuel Tsouderos walked through the Samaria Gorge to Agia Roumeli to be evacuated to Egypt.

The Cretan Resistance

Most of the Allied soldiers that were not evacuated were hidden by the Cretans and helped to escape. During the German occupation Allied undercover agents supplied from North Africa coordinated the guerilla warfare waged by the Cretan fighters, known as *andartes*. Allied soldiers and Cretans alike were under constant threat from the Nazis while they lived in caves, sheltered in monasteries, trekked across peaks or unloaded cargo on the south coast. One of the most daring feats of the resistance movement was the kidnapping of General Kreipe in 1944. The German commander was snatched outside Iraklio and spirited down to the south coast and away to Egypt. For a moving account of the Cretan resistance, read *The Cretan Runner*, by George Psychoundakis.

German reprisals against the civilian population were fierce, especially after the kidnapping of General Kreipe. Cities were bombed and villages were annihilated with the men, women and children lined up and shot. When the Germans finally surrendered in 1945 they insisted on surrendering to the British fearing that the Cretans would inflict upon them some of the same punishment they had suffered for four years.

Postwar Crete

With the defeat of the Germans, the Allies turned their attention to the political complexion of postwar Greece. Throughout the occupation of mainland Greece, the resistance was dominated by the Greek Communists. Winston Churchill wanted the king back and was afraid of a communist takeover, especially after the two leading resistance organisations formed a coalition and declared a provisional government in the summer of 1944.

An election held in March 1946, and boycotted by the Communists, was won by the royalists with British backing. A rigged plebiscite put George II back on the throne and civil war broke out, lasting until 1949.

On Crete the situation was different. The close cooperation between the Cretans and British soldiers left the islanders with strong pro-British sentiments that left little room for communist infiltration.

The British also made sure that the scarce supplies and equipment available went to non-communist resistance organisations. The result was that Crete was largely spared the bloodshed and bitterness that left Greece a political and economic basket case in the 1950s.

A national election was held in 1950. The system of proportional representation resulted in a series of unworkable coalitions. The electoral system was changed to majority voting in 1952, which excluded the communists from future governments. The following election was a victory for the newly formed right-wing Ellinikos Synagermos (Greek Rally) party led by General Papagos, who had been a field marshal during the civil war.

Greece joined NATO in 1951, and in 1953 the US was granted the right to operate sovereign bases. Intent on maintaining a right-wing government, the US gave generous aid and even more generous military support. Despite improved living standards during the 1950s, Greece remained a poor country.

A succession of right-wing governments was supplanted by the centrist EK (Centre Union) led by Georgos Papandreou in 1964. His government was short-lived; a group of army colonels led by Georgos Papadopoulos and Stylianos Patakos staged a coup d'etat on 21 April 1967 and established a military junta with Papadopoulos as prime minister.

The colonels imposed martial law, abolished all political parties, banned trade unions, imposed censorship, and imprisoned, tortured and exiled thousands of Greeks who opposed them. Cretan resentment towards the colonels intensified when the colonels muscled through major tourist development projects on the island that were rife with favouritism. Suspicions that the coup had been aided by the CIA remain conjecture, but criticism of the coup, and the ensuing regime, was certainly not forthcoming from the CIA or the US government. The perception of US involvement in the coup has left a residue of ill feeling that has not entirely dissipated.

After the Colonels

Discredited by the Turkish invasion of Cyprus, the junta stepped down in July 1974. An election was arranged for November 1974, and the ban on communist parties was lifted. Andreas Papandreou (son of Georgos) formed PASOK (the Panhellenic Socialist Union), and a national plebiscite voted 69% against restoration of the monarchy with Cretans even more overwhelmingly in favour of a republican system.

Karamanlis' right-wing New Democracy (ND) party won the election in 1977, but his personal popularity, which was never very high in Crete, began to decline. One of his biggest achievements before accepting the largely ceremonial post of president was to engineer Greece's entry into the European

Community (now the European Union), which involved jumping the queue ahead of other countries who had waited patiently to be accepted. On 1 January 1981 Greece became the 10th member of the EC.

The Socialist 1980s

Andreas Papandreou's PASOK party won the election of October 1981 with 48% of the vote, giving Greece its first socialist government. PASOK promised removal of US bases and withdrawal from NATO.

Their international stance was and is particularly popular in Crete where the US naval base at Souda Bay is a regular target for protests. Crete's history of foreign occupation has given islanders a strong antipathy to the presence of foreign troops in any way, shape, manner or form.

After seven years in government, these promises remained unfulfilled (although the US military presence was reduced), unemployment was high and reforms in education and welfare had been limited. Women's issues had fared better, though: the dowry system was abolished, abortion legalised, and civil marriage and divorce were implemented. The crunch came in 1988 when Papandreou's love affair with air hostess Dimitra Liani (whom he subsequently married) hit the headlines, and PASOK became embroiled in a financial scandal involving the Bank of Crete.

In July 1989 an unlikely coalition of conservatives and communists took over to implement a *katharsis* (campaign of purification) to investigate the scandal. In September it ruled that Papandreou and four former ministers should be tried for embezzlement, telephone tapping and illegal grain sales. The trial of Papandreou ended in January 1992 with his acquittal on all counts.

The 1990s

An election in 1990 brought the ND back to power with a majority of only two seats, and with Konstantinos Mitsotakis, a Cretan, as prime minister. Intent on redressing the country's economic problems – high inflation and high government spending – the government imposed austerity measures,

including a wage freeze for civil servants and steep increases in public-utility costs and basic services. It also announced a privatisation program aimed at 780 state-controlled enterprises; OTE (the telecommunications company), electricity and Olympic Airways were first on the list. The government also cracked down on tax evasion, which is still so rife it's described as the nation's favourite pastime. None of Mitsotakis' reforms were popular in Crete although the prime minister himself retained strong personal popularity.

By late 1992 corruption allegations were being made against the government and it was claimed that Mitsotakis had a large, secret collection of Minoan art, and in mid-1993 there were allegations of government telephone tapping. Former Mitsotakis supporters began to cut their losses: in June 1993 Antonis Samaras, the ND's former foreign minister, founded the Political Spring party and called upon ND members to join him. So many of them joined that the ND lost its parliamentary majority and hence its capacity to govern.

An early election was held in October, in which Andreas Papandreou's PASOK party won with 47% of the vote against 39% for ND and 5% for Political Spring. Through the majority voting system, this translated into a handsome parliamentary majority for PASOK.

In light of 74-year-old Papandreou's heart condition and ailing health, the focus of political interest now shifted to speculation on the succession. Papandreou was rarely sighted outside his villa, where he lived surrounded by his ministerial coterie of family and friends. He was finally forced to step down as PASOK leader in early 1996 after another bout of ill-health, and his death on June 26 marked the end of an era in Greek politics.

Papandreou's departure produced a dramatic change of direction for PASOK, with the party abandoning his left-leaning politics and electing economic reformer Costas Simitis as prime minister. The new leader had been an outspoken critic of Papandreou and had been sacked as industry minister

Facts & Figures

- Crete has a population of 540,000
- Over two million tourists visit Crete each year
- 80% of tourists to the island are on package tours
- The annual turnover from the tourist sector is about US$1.5 billion
- There are 25 million olive trees
- A one-bedroom house in Hania's Old Town costs about 20,000,000 dr
- 3500 square kilometres of land is devoted to agriculture

four months previously. He surprised many by calling a snap poll in September 1996, and campaigned hard in support of his 'Mr Clean' image. He was rewarded with almost 42% of the vote, which translated into a comfortable parliamentary majority.

Simitis belongs to much the same school of politics as Britain's Tony Blair. Since he took power, PASOK policy has shifted right to the extent that it now agrees with the opposition New Democracy on all major policy issues, including further integration with Europe and monetary union. With elections scheduled to take place in 2000, Simitis is running into political trouble with an austerity package designed to whip Greece into fiscal shape to qualify for monetary union by 2001. Securing the 2004 Olympic Games was an enormous coup for Simitis bringing a flood of money into Greece for improvements to the infrastructure.

Although anti-Turkish sentiment still runs strong, the earthquakes that slammed Turkey and Athens in 1999 prompted an exchange of relief workers that may herald a thaw in relations between the two countries. Relations with the United States have grown increasingly testy since the 1999 NATO bombardment of Kosovo which was wildly unpopular in Greece.

GEOGRAPHY

Crete is the largest island in the Greek archipelago with an area of 8335 kilometres. It includes Gavdos Island, the most southerly point in Europe, just 300km from Africa. Crete is 250km long, about 60km at its widest point and 12km at its narrowest. Three major mountain groups – the Lefka Ori (White Mountains) in the west, Mt Psiloritis (also known as Mt Ida) in the centre and the Lassithi Mountains in the east – define the rugged interior. The Lefka Ori are known for their spectacular gorges, such as Samaria, as well as the snow that lingers on the mountains well into spring. The Omalos Plain is in the Lefka Ori at an altitude of 1000m. The Psiloritis contains hundreds of caves, including the Ideon Andron Cave where Zeus allegedly grew up, and the Rouva Forest on the southern slopes. The highest mountain peak in Crete is Timios Stavros at 2447m, part of the Psiloritis Range.

The Lassithi Mountains harbour the famous Lassithi Plateau and Mt Dikti (2148m) whose southern slopes preserve an example of the magnificent forests that once blanketed the island.

Western Crete is the most mountainous and greenest part of the island while eastern Crete tends to be barren and rocky. Most of the interior is mountainous and marked by olive trees, scrub *(phrygana)* and wild herbs. High upland plains are either cultivated like the Lassithi Plain or used for pasturing goats like the Omalos Plain. The largest cultivable area in the south is the fertile Mesara Plain which is about 40km long and up to 20km wide. Steep mountains in the south and gently sloping mountains in the north border the 1046km coastline. There is only one lake on the island, Lake Kournas, outside of Hania. The populous northern cities of Hania, Souda, Rethymno, Iraklio and Mirabello Bay are located on wide bays.

CLIMATE

Crete has a Mediterranean climate, with hot, dry summers and mild winters. With 300 days of sunshine every year, it's the sunniest island in the Mediterranean after Cyprus. It also stays warm the longest of all the Greek islands – you can swim off its southern coast from mid-April to November.

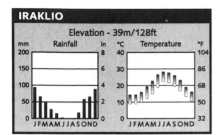

There's no rain at all in July and August and the sea temperature hovers at a comfortable 25°C. During these months, the mercury can soar to 40°C in the shade just about anywhere on the coast although the highlands are much cooler. July and August are also the months of the *meltemi*, a strong northerly wind that sweeps the eastern coast of mainland Greece (including Athens) through the Aegean islands, the Cyclades and Crete. The wind is caused by air pressure differences between North Africa and the Balkans. The wind is a mixed blessing: it reduces humidity, but plays havoc with ferry schedules and sends everything flying – from beach umbrellas to washing hanging out to dry. Between May and August you may encounter the sirocco wind which blows up from Africa bringing dust and sand. The air becomes stifling but fortunately the wind only lasts from 24 to 72 hours.

The island begins to cool down in September and there is occasional rain. December, January and February are the rainiest months especially in the interior mountains, and there is snow on the peaks of the Lefka Ori. The clouds begin to lift in March when the temperature is mild enough to make outdoor activities such as hiking through the hills a pleasure.

ECOLOGY & ENVIRONMENT

Crete has not achieved a very high level of environmental awareness and environmental regulation is practically non-existent.

Despite severe water shortages in many parts of the island, you will still see storekeepers wash the footpaths with water. There are no recycling programs even though the huge influx of summer visitors entails tons of rubbish. Most tourist areas are kept relatively rubbish-free but in the interior you will often be treated to the pungent odour of garbage decomposing in a dump.

Crete's air and water outside the major cities is clean but the flora and fauna are under pressure from deforestation. Olive cultivation, firewood gathering, shipbuilding, uncontrolled livestock breeding and arson over the centuries have laid waste to the forests that had carpeted the island at one time. There is no tree replanting program, possibly because the 90,000 goats living on the island would chew through the sapplings. The use of pesticides and herbicides in farming has eliminated many bird and plant species and hunting has decimated the animal population.

It is along Crete's shoreline that environmental damage is most acute. Marine life has suffered from the local habit of fishing with dynamite and overdevelopment of the north coast is chasing away migratory birds. Worldwide concern has been roused for the plight of the loggerhead sea turtle, that nest on the same sandy beaches that tourists prize. *Caretta Caretta* is the Latin name for the turtle that has been nesting on Crete since the days of the dinosaurs. The beaches of Rethymno, Hania and the Messara Gulf in the south can host from 500 to 800 nests each summer. Sadly, the ribbon of taverns and hotels on the beachfront has seriously disturbed the nesting habits of this ancient species. Because these bulky creatures are so vulnerable on land, the females are frightened by objects on the beach at night and can refuse to lay eggs. When the hatchlings emerge at night they find the sea by the reflection of moon and starlight but are easily disoriented by tavern lights.

As tourism on Crete has ballooned over the last two decades, the island has had to cope with increasing demands for electricity. Although the power supply had long been reliant on fossil fuels, Greenpeace launched a major campaign in 1996 and persuaded the Greek government to help build the world's largest solar power plant on Crete. When completed in 2003, the

Loggerhead Turtles

The Sea Turtle Protection Society of Greece has the following advice for visitors:

- Leave the beaches clear at night during the May to October nesting season
- Remove umbrellas and lounge chairs at night
- Don't touch baby turtles on the way to the sea; they must orient themselves and the walk strengthens them
- Urge hotel and tavern owners to cooperate with the Society and shade their lights when necessary
- Dispose of rubbish properly; plastic bags, mistaken by the turtles as jellyfish, are lethal

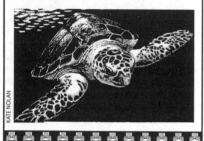

KATE NOLAN

plant will provide 50MW of solar power, which is enough power for almost 100,000 people. In order to encourage the installation of solar materials the government has offered subsidies and tax deductions to businesses and households. It is expected that the cost of electricity will be low enough to make the Crete installation a prototype for other solar power projects in the Mediterranean.

FLORA & FAUNA
Flora
One of the major attractions of a visit to Crete is the opportunity to enjoy the amazing variety of plants and wildflowers growing on the island. It has been estimated that there are about 2000 species of plants on the island and about 160 species of those are found only on Crete.

As a rule, a visit in March or April is the surest way to see the island in full flower but mountain plants and flowers often bloom later and late rains can also extend the growing season.

What you see depends upon when you come and where you are. Along the coast you'll come across sea daffodils that flower in August and September, and knapsweeds on the west coast that flower in April and May. The purple or violet petals of stocks provide pretty splashes of colour on sandy beaches from April to May. In eastern Crete, especially around Sitia, watch for crimson poppies on the borders of the beach in April and May. At the edge of sandy beaches that are not yet lined with a strip of hotels you'll find delicate pink bindweeds and jujube trees that flower from May to June and bear fruit in September and October. In the same habitat is the tamarisk tree that flowers in the spring.

Further away from the beach in the lowlands are junipers and holm oak trees as well as poppies and purple lupins that flower in the spring. If you come in the summer, you won't be deprived of colour since milky white and magenta oleanders bloom from June through August.

On the hillsides look for cistus and brooms in the early summer and in the fields fabulous yellow chrysanthemums flower from March to May.

Orchid buffs will find a lot to appreciate on Crete. Many varieties of orchids and ophrys bloom in the spring on the lower slopes of the mountains turning the hills and meadows bright with pink, purple and violet flowers. Dense-flowered orchids, pink-flowered butterfly orchids and Cretan cyclamens are found on the Lassithi Plateau. Purple and crimson anemones are found in the same habitat in early spring followed by yellow buttercups and crow-foots in late spring.

Cretan mountainsides are fragrant with the scents of oregano, thyme, sage and rosemary. One of the island's more unusual herbs is dittany *(Origanum dictamnus)* which is covered with small, round, grey leaves with small pink flowers at the end.

Drunk as an herbal tea, dittany is reputed to be both an aphrodisiac and an abortofacient. Its ability to induce an abortion if taken in large quantities early in the pregnancy has been scientifically verified. Its reputation as an aphrodisiac is purely anecdotal.

Fauna

Bird life is varied on Crete and includes both resident and migratory species. Along the coast you'll find birds of passage such as egrets and herons during the spring and autumn migration. Various species of gulls nest on coastal cliffs and offshore islets. Rare hawks migrate up from Africa during the summer to nest on the offshore islets. Woodpigeons still nest in cliffs along the sea but have been hunted to near extinction.

The mountains host a wealth of interesting birds. Look for blue rock thrushes, buzzards and huge vultures such as the griffon vulture. In the Samaria Gorge you may spot the rare *lammergeier*, or bearded vulture, now threatened with extinction. Other birds in the mountains include Alpine swifts, stonechats, blackbirds and Sardinian warblers. The fields around Malia host tawny and red-throated pipits, stone-curlews, fantailed warblers and short-toed larks. On the hillsides below the Moni Preveli you may find ruppell's and subalpine warblers. The Akrotiri Peninsula is a good place to look for birds. Migrating species such as waders, egrets and gulls are found on Souda Bay. Around the Agia Triada and Gouvernetou monasteries you'll find collared and pied flycatchers, wrynecks, tawny pipits, black-eared wheatears, blue rock thrushes, stonechats, chukars and northern wheatears.

Mammal life on Crete is divided between livestock and endangered species. Sheep, goats, and cows are treated with the respect appropriate to any money-making endeavour but all other mammals have been hunted ferociously. Crete's most famous animal is the *kri kri*, or wild goat, only a few of which survive in and around the Samaria Gorge. Apparently the animal was more prevalent in Minoan times and was often depicted in Minoan art.

One of the more intriguing rare animals on Crete is the *fourokattos* (wild cat). Shepherds have been telling tales for centuries about the mysterious wild cat but scientists assumed that the cat existed in legend only. The first indication that the cat may have been real occurred in 1905 when a British scientist bought two pelts at a market in Hania. Proof of the cat's existence occurred in 1996 when Italian scientists studying Cretan fauna found the 5½ kilogram cat in a trap one morning. It remains unclear whether the cat was indigenous to the island or whether it was a domesticated animal that ran wild. No further cats have been found.

Other mammals found on Crete include the indigenous Cretan spiny mouse and a large population of bats.

National Parks

The only national park in Crete is the Samaria Gorge, the largest and most impressive gorge in Europe. It is 18km long and has a visitor's centre. The Samaria Gorge is an important sanctuary for birds and animals; no one lives in the gorge.

GOVERNMENT & POLITICS

Greece is a parliamentary republic with a president as head of state. It is divided into regions and island groups. The regions of the mainland are the Peloponnese, Central Greece (officially called Sterea Ellada), Epiros, Thessaly, Macedonia and Thrace.

The island groups are the Cyclades, Dodecanese, North-Eastern Aegean, Sporades and Saronic Gulf, all in the Aegean Sea, and the Ionian Islands, which are in the Ionian Sea. The large islands of Evia and Crete do not belong to any group. For administrative purposes these regions and groups are divided into 51 prefectures or nomes (*nomoi* in Greek). Crete contains four of these: Lassithi, Iraklio, Rethymno and Hania. The island's capital and Greece's fifth-largest city is Iraklio, with a population of 127,600. As the island's capital until 1971, Hania considers itself the historical heart of the island and Rethymno claims to be its cultural centre. Rivalries between the prefectures are strong as each competes for investment, tourism and, more recently, distribution of the island's water supply.

Centuries of battling foreign occupiers have left the island with a stubbornly independent streak that sometimes leads to clashes with Athens. NATO bases on the island are a sore point with the local population who would like to see them removed despite foreign policy commitments by the national government. National laws that conflict with local customs are simply disregarded. Guns are strictly regulated in Greece but nearly every household in Crete has at least one illegal firearm and many harbour small arsenals.

Politically, the island is more moderate. The dominant ideology is left-of-centre with the socialist PASOK party repeatedly outdrawing the conservative New Democracy party in local and national elections. Extremists on either the right or left have little support.

ECONOMY

Greece is an agricultural country, but the importance of agriculture to the economy has declined rapidly since WWII. Some 50% of the workforce is now employed in services (contributing 59% of GDP), 22% in agriculture (contributing 15%), and 27% in industry and construction (contributing 26%). Tourism is by far the biggest industry; shipping comes next. The eight million tourists who visit Greece each year contribute around US$3 billion to the economy.

Although Greece has the second-lowest income per capita of all the EU countries (after Portugal), its economic future looks brighter now than it has for some time. The economy suffered badly from the fighting in the Balkans in the early 90s, which cut Greece's major overland trade route to the rest of Europe. Peace in the Balkans has done much to restore business confidence. The austerity measures imposed by successive governments also appear to have had the desired effect, with inflation cut to single figures (8.5%) for the first time in 22 years, and unemployment officially running at 10%. Its economy is unlikely to be in good enough health to meet the criteria for the first phase of European monetary union in 1999, but the government is confident that it will be ready for the second phase.

Agriculture and tourism are the twin engines of the Cretan economy leaving the island with an unemployment rate of only 5.5% – almost half the national rate. Olives, olive oil, sultanas, wine, vegetables and fruit are produced in quantity for export. Although fewer people are working in agriculture than in the postwar period, improvements in roads and better techniques are allowing the output to remain the same and in some cases increase. Tourism has expanded to the point where it constitutes two-thirds of the Gross Regional Product of Crete and provides employment to 40% of the island's workforce. The labour-intensive tourism sector draws seasonal workers from mainland Greece, the EU and Eastern Europe to work in hotels, restaurants, shops and bars.

POPULATION & PEOPLE

Crete is Greece's most populous island with 537,000 people. The population figures of the island's major cities are: Iraklio (127,600), Hania (65,000), Rethymno (24,000), Agios Nikolaos (9000). After the exodus of the Turkish population in 1923 Crete became ethnically homogenous, consisting solely of Greek Orthodox residents. Modern Cretans are a mixture of all the races and ethnic groups that occupied them over the centuries.

EDUCATION

Education in Greece is free at all levels of the state system from kindergarten to tertiary. Primary schooling begins at the age of six, but most children attend a state-run kindergarten from the age of five. Private kindergartens are popular with those who can afford them.

Primary school classes tend to be larger than those in most European countries – usually 30 to 35 children. Primary school hours are short (8 am to 1pm), but children get a lot of homework.

(continued on page 41)

CRETAN
ART

CRETAN ART

One of the great joys of visiting Crete is discovering the sculpture, pottery, frescoes and icons that express thousands of years of Cretan culture. From prehistoric pottery to 17th-century icons, Cretan art has influenced and been influenced by the civilisations that have come into contact with the island. The interchange between Crete, its colonies and its conquerors has left a profound impact on the development of Aegean culture. Although there are fine museums in all Crete's major cities, Iraklio's Archaeological Museum has the best collection of Cretan art from the prehistoric through the Roman eras.

Title page: The walls of the palace at Knossos were adorned with frescoes, such as the *Priest King Fresco*, which often depicted religious ceremonies. (photo by Heracleion Museum)

Left: The *La Parisienne* fresco is one of the many that decorated the palace at Knossos.

Neolithic & Early Minoan Periods

Little is known about the Neolithic cave dwellers of Crete but it appears that they made crude and undecorated pottery. Since the potter's wheel had not yet been invented, the pots were simply baked in a fire resulting in uneven colouring. The first figurines depicted human forms and were usually carved from stone. The male marble figurine found at Knossos is a good example of this early style that seems related to similar figurines in the Cyclades. Pottery technique advanced in the early Minoan years. Spirals and curvilinear motifs in white were painted on dark vases and several distinct styles emerged. Pyrgos pottery was characterised by black, grey or brown colours and, later on, Vasiliki pottery, made near Ierapetra, displayed polychrome surfaces. Gold, silver and bronze jewellery and daggers were finely crafted and foreshadowed the later achievements of Minoan art.

Protopalatial Period

The founding of the first Minoan palaces on Crete in 2000 BC coincided with the production of the so-called Kamares pottery in the workshops of Knossos and Phaestos. Named after the cave at Kamares where the pottery was first found, this elegant, beautifully crafted pottery flourished during the entire Middle Minoan period. Cups, spouted jars and pithoi (large Minoan storage jars) could now be produced quickly with the invention of the potter's wheel. The use of the wheel also gave a new crispness to the designs. The stylised motifs were derived from plant and marine life and were balanced with curvilinear abstract patterns. The finely worked designs were usually painted in white, red, orange and yellow on black or grey backgrounds. The most striking pottery was the 'eggshell' vases characterised by extremely thin walls. Kamares pottery was exported to Cyprus, Egypt and the Levant.

Right: The finely worked designs of the Kamares style balanced plant and marine life with abstract patterns as seen in this pottery vase.

Other crafts also reached a high degree of artistry during this period. Using semi-precious stones and clay, artisans made miniature master-pieces out of carved sealstones which sometimes contained hiero-glyphic letters. The exquisite bee pendant found at Malia displays extraordinary delicacy and imagination in jewellery making.

Neopalatial Period

From 1700 to 1400 BC Minoan civilisation reached its 'golden age'. Al-though fresco painting probably existed before 1700 BC, all remnants were destroyed in the cataclysm that destroyed Minoan palaces around that date. The palace at Knossos yielded the richest trove of frescoes from the Neopalatial period. Although only fragments survive, they were very carefully restored and the technique of using plant and mineral dyes has kept the colours relatively fresh. The subjects reflect the full variety of Minoan experience and influenced wall paintings on the Greek mainland. Landscapes rich with animals and birds, marine life teaming with fish and octopus, banquets, games and rituals are rendered with vivid naturalism. Griffins are repeatedly represented in-dicating that they may have had a protective function. Minoan fresco painters borrowed heavily from certain Egyptian conventions – men's skin was bronze and women's was white, for example – but the figures are far less rigid than most Egyptian wall paintings.

Pottery also flourished in the Neopalatial era. In the early years there was the marine style and a floral style that reflected the same themes

Top Left: This fine piece of gold jewellery depict-ing two bees dropping honey into a comb was found at Malia.

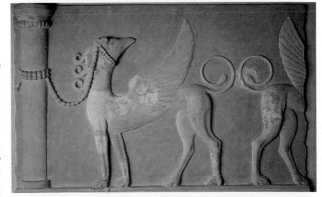

Top left: This *Bull's Head* stone rhyton is an example of Minoan pottery which often took the shape of animal's heads.

Top right: The faience figurine of the *snake goddess*, which was found at Knossos, is a fine example of Minoan sculpture.

Middle: Griffins were believed to offer protection against invaders and were often used in Minoan frescoes. The *Griffin Fresco* was found in the Throne Room at Knossos.

Bottom: Minoan frescoes offered landscapes rich with animal life, as can be seen in the *Dolphin Fresco*.

ALL PHOTOS BY HERACLEION MUSEUM

as the era's frescoes. Octopuses, dolphins and fish appeared on some pottery while others showed flowers, leaves and branches along with religious symbols. In contrast to earlier pottery the decoration was often in dark colours such as brown and rust painted on light backgrounds. After 1500 BC, vases spouted three handles and were frequently shaped as animal heads. The stone rhyton in the shape of a bull's head is a particularly fine example from this period.

The art of sealstone carving also advanced in the palace workshops. Knossos, Zakros and Agia Triada were the most productive. Naturalistic subjects such as goats, lions and griffins were rendered in minute detail on hard stones, usually in an almond shape. Minoan sculptors also created fine idols in faience, gold, ivory bronze and stone. The

Left: The *Harvesters Vase* is one of three celebrated vases found at the small Minoan site of Agia Triada.

serpent goddess in faience (tin-glazed earthenware) is one of the most outstanding surviving examples.

Post Palatial Period

The second cataclysm of 1750 that destroyed Minoan palaces saw the decline of Minoan culture. The lively marine pottery of previous centuries degenerated into dull rigidity. Whether because of less trade with Egypt or the loss of the palace workshops, frescoes became uninspired. The production of jewellery and sealstones was replaced by the production of weaponry reflecting the influence of the warlike Myceaneans.

Dorian & Roman Periods

There was a brief artistic renaissance on Crete that lasted from the 8th to the 7th centuries BC. A new movement in sculpture emerged called the Daedalic movement after a sculptor called Daedalos. Although the existence of this sculptor is uncertain, it is clear that a group of sculptors called the Daedalids perfected a new technique of making

Right: The hieroglyphic inscription on the famous *Phaestos Disc*, found just north of the palace at Phaestos, has yet to be deciphered.

HERACLEION MUSEUM

sculptures in hammered bronze. They worked in a style that combined Eastern and Greek aesthetics and their influence spread to mainland Greece. Cretan culture went into decline again at the end of the 7th century BC. There was a brief revival under the Romans, mainly notable for the richly decorated mosaic floors and marble sculpture such as the colossal statue of Apollo.

Byzantine & Venetian Periods

Although Byzantine icons and frescoes were created from the earliest years of Byzantine rule much was destroyed in the rebellions of the 13th and 14th centuries. In the 11th century, emigres from Constantinople brought portable icons to Crete but the only surviving example from this period is the icon of the virgin at Mesopantitissa, now in Venice. From the 13th to the early-16th centuries, churches around Crete were decorated with frescoes – many of which can still be seen. Byzantine art flowered under the Palaeologan emperors who ruled from 1258 to 1453, and its influence spread to Crete. The great icon painter of the 14th century was Ioannis Pagomenos who worked in West Crete.

With the fall of Constantinople in 1453 many Byzantine artists fled to Crete. At the same time, the Italian Renaissance was in full bloom and many Cretan artists studied in Italy. The result was the 'Cretan school' of icon painting that combined technical brilliance and dramatic richness. In Hania alone there were over 200 painters working from the mid-16th to mid-17th centuries who were equally at ease in Venetian and Byzantine styles. The Cretan Theophanes Sterlitzas painted monasteries throughout Greece that spread the techniques of the Cretan school.

Too few examples of the Cretan school are on display in Crete but visitors to Iraklio are fortunate to have the church and museum of Agia Ekaterini. Six portable icons from the great Michael Damaskinos, the finest exponent of the Cretan school, form the centrepiece of the collection. Damaskinos' long sojourn in Venice introduced him to new techniques of rendering perspective, which he brought to the Byzantine style of icon painting.

(continued from page 32)

At 12, children enter the *gymnasio*, and at 15 they may leave school, or enter the *lykeio*, from where they take university entrance examinations. Although there is a high percentage of literacy, many parents and pupils are dissatisfied with the education system, especially beyond primary level. The private sector therefore flourishes, and even relatively poor parents struggle to send their children to one of the country's 5000 *frontistiria* (intensive coaching colleges) to prepare them for the very competitive university entrance exams. Grievances reached a peak in 1991, when lykeio students staged a series of sit-ins in schools throughout the country, and organised protest marches. In 1992, gymnasio pupils followed suit, and the government responded by calling for stricter discipline and a more demanding curriculum. After more sit-ins the government changed its plans and is still reassessing the situation.

ARTS

See the 'Cretan Art' special section for a detailed look at the history of art in Crete.

Music & Dance

In addition to its own traditional music and dances, Crete incorporates music and dance from all over Greece. The folk dances of today derive from the ritual dances performed in ancient Greek temples. One of these dances, the *syrtos*, is depicted on ancient Greek vases, and there are references to dances in Homer's works. Homer commented on the ability of Cretan dancers, which were often depicted in Minoan frescoes.

Many Greek folk dances, including the syrtos, are performed in a circular formation. In ancient times, dancers formed a circle to seal themselves off from evil influences.

Dancing has always been a large part of Cretan celebrations. In addition to Greek dances Cretans dance the *pentozalis*, a circle dance involving male dancers leaping to a fast beat. Other Cretan dances include the

kastrinos and *maleveziotiko*, also fast dances, and the *sousta* dance for couples.

Each region of Greece has its own dances, but one dance you'll see performed everywhere is the *kalamatianos*, originally from Kalamata in the Peloponnese. It's the dance in which dancers stand in a row with their hands on one another's shoulders.

Singing and the playing of musical instruments have also been an integral part of life in Greece since ancient times. Cycladic figurines holding musical instruments resembling harps and flutes date back to 2000 BC. Musical instruments of ancient Greece included the lyre, lute, *piktis* (pipes), *kroupeza* (a percussion instrument), *kithara* (a stringed instrument), *aulos* (a wind instrument), *barbitos* (similar to a violin cello) and the *magadio* (similar to a harp).

If ancient Greeks did not have a musical instrument to accompany their songs, they imitated the sound of one. It is believed that unaccompanied Byzantine choral singing derived from this custom.

The *bouzouki*, heard everywhere in Greece, is a mandolin-like instrument. It is one of the main instruments of *rembetika* music – the Greek equivalent of the American Blues. The name rembetika may come from the Turkish word *rembet* which means outlaw. Opinions differ as to the origins of

The bouzouki is one of the main instruments used in *rembetika* music

rembetika, but it is probably a hybrid of several different types of music. One source was the music that emerged in the 1870s in the 'low life' cafes, called *tekedes* (hashish dens), in urban areas and especially around ports. Another source was the Arabo-Persian music played in sophisticated Middle Eastern music cafes *(amanedes)* in the 19th century. Rembetika was popularised in Greece by the refugees from Asia Minor.

The songs that emerged from the tekedes had themes concerning hashish, prison life, gambling, knife fights etc, whereas cafe aman music had themes that centred around erotic love. These all came together in the music of the refugees, from which a subculture of rebels, called *manges*, emerged. The manges wore showy clothes even though they lived in extreme poverty. They worked long hours in menial jobs, and spent their evenings in the tekedes, smoking hashish and singing and dancing. Although hashish was illegal, the law was rarely enforced until Metaxas did his clean-up job in 1936. It was in a tekedes in Piraeus that Markos Vamvakaris, now acknowledged as the greatest rembetis, was discovered by a recording company in the 1930s.

Metaxas' censorship meant that themes of hashish, prison, gambling and the like disappeared from recordings of rembetika in the late 1930s, but continued clandestinely in some tekedes. This polarised the music, and the recordings, stripped of their 'meaty' themes and language, became insipid and bourgeois; recorded rembetika even adopted another name – *laiko tragoudi* – to disassociate it from its illegal roots. Although WWII brought a halt to recording, a number of composers emerged at this time. They included Apostolos Kaldaras, Yiannis Papaïoanou, Georgos Mitsakis and Manolis Hiotis, and one of the greatest female rembetika singers, Sotiria Bellou, also appeared at this time.

During the 1950s and 1960s rembetika became increasingly popular, but less and less authentic. Much of the music was glitzy and commercialised, although the period also produced two outstanding composers of popular music (including rem-

betika) in Mikis Theodorakis and Manos Hatzidakis. The best of Theodorakis' work is the music which he set to the poetry of Seferis, Elytis and Ritsos. During the junta years, many rembetika clubs were closed down, but interest in genuine rembetika revived in the 1980s – particularly among students and intellectuals.

In Crete, music is woven into the fabric of everyday life and accompanies weddings, births, deaths, holidays, harvesting and simply relaxing. The main instruments are the *lyra*, which is similar to a violin and the eight-stringed *lute*, which is played like a guitar. One of Crete's favourite forms of musical expression is *mantinades*, improvised couplets of 30 syllables that express the age-old concerns of love, death and the vagaries of fate. Probably originating as love songs in 15th-century Venice, thousands of mantinades helped forge a sense of national identity during the long centuries of occupation. Since the verses are improvised, 'rhymers' at Cretan festivals tailor the songs to the people present at the event and try to outdo each other in skill.

Another popular form is *rizitika* which are centuries-old songs from the Lefka Ori that derived from the songs of the border guards of the Byzantine Empire.

There are two kinds of rizitika – *tavla* (table) songs that accompany feasts and *strata* (round) songs which accompany travellers. Many of the rizitika songs deal with historical or heroic themes. One of the most popular is the song of Daskalogiannis, the Sfakian hero who led the rebellion against the Turks in 1770. The song has 1034 verses and is still sung throughout Sfakia.

Literature

Crete has a rich literary tradition that sprang from the Cretan love of songs, verses and word play. In the late 16th or early 17th centuries, Crete had a tremendous literary flowering under Venetian rule. The era's greatest masterpiece was undoubtedly the epic poem *Erotokritos* written by Vitzentzos Kornaros of Sitia. More than 10,000 lines long, this poem of courtly love is full of nostalgia for the dying Venetian regime that was threatened by the rise in Turkish power. The poem was recited for centuries by illiterate peasants and professional singers alike, embodying the dreams of freedom that enabled Cretans to endure their many privations. Many of the verses were incorporated into Crete's beloved mantinades.

Greece's best-known writer since Homer is Nikos Kazantzakis, born in Iraklio in 1883 amid the last spasms of Crete's struggle for independence from the Turks. Educated as a lawyer in Athens and abroad, Kazantzakis continued his studies at the Sorbonne in Paris. His first works were travel books on a variety of European, Middle East and eastern destinations. He then began translating classics into modern Greek and wrote his own epic poem, *The Odyssey*, a sequel to Homer's original. Throughout his career this prolific writer produced 12 novels, 22 plays, nine screenplays, a history of Russian literature, three philosophical studies and hundreds of articles. His best-known novel in Greece is *Freedom or Death* which deals with the Turkish occupation but his international fame rests upon *Zorba the Greek*, a lively portrait of Crete and the irrepressible free spirit Zorba. Although Zorba is an engaging and unforgettable character, the author's undisguised misogyny has not worn well. Kazantzakis was nominated several times for the Noble Prize and both *Zorba the Greek* and *The Last Temptation of Christ* were made into movies. His tomb in Iraklio is inscribed with his quotation: 'I hope for nothing. I fear nothing. I am free.'

Iraklio may have Kazantzakis but Rethymno has Pandelis Prevelakis. Born in Rethymno in 1900, Prevelakis also studied in Athens and at the Sorbonne. Primarily known as a poet, Prevelakis also wrote plays and novels. His best-known work is *The Tale of a Town* about Rethymno.

Film

Cretans are avid cinema-goers, although most of the films shown are North American or British. The Greek film industry is in the doldrums, largely due to inadequate government funding. The problem is compounded by the type of films the Greeks produce which have a reputation for being slow moving, loaded with symbolism and generally too avant-garde to have mass appeal, despite being well-made with some outstanding cinematography.

Greece's most acclaimed film director is Theodoros Angelopoulos, whose films include *The Beekeeper*, *Alexander the Great*, *Travelling Players*, *Landscapes in the Mist* and *The Hesitant Step of the Stork*. All have received awards at both national and international festivals.

SOCIETY & CONDUCT
Traditional Culture

Proud, patriotic, hospitable and religious, today's Cretan's strong connection to their ancestors is apparent as soon as you leave the major tourist centres. Mountain villages are repositories of traditional culture and you'll find that most older women and many men are still clad in black garb. During weddings and festivals even young men don black boots, shirt and baggy pants, tucking a pistol into their belt to be fired into the air as the evening wears on.

One of the more remarkable features of Cretan life is the ability of the islanders to

Nights of the Undead

As though hazards like wars and vendettas weren't frightening enough, older Cretans believed they were also subject to vampires called *vrykolakas*. Suicides, unbaptised children and excommunicates could all become *vrykolakas*. Every night, except Saturday, these flesh-eating ghouls allegedly roamed the hills searching for victims in remote mountain villages. Villagers said that if the vampire's blood touched you it would burn through your skin. The only way a *vrykolakas* could achieve final rest was being hit by lightning or consumed by fire.

Cretan Knives

Given the island's unruly history, it's not surprising that Cretans have a highly developed tradition of cutlery. Traditional Cretan dress for men always includes a knife, often white-handled, as part of the standard black shirt, trousers and boots outfit. Knives have acquired a power that borders on the mystical. Older Cretans believe that knives made during Holy Week offer protection from evil spirits. In eastern Crete, it's considered bad luck to give a knife as a present while in western Crete, it's considered good luck for the best man or godfather at a wedding to be presented with a knife.

Although the Minoans certainly produced knives, the current method probably developed under Turkish rule. At that time, the handles were made from buffalo horn or mountain goat antlers but since horns have become rarer, cutlers sometimes use cattle bones. Unfortunately, customers are also becoming more scarce and the cutlers' craft is slowly disappearing.

A good Cretan knife is hard to find now but you can always make your own. Here's how:

1. If you don't have a goat horn, get a good slab of cattle bone.
2. Boil it for 4 to 5 hours in water, ashes and lime.
3. Carve it into shape.
4. Forge a stainless steel blade with a single edge.
5. Emboss the knife with designs or a verse from a *mantinade*.
6. Find some oleander wood for the sheath. Make sure to cut it when the moon is waning or it will soon be oozing worms.
7. Split the wood in the middle and carve out the interior to fit the blade.
8. Cut a thin piece of leather into shape and glue it to the sheath.
9. Fit handle, blade and sheath together, tuck it into your black trousers and look for some *raki*.

maintain many aspects of their traditional culture in the face of a seasonal invasion of foreign tourists. Cretans have learned to co-exist partly by operating in a different time-space continuum than their guests. From April to around October, the islanders live in the hurly-burly of the coastal resorts running shops, pensions or tavernas and then return to their traditional life in the hills for the autumn olive and grape harvest. Tourists eat early in the evening in restaurants along a harbour or beach while Cretans drive out to a village taverna for a dinner that begins around 11 pm. Dance clubs play Western music until around 3 am when the Greek crowd arrives and the music switches to Cretan or Greek music.

Men and women also occupy different spheres. When not tending livestock or olive trees, Cretan men can usually be found in a *kafeneio* playing cards and drinking coffee or *raki*. Although exceptions are made for foreign women, kafeneia are off-limits to Cretan women who are usually occupied with housework and child rearing. In their off-hours, women busy themselves with sewing, crocheting or embroidery, often in a circle of other women. Old attitudes towards the 'proper role' for women are changing, however, as more women enter the workforce. Young Cretan women have discarded shapeless dresses in favour of skin-tight slacks and are more likely to be found in a disco than behind a loom. Friction has developed between the older generation and a younger generation more attuned to European influences. Fortunately the employment opportunities brought by the tourist business has discouraged young people from leaving the island, thus allowing them to retain at least a nominal contact with their parent's culture.

Dos & Don'ts

If you go into a kafeneio, taverna or shop, it is customary to greet the waiters or assistants with '*kalimera*' (good day) or '*kalispera*' (good evening). Personal questions are not considered rude, so prepare to be inundated with queries about your age, salary, marital status etc, and to be given sympathy if you are over 25 and not married!

Cretans have a well-justified reputation for hospitality. The tradition was to treat strangers as honoured guests and invite them for coffee, a meal or to spend the night. Obviously Cretans are no longer offering free food and lodging to several million tourists a year but if you wander off the beaten track into mountain villages you may be invited to someone's home. If you're served a glass of water, coffee and some preserves it is the custom to first drink the water then eat the preserves and then drink the coffee. When visiting someone, it is bad manners to refuse the coffee or raki they'll offer you. You may feel uneasy, especially if your host is poor, but don't offend them by offering money. Give a gift, perhaps to a child in the family, instead.

If you go out for a meal with Cretans, the bill is not shared but rather paid by the host. When drinking wine, only half fill the glass and don't let it become empty (a no-no).

Cretans have a long tradition of welcoming foreigners which has made them tolerant of different customs. Although Greek women are unlikely to go topless, in most places topless sunbathing is allowed. The few south coast beaches where it is frowned upon post signs to that effect.

Treatment of Animals

The Cretan attitude to animals depends on whether the animal is a cat or not. It's definitely cool to be a cat. Even the mangiest-looking stray can be assured of a warm welcome and a choice tidbit on approaching the restaurant table of a Greek. Most other domestic animals are greeted with a certain indifference or put to work. Most shepherds have dogs for guarding the flock but they are treated poorly, often chained to a post for days and fed inadequately.

The main threat to animal welfare is hunting. Cretan hunters are notorious for blasting anything that moves, and millions of animals are killed during the long 'open' season, from 20 August to 10 March, which encompasses the bird migratory period. The Hellenic Wildlife Hospital (☎ 0297-22 882), on the island of Aegina, reports that 80% of the animals it treats have been shot.

RELIGION

About 98% of Greeks belong to the Greek Orthodox Church. Most of the remainder are either Roman Catholic, Jewish or Muslim.

The Greek Orthodox Church is closely related to the Russian Orthodox Church and together with it forms the third-largest branch of Christianity. Orthodox, meaning 'right belief', was founded in the 4th century by Constantine the Great, who was converted to Christianity by a vision of the Cross.

By the 8th century, there were a number of differences of opinion between the pope in Rome and the patriarch of Constantinople, as well as increasing rivalry between the two. One dispute was over the wording of the Creed. The original Creed stated that the Holy Spirit proceeds 'from the Father', which the Orthodox Church adhered to, whereas Rome added 'and the Son'. Another bone of contention concerned the celibacy of the clergy. Rome decreed priests had to be celibate; in the Orthodox Church, a priest could marry before he became ordained. There were also differences in fasting: in the Orthodox Church, not only was meat forbidden during Lent, but wine and oil were also.

By the 11th century these differences had become irreconcilable, and in 1054 the pope and the patriarch excommunicated one another. Ever since, the two have gone their own ways as the (Greek/Russian) Orthodox Church and the Roman Catholic Church.

During Ottoman times membership of the Orthodox Church was one of the most important criteria in defining a Greek, regardless of where he or she lived. The church was the principal upholder of Greek culture and traditions.

(Continued on page 50)

MYTHOLOGY

Mythology was an integral part of life in ancient times. The myths are accounts of the lives of the deities whom the Greeks worshipped and of the heroes they idolised.

The myths are all things to all people – a ripping good yarn, expressions of deep psychological insights, words of spine-tingling poetic beauty and food for the imagination. They have inspired great literature, art and music – as well as the odd TV show.

The myths we know are thought to be a blend of Dorian and Mycenaean mythology. Most accounts derive from the works of the poets Hesiod and Homer, produced in about 900 BC. The original myths have been chopped and changed countless times – dramatised, moralised and even adapted for ancient political propaganda – so numerous versions exist.

The Greek Myths by Robert Graves is regarded as being the ultimate book on the subject. It can be heavy going, though. *An Iconoclast's Guide to the Greek Gods* by Maureen O'Sullivan makes more entertaining reading.

The Twelve Deities

The main characters of the myths are the 12 deities who lived on Mt Olympus – which the Greeks thought to be at the exact centre of the world.

The supreme deity was **Zeus**, who was also god of the heavens. His job was to make laws and keep his unruly family in order by brandishing his thunderbolt. He was also the possessor of an astonishing libido and vented his lust on just about everyone he came across, including his own mother. Mythology is littered with his offspring.

Zeus was married to his sister, **Hera**, the protector of women and the family. Hera was able to renew her virginity each year by bathing in a spring. She was the mother of Ares, Hephaestus and Hebe.

Ares, god of war, was the embodiment of everything warlike. Strong and brave, he was definitely someone to have on your side in a fight – but he was also hot-tempered and violent, liking nothing better than a good massacre. Athenians, who fought only for such noble ideals as liberty, thought that Ares must be a Thracian – whom they regarded as bloodthirsty barbarians.

RICARDO BUSTOS

Hephaestus was worshipped for his matchless skills as a craftsman. When Zeus decided to punish man, he asked Hephaestus to make a woman. So Hephaestus created Pandora from clay and water, and, as everyone knows, she had a box, from which sprang all the evils afflicting humankind.

RICARDO BUSTOS

The next time you have a bowl of corn flakes, give thanks to **Demeter**, the goddess of earth and fertility. The English word 'cereal', for products of corn or edible grain, derives from the goddess' Roman name, Ceres. The Greek word for such products is *demetriaka*.

The goddess of love (and lust) was the beautiful **Aphrodite**. Her *tour de force* was her magic girdle which made everyone fall in love with its wearer. The girdle meant she was constantly pursued by both gods and goddesses – the gods because they wanted to make love to her, the goddesses because they wanted to borrow the girdle. Zeus became so fed up with her promiscuity that he married her off to Hephaestus, the ugliest of the gods.

Athena, the powerful goddess of wisdom and guardian of Athens, is said to have been born (complete with helmet, armour and spear) from Zeus' head, with Hephaestus acting as midwife. Unlike Ares, she derived no pleasure from fighting, preferring to use her wisdom to settle disputes peacefully. If need be, however, she went valiantly into battle.

Poseidon, the brother of Zeus, was god of the sea and preferred his sumptuous palace in the depths of the Aegean to Mt Olympus. When he was angry (which was often) he would use his trident to create massive waves and floods. His moods could also trigger earthquakes and volcanic eruptions. He was always on the lookout for some real estate on dry land and challenged Dionysos for Naxos, Hera for Argos and Athena for Athens.

Apollo, god of light, was the son of Zeus by the nymph Leto. He was the sort of person everybody wanted to have around. The ancient Greeks associated sunshine with spiritual and intellectual illumination. Apollo was also worshipped as the god of music and song, which the ancients believed were heard only where there was light and security. His twin sister, **Artemis**, seems to have been a bit confused by her portfolio. She was worshipped as the goddess of childbirth, yet she asked Zeus to grant her eternal virginity; she was also the protector of suckling animals, but loved hunting!

Hermes, messenger of the gods, was another son of Zeus – this time by Maia, daughter of Atlas. He was a colourful character who smooth-talked his way into the top ranks of the Greek pantheon. Convicted of rustling Apollo's cattle while still in his cradle, he emerged from the case as the guardian of all divine property. Zeus then made Hermes his messenger, and fitted him out with a pair of winged golden sandals to speed him on his way. His job included responsibility for commerce, treaties and the safety of travellers. He remained, however, the patron of thieves.

Hermes completes the first XI – the gods whose position in the pantheon is agreed by everyone. The final berth is normally reserved for **Hestia**, goddess of the hearth. She was as pure as driven snow, a symbol of security, happiness and hospitality. She spurned disputes and wars and swore to be a virgin forever.

She was a bit too virtuous for some, who relegated her to the ranks of the Lesser Gods and promoted the fun-loving **Dionysos**, god of wine, in her place. Dionysos was a son of Zeus by another of the supreme deity's dalliances. He had the job of touring the world with an entourage of fellow revellers spreading the word about the vine and wine.

Lesser Gods

After his brothers Zeus and Poseidon had taken the heavens and seas, **Hades** was left with the underworld (the earth was common ground). This vast and mysterious region was thought by the Greeks to be as far beneath the earth as the sky was above it. The underworld was divided into three regions: the Elysian Fields for the virtuous, Tartarus for sinners and the Asphodel Meadows for those who fitted neither category. Hades was also the god of wealth, in the form of the precious stones and metals found deep in the earth.

Pan, the son of Hermes, was the god of the shepherds. Born with horns, beard, tail and goat legs, his ugliness so amused the other gods that eventually he fled to Arcadia where he danced, played his famous pipes and watched over the pastures, shepherds and herds.

Other gods included: **Asclepius**, god of healing; **Eros**, god of love; **Hypnos**, god of sleep; **Helios**, god of the sun; and **Selene**, goddess of the moon.

Mythology & the Islands

The Gods may have lived on Mt Olympus, but their influence extended to the farthest reaches of Greek territory and the islands feature prominently in mythology.

RICARDO BUSTOS

The sacred island of **Delos** was the birthplace of the twins Apollo and Artemis, while Zeus himself was raised in Dikteon Cave on **Crete**.

The island of **Ikaria** is named after Icarus, who plunged into the sea after he flew too close to the sun. **Aegina** is named after a daughter of the river god, Asopus. She was taken to the island by Zeus on another of his lecherous sorties.

Olympian Creation Myth

According to mythology, the world was formed from a great shapeless mass called Chaos. From Chaos came forth Gaea, the earth goddess. She bore a son, Uranus, the Firmament, and their subsequent union produced three 100-handed giants and three one-eyed Cyclopes. Gaea dearly loved her hideous offspring, but not so Uranus, who hurled them into Tartarus (the underworld).

The couple then produced the seven Titans, but Gaea still grieved for her other children. She asked the Titans to take vengeance upon their father, and free the 100-handed giants and the Cyclopes. The Titans did as they were requested, castrating the hapless Uranus, but Cronos (the head Titan), after setting eyes on Gaea's hideous offspring, hurled them back into Tartarus, whereupon Gaea foretold that Cronos would be usurped by one of his own offspring.

Cronos married his sister Rhea, but wary of his mother's warning, he swallowed every child Rhea bore him. When Rhea bore her sixth child, Zeus, she smuggled him to Crete, and gave Cronos a stone in place of the child, which he duly swallowed. Rhea hid the baby Zeus in the Dikteon Cave in the care of three nymphs.

On reaching manhood, Zeus, determined to avenge his swallowed siblings, became Cronos' cupbearer and filled his cup with poison. Cronos drank from the cup, then disgorged first the stone and then his children Hestia, Demeter, Hera, Poseidon and Hades, all of whom were none the worse for their ordeal. Zeus, aided by his regurgitated brothers and sisters, deposed Cronos, and went to war against the Titans who wouldn't acknowledge him as chief god. Gaea, who still hadn't forgotten her imprisoned, beloved offspring, told Zeus he would only be victorious with the help of the Cyclopes and the 100-handed giants, so he released them from Tartarus.

The Cyclopes gave Zeus a thunderbolt, and the three 100-handed giants threw rocks at the Titans, who eventually retreated. Zeus banished Cronos, as well as all of the Titans except Atlas (Cronos' deputy), to a far-off land. Atlas was ordered to hold up the sky.

Mt Olympus became home-sweet-home for Zeus and his family. Zeus soon took a fancy to his sister Hera. He tricked the unsuspecting Hera into holding him to her bosom by turning himself into a dishevelled cuckoo, then violated her. Hera reluctantly agreed to marry him and they had three children: Ares, Hephaestus and Hebe.

RICARDO BUSTOS

(Continued from page 45)

Vendettas

Cretans are an ethnic mix, formed from the races and ethnicities that occupied the island over the millennia. However, ethnic and religious homogeneity has not brought harmony. Cretans are notorious throughout Greece for murderous vendettas that have lasted for generations and caused hundreds of Cretans to flee the island.

Particularly prevalent in Sfakia, the south-west of Crete, a vendetta can start over the theft of some sheep, an errant bullet at a wedding or anything deemed an insult to family honour. The insult is avenged with a murder, which must be avenged with another murder and so on. Modernity has in no way stemmed the carnage and, in fact, prosperity has allowed avengers to pursue their targets across Greece.

Religion is still integral to life in Greece, and the Greek year is centred on the festivals of the church calendar. Most Greeks, when they have a problem, will go into a church and light a candle to the saint they feel is most likely to help them. On the islands you will see hundreds of tiny churches dotted around the countryside. Most have been built by individual families in the name of their family's selected patron saint as thanksgiving for God's protection.

The Orthodox religion held Cretan culture together during the many dark centuries of repression despite numerous, largely futile efforts by the Venetians and Turks to turn the Cretans toward Catholicism and Islam.

Cretans still celebrate Greek Orthodox holidays with enthusiasm, though it's interesting to note that the Orthodox Church of Crete is independent from the Greek Orthodox Church and answers directly to the Patriarch of Constantinople.

If you wish to look around a church, you should dress appropriately. Women should wear skirts that reach below the knees, men should wear long trousers and arms should be covered. Regrettably, many churches are kept locked nowadays, but it's usually easy enough to locate caretakers, who will be happy to open them up for you.

LANGUAGE

Greek is the official language in Crete. English is spoken only in areas catering to large numbers of tourists, so away from major towns you'll need at least some Greek. See the Language chapter at the back of this book for a brief guide to Greek and a list of useful words and phrases.

Facts for the Visitor

The Best

It's tough trying to pick just 10 of the best things about Crete. These are personal favourites; the places, things and activities the authors of this book would most like to dedicate a lot more of their time to:

- Swimming at uncrowded beaches
- Traditional villages
- Late night dinners at village tavernas
- Eating fresh seafood by the sea
- Cretan music
- Exploring the island on foot
- Easter festivities
- Cretan hospitality
- Siesta time
- Wedding feasts that include an entire village

The Worst

We'd be very happy not to experience the following again:

- Concrete-box domatia spoiling landscapes
- The attitude to rubbish
- Hot, mosquito-ridden hotel rooms
- The loss of traditional lifestyles as every man, woman and dog tries to make a fast buck out of tourism
- Brash restaurant touts accosting passers-by
- Smoking
- Demon drivers
- Ouzo-induced hangovers
- Iraklio airport
- Poorly marked and potholed roads

PLANNING
When to Go

The best times to visit Crete are in late spring/early summer and in autumn. Winter is pretty much a dead loss. Most of the tourist infrastructure goes into hibernation from November until the beginning of April – hotels and restaurants are closed and bus and ferry services are either drastically reduced or plain cancelled.

The cobwebs are dusted off in time for Easter, when the first tourists start to arrive. Conditions are perfect between Easter and mid-June, when the weather is pleasantly warm in most places, but not too hot; beaches and ancient sites are relatively uncrowded; public transport operates on close to full schedules; and accommodation is cheaper and easy to find.

Mid-June until the end of August is the high season. It's party time on the island and everything is in full swing. It's also very hot – in July and August the mercury can soar to 40°C (100°F) in the shade, the beaches are crowded, the ancient sites are swarming with tour groups, and in many places accommodation is booked solid.

The season starts to wind down in September, and conditions are ideal once more until the end of October.

Maps

Mapping is an important feature of this guide. Unless you are going to trek or drive, you probably won't need additional maps.

Most tourist offices hand out free maps, but they are often out of date and not particularly accurate. The same applies to the cheap (400 dr to 500 dr) 'tourist maps'.

The best maps are published by the Greek company Road Editions. Crete is covered by the company's 1:250,000 maroon-cover mainland series. Even the smallest roads and villages are clearly marked, and the distance indicators are spot-on – important when negotiating your way around the backblocks.

What to Bring

Sturdy shoes are essential for clambering around ancient sites and wandering around historic towns and villages, which tend to have lots of steps and cobbled streets.

A day-pack is useful for the beach, and for sightseeing or trekking. A compass is essential if you are going to trek in remote areas, as is a whistle, which you can use should you become lost or disorientated. A torch (flashlight) is not only needed if you intend to explore caves, but comes in handy during occasional power cuts. If you like to fill a washbasin or bathtub (a rarity in Crete), bring a universal plug as Greek bathrooms rarely have plugs.

Many camping grounds in Crete have covered areas where tourists without tents can sleep in summer, so you can get by with a lightweight sleeping bag and foam bedroll.

You will need only light clothing – preferably cotton – during the summer months. During spring and autumn you'll need a light sweater or jacket in the evening.

In summer, a broad-rimmed sunhat and sunglasses are essential (see the Health section later in this chapter). Sunscreen creams are expensive in Crete, as are moisturising and cleansing creams.

If you read a lot, it's a good idea to bring along a few disposable paperbacks to read and swap.

TOURIST OFFICES

Tourist information is handled by the Greek National Tourist Organisation, known by the initials GNTO abroad and EOT (Ellinikos Organismos Tourismou) in Greece.

Local Tourist Offices

The address of the EOT's head office (☎ 01-322 3111) is Amerikis 2, Athens 105 64. There are about 25 EOT offices throughout Crete. Most EOT staff speak English, but they vary in their enthusiasm and helpfulness.

Some offices, like that in Agios Nikolaos, have loads of useful local information, but most have nothing more than glossy brochures and a few maps. Some have absolutely nothing to offer.

In addition to EOT offices, there are also municipal tourist offices. They are often more helpful.

Tourist Offices Abroad

GNTO offices abroad include:

Australia
  (☎ 02-9241 1663/4/5)
  51 Pitt St, Sydney NSW 2000
Austria
  (☎ 1-512 5317/8)
  Opernring 8, Vienna A-10105
Belgium
  (☎ 2-647 5770)
  172 Ave Louise Louizalaan, B-1050 Brussels
Canada
  (☎ 416-968 2220)
  1300 Bay St, Toronto, Ontario M5R 3K8
Denmark
  (☎ 3-325 332)
  Vester Farimagsgade 1, 1606 Copenhagen
France
  (☎ 01-42 60 65 75)
  3 Ave de l'Opéra, Paris 75001
Germany
  (☎ 69-237 735)
  Neue Mainzerstrasse 22, 60311 Frankfurt
  (☎ 89-222 035/036)
  Pacellistrasse 5, W 80333 Munich 2
  (☎ 40-454 498)
  Abteistrasse 33, 20149 Hamburg 13
  (☎ 30-217 6262)
  Wittenbergplatz 3A, 10789 Berlin 30 Israel
  (☎ 23-517 0501)
  5 Shalom Aleichem St, Tel Aviv 61262
Italy
  (☎ 06-474 4249)
  Via L Bissolati 78-80, Rome 00187
  (☎ 02-860 470)
  Piazza Diaz 1, 20123 Milan
Japan
  (☎ 03-350 55 911)
  Fukuda Building West, 5F 2-11-3 Akasaka, Minato-Ku, Tokyo 107
Netherlands
  (☎ 020-625 4212/3/4)
  Leidsestraat 13, Amsterdam NS 1017
Norway
  (☎ 2-426 501)
  Ovre Slottsgate 15B, 0157 Oslo 1
Sweden
  (☎ 8-679 6480)
  Birger Jarlsgatan 30, Box 5298 S, 10246 Stockholm
Switzerland
  (☎ 01-221 0105)
  Loewenstrasse 25, CH 8001 Zurich
UK
  (☎ 020-7499 4976)
  4 Conduit St, London W1R ODJ

USA
(☎ 212-421 5777)
Olympic Tower, 645 5th Ave, New York, NY 10022
(☎ 312-782 1084)
Suite 600, 168 North Michigan Ave, Chicago, Illinois 60601
(☎ 213-626 6696)
Suite 2198, 611 West 6th St, Los Angeles, California 92668

Tourist Police

The tourist police work in cooperation with the regular Cretan police and EOT. Each tourist police office has at least one member of staff who speaks English. Hotels, restaurants, travel agencies, tourist shops, tourist guides, waiters, taxi drivers and bus drivers all come under the jurisdiction of the tourist police. If you think that you have been ripped off by any of these, report it to the tourist police and they will investigate.

If you need to report a theft or loss of passport, the tourist police will act as interpreters between you and the regular police. The tourist police also fulfil the same functions as the EOT and municipal tourist offices, dispensing maps and brochures, and giving information on transport.

VISAS & DOCUMENTS
Passport

To enter Greece you need a valid passport or, for EU nationals, travel documents (ID cards). You must produce your passport or EU travel documents when you register in a hotel or pension in Crete. You will find that many accommodation proprietors will want to keep your passport during your stay. This is not a compulsory requirement; they need it only long enough to take down the details.

Visas

The list of countries whose nationals can stay in Greece for up to three months without a visa include Australia, Canada, all EU countries, Iceland, Israel, Japan, New Zealand, Norway, Switzerland and the USA. Other countries included are Cyprus, Malta, the European principalities of Monaco and San Marino, and most South American countries. The list changes, so contact Greek embassies for the full list. Those not on the list can expect to pay about $20 for a three month visa.

Turkish-Occupied North Cyprus Greece will refuse entry to people whose passport indicates that they have visited Turkish-occupied North Cyprus since November 1983. This can be overcome if, upon entering North Cyprus, you ask the immigration officials to stamp a piece of paper (looseleaf visa) rather than your passport. If you enter North Cyprus from the Greek Republic of Cyprus (only possible for a day visit), an exit stamp is not put into your passport.

Visa Extensions If you want to stay in Greece for longer than three months, apply at a consulate abroad or at least 20 days in advance to the Aliens Bureau (☎ 01-770 5711), Leoforos Alexandras 173, Athens. Take your passport and four passport photographs along. You may be asked for proof that you can support yourself financially, so keep all your bank exchange slips (or the equivalent from a post office). These slips are not always automatically given – you may have to ask for them. The Aliens Bureau is open 8 am to 1 pm weekdays. In Crete apply to the main prefecture in Iraklio. You will be given a permit which will authorise you to stay in Greece for a period of up to six months. Most travellers get around this by visiting Bulgaria or Turkey briefly and then reentering Greece.

Travel Insurance

A travel insurance policy to cover theft, loss and medical problems is a good idea. The policies handled by STA Travel and other student travel organisations are usually good value. There is a wide variety of policies available; check the small print. Some policies specifically exclude 'dangerous activities' which can include scuba diving, motorcycling, even trekking. A locally acquired motorcycle licence is not valid under some policies.

You may prefer a policy that pays doctors or hospitals direct rather than you having to pay on the spot and claim later. If you have to claim later make sure you keep all documentation. Some policies ask you to call back (reverse charges) to a centre in your home country where an immediate assessment of your problem is made.

Check that the policy covers ambulances or an emergency flight home.

Driving Licence & Permits

Crete recognises all national driving licences, provided the licence has been held for at least one year. It also recognises an International Driving Permit, which should be obtained before you leave home.

Hostel Cards

A Hostelling International (HI) card is of no use in Crete.

Student & Youth Cards

The most widely recognised (and thus the most useful) form of student ID is the International Student Identity Card (ISIC). Holders qualify for half-price admission to some museums and ancient sites. There are no travel agencies authorised to issue ISICs in Crete, so it would be wise to arrange for one before leaving home.

Air Crete and Cronus Airlines both offer student discounts on domestic flights, but there are no discounts on buses, ferries or trains.

Photocopies

All important documents (passport data page and visa page, credit cards, travel insurance policy, air/bus/train tickets, driving licence etc) should be photocopied before you leave home. Leave one copy with someone at home and keep another with you, separate from the originals.

It is also a good idea to store details of your vital travel documents in Lonely Planet's free online Travel Vault at www.ekno.lonelyplanet.com.in case you lose the photocopies or can't be bothered with them. Your password-protected Travel Vault is accessible online anywhere in the world.

Student Cards

An ISIC (International Student Identity Card) is a plastic ID-style card displaying your photograph. These cards are widely available from budget travel agencies (take along proof that you are a student). In Athens you can get one from the International Student & Youth Travel Service (ISYTS; ☎ 01-323 3767, 2nd floor, Nikis 11, Athens).

Some travel agencies in Greece offer discounts on organised tours to students. However, there are no student discounts for travel within Greece (although Olympic Airways gives a 25% discount on domestic flights that are part of an international flight). Turkish Airlines (THY) gives 55% student discounts on its international flights. THY has flights from Athens to Istanbul and Izmir. Most ferries to Cyprus, Israel and Egypt from Piraeus give a 20% student discount and a few of the services between Greek and Italian ports do so also. If you are under 26 years but not a student, the Federation of International Youth Travel Organisation (FIYTO) card gives similar discounts. Many budget travel agencies issue FIYTO cards including London Explorers Club (☎ 020-7792 377033, Princes Square, Bayswater, London W2) and SRS Studenten Reise Service (☎ 030-2 83 30 93, Marienstrasse 23, Berlin).

EMBASSIES & CONSULATES
Greek Embassies & Consulates

The following is a selection of Greek diplomatic missions abroad:

Australia
    (☎ 02-6273 3011)
    9 Turrana St, Yarralumla, Canberra ACT 2600
Bulgaria
    (☎ 92-946 1027)
    San Stefano 33, Sofia 1504
Canada
    (☎ 613-238 6271)
    76-80 Maclaren St, Ottawa, Ontario K2P OK6
Cyprus
    (☎ 02-441 880/8801)
    Byron Boulevard 8-10, Nicosia

Denmark
(☎ 33-11 4533)
Borgergade 16, 1300 Copenhagen K
Egypt
(☎ 02-355 1074)
18 Aisha el Taymouria, Garden City, Cairo
France
(☎ 01-47 23 72 28)
17 Rue Auguste Vacquerie, 75116 Paris
Germany
(☎ 228-83010)
An Der Marienkapelleb 10, 53 179 Bonn
Ireland
(☎ 01-676 7254)
1 Upper Pembroke St, Dublin 2
Israel
(☎ 03-605 5461)
47 Bodenheimer St, Tel Aviv 62008
Italy
(☎ 06-854 9630)
Via S Mercadante 36, Rome 00198
Japan
(☎ 03-340 0871/0872)
3-16-30 Nishi Azabu, Minato-ku,
Tokyo 106
Netherlands
(☎ 070-363 87 00)
Koninginnegracht 37, 2514 AD, Den Hague
New Zealand
(☎ 04-473 7775)
5-7 Willeston St, Wellington
Norway
(☎ 22-44 2728)
Nobels Gate 45, 0244 Oslo 2
South Africa
(☎ 12-437 351/352)
995 Pretorius Street, Arcadia, Pretoria 0083
Spain
(☎ 01-564 4653)
Avenida Doctor Arce 24, Madrid 28002
Sweden
(☎ 08-663 7577)
Riddargatan 60, 11457 Stockholm
Switzerland
(☎ 31-951 0814)
Postfach, 3000 Berne 6, Kirchenfeld
Turkey
(☎ 312-436 8860)
Ziya-ul-Rahman Caddesi 9-11,
Gaziosmanpasa 06700, Ankara
UK
(☎ 020-7229 3850)
1A Holland Park, London W11 3TP
USA
(☎ 202-939 5818)
2221 Massachusetts Ave NW, Washington DC
20008

Embassies & Consulates in Crete
The UK embassy in Iraklio is the only foreign embassy in Crete. The rest are in Athens and its suburbs (telephone code 01).
They include:

Australia
(☎ 645 0404)
Dimitrou Soutsou 37, Athens 115 21
Bulgaria
(☎ 647 8105)
Stratigou Kalari 33A, Psyhiko,
Athens 154 52
Canada
(☎ 727 3400)
Genadiou 4, Athens 115 21
Cyprus
(☎ 723 7883)
Irodotou 16, Athens 106 75
Egypt
(☎ 361 8613)
Leoforos Vasilissis Sofias 3, Athens 106 71
France
(☎ 339 1000)
Leoforos Vasilissis Sofias 7, Athens 106 71
Germany
(☎ 728 5111)
Dimitriou 3 & Karaoli, Kolonaki,
Athens 106 75
Ireland
(☎ 723 2771)
Leoforos Vasileos Konstantinou 7,
Athens 106 74
Israel
(☎ 671 9530)
Marathonodromou 1, Psyhiko,
Athens 154 52
Italy
(☎ 361 7260)
Sekeri 2, Athens 106 74
Japan
(☎ 775 8101)
Athens Tower, Leoforos Messogion 2-4,
Athens 115 27
Netherlands
(☎ 723 9701)
Vasileos Konstantinou 5-7,
Athens 106 74
New Zealand (Consulate)
(☎ 771 0112)
Xenias 24, Athens 115 28
South Africa
(☎ 680 6645)
Kifissias 60, Maroussi, Athens 151 25
Turkey
(☎ 724 5915)
Vasilissis Georgiou 8, Athens 106 74

UK
  (☎ 723 6211)
  Ploutarhou 1, Athens 106 75
  (☎ 081-22 4012)
  Apalexandrou 16, Iraklio
USA
  (☎ 721 2951)
  Leoforos Vasilissis Sofias 91, Athens 115 21
Yugoslavia
  (☎ 031-244 266, fax 240 412)
  Komninon 4, Thessaloniki

Generally speaking, your own country's embassy won't be much help in emergencies if the trouble you're in is remotely your own fault. Remember that you are bound by Greek laws. Your embassy will not be sympathetic if you end up in jail after committing a crime locally, even if such actions are legal in your own country.

In genuine emergencies you might get some assistance, but only if other channels have been exhausted. For example, if you need to get home urgently, a free ticket home is exceedingly unlikely – the embassy would expect you to have insurance. If you have all your money and documents stolen, it might assist with getting a new passport, but a loan for onward travel is out of the question.

CUSTOMS

There are no longer duty-free restrictions within the EU. This does not mean, however, that customs checks have been dispensed with – random searches are still made for drugs.Upon entering the country from outside the EU, customs inspection is usually curs-ory for foreign tourists. There may be spot checks, but you probably won't have to open your bags. You may bring the following into Crete duty-free: 200 cigarettes or 50 cigars; 1L of spirits or 2L of wine; 50g of perfume; 250ml of eau de Cologne; one camera (still or video) and film; a pair of binoculars; a portable musical instrument; a radio or tape recorder; a typewriter; sports equipment; and dogs and cats (with a veterinary certificate).

Importation of works of art and antiquities is free, but they must be declared on entry, so that they can be re-exported. Import regulations for medicines are strict; if you are taking medication, make sure you get a statement from your doctor before you leave home. It is illegal, for instance, to take codeine into Crete without an accompanying doctor's certificate.

An unlimited amount of foreign currency and travellers cheques may be brought into Crete. If, however, you intend to leave the country with foreign banknotes in excess of $1000, you must declare the sum upon entry.

Restrictions apply to the importation of sailboards into Crete. See the Activities section later in this chapter for more details.

It is strictly forbidden to export antiquities (anything over 100 years old) without an export permit. This crime is second only to drug smuggling in the penalties imposed. It is an offence to remove even the smallest article from an archaeological site.

The place to apply for an export permit is the Antique Dealers & Private Collections Section, Archaeological Service, Polygnotou 13, Athens.

Cars can be brought into Crete for four months without a carnet (a customs licence); only a green card (international third party insurance) is required. Your vehicle will be registered in your passport when you enter Crete to prevent you leaving the country without it.

MONEY
Currency

The unit of currency in Crete is the drachma (dr). Coins come in denominations of five, 10, 20, 50 and 100 dr. Banknotes come in 100, 200, 500, 1000, 5000 and 10,000 dr.

Exchange Rates

country	unit		drachma
Australia	A$1	=	207 dr
Canada	C$1	=	221 dr
euro	€1	=	328 dr
France	10FF	=	500 dr
Germany	DM1	=	168 dr
Italy	L1000	=	169 dr
Japan	¥100	=	318 dr
New Zealand	NZ$1	=	166 dr
United Kingdom	UK£1	=	521 dr
United States	US$1	=	325 dr

Exchanging Money

Banks will exchange all major currencies in either cash, travellers cheques or Eurocheques. The best-known travellers cheques in Crete are Thomas Cook and American Express. A passport is required to change travellers cheques, but not cash.

Commission charged on the exchange of banknotes and travellers cheques varies not only from bank to bank but from branch to branch. It's less for cash than for travellers cheques. For travellers cheques the commission is 350 dr for up to 20,000 dr; 450 dr for amounts between 20,000 and 30,000 dr; and a flat rate of 1.5% on amounts over 30,000 dr.

Post offices can exchange banknotes – but not travellers cheques – and charge less commission than banks. Many travel agencies and hotels will also change money and travellers cheques at bank rates, but their commission charges are higher.

If there is a chance that you may apply for a visa extension, make sure you receive, and keep hold of, a bank exchange slip after each transaction.

Cash Nothing beats cash for convenience – or for risk. If you lose it, it's gone for good and very few travel insurers will come to your rescue. Those that will, normally limit the amount to about $300. It's best to carry no more cash than you need for the next few days, which means working out your likely needs when you change travellers cheques or withdraw cash from an ATM (automatic teller machines).

It's also a good idea to set aside a small amount of cash, say $50, as an emergency stash.

Travellers Cheques The main reason to carry travellers cheques rather than cash is the protection they offer against theft. They are, however, losing popularity as more and more travellers opt to put their money in a bank at home and withdraw it at ATMs as they go along.

American Express, Visa and Thomas Cook cheques are all widely accepted and have efficient replacement policies. Maintaining a record of the cheque numbers and recording when you use them is vital when it comes to replacing lost cheques. Keep this record separate from the cheques themselves. US dollars is a good currency to use.

ATMs ATMs are to be found in almost every town large enough to support a bank – and certainly in all the tourist areas. If you've got MasterCard or Visa/Access, there are plenty of places to withdraw money.

Cirrus, Plus and Maestro users can make withdrawals in all major towns and tourist areas.

AFEMs (Automatic Foreign Exchange Machines) are common in major tourist areas. They take all the major European currencies, Australian and US dollars and Japanese yen, and are useful in an emergency.

Credit Cards The great advantage of credit cards is that they allow you to pay for major items without carrying around great wads of cash. Credit cards are now an accepted part of the commercial scene just about everywhere in Crete. They can be used to pay for a wide range of goods and services such as upmarket meals and accommodation, car hire and souvenir shopping.

If you are not familiar with the card options, ask your bank to explain the workings and relative merits of the various schemes: cash cards, charge cards and credit cards. Ask whether the card can be replaced in Crete if it is lost or stolen.

The main credit cards are MasterCard, Visa (Access in the UK) and Eurocard, all of which are widely accepted in Crete. They can also be used as cash cards to draw drachma from ATMs of affiliated Greek banks in the same way as at home. Daily withdrawal limits are set by the issuing bank. Cash advances are given in local currency only. Credit cards can be used to pay for accommodation in all the classier hotels. Some C-class hotels will accept credit cards, but D- and E-class hotels rarely do. Most upmarket shops and restaurants accept credit cards but the village tavernas do not.

The main charge cards are American Express and Diner's Club card, which are widely accepted in tourist areas but unheard of elsewhere.

International Transfers If you run out of money, or need more for whatever reason, you can instruct your bank back home to send you a draft. Specify the city and the bank as well as the branch that you want the money sent to. If you have the choice, select a large bank and ask for the international division. Money sent by electronic transfer should reach you within 24 hours.

Warning It's all but impossible to exchange Turkish lira in Greece. The only place you can change it is at the head office of the National Bank of Greece, Panepistimiou 36, Athens – and it'll give only about 75% of the going international rate.

Security

The safest way of carrying cash and valuables (passport, travellers cheques, credit cards etc) is a favourite topic of travel conversation. The simple answer is that there is no foolproof method. The general principle is to keep things out of sight. The front pouch belt, for example, presents an obvious target for a would-be thief – only marginally less inviting than a fat wallet bulging from your back pocket.

The best place is under your clothes in contact with your skin where, hopefully, you will be aware of an alien hand before it's too late. Most people opt for a money belt, while others prefer a leather pouch hung around the neck. Whichever method you choose, put your valuables in a plastic bag first – otherwise they will get soaked in sweat as you wander around in the heat.

Costs

Crete is cheap by northern European standards, but it is no longer dirt-cheap, especially in the high season (July and August). A rock-bottom daily budget would be 6000 dr.

This would mean hitching, staying in youth hostels or camping, staying away from bars, and only occasionally eating in restaurants or taking ferries. Allow at least 12,000

dr per day in the summer for a simple room, meals in local tavernas, drinks at night and some sightseeing. Outside of the high season you could get by on about 25% less. If you really want a holiday – comfortable rooms and restaurants all the way – you will need closer to 20,000 dr per day. These budgets are for individuals. Couples sharing a double room can get by on less.

Tipping & Bargaining

In restaurants the service charge is included in the bill but it is the custom to leave a small tip. The practice is often just to round off the bill. Likewise for taxis – a small amount is appreciated.

Bargaining is not as widespread in Crete as it is further east. Prices in most shops are clearly marked and non-negotiable. The same applies to restaurants and public transport. However, it is always worth bargaining over the price of hotel rooms or *domatia* (the Greek equivalent of the British bed and breakfast, minus the breakfast), especially if you are intending to stay a few days. You may get short shrift in peak season, but prices can drop dramatically in the off season. Souvenir shops and market stalls are other places where your negotiating skills will come in handy. If you feel uncomfortable about haggling, walking away can be just as effective – you can always go back.

POST & COMMUNICATIONS

Post offices *(tahydromio)* are easily identifiable by means of the yellow signs outside. Regular post boxes are also yellow. The red boxes are for express mail only.

Postal Rates

The postal rate for postcards and airmail letters to destinations within the EU is 170 dr for up to 20g and 270 dr for up to 50g. To other destinations the rate is 200 dr for up to 20g and 300 dr for up to 150g. Post within Europe takes five to eight days and to the USA, Australia and New Zealand, nine to 11 days. Some tourist shops also sell stamps, but with a 10% surcharge.

Express mail costs an extra 400 dr and should ensure delivery in three days within the EU – use the special red post boxes. Valuables should be sent registered post, which costs an extra 350 dr.

Sending Mail

Do not wrap a parcel until it has been inspected at a post office. In Iraklio, take your parcel to the central post office on Plateia Daskalogianni, and elsewhere to the parcel counter of a regular post office.

Receiving Mail

You can receive mail poste restante (general delivery) at any main post office.

The service is free, but you are required to show your passport. Ask senders to write your family name in capital letters on the envelope and underline it, and to mark the envelope 'poste restante'. It is a good idea to ask the post office clerk to check under your first name as well if letters you are expecting cannot be located. After one month, uncollected mail is returned to the sender. If you are about to leave a town and expected mail hasn't arrived, ask at the post office to have it forwarded to your next destination, c/o poste restante.

Parcels are not delivered in Crete, they must be collected from the post office.

Telephone

The Greek telephone service is maintained by the public corporation known as Organismos Tilepikoinonion Ellados, which is always referred to by the acronym OTE (pronounced o-tay). The system is modern and efficient. Public telephones all take phonecards, which cost 1000 dr for 100 units, 1800 dr for 200 units, 4200 dr for 500 units, and 8200 dr for 1000 units. The 100-unit cards are widely available at *periptera*, corner shops and tourist shops; the others can be bought at OTE offices.

The phones are easy to operate and can be used for local, long distance and international calls. The 'i' at the top left of the push-button dialling panel brings up the operating instructions in English. Don't remove your card before you are told to do so or you will wipe out the remaining credit. Local calls cost one unit per minute.

It is possible to use various national card schemes, such as Telstra Australia's Telecard, to make international calls. You will still need a phonecard to dial the scheme's access number, which will cost you one unit, and the time you spend on the phone is charged at local call rates.

International calls can also be made from OTE offices. A counter clerk directs you to a cubicle equipped with a metered phone, and payment is made afterwards.

Villages and remote islands without OTE offices almost always have at least one metered phone for international and long distance calls – usually in a shop, *kafeneio* (cafe) or taverna.

Reverse charge (collect) calls can be made from an OTE office. If you are using a private phone to make a reverse charge call, dial the operator (domestic ☎ 151, international ☎ 161).

To call overseas direct from Crete, dial the Greek overseas access code (☎ 00), followed by the country code for the country you are calling, then the local area code (dropping the leading zero if there is one) and then the number. The table below lists some country codes and per-minute charges:

country	code	cost per minute (dr)
Australia	☎ 61	236
France	☎ 33	183
Germany	☎ 49	183
Ireland	☎ 353	183
Italy	☎ 39	183
Japan	☎ 81	319
Netherlands	☎ 31	183
New Zealand	☎ 64	319
Turkey	☎ 90	183
UK	☎ 44	183
USA & Canada	☎ 1	236

Off-peak rates are 25% cheaper. They are available to Africa, Europe, the Middle East and India between 10 pm and 6 am; to the Americas between 11 pm and 8 am; and to Asia and Oceania between 8 pm and 5 am.

To call Crete the international access code is ☎ 30.

Useful Phone Numbers

Directory inquiries	☎ 131
International dialling instructions in English, French and German	☎ 169
International access code to call Greece	☎ 30
International access code from within Greece	☎ 00

Toll-free 24 hour emergency phone numbers:

Police	☎ 100
Tourist Police	☎ 171
Ambulance (Athens)	☎ 166
Fire Brigade	☎ 199
Roadside Assistance (ELPA)	☎ 104

Fax & Telegraph
Most post offices have fax machines; telegrams can be sent from any OTE office.

Email & Internet Access
Crete was slow to embrace the wonders of the Internet, but is now striving to make up for lost time. Internet cafes are springing up everywhere, and are listed under the Information section for cities where available.

There has also been a huge increase in the number of hotels and businesses using email, and these addresses have been listed where available. Some hotels catering for travellers offer Internet access.

INTERNET RESOURCES
The Lonely Planet Web site (www.lonely planet.com) has information on Crete, as well as travel news, updates to our guidebooks and links to other travel resources. You may also find these sites useful:

Athens News
  athensnews.dolnet.gr/
  (The daily English language newspaper's site)
GNTO
  www.areianet.gr/infoxenios/english/crete/crete
  .html
  (GNTO's page for Crete)

goCrete.com
  www.gocrete.com/
  (Internet Guide to Crete)
GTP schedule
  www.gtpnet.gr
  (Greek ferry schedules)
Interkriti
  www.interkriti.gr
  (Links to hotels, apartments, shops and restaurants as well as an active bulletin board)
Ktel
  www.ktel.org
  (Maps and schedules of buses around the island)
OTE
  www.ote.gr
  (Online telephone directory for Crete with white pages in Greek and yellow pages in English.)
Stigmes
  www.forthnet.gr/stigmes/destcret.htm
  (Magazine of Crete)

BOOKS
Most books are published in different editions by different publishers in different countries.

As a result, a book might be a hardcover rarity in one country while it's readily available in paperback in another. Fortunately, bookshops and libraries search by title or author, so your local bookshop or library is best placed to advise you on the availability of the following recommendations.

Lonely Planet
The 4th edition of Lonely Planet's guide to *Greece* has comprehensive coverage of mainland Greece as well as the islands (including Crete), while the Lonely Planet guides to *Mediterranean Europe* and *Western Europe* also include coverage of Crete, as does *Europe on a shoestring*. The handy *Greek phrasebook* will help enrich your visit.

Katherine Kizilos vividly evokes Greece's landscapes, people and politics in her book *The Olive Grove: Travels in Greece*. She explores the islands and borderlands of her father's homeland, and life in her family's village in the Peloponnese Mountains. The book is part of the Journeys travel literature series.

These titles are available at major English-language bookshops in Iraklio, Hania and Rethymno. See the Bookshops entries in these sections for more details.

Guidebooks

For archaeology buffs, the *Crete Blue Guide* is hard to beat. They go into tremendous detail about all the major sites, and many of the lesser known ones.

Travel

Winds of Crete by David MacNeill Doren is widely available on Crete. It's an amusing account of island life as experienced by an American and his Swedish wife.

Under Mount Ida: A Journey into Crete by Oliver Burch is a compelling portrayal of this diverse and beautiful island – full of insights into its landscape, history and people.

The Colossus of Maroussi by Henry Miller is now regarded as a classic. Miller relates his travels in Crete and Crete at the outbreak of WWII with feverish enthusiasm.

Roughing It in Crete by JE Hilary Skinner is an Englishman's account of his experiences fighting the Turks with Cretan rebels in the mid-19th century.

People & Society

Tale of a Town by Pandelis Prevelakis recounts the author's life in early 20th-century Rethymno and includes a moving account of the arrival of refugees from Smyrna in 1923.

Greek Men Made Simple was written by an anonymous English woman to explain the mating habits and peculiarities of Greek men. Essential reading for foreign women contemplating an affair in Crete.

History & Mythology

A Traveller's History of Crete by Timothy Boatswain & Colin Nicholson gives the layperson a good general reference on the historical background of Crete, from Neolithic times to the present day.

Modern Crete: A Short History by CM Woodhouse is in a similar vein, although it has a right-wing bent. It covers the period from Constantine the Great to 1990.

Mythology was an intrinsic part of life in ancient Crete, and some knowledge of it will enhance your visit. *The Greek Myths* by Robert Graves is regarded as the definitive book on the subject. Maureen O'Sullivan's *An Iconoclast's Guide to the Greek Gods* presents entertaining and accessible versions of the myths.

There are many translations of Homer's *Iliad* and *Odyssey*, which tell the story of the Trojan War and the subsequent adventures of Odysseus. The translations by EV Rien are among the best.

The Argonautica Expedition by Theodor Troev encompasses Greek mythology, archaeology, travel and adventure. It relates the voyage undertaken by the author and his crew in the 1980s that followed in the footsteps of Jason and the Argonauts.

Mary Renault's novels provide an excellent feel for ancient Crete. *The King Must Die* and *The Bull from the Sea* are vivid tales of Minoan times.

The Archaeology of Crete by JDS Pendlebury is an excellent guide to the archaeological sights on the island and *Handbook to the Palace of Minos* tells you all you need to know about the Palace of Knossos.

History of Crete by Theocharis E Detorakis is an extraordinarily complete guide to Cretan history from the Minoan times up to, but not including, the Battle of Crete.

The Cretan Runner by George Psychoundakis is an exciting and personal account of the Cretan resistance. The author was a runner delivering messages to the Allies.

Crete: The Battle and the Resistance by Antony Beevor is a short and readable analysis of the Allied defeat.

Officers and Gentlemen by Evelyn Waugh recounts the hair-raising evacuation of the Allied soldiers.

Poetry

Sappho: A New Translation by Mary Bernard is the best translation of this great ancient poet's works.

Collected Poems by George Seferis, *Selected Poems* by Odysseus Elytis and

Collected Poems by Constantine Cavafy are all excellent translations of Crete's greatest modern poets.

Novels
The most well known and widely read Greek author is the Cretan writer Nikos Kazantzakis, whose novels are full of drama and larger-than-life characters. His most famous works are *The Last Temptation*, *Zorba the Greek*, *Christ Recrucified* and *Freedom or Death*. The first two have been made into films. *Zorba the Greek* takes place on Crete and provides a fascinating glimpse of the harsher side of Cretan culture. Zorba is one of the world's greatest literary characters but women need to be prepared for a mega-dose of misogyny.

Botanical Field Guides
The Flowers of Crete & the Aegean by William Taylor & Anthony Huxley is the most comprehensive field guide to Crete. The Greek writer, naturalist and mountaineer George Sfikas has written many books on wildlife in Crete. Among them are

MARTIN HARRIS

Nikos Kazantzakis

Wildflowers of Crete, *Trees & Shrubs of Crete* and *Medicinal Plants of Crete*.

Children's Books
The Greek publisher Malliaris-Paedia puts out a good series of books on the Greek myths, retold in English for young readers by Aristides Kesopoulos. The titles are *The Gods of Olympus and the Lesser Gods*, *The Labours of Hercules*, *Theseus and the Voyage of the Argonauts*, *The Trojan War and the Wanderings of Odysseus* and *Heroes and Mythical Creatures*.

Robin Lister's retelling of *The Odyssey* is aimed at slightly older readers (ages 10 to 12), but makes compelling listening for younger children.

Bookshops
There are several English-language bookshops in Iraklio, as well as shops selling books in French, German and Italian. There are also good foreign-language bookshops in Hania, Rethymno and Agios Nikolaos (see those sections for details).

All other major towns and tourist resorts have bookshops that sell some foreign-language books. Imported books are expensive – normally two to three times the recommended retail price in the UK and the USA. Many hotels have second-hand books to read or swap.

Abroad, the best bookshop for new and second-hand books about Crete, written in both English and Greek, is the Hellenic Book Service (☎ 020-7267 9499, fax 020-7267 9498), 91 Fortress Rd, Kentish Town, London NW5 1AG. It stocks almost all of the books recommended here.

FILMS
The most famous movie filmed on Crete was undoubtedly *Zorba the Greek* which was shot in Stavros on the Akrotiri Peninsula as well as other locations. In 1956, the American director Jules Dassin *(Never On Sunday)* chose Kritsa as the backdrop for *He Who Must Die*, the film version of Katzantzakis' novel *Christ Recrucified* starring Dassin's wife, Melina Mercouri. The film lovingly captured the worn faces

of the villagers, many of whom acted in the film.

NEWSPAPERS & MAGAZINES

Greeks are great newspaper readers. There are 15 daily newspapers, of which the most widely read are *Ta Nea*, *Kathimerini* and *Eleftheros Typos*.

The main English-language newspapers are the daily (except Monday) *Athens News* (250 dr) which carries Greek and international news, and the weekly *Hellenic Times* (300 dr), with predominantly Greek news. The English and German newspaper, *Cretasummer*, is published monthly during the summer in Rethymno and contains Greek news, Cretan features and many ads. The monthly magazine, *Kreta*, is on sale in a variety of languages and contains some useful information amidst the ads. In addition to these, the Athens edition of the *International Herald Tribune* (350 dr) includes an eight page English-language edition of the Greek daily *Kathimerini*. All are widely available in Iraklio and at major resorts. You'll find the *Athens News* electronic edition at athensnews.dolnet.gr on the Internet. The site's archives date back to 1995.

Foreign newspapers are also widely available. You'll find all the British and other major European dailies, as well as international magazines such as *Time*, *Newsweek* and the *Economist*.

RADIO & TV

Crete has two state-owned radio channels, ET 1 and ET 2. ET 1 runs three programs; two are devoted to popular music and news, while the third plays mostly classical music. It has a news update in English at 7.30 am Monday to Saturday, and at 9 pm Monday to Friday. It can be heard on 91.6 MHz and 105.8 MHz on the FM band, and 729 KHz on the AM band. ET 2 broadcasts mainly popular music.

Commercial radio stations tend to confine their broadcasts to major urban areas. The hills around Athens are bristling with radio transmitters, but the choice is very limited on the islands.

The best short-wave frequencies for picking up the BBC World Service are:

GMT	frequency
3 to 7.30 am	9.41 MHz (31m band)
	6.18 MHz (49m band)
	15.07 MHz (19m band)
7.30 am to 6 pm	12.09 MHz (25m band)
	15.07 MHz (19m band)
6.30 to 11.15 pm	12.09 MHz (25m band)
	9.41 MHz (31m band)
	6.18 MHz (49m band)

As far as Greek TV is concerned, it's a case of quantity rather than quality. There are nine TV channels and various pay-TV channels. All the channels show English and US films and soapies with Greek subtitles. A bit of channel-swapping will normally turn up something in English. Local Cretan channels include Creta Channel, Kastro TV, Kidon TV, CreteTV, Crete 1, and Sitia TV. Most of the better quality hotels have satellite TV where you can pick up CNN.

VIDEO SYSTEMS

If you want to record or buy video tapes to play back home, you won't get a picture unless the image registration systems are the same. Crete uses PAL, which is incompatible with the North American and Japanese NTSC system. Australia and most of Europe use PAL.

PHOTOGRAPHY & VIDEO
Film & Equipment

Major brands of film are widely available. In Iraklio, expect to pay about 1500 dr for a 36 exposure roll of Kodak Gold ASA 100; less for other brands. You'll find all the gear you need in the photography shops of Iraklio and other major towns and tourist areas.

Because of the brilliant sunlight in summer, you'll get better results using a polarising lens filter.

As elsewhere in the world, developing film is a competitive business. Most places charge around 80 dr per print, plus a 400 dr service charge.

Restrictions

Never photograph a military installation or anything else that has a sign forbidding photography. Flash photography is not allowed inside churches, and it's considered taboo to photograph the main altar.

Cretans usually love having their photos taken, but always ask permission first. The same goes for video cameras.

TIME

Crete is two hours ahead of GMT/UTC and three hours ahead on daylight-saving time, which begins on the last Sunday in March when clocks are put forward one hour. Daylight saving ends on the last Sunday in September.

So, when it is noon in Crete it is 10 am in London, 11 am in Rome, 2 am in San Francisco, 5 am in New York and Toronto, 8 pm in Sydney and 10 pm in Auckland.

ELECTRICITY

Electricity is 220V, 50 cycles. Plugs are the standard continental type with two round pins. All hotel rooms have power points and most camping grounds have supply points.

WEIGHTS & MEASURES

Crete uses the metric system. Liquids – especially barrel wine – are sold by weight rather than volume: 959g of wine, for example, is equivalent to 1000mL.

Remember that, like other continental Europeans, Greeks indicate decimals with commas and thousands with points.

LAUNDRY

Large towns and some islands have laundrettes. They charge from 2000 dr to 2500 dr to wash and dry a load whether you do it yourself or have it service-washed. Hostels and room owners will usually provide you with a washtub.

TOILETS

Most places in Crete have western-style toilets, especially hotels and restaurants which cater for tourists. You'll occasionally come across Asian-style squat toilets in older houses, *kafeneia* and public toilets.

Public toilets are rare, except at airports and bus and train stations. Cafes are the best option if you get caught short, but you'll be expected to buy something for the privilege.

One peculiarity of the Cretan plumbing system is that it can't handle toilet paper, apparently the pipes are too narrow. Whatever the reason, anything larger than a postage stamp seems to cause a problem. Flushing away tampons and sanitary napkins is guaranteed to block the system. Toilet paper etc should be placed in the small bin provided in every toilet.

HEALTH

Travel health depends on your pre-departure preparations, your day-to-day health care while travelling and how you handle any medical problem or emergency that does develop. While the list of potential dangers can seem quite frightening, few travellers experience more than upset stomachs.

Pre-departure Planning

Health Insurance See Travel Insurance under Visas & Documents earlier in this chapter for information.

Warning Codeine, which is commonly found in headache preparations, is banned in Crete; check labels carefully, or risk prosecution.

There are strict regulations applying to the importation of medicines into Crete, so obtain a certificate from your doctor which outlines any medication you may have to carry into the country with you.

Health Preparations Make sure you're healthy before you start travelling. If you are embarking on a long trip make sure your teeth are OK.

If you wear glasses take a spare pair and your prescription.

If you require a particular medication take an adequate supply with you, as it may not be available locally in Crete. Take the prescription or, better still, part of the packaging showing the generic rather than the brand name you use at home (which

Medical Kit Check List

Following is a list of items you should consider including in your medical kit – consult your pharmacist for brands available in your country.

☐ **Aspirin or paracetamol (acetaminophen in the USA)** – for pain or fever
☐ **Antihistamine** – for allergies, eg, hay fever; to ease the itch from insect bites or stings; and to prevent motion sickness
☐ **Cold and flu tablets, throat lozenges and nasal decongestant**
☐ **Multivitamins** – consider for long trips, when dietary vitamin intake may be inadequate
☐ **Antibiotics** – consider including these if you're travelling well off the beaten track; see your doctor, as they must be prescribed, and carry the prescription with you
☐ **Loperamide or diphenoxylate** – 'blockers' for diarrhoea
☐ **Prochlorperazine or metaclopramide** – for nausea and vomiting
☐ **Rehydration mixture** – to prevent dehydration, which may occur, for example, during bouts of diarrhoea; particularly important when travelling with children
☐ **Insect repellent, sunscreen, lip balm and eye drops**
☐ **Calamine lotion, sting relief spray or aloe vera** – to ease irritation from sunburn and insect bites or stings
☐ **Antifungal cream or powder** – for fungal skin infections and thrush
☐ **Antiseptic (such as povidone-iodine)** – for cuts and grazes
☐ **Bandages, Band-Aids (plasters) and other wound dressings**
☐ **Water purification tablets or iodine**
☐ **Scissors, tweezers and a thermometer** – note that mercury thermometers are prohibited by airlines

may not be locally available), as it will make getting replacements easier while you are in Crete.

Immunisations No jabs are required for travel to Crete but a yellow fever vaccination certificate is required if you are coming from an infected area. There are, however, a few routine vaccinations that are recommended. These should be recorded on an international health certificate, available from your doctor or government health department. Don't leave your vaccinations until the last minute as some require more than one injection. Recommended vaccinations include:

Tetanus & Diphtheria Boosters are necessary every 10 years and protection is highly recommended.

Polio A booster of either the oral or injected vaccine is required every 10 years to maintain immunity after childhood vaccination. Polio is still prevalent in many developing countries.

Hepatitis A The most common travel-acquired illness that can be prevented by vaccination. Protection can be provided in two ways – either with the antibody gamma globulin or the vaccine Havrix 1440. Havrix 1440 provides long-term immunity (possibly more than 10 years) after an initial injection and a booster at six to 12 months. Gamma globulin, a ready-made antibody, should be given as close as possible to departure because it is at its most effective in the first few weeks after administration and the effectiveness tapers off gradually between three and six months.

Rabies Pre-travel rabies vaccination involves having three injections over 21 to 28 days and should be considered by those who will spend a month or longer in a country where rabies is common, especially if they are cycling, handling animals, caving, travelling to remote areas, or taking children (who may not report a bite). If someone who has been vaccinated is bitten or scratched by an animal they will require two booster injections of vaccine; those not vaccinated will require more.

Basic Rules

Care in what you eat and drink is the most important health rule. Stomach upsets are the most likely travel health problem (between 30% and 50% of travellers in a two week stay experience this) but the majority of these upsets will be relatively minor. Don't become paranoid; trying the local food is part of the experience of travel, after all.

Food & Water Tap water is safe to drink in Crete, but mineral water is widely available if you prefer it. You might experience mild intestinal problems if you're not used to copious amounts of olive oil; however, you'll get used to it and current research says it's good for you.

If you don't vary your diet, are travelling hard and fast and missing meals, or simply lose your appetite, you can soon start to lose weight and place your health at risk. Fruit and vegetables are good sources of vitamins and Crete produces a greater variety of these than almost any other European country. Eat plenty of grains (including rice) and bread. If your diet isn't well-balanced or if your food intake is insufficient, it's a good idea to take vitamin and iron pills.

In hot weather make sure you drink enough – don't rely on feeling thirsty to indicate when you should drink. Not needing to urinate or very dark yellow urine is a danger sign.

Always carry a water bottle with you on long trips. Excessive sweating can lead to loss of salt and therefore muscle cramping. Salt tablets are not a good idea as a preventative, but in places where salt is not used much, adding salt to food can help.

Everyday Health

Normal body temperature is up to 37°C (98.6°F); more than 2°C (4°F) higher indicates a high fever. The normal adult pulse rate is 60 to 100 per minute (children 80 to 100, babies 100 to 140). As a general rule the pulse increases about 20 beats per minute for each 1°C (2°F) rise in fever.

Respiration (breathing) rate is also an indicator of illness. Count the number of breaths per minute: Between 12 and 20 is normal for adults and older children (up to 30 for younger children, 40 for babies). People with a high fever or serious respiratory illness breathe more quickly than normal. More than 40 shallow breaths a minute may indicate pneumonia.

Environmental Hazards

Sunburn By far the biggest health risk in Crete comes from the intensity of the sun. You can get sunburnt surprisingly quickly, even through cloud. Using a sunscreen and taking extra care to cover the areas which don't normally see sun helps, as does zinc cream or some other barrier cream for your nose and lips. Calamine lotion is good for mild sunburn. Cretans claim that yogurt applied to sunburn is soothing. Protect your eyes with good quality sunglasses.

Prickly Heat Prickly heat is an itchy rash caused by excessive perspiration trapped under the skin. Keeping cool but bathing often, using a mild talcum powder or even resorting to air-conditioning may help until you acclimatise.

Heat Exhaustion Dehydration or salt deficiency can cause heat exhaustion. Take time to acclimatise to high temperatures, and drink sufficient liquids. Wear loose clothing and a broad-brimmed hat. Do not do anything too physically demanding.

Salt deficiency is characterised by fatigue, lethargy, headaches, giddiness and muscle cramps and in this case salt tablets may help. Vomiting or diarrhoea can deplete your liquid and salt levels.

Heat Stroke This serious, sometimes fatal, condition can occur if the body's heat-regulating mechanism breaks down and the body temperature rises to dangerous levels. Long, continuous periods of exposure to high temperatures can leave you vulnerable to heat stroke. You should avoid excessive alcohol consumption or strenuous activity when you first arrive in a hot climate.

The symptoms are feeling unwell, not sweating very much or at all and a high body temperature (39°C to 41°C or 102°F to 106°F). Where sweating has ceased, the skin becomes flushed and red. Severe, throbbing headaches and lack of coordination will also occur, and the sufferer may be confused or aggressive. Eventually the victim will become delirious or convulsive. Hospitalisation is essential, but in the interim get victims out of the sun, remove their clothing, cover them with a wet sheet or towel and then fan continually. Give fluids if they are conscious.

Fungal Infections Fungal infections, which occur with greater frequency in hot weather, are most likely to occur on the scalp, between the toes or fingers, in the groin and on the body. You get ringworm (which is a fungal infection, not a worm) from infected animals or by walking on damp areas like shower floors.

To prevent fungal infections wear loose, comfortable clothes, avoid artificial fibres, wash frequently and dry carefully. If you do get an infection, wash the infected area daily with a disinfectant or medicated soap and water, and rinse and dry well. Apply an antifungal cream or powder like the widely available Tinaderm. Try to expose the infected area to air or sunlight as much as possible and wash all towels and underwear in hot water as well as changing them often.

Motion Sickness Sea sickness can be a problem. The Aegean is very unpredictable and gets very rough when the *meltemi* wind blows. If you are prone to motion sickness, eat lightly before and during a trip and try to find a place that minimises disturbance – near the wings on aircraft, close to midships on boats, near the centre on buses. Fresh air usually helps; reading and cigarette smoke don't. Commercial motion-sickness preparations, which can cause drowsiness, have to be taken before the trip commences; when you're feeling sick it's too late. Ginger (available in capsule form) and peppermint (including mint-flavoured sweets) are natural preventatives.

Infectious Diseases

Diarrhoea Simple things like a change of water, food or climate can all cause a mild bout of diarrhoea, but a few rushed toilet trips with no other symptoms is not indicative of a major problem.

Dehydration is the main danger with any diarrhoea, particularly in children or the elderly as dehydration can occur quite quickly.

Under all circumstances *fluid replacement* (at least equal to the volume being lost) is the most important thing to remember. Weak black tea with a little sugar, soda water, or soft drinks allowed to go flat and diluted 50% with clean water are all good.

Hepatitis Hepatitis is a general term for inflammation of the liver. It is a common disease worldwide. The symptoms are fever, chills, headache, fatigue, feelings of weakness and aches and pains, followed by loss of appetite, nausea, vomiting, abdominal pain, dark urine, light-coloured faeces, jaundiced (yellow) skin and the whites of the eyes may turn yellow.

Hepatitis A is transmitted by contaminated food and drinking water. The disease poses a real threat to the Western traveller. You should seek medical advice, but there is not much you can do apart from resting, drinking lots of fluids, eating lightly and avoiding fatty foods. People who have had hepatitis should avoid alcohol for some time after the illness, as the liver needs time to recover.

Hepatitis E is transmitted in the same way, and can be very serious in pregnant women.

There are almost 300 million chronic carriers of **Hepatitis B** in the world. It is spread through contact with infected blood, blood products or body fluids; for example, through sexual contact, unsterilised needles and blood transfusions, or contact with blood via small breaks in the skin. Other risky situations include having a shave, tattoo, or having your body pierced with contaminated equipment. The symptoms of type B may be more severe and may lead to long-term problems. **Hepatitis D** is spread in the same way, but the risk is mainly in shared needles.

Hepatitis C can lead to chronic liver disease. The virus is spread by contact with blood and blood products – usually via contaminated transfusions or shared needles – or bodily fluids.

Tetanus This potentially fatal disease is found worldwide. It is difficult to treat but is preventable with immunisation.

Rabies Rabies is a fatal viral infection caused by a bite or scratch by an infected animal. It's rare, but it is found in Crete. Dogs are noted carriers, as are cats. Any bite, scratch or even lick from a warm-blooded, furry animal should be cleaned immediately and thoroughly. Scrub with soap and running water, and then clean with an alcohol or iodine solution. If there is any possibility that the animal is infected medical help should be sought immediately to prevent the onset of symptoms and death. Even if the animal is not rabid, all bites should be treated seriously as they can become infected or can result in tetanus. A rabies vaccination is now available and should be considered if you are in a high risk category – eg if you intend to explore caves (bat bites can be dangerous), work with animals, or travel so far off the beaten track that medical help is more than two days away.

Sexually Transmitted Diseases Sexual contact with an infected sexual partner spreads these diseases. While abstinence is the only 100% preventative, using condoms is also effective. Gonorrhoea, herpes and syphilis are among these diseases; sores, blisters or rashes around the genitals, discharges or pain when urinating are common symptoms. In some STDs, such as wart virus or chlamydia, symptoms may be less marked or not observed at all in women. Syphilis symptoms eventually disappear completely but the disease continues and can cause severe problems in later years. The treatment of gonorrhoea and syphilis is with antibiotics.

There are numerous other sexually transmitted diseases, for most of which effective treatment is available. But there is no cure for herpes and currently no cure for AIDS.

HIV/AIDS Infection with the human immunodeficiency virus (HIV) may lead to acquired immune deficiency syndrome (AIDS), which is a fatal disease. Any exposure to blood, blood products or body fluids may put the individual at risk. The disease is often transmitted through sexual contact or dirty needles – vaccinations, acupuncture, tattooing and body piercing can be potentially as dangerous as intravenous drug use.

If you do need an injection, ask to see the syringe unwrapped in front of you, or take a needle and syringe pack with you.

Fear of HIV infection should never preclude treatment for serious medical conditions.

Insect-Borne Diseases
Typhus Tick typhus is a problem from April to September in rural areas, particularly areas where animals congregate. Typhus begins with a fever, chills, headache and muscle pain, followed a few days later by a body rash. There is often a large painful sore at the site of the bite and nearby lymph nodes are swollen and painful. There is no vaccine available. The best protection is to check your skin carefully after walking in danger areas such as long grass and scrub. A strong insect repellent can help, and walkers in tick areas should consider having their boots and trousers impregnated with benzyl benzoate and dibutylphthalate. (See the Cuts, Bites & Stings section following for information about ticks.)

Lyme Disease Lyme disease is a tick-transmitted infection which may be acquired throughout Europe. The illness usually begins with a spreading rash at the site of the bite and is accompanied by fever, headache, extreme fatigue, aching joints and muscles and mild neck stiffness. If untreated, these symptoms usually resolve over several weeks but over subsequent weeks or months disorders of the nervous system, heart and joints may develop. The response to treatment is best early in the illness. The longer the delay, the longer the recovery period.

Cuts, Bites & Stings
Skin punctures can easily become infected in hot climates and may be difficult to heal. Treat any cut with an antiseptic such as povidone-iodine. Where possible avoid bandages and Band-Aids, which can keep wounds wet.

Although there are a lot of bees and wasps in Crete, their stings are usually painful rather than dangerous. Calamine lotion or sting relief spray will give relief and ice packs will reduce the pain and swelling.

Snakes Always wear boots, socks and long trousers when walking through undergrowth where snakes may be present. Don't put your hands into holes and crevices, and be careful when collecting firewood.

Snake bites do not cause instantaneous death and antivenenes are usually available. Keep the victim calm and still, wrap the bitten limb tightly, as you would for a sprained ankle, and attach a splint to immobilise it. Then seek medical help, if possible with the dead snake for identification. Don't attempt to catch the snake if there is even a remote possibility of being bitten again. Tourniquets and sucking out the poison are now comprehensively discredited.

Jelly Fish, Sea Urchins & Weever Fish Watch out for sea urchins around rocky beaches; if you get some of their needles embedded in your skin, olive oil will help to loosen them. If they are not removed they will become infected. Be wary also of jelly fish, particularly during the months of September and October. Although they are not lethal in Crete, their stings can be painful. Dousing in vinegar will deactivate any stingers which have not 'fired'. Calamine lotion, antihistamines and analgesics may reduce the reaction and relieve the pain.

Much more painful than either of these, but thankfully much rarer, is an encounter with the weever fish. It buries itself in the sand of the tidal zone with only its spines protruding, and injects a painful and powerful toxin if trodden on. Soaking your foot in very hot water (which breaks down the poison) should solve the problem. In the worst instance, it can cause permanent local paralysis.

Bedbugs & Lice Bedbugs live in various places, but particularly in dirty mattresses and bedding. Spots of blood on bedclothes or on the wall around the bed can be read as a suggestion to find another hotel. Bedbugs leave itchy bites in neat rows. Calamine lotion or sting relief spray may help.

All lice cause itching and discomfort. They make themselves at home in your hair, your clothing or in your pubic hair. You catch lice through direct contact with infected people or by sharing combs, clothing and the like. Powder or shampoo treatment will kill the lice and infected clothing should then be washed in very hot water.

Leeches & Ticks Leeches may be present in damp areas; they attach themselves to your skin to suck your blood. Trekkers often get them on their legs or in their boots. Salt or a lighted cigarette end will make them fall off. Do not pull them off, as the bite is then more likely to become infected. An insect repellent may keep them away. You should always check your body if you have been walking through a potentially tick-infested area as ticks can cause skin infections and other more serious diseases.

Sheepdogs These dogs are trained to guard sheep, and are often underfed and sometimes ill-treated by their owners. They are almost always 'all bark and no bite', but if you are going to trek into remote areas, you should consider having rabies injections (see Rabies section earlier in the chapter). You are most likely to encounter these dogs in the mountainous regions of Crete. Wandering through a flock of sheep over which one of these dogs is watching is asking for trouble.

Women's Health

Antibiotic use, synthetic underwear, sweating and contraceptive pills can lead to fungal vaginal infections, especially when travelling in hot climates. Fungal infections are characterised by a rash, itch and discharge and can be treated with a vinegar or lemon-juice douche, or with yogurt. Nystatin, miconazole or clotrimazole pessaries or vaginal cream are the usual treatment. Maintaining good personal hygiene and wearing loose-fitting clothes and cotton underwear may help prevent these infections.

Sexually transmitted diseases are a major cause of vaginal problems. Symptoms include a smelly discharge, painful intercourse and sometimes a burning sensation when urinating. Medical attention should be sought and sexual partners must also be treated. For more details see the section on Sexually Transmitted Diseases earlier. Besides abstinence, the best thing is to practise safer sex using condoms.

Hospital Treatment

Citizens of EU countries are covered for free treatment in public hospitals within Crete on presentation of an E111 form. Inquire at your national health service or travel agent in advance. Emergency treatment is free to all nationalities in public hospitals. In an emergency, dial ☎ 166. Pharmacies can dispense medicines which are available only on prescription in most European countries, so you can consult a pharmacist for minor ailments.

All this sounds fine, but although medical training is of a high standard in Greece, the health service is badly underfunded and one of the worst in Europe.

Hospitals are overcrowded, hygiene is not always what it should be and relatives are expected to bring in food for the patient – which could be a problem for a tourist. Conditions and treatment are better in private hospitals, which are expensive. All this means that a good health insurance policy is essential.

WOMEN TRAVELLERS

Many women travel alone in Crete. The crime rate remains relatively low, and solo travel is probably safer than in most European countries. This does not mean that you should be lulled into complacency; bag snatching and rapes do occur, although violent offences are rare.

The biggest nuisance to foreign women travelling alone are the guys the Greeks have nicknamed *kamaki*. The word means 'fishing trident' and refers to the kamaki's favourite pastime, 'fishing' for foreign women. You'll find them everywhere there are lots of tourists; young (for the most part),

smooth-talking guys who aren't in the least bashful about sidling up to foreign women in the street. They can be very persistent, but they are a hassle rather than a threat.

The majority of Greek men treat foreign women with respect, and are genuinely helpful.

GAY & LESBIAN TRAVELLERS

In a country where the church still plays a prominent role in shaping society's views on issues such as sexuality, it should come as no surprise that homosexuality is generally frowned upon. While there is no legislation against homosexual activity, it pays to be discreet and to avoid public displays of togetherness.

Although other islands have a thriving gay scene, Crete does not. Since homosexuality is generally frowned upon and Crete has never been marketed as a gay destination to package tourists there is no overtly gay nightlife.

There are a number of venues in Iraklio that are gay-friendly although not exclusively gay. Relaxed Paleohora is gay-friendly and most nude beaches are welcoming to gays.

Information The *Spartacus International Gay Guide*, published by Bruno Gmunder (Berlin), is widely regarded as the leading authority on the gay travel scene. The 1998/99 edition has a wealth of information on gay venues around the Greek Islands.

There's also stacks of information on the Internet. *Roz Mov* at www.geocities.com/WestHollywood/2225/index.html, is a good place to start. It has pages on travel info, gay health, the gay press, organisations, events and legal issues – and links to lots more sites.

Gayscape has a useful site with lots of links at www.gayscape.com.

Organisations The main gay rights organisation in Greece is the Elladas Omofilofilon Kommunitas (☎ 01-341 0755, fax 883 6942, email eok@nyx.gr), upstairs at Apostolou Pavlou 31 in the Athens suburb of Thisio.

DISABLED TRAVELLERS

If mobility is a problem, visiting Crete presents some serious challenges. The hard fact is that most hotels, ferries, museums and ancient sites are not wheelchair accessible.

If you are determined, then take heart in the knowledge that disabled people do go to Crete for holidays. But the trip needs careful planning, so get as much information as you can before you go. The British-based Royal Association for Disability and Rehabilitation (RADAR) publishes a useful guide called *Holidays & Travel Abroad: A Guide for Disabled People*, which gives a good overview of facilities available to disabled travellers in Europe. Contact RADAR (☎ 020-7250 3222, fax 020-7250 0212, email radar@radar.org.uk), at 12 City Forum, 250 City Road, London EC1V 8AF.

SENIOR TRAVELLERS

Card-carrying EU pensioners can claim a range of benefits such as reduced admission charges at museums and ancient sites and discounts on trains.

TRAVEL WITH CHILDREN

Crete is a safe and relatively easy place to travel with children. It's especially easy if you're staying by the beach or at a resort hotel. If you're travelling around, the main problem is a shortage of decent playgrounds and recreational facilities.

Don't be afraid to take children to ancient sites. Many parents are surprised by how much their children enjoy them. Young imaginations go into overdrive when let loose somewhere like the 'labyrinth' at Knossos.

Hotels and restaurants are usually very accommodating when it comes to meeting the needs of children, although highchairs are a rarity outside resorts. The service in restaurants is normally very quick, which is great when you've got hungry children on your hands.

Fresh milk is readily available in large towns and tourist areas, but hard to find in small villages. Supermarkets are the best place to look. Formula is available everywhere, as is condensed and heat-treated milk.

Mobility is an issue for parents with very small children. Strollers (pushchairs) aren't much use in Crete unless you're going to spend all your time in one of the few flat spots. They are hopeless on rough stone paths and up steps, and a curse when getting on/off buses and ferries. Backpacks or front pouches are best.

Children under four travel for free on ferries and buses. They pay half fare up to the age of 10 (ferries) and 12 (buses). Full fare applies otherwise. On domestic flights, you'll pay 10% of the fare to have a child under two sitting on your knee. Kids aged two to 12 pay half fare.

USEFUL ORGANISATIONS

ELPA (☎ 01-779 1615), the Greek automobile club, has its headquarters on the ground floor of Athens Tower, Messogion 2-4, Athens 115 27. ELPA offers reciprocal services to members of national automobile associations on production of a valid membership card. If your vehicle breaks down, dial ☎ 104.

DANGERS & ANNOYANCES
Theft

Crime, especially theft, is low in Crete, but unfortunately it is on the increase. Keep track of your valuables on public transport and in markets. Do not leave luggage unattended in cars. The vast majority of thefts from tourists are still committed by other tourists; the biggest danger of theft is probably in dormitory rooms in hostels and at camp sites. So make sure you do not leave valuables unattended in such places. If you are staying in a hotel room, and the windows and door do not lock securely, ask for your valuables to be locked in the hotel safe – hotel proprietors are happy to do this.

LEGAL MATTERS
Consumer Advice

The Tourist Assistance Programme exists to help people who are having trouble with any tourism-related service. Free legal advice is available in English, French and German from July 1 to September 30. The main office (☎ 081-240 666) in Crete is in

Iraklio at Milatou 1 and Agiou Titou. It's open 10 am to 2 pm Monday to Friday.

Drugs

Greek drug laws are the strictest in Europe. Greek courts make no distinction between possession and pushing. Possession of even a small amount of marijuana is likely to land you in jail.

BUSINESS HOURS

Banks are open 8 am to 2 pm Monday to Thursday, and 8 am to 1.30 pm Friday. Some banks in large towns and cities open between 3.30 and 6.30 pm in the afternoon and on Saturday morning.

Post offices are open 7.30 am to 2 pm Monday to Friday. In the major cities they stay open until 8 pm, and open from 7.30 am to 2 pm on Saturday.

The opening hours of OTE offices (for long distance and overseas telephone calls) vary according to the size of the town. In smaller towns they are usually open 7.30 am to 3 pm daily; from 6 am until 11 pm in larger towns; and 24 hours in major cities like Athens and Thessaloniki.

In summer, shops are open 8 am to 1.30 pm and 5.30 to 8.30 pm Tuesday, Thursday and Friday, and 8 am to 2.30 pm Monday, Wednesday and Saturday. They open 30 minutes later in winter. These times are not always strictly adhered to. Many shops in tourist resorts are open seven days a week. *Periptera* (street kiosks) are open from early morning until late at night. They sell everything from bus tickets and cigarettes to hard-core pornography.

Opening times of museums and archaeological sites vary, but most are closed on Monday.

PUBLIC HOLIDAYS

All banks and shops and most museums and ancient sites close public holidays. Greek national public holidays observed in Crete are:

New Year's Day	1 January
Epiphany	6 January
First Sunday in Lent	February

Greek Independence Day	25 March
Good Friday	March/April
(Orthodox) Easter Sunday	March/April
Spring Festival/Labour Day	1 May
Feast of the Assumption	15 August
Ohi Day	28 October
Christmas Day	25 December
St Stephen's Day	26 December

SPECIAL EVENTS

The Greek year is a succession of festivals and events, some of which are religious, some cultural, others an excuse for a good knees-up, and some a combination of all three. The following is by no means an exhaustive list, but it covers the most important events, both national and regional. If you're in the right place at the right time, you'll certainly be invited to join the revelry.

January
Feast of Agios Vasilios (St Basil)
The year kicks off with this festival on 1 January. A church ceremony is followed by the exchanging of gifts, singing, dancing and feasting; the New Year pie *(vasilopitta)* is sliced and the person who gets the slice containing a coin will supposedly have a lucky year.

Epiphany (the Blessing of the Waters)
On 6 January, Christ's baptism by St John is celebrated throughout Greece. Seas, lakes and rivers are blessed and crosses immersed in them.

February-March
Shrove Monday (Clean Monday)
On the Monday before Ash Wednesday (the first day of Lent), people take to the hills throughout Greece to have picnics and fly kites.

March
Independence Day
The anniversary of the hoisting of the Greek flag by Bishop Germanos at Moni Agias Lavras is celebrated on 25 March with parades and dancing. Germanos' act of revolt marked the start of the War of Independence. Independence Day coincides with the Feast of the Annunciation, so it is also a religious festival.

March-April
Easter
Easter is taken much more seriously than any other religious holiday. On Palm Sunday (the

Sunday before Orthodox Easter), worshippers return from church services with a cross woven of palm and myrtle.

The Monday evening service is the 'Bridegroom Service' because the priest carries an icon of Christ, 'the bridegroom' through the church.

Tuesday is dedicated to Mary Magdalene and Wednesday is the 'Day of Atonement'.

On Thursday worshippers mourn for Christ in the evening service an d on Good Friday, the symbolic body of Christ is carried through the streets in a funeral procession.

The climax of the week is the Saturday evening service.

At midnight all lights in the churches are extinguished until the priest appears with a lighted candle and the cry *Christos Anesti!* 'Christ has arisen'.

He lights each worshipper's candle and people make their way home, trying to keep the candle lit. Fireworks and gunshots herald the start of feasting that lasts through Easter Sunday.

The ceremony of the lighting of candles is the most significant moment in the Orthodox year, for it symbolises the Resurrection. Its poignancy and beauty are spellbinding.

If you are in Crete at Easter you should endeavour to attend this ceremony, which ends with fireworks and a candle-lit procession through the streets.

The Lenten fast ends on Easter Sunday with the cracking of red-dyed Easter eggs and an outdoor feast of roast lamb followed by Greek dancing.

Feast of Agios Georgos (St George)

The feast day of St George, Crete's patron saint and patron saint of shepherds, takes place on 23 April or the Tuesday following Easter (whichever comes first).

The most elaborate celebration is in Asi Gonias where thousands of goats and sheep are gathered at the town church for shearing, milking and blessing.

Fresh milk accompanies the ensuing feast.

May
May Day

On the first day of May there is a mass exodus from towns to the country.

During picnics, wildflowers are gathered and made into wreaths to decorate houses.

Battle of Crete

During the last week of May, the town of Hania commemorates the Battle of Crete in athletic competitions, folk dancing and ceremonial events.

June
Navy Week

Navy Week is celebrated in even-numbered years during the last week in June and commemorates Crete's relationship with the sea. In Crete's harbour cities there are music and dancing events on land and swimming and sailing competitions on the water.

Feast of St John the Baptist

This feast day on 24 June is widely celebrated. Wreaths made on May Day are kept until this day, when they are burned on bonfires.

July
Feast of Agia Marina (St Marina)

This feast day is celebrated on 17 July in many parts of Crete, and is a particularly important event in Agia Marina outside of Hania.

Feast of Profitis Ilias

This feast day is celebrated on 20 July at hilltop churches and monasteries dedicated to the prophet, especially in the Cyclades.

Wine Festival

The Wine Festival of Rethymno is held in the municipal park with wine tastings and local cuisine

August
Assumption Day

Greeks celebrate Assumption Day (15 August) with family reunions. The whole population is on the move either side of the day, so it's a good time to avoid public transport. The island of Tinos gets particularly busy because of its miracle-working icon of Panagia Evangelistria. It becomes a place of pilgrimage for thousands, who come to be blessed, healed or baptised, or just for the excitement of being there. Many are unable to find hotels and sleep out on the streets.

Paleohora Music Festival

Paleohora Music Festival is devoted to music. The first ten days of August are filled with song contests and concerts staged every night.

Cultural Festival

In Ano Viannos, there's a three-day Cultural Festival at the beginning of August with concerts, plays and art exhibits.

Wine Festival

In the town of Arhanes, August 15 is the conclusion of a five-day Wine Festival celebrating their excellent local wine.

Sultana Festival

Sitia celebrates their superior sultana raisins with wine, music and dancing in a Sultana Festival held the last week of the month.

Potato Festival

Lassithi produces superior potatoes, a product which is celebrated in the Potato Festival held for three days at the end of August in Tzermiado.

Traditional Cretan wedding

In late August Kritsa stages a traditional Cretan wedding replete with songs, dancing and traditional food for an admission of about 3000 dr.

September
Genesis tis Panagias
(the Virgin's Birthday)

This day is celebrated on 8 September throughout Greece with various religious services and feasting.

October
Chestnut Festival

The village of Elos stages a chestnut festival on the third Sunday of the month when everyone is offered roasted chestnuts, chestnut sweets and *tsikoudia*.

Ohi (No) Day

Metaxas' refusal to allow Mussolini's troops free passage through Crete during WWII is commemorated on 28 October with a number

LLP

Many of Crete's local festivals celebrate the harvesting of crops. A five-day Wine Festival in the town of Arhanes celebrates the region's excellent wines.

of remembrance services, military parades, folk dancing and feasting.

November

One of the most important local holidays celebrated in Crete is the anniversary of the explosion at Moni Arkadiou. From November 7 to 9, this tragic event is commemorated at Moni Arkadiou.

December
Christmas Day

Although not as important as Easter, Christmas is still celebrated with religious services and feasting. Nowadays much 'western' influence is apparent, including Christmas trees, decorations and presents.

Summer Festivals & Performances

There are cultural festivals throughout Crete in summer. The most important are the annual Renaissance Festival in Rethymno that features dance, drama and films as well as art exhibitions; the Krvia Festival in Ierapetra includes various musical, theatrical and artistic presentations.

Sitia's Kornaria Festival that presents music, theatre, art exhibits, races and a beach volleyball competition; Iraklio's Summer Arts Festival that attracts international artists as well as local singers and dancers to perform in the Kazantzakis Open Air Theatre, and the Lato Festival in Agios Nikolaos that features traditional and modern works performed by local and international orchestras and dance troupes.

ACTIVITIES
Water Sports

Parasailing, water-skiing, jet skiing, pedal boating, canoeing and windsurfing are available on most of the major beaches.

On the north coast, you'll find a water sports centre attached to most luxury hotels and you don't need to stay there to avail yourself of the facilities.

Outside Iraklio, try the water sports centre at the Grecotel Agapi Beach (☎ 081-250 502) in Ammoudara.

Outside Hania in nearby Platanias, there's Argiris Sea Sports (☎ 0821-093 493 449). If you're staying in Agios Nikolaos, head out to the beach resort of Elounda, 12km north of town. There's a water sports centre at the Elounda Bay Hotel (☎ 0841-41 502) and the neighbouring Elounda Beach Hotel (☎ 0841-41 412). In Bali, there's the Water Sports Lefteris (☎ 0834-94 102) and in Vai, there's Vai Watersports (☎ 0843-61 070).

The best windsurfing is at Kouremenos beach, the town beach of Palekastro, east of Sitia. Call the Kouremenos Watersports Centre (☎ 0843-093 751 7444). Windsurfing is also good in Paleohora. Try Westwind (☎ 0823-094 681 9777) near the Pal Beach Hotel.

Snorkelling & Diving
The warm, clear waters of Crete make snorkelling and diving a pleasure. Some of the best snorkelling is around the sunken city of Olous in Elounda.

In the shallow water you can see the foundations of ancient houses. There are a number of diving centres that allow you to get acquainted with diving, become a certified diver or explore the underwater wonders if you're already certified. Under Greek law, you must dive as part of a licensed diving operation and you are forbidden to disturb any antiquities you may come across. In Hania, you have a choice of Blue Adventures Diving (☎ 0821-40 608), Daskalogianni 69, or Creta's Diving Centre (☎ 0821-93 616), Papanikoli 6, Nea Hora. In Bali, there's Hippocampos (☎ 0834-94 193) near the port. In Agios Nikolaos, there's a diving centre affiliated with the aquarium and a diving centre on the beach of the Coral Hotel (☎ 0841-82 546). In Rethymno, there's The Paradise Dive Centre (☎ 0831-53 258), El Venizelou 76. It's wise to call at least a day in advance.

Trekking
Crete is a veritable paradise for trekkers – at the right time of the year. Trekking is no fun at all in June, July and August, when the temperatures are constantly up around 40°C. Spring (April-May) is the perfect time.

There are dozens of interesting hikes throughout Crete that will take you through remote villages, across plains and into gorges.

Some of the most popular treks, such as the Samaria Gorge, are detailed in this book. There are a number of companies running organised treks. One of the biggest is Trekking Hellas (☎ 01-323 4548, fax 325 1474, email trekking@compulink.gr), at Filellinon 7, Athens 105 57. You'll find more information at www.trekking.gr. Also, try The Happy Walker (☎ 0831-52 920), Tobazi 56, Rethymno, or Trekking Plan (☎ 0821-60 861) in Agia Marina just outside Hania.

WORK
Permits
EU nationals don't need a work permit, but they need a residency permit if they intend to stay longer than three months. Nationals of other countries are supposed to have a work permit.

Bar & Hostel Work
The best bar and hotel jobs can pay quite well, so well that they are usually taken by young Greeks from the mainland. Language training has improved dramatically in recent years eliminating the need for multilingual foreign workers. Resorts such as Hersonisos and Malia that cater to British travellers are the best bet for Brits looking for bar work.

Courier
As a package tour destination par excellence Crete provides excellent opportunities for those interested in working as a courier for a package tour company. Package tour companies based in Britain begin looking for personnel around February to fill the summer season needs.

You need to have a good presentation and outgoing personality and, usually, some college education. The pay is poor but you can make tips and some companies allow couriers to earn a percentage of the excursions they sell.

Summer Harvest
Seasonal harvest work seems to be monopolised by migrant workers from Albania, and is no longer a viable option for travellers.

Volunteer Work

The Sea Turtle Protection Society of Crete
(☎/fax 01-523 1342, email stps@compulink
.gr), at Solomou 57, Athens 104 32, uses
volunteers for their monitoring programs
on Crete.

Other Work

There are often jobs advertised in the classi-
fieds of the English-language newspapers, or
you can place an advertisement yourself. EU
nationals can also make use of the OAED
(Organismos Apasholiseos Ergatikou Dy-
namikou), the Greek National Employment
Service, in their search for a job.

ACCOMMODATION

There is a range of accommodation available in Crete to suit every taste and pocket.
All places to stay are subject to strict price
controls set by the tourist police. By law, a
notice must be displayed in every room,
which states the category of the room and
the price charged in each season.

Accommodation owners may add a 10%
surcharge for a stay of less than three
nights, but this is not mandatory. A mandatory charge of 20% is levied if an extra bed
is put into a room.

During July and August, accommodation
owners will charge the maximum price, but
in spring and autumn, prices will drop by up
to 20%, and perhaps by even more in winter. These are the times to bring your bargaining skills into action.

Rip-offs rarely occur, but if you suspect
you have been exploited by an accommodation owner, report it to either the tourist police or regular police and they will act swiftly.

Camping

There are only about a dozen or so camping
grounds in Crete. Most are privately run
and very few are open outside the high season (April-October). The Panhellenic
Camping Association (☎/fax 01-362 1560),
at Solonos 102, Athens 106 80, publishes an
annual booklet listing all the camp sites and
their facilities.

Camping fees are highest from 15 June to
the end of August. Most camping grounds

charge from 1200 dr to 1500 dr per adult
and 600 dr to 800 dr for children aged four
to 12. There's no charge for children aged
under four. Tent sites cost from 900 dr per
night for small tents, and from 1200 dr per
night for large tents. Caravan sites start at
around 2500 dr.

Between May and mid-September it is
warm enough to sleep out under the stars,
although you will still need a lightweight
sleeping bag to counter the pre-dawn chill.
It's a good idea to have a foam pad to lie on
and a waterproof cover for your sleeping
bag.

Freelance (wild) camping is illegal, but
the law is not always strictly enforced. It's
wise to ask around before camping wild.

Hostels

There are youth hostels in Iraklio,
Rethymno, Sitia and Plakias that are run by
the Greek Youth Hostel Organisation (☎ 01-
751 9530, fax 751 0616, email y-hos
tels@otenet.gr), at Damareos 75, 116 33 in
Athens.

Hostel rates vary from 1600 dr to 2000 dr
and you don't have to be a member to stay
in any of them.

Domatia

Domatia are the Greek equivalent of the
British bed and breakfast, minus the breakfast. Once upon a time domatia comprised
little more than spare rooms in the family
home which could be rented out to travellers in summer; nowadays, many are
purpose-built appendages to the family
house. Some come complete with fully
equipped kitchens.

Standards of cleanliness are generally
high. The decor runs the gamut from cool
grey marble floors, coordinated pine furniture, pretty lace curtains and tasteful pic-
tures on the walls, to so much kitsch you are
almost afraid to move in case you break an
ornament.

Domatia remain a popular option for
budget travellers. They are classified A, B
or C. Expect to pay from 4000 dr to 9000 dr
for a single, and 6000 dr to 15,000 dr for a
double, depending on the class, whether

bathrooms are shared or private, the season and how long you plan to stay.

Many domatia are open only between April and October.

Hotels

Hotels in Crete are divided into six categories: deluxe, A, B, C, D and E. Hotels are categorised according to the size of the room, whether or not they have a bar, and the ratio of bathrooms to beds, rather than standards of cleanliness, comfort of the beds and friendliness of staff – all elements which may be of greater relevance to guests.

As one would expect, deluxe, A- and B-class hotels have many amenities, private bathrooms and constant hot water.

They usually, but not always, have air-conditioning. Even in expensive hotels the air-conditioning may only function part of the day. Often it is turned off at night. C-class hotels have a snack bar, rooms have private bathrooms, but hot water may only be available at certain times of the day. D-class hotels may or may not have snack bars, most rooms will share bathrooms, but there may be some with private bathrooms, and they may have solar heated water, which means hot water is not guaranteed. E-class hotels do not have a snack bar, bathrooms are shared and you may have to pay extra for hot water - if it exists at all.

Prices are controlled by the tourist police and the maximum rate that can be charged for a room must be displayed on a board behind the door of each room. The classification is not often much of a guide to price. Rates in D- and E-class hotels are generally comparable with domatia. You can pay anywhere from 10,000 dr to 20,000 dr for a C-class single in high season and 15,000 dr to 25,000 dr for a double. Prices in B-class range from 15,000 dr to 25,000 dr for singles, and from 25,000 dr to 35,000 dr for doubles. A-class prices are not much higher.

Apartments

Self-contained family apartments are available in some hotels and domatia. There are also a number of purpose-built apartments, available for either long or short-term rental. Prices vary considerably according to the amenities offered.

Traditional Settlements

Traditional settlements are old buildings of architectural merit that have been renovated and converted into tourist accommodation. The best in Crete are at Vamos and Milia. They're not cheap but traditional features such as fireplaces and stone kitchens provide an unusual and appealing lodging experience.

Mountain Refuges

Mountain refuges are not plentiful on Crete but there are some lodges scattered in the Lefka Ori, Mt Psiloritis and Kallergi.

FOOD

Greek food does not enjoy a reputation as one of the world's great cuisines. Maybe that's because many travellers have experienced Greek cooking only in tourist resorts. The old joke about the Greek woman who, on summer days, shouted to her husband 'Come and eat your lunch before it gets hot' is based on truth.

Until recently, food was invariably served lukewarm – which is how Greeks prefer it. Most restaurants that cater to tourists have now cottoned on to the fact that foreigners expect cooked dishes to be served hot, and improved methods of warming meals (including the dreaded microwave) have made this easier. If your meal is not hot, ask that it be served zesto, or order grills, which have to be cooked to order. Greeks are fussy about fresh ingredients, and frozen food is rare.

Cretans eat out regularly, regardless of socioeconomic status. Enjoying life is paramount to Greeks and a large part of this enjoyment comes from eating and drinking with friends.

By law, every eating establishment must display a written menu including prices. Restaurant staff will automatically put bread on your table and usually costs between 100 dr and 200 dr, depending on the restaurant's category.

Where to Eat

Tavernas Traditionally, the taverna is a basic eating place with a rough-and-ready ambience, although some are more upmarket, particularly in Athens, and resorts and big towns. All tavernas have a menu, often displayed in the window or on the door, but it's usually not a good guide to what's actually available on the day. You'll be told about the daily specials – or ushered into the kitchen to peer into the pots and point to what you want. This is not merely a privilege for tourists; Cretans also do it because they want to see the taverna's version of the dishes on offer. Some tavernas don't open until 8 pm, and then stay open until the early hours. Some are closed on Sunday.

Psistaria These places specialise in spit roasts and charcoal-grilled food – usually lamb, pork or chicken.

Restaurants A restaurant *(estiatorio)* is normally more sophisticated than a taverna or psistaria with damask tablecloths, smartly attired waiters and printed menus at each table with an English translation. Ready-made food is usually displayed in a *bain-marie* and there may also be a charcoal grill.

Ouzeria An *ouzeri* serves ouzo. Greeks believe it is essential to eat when drinking alcohol so, in traditional establishments, your drink will come with a small plate of titbits or *mezedes* (appetisers) – perhaps olives, a slice of feta and some pickled octopus. Ouzeria are becoming trendy and many now offer menus with both appetisers and main courses.

Galaktopoleia A *galaktopoleio* (literally 'milk shop') sells dairy produce including milk, butter, yogurt, rice pudding, cornflour pudding, custard, eggs, honey and bread. It may also sell home-made ice cream – look for the sign *'pagoto politiko'* displayed outside. Most have seating and serve coffee and tea. They are inexpensive for breakfast and usually open from very early in the morning until evening.

Zaharoplasteia A *zaharoplasteio* (patisserie) sells cakes (both traditional and western), chocolates, biscuits, sweets, coffee, soft drinks and, possibly, bottled alcoholic drinks. They usually have some seating.

Kafeneia Kafeneia are often regarded by foreigners as the last bastion of male chauvinism in Europe. With bare light bulbs, nicotine-stained walls, smoke-laden air, rickety wooden tables and raffia chairs, they are frequented by middle-aged and elderly Cretan men in cloth caps who while away their time fiddling with worry beads, playing cards or backgammon, or engaged in heated political discussion.

It was once unheard of for women to enter a kafeneia but in large cities this situation is changing.

In rural areas, Cretan women are rarely seen inside kafeneia. When a female traveller enters one, she is invariably treated courteously and with friendship if she manages a few Greek words of greeting. If you feel inhibited about going into a kafeneio, opt for outside seating. You'll feel less intrusive.

Kafeneia originally only served Greek coffee but now, most also serve soft drinks, Nescafé and beer. They are generally fairly cheap, with Greek coffee costing about 150 dr and Nescafé with milk 250 dr or less. Most kafeneia are open all day every day, but some close during siesta time (roughly from 3 to 5 pm).

Meals

Breakfast Most Cretans have Greek coffee and perhaps a cake or pastry for breakfast. Budget hotels offering breakfast generally provide it continental-style (rolls or bread with jam, and tea or coffee), while more upmarket hotels serve breakfast buffets (western and continental-style). Otherwise, restaurants and galaktopoleia serve bread with butter, jam or honey; eggs; and the budget travellers' favourite, yogurt *(yiaourti)* with honey. In tourist areas, many menus offer an 'English' breakfast – which means bacon and eggs.

A Greek Feast

Greek dishes are easy to prepare at home. Here's a simple lunch or dinner to share with friends. Recipes serve four people.

Tzatziki (Cucumber and Yogurt Dip) Peel and grate a medium cucumber. Add a cup of yoghurt, a tablespoon of olive oil, a pinch of salt, a teaspoon of vinegar, a teaspoon of freshly chopped dill and a minced garlic clove and refrigerate for two hours. Garnish with an olive and serve with fresh crusty bread or as an accompaniment to vegetables or fried fish.

Soupa Avgolemono (Egg and Lemon Soup) Add six tablespoons of uncooked rice to six cups of boiling chicken, fish or beef stock, then cover and simmer until the rice is tender. Beat two eggs, adding a pinch of salt and the juice of a large lemon. Add the stock to this mixture slowly, so that it doesn't curdle, then pour the mixture into a pot for reheating. Stir and ensure it does not boil.

Soutzoukakia (Sausages from Smyrna) This hearty dish originated in Smyrna in the days of Greek occupation and has subsequently been adopted by the cooks of Thessaloniki. Soak two slices of white bread in half a cup of water, mash and add three garlic cloves finely chopped, half a teaspoon of pepper and a dessertspoon of cumin.

Add 500g (1lb) of minced lamb or beef and a beaten egg, mix well and form into small sausages. Place in an oiled roasting pan and bake in a medium to hot oven until the sausages brown on the base side. Turn the sausages and add 500g (1lb) of tomatoes, a dollop of butter and teaspoon of sugar and return to the oven for about 15 minutes – or until the tomatoes are soft and the *soutzoukakia* are brown on the other side. Serve with fried potatoes or rice, and salad.

Halvas tou Fournou (Baked Halva) Here's a delightful dessert that is simple to make. Sift half a cup of flour with two teaspoons of baking powder and a pinch of salt. Add two cups of semolina and a cup of finely chopped nuts. Cream ¾ of a cup of butter or margarine with a cup of sugar and add three beaten eggs and grated lemon peel. Combine the mixtures well, then pour into a greased 25cm (10 inch) square pan. Bake in a medium oven until golden.

Boil three cups of water with three cups of sugar, add four cloves and a half stick of cinnamon, then pour over the rest of the dessert. Leave it to stand until the cinnamon and clove mixture has been absorbed, then serve with or without cream, warm or cold. It's filling and keeps for days.

Lunch This is eaten late – between 1 and 3 pm – and may be either a snack or a complete meal.

The main meal in a Cretan's day can be lunch or dinner – or both. Cretans enjoy eating and it is quite common for them to have two large meals a day.

Dinner Cretans also eat dinner late. Many people don't start to think about food until about 9 pm, which is why some restaurants don't bother to open their doors until after 8 pm. In tourist areas dinner is often served earlier. A full dinner in Crete begins with appetisers and/or soup, followed by a main course of either ready-made food, grilled meat, or fish.

Only very posh restaurants or those pandering to tourists include Western-style desserts on the menu.

Cretans usually eat cakes separately in a galaktopoleio or zaharoplasteio.

Greek Specialities

Snacks Favourite Greek snacks include pretzel rings sold by street vendors, *tyropitta* (cheese pie), *bougatsa* (custard-filled pastry), *spanakopitta* (spinach pie) and *sandouits* (sandwiches). Street vendors sell various nuts and dried seeds such as pumpkin for 200 dr to 400 dr a bag.

Mezedes In a simple taverna, possibly only three or four mezedes (appetisers) will be offered – perhaps *taramasalata* (fish-roe dip), *tzatziki* (yogurt, cucumber and garlic dip), olives and feta. Ouzeria and restaurants usually offer wider selections.

Mezedes include *ohtapodi* (octopus), *garides* (shrimps), *kalamaria* (squid), *dolmades* (stuffed vine leaves), *melitzanosalata* (aubergine or eggplant dip) and *mavromatika* (black-eyed beans). Hot mezedes include *keftedes* (meatballs), *fasolia* (white haricot beans), *gigantes* (lima beans), *loukanika* (little sausages), tyropitta, spanakopitta, *bourekaki* (tiny meat pie), *kolokythakia* (deep-fried zucchini), *melitzana* (deep-fried aubergine) and *saganaki* (fried cheese).

It is quite acceptable to make a full meal of these instead of a main course. Three plates of mezedes are about equivalent in price and quantity to one main course. You can also order a *pikilia* (mixed plate).

Soups Soup is normally eaten as a starter, but can be an economical meal in itself with bread and a salad. *Psarosoupa* is a filling fish soup with vegetables, while *kakavia* (Greek bouillabaisse) is laden with seafood and is more expensive. *Fasolada* (bean soup) is also a meal in itself. *Avgolemano soupa* (egg and lemon soup) is usually prepared from a chicken stock. If you're into offal, don't miss the traditional Easter soup, *mayiritsa*, at this festive time.

Salads The ubiquitous (and no longer inexpensive) Greek or village salad, *horiatiki*

Another helping of horta?

An influential study concluded in 1960, after 15 years of research, found that Cretan men had the lowest rate of heart disease and cancer of all seven countries studied (Finland, USA, Netherlands, Italy, Yugoslavia, Japan and Kerkyra Island in Crete). The extraordinary longevity of Cretan men is a puzzle. Doctors noted that the traditional Cretan diet was high in fruits, vegetables, beans, whole grains and olive oil – the so-called "Mediterranean diet". Another important factor may be the wild greens that Cretans were accustomed to gathering in the hills. Used in pies, salads, or *horta*, the greens may have protective properties that are not yet fully understood. Unfortunately the Cretan beans and greens diet is changing as the island has prospered and urbanised. As Cretans have included more meat and cheese in their diets and no longer work (out) in the fields, heart disease and cancer rates are rising. Cretans have not completely abandoned their old ways however. Anyone who wants to clean up their coronaries will find plenty of healthy choices on Cretan menus.

salata, is a side dish for Greeks, but many drachma-conscious tourists make it a main dish. It consists of peppers, onions, olives, tomatoes and feta cheese, sprinkled with oregano and dressed with olive oil and lemon juice. A tomato salad often comes with onions, cucumber and olives, and, with bread, makes a satisfying lunch. In spring, try *radikia salata* (dandelion salad).

Main Dishes The most common main courses are *moussaka* (layers of eggplant or zucchini, minced meat and potatoes topped with cheese sauce and baked), *pastitsio* (baked cheese-topped macaroni with or without minced meat), dolmades, and *yemista* (stuffed tomatoes or green peppers). Other main courses include *giouvetsi* (casserole of lamb or veal and pasta), *stifado* (meat stewed with onions), *soutzoukakia* (spicy meatballs in tomato sauce) and *salingaria* (snails in oil with herbs). *Melizanes papoutsakia* is baked eggplant stuffed with meat and tomatoes and topped with cheese, which looks, as its Greek name suggests, like a little shoe. Spicy *loukanika* (sausage) is a good budget choice and comes with potatoes or rice. *Arni fricassée me maroulia* (lamb fricassee, cooked with lettuce) is usually filling enough for two to share.

Fish is usually sold by weight in restaurants, but is not as cheap nor as widely available as it used to be. Calamari (squid), deep-fried in batter, remains a tasty option for the budget traveller at 1000 dr to 1400 dr for a generous serve. Other reasonably priced fish (about 1000 dr a portion) are *marides* (whitebait), sometimes cloaked in onion, pepper and tomato sauce, and *gopes*, which are similar to sardines. More expensive are *ohtapodi* (octopus), *bakaliaros* (cod), *xifias* (swordfish) and *glossa* (sole). Ascending the price scale further are *synagrida* (snapper) and *barbounia* (red mullet). *Astakos* (lobster) and *karabida* (crayfish) are top of the range at about 10,000 dr per kg.

Fish is mostly grilled or fried. More imaginative fish dishes include shrimp casserole and mussel or octopus *saganaki* (fried with tomato and cheese).

Desserts Greek cakes and puddings include *baklava*, *loukoumades* (puffs or fritters with honey or syrup), *katafi* (chopped nuts inside shredded wheat pastry or filo soaked in honey), *rizogalo* (rice pudding), *loukoumi* (Turkish delight), *halva* (made from semolina or sesame seeds) and *pagoto* (ice cream). Tavernas and restaurants usually only have a few of these on the menu. The best places to go for these delights are *galaktopoleia* or *zaharoplasteia*.

Cretan Specialities
Greek and Cretan dishes often overlap but there are a few Cretan specialties worth searching out. Cretan food is based upon the vegetables, grain and livestock produced on the island. Barley *tako* is made into rusk that is softened in water and soaked in oil and tomato. Crete also produces some wonderful cheeses including sweet *myzithres*, and the yellow, sheep's milk cheese, *graviera*. Cretans are also fond of rabbit which is made into stifado, or stew. Snails are gathered on hillsides after a rainfall and prepared in dozens of interesting ways. Try *chochliii boubouristi*, snails simmered in vinegar or snails with barley. For centuries Cretans have been gathering wild greens from the hills and making them into *horta*, a delicious, tart vegetable side dish.

Vegetarian Food
Crete has few vegetarian restaurants, and unfortunately, many vegetable soups and stews are based on meat stocks. Fried vegetables are a safe bet as olive oil is always used – never lard. The Cretans do wonderful things with artichokes *(aginares)*. They can be served stuffed, as a salad, as a mezes (particularly with *raki*) or used as the basis of a vegetarian stew. Vegetarians who eat eggs can rest assured that an economical omelette can be whipped up anywhere. Salads are cheap, fresh, substantial and nourishing. Other options are yogurt, rice pudding, cheese and spinach pies, and nuts.

Lent, incidentally, is a good time for vegetarians because the meat is missing from many dishes.

Fast Food
Western-style fast food has arrived in Crete in a big way – creperies, hamburger joints and pizza places are to be found in all the major towns and resort areas.

It's hard, though, to beat eat-on-the-street Greek offerings. Foremost among them are the *gyros* and the souvlaki. The gyros is a giant skewer laden with slabs of seasoned meat which grills slowly as it rotates and the meat is trimmed steadily from the outside; souvlaki are small individual kebab sticks. Both are served wrapped in pitta bread, with salad and lashings of tzatziki.

Another favourite is *tost*, which is a bread roll cut in half, stuffed with the filling(s) of your choice, buttered on the outside and then flattened in a heavy griddle iron. It's the speciality of the Everest fast-food chain, which has outlets nationwide.

Fruit

Crete grows many varieties of fruit. Most visitors will be familiar with *syka* (figs), *rodakina* (peaches), *stafylia* (grapes), *karpouzi* (watermelon), *milo* (apples), *portokalia* (oranges) and *kerasia* (cherries).

Many will not, however, have encountered the *frangosyko* (prickly pear). Also known as the Barbary fig, it is the fruit of the opuntia cactus, recognisable by the thick green spiny pads that form its trunk. The fruit are borne around the edge of the pads in late summer and autumn and vary in colour from pale orange to deep red. They are delicious but need to be approached with extreme caution because of the thousands of tiny prickles (invisible to the naked eye) that cover their skin. Never pick one up with your bare hands. They must be peeled before you can eat them. The simplest way to do this is to trim the ends off with a knife and then slit the skin from end to end.

Another fruit that will be new to many people is the *mousmoula* (loquat). These small orange fruit are among the first of summer, reaching the market in mid-May. The flesh is juicy and pleasantly acidic.

Self-Catering

Eating out in Crete is as much an entertainment as a gastronomic experience, so to self-cater is to sacrifice a lot. But if you are on a low budget you will need to make the sacrifice – for breakfast and lunch at any rate.

All towns and villages of any size have supermarkets, fruit and vegetable stalls and bakeries.

Only in isolated villages and on remote islands is food choice limited. There may only be one all-purpose shop – a *pantopoleio* which will stock meat, vegetables, fruit, bread and tinned foods.

Markets Most larger towns have huge indoor *agora* (food markets) which feature fruit and vegetable stalls, butchers, dairies and delicatessens, all under one roof. They are lively places that are worth visiting for the atmosphere as much as for the shopping. The markets at Hania are a good example.

Smaller towns have a weekly *laki agora* (street market) with stalls selling local produce.

DRINKS
Nonalcoholic Drinks

Coffee & Tea Greek coffee is the national drink. It is a legacy of Ottoman rule and, until the Turkish invasion of Cyprus in 1974, the Greeks called it Turkish coffee. It is served with the grounds, without milk, in a small cup. Connoisseurs claim there are at least 30 variations of Greek coffee, but most people know only three – *glyko* (sweet), *metrio* (medium) and *sketo* (without sugar).

The next most popular coffee is instant, called Nescafe (which it usually is). Ask for Nescafe *me ghala* (pronounced 'me **ga**-la') if you want it with milk. In summer, Cretans drink Nescafe chilled, with or without milk and sugar – this version is called *frappé*. Espresso and filtered coffee, once sold only in trendy cafes, are now also widely available.

Tea is not the beverage of choice in Crete but it is available, usually in bags. Herbal tea is becoming popular, especially *diktamos* or dittany tea.

Fruit Juice & Soft Drinks Packaged fruit juices are available everywhere. Fresh orange juice is also widely available, but doesn't come cheap.

The products of all the major soft-drink multinationals are available everywhere in cans and bottles, along with local brands.

Milk Fresh milk can be hard to find in remote areas. Elsewhere, you'll have no problem. A litre costs about 350 dr. UHT milk is available almost everywhere, as is condensed milk.

Water Tap water is safe to drink in Crete, although sometimes it doesn't taste too good. Many tourists prefer to drink bottled spring water, sold widely in 500mL and 1.5L plastic bottles. If you're happy with tap water, fill a container with it before embarking on ferries or you'll wind up paying through the nose for bottled water. Sparkling mineral water is rare.

Alcoholic Drinks

Beer Beer lovers will find the market dominated by the major northern European breweries. The most popular beers are Amstel and Heineken, both brewed locally under licence. Other beers brewed locally are Henniger, Kaiser, Kronenbourg and Tuborg.

The only local beer is Mythos, launched in 1997 and widely available. It has proved popular with drinkers who find the northern European beers a bit sweet.

Imported lagers, stouts and beers are found in tourist spots such as music bars and discos. You might even spot Newcastle Brown, Carlsberg, Castlemaine XXXX and Guinness.

Supermarkets are the cheapest place to buy beer, and bottles are cheaper than cans. A 500mL bottle of Amstel or Mythos costs about 200 dr (including 25 dr deposit on the bottle), while a 500mL can costs about 260 dr. Amstel also produces a low-alcohol beer and a bock, which is dark, sweet and strong.

Wine According to mythology, the Greeks invented or discovered wine and have produced it in Crete on a large scale for more than 3000 years.

The modern wine industry, though, is still very much in its infancy. Until the 1950s, most Greek wines were sold in bulk and were seldom distributed any farther afield than the nearest town. It wasn't until industrialisation (and the resulting rapid urban growth) that there was much call for bottled wine. Quality control was unheard of up until 1969, when appellation laws were introduced as a precursor to applying for membership of the then European Community. Wines have improved significantly since then.

Cretan wine may not make wine connoisseurs tremble with delight but it can be pleasant and even distinguished. The quality is uneven but the best brands tend to come from Peza, Daphnes, Sitia and Arhanes. There's also the popular Vin de Crete which is a mediocre blend of local wines. The best wines are labelled with the region of origin clearly stated. The house wine is usually *kokkino*, a cloudy rosé that ranges from drinkable to dreadful. It only costs about 1000 dr a carafe while a good regional wine is at least three times as much for a bottle.

Don't expect Cretan wines to taste like French wines. The grape varieties grown in Crete are quite different. The most popular grapes are Villana and Thrapsathiri. The oldest grape variety is Liatiko which has been used to make red wine for the last 4000 years.

Spirits Ouzo is the most popular aperitif in Crete. Distilled from grape stems and flavoured with anise, it is similar to the Middle Eastern *arak*, Turkish *raki* and French Pernod. Clear and colourless, it turns white when water is added. A 700mL bottle of a popular brand like Ouzo 12, Olympic or Sans Rival costs about 1200 dr in supermarkets. In an ouzeri, a glass costs from 250 dr to 500 dr. It will be served neat, with a separate glass of water to be used for dilution.

The second-most popular spirit is Greek brandy, which is dominated by the Metaxa label. Metaxa comes in a wide choice of grades, starting with three star – a high-octane product without much finesse. You can pick up a bottle in a supermarket for about 1500 dr.

The quality improves as you go through the grades: five star, seven star, VSOP, Golden Age and finally the top-shelf Grand Olympian Reserve (5600 dr). Other reputable brands include Cambas and Votrys. The Cretan speciality is raki, a fiery clear spirit that is served as a greeting (regardless of the time of day).

If you're travelling off the beaten track, you may come across *chipura*. Like ouzo, it's made from grape stems but without the anise. It's an acquired taste, much like Irish poteen – and packing a similar punch. You'll most likely encounter chipura in village kafeneia or private homes.

ENTERTAINMENT
Discos & Music Bars
Discos can be found in big cities and resort areas, though not in the numbers of a decade ago.

Most young Greeks prefer to head for the music bars that have proliferated to fill the void.

These bars normally specialise in a particular style of music – Greek, modern rock, 60s rock, techno and, very occasionally, jazz.

Rock
Western rock music continues to grow in popularity, but live music remains a rarity.

Traditional Music & Dancing
Cretans are proud of their rich tradition of folk songs and dances. In village tavernas late at night someone is bound to produce a lyra and inspire a group sing along. Weddings are great opportunities to catch a glimpse of authentic local culture. Cretan music is often played in restaurants and clubs during the tourist season although it's usually altered to appeal to tourists.

Cinemas
Greeks are keen movie-goers and almost every town of consequence has a cinema. English-language films are shown in English with Greek subtitles. Admission ranges from 1000 dr in small-town movie houses to 1800 dr at plush big-city cinemas.

Theatre
The highlight of the Cretan dramatic year is the staging of ancient Greek dramas during Iraklio's Summer Festival. See Iraklio's special events section for more details.

Ballet, Classical Music & Opera
High-brow European culture has never caught on in Crete, perhaps because local music and dancing are so complex and interesting. Very few international troupes come to Crete but if they do it would be during the Iraklio Summer Festival.

SPECTATOR SPORTS
Cretan men are football (soccer) and basketball mad, both as spectators and participants. If you happen to be eating in a taverna on a night when a big match is being televised, expect indifferent service.

SHOPPING
Crete has a long tradition of artisanship that has metamorphosed into a giant industry. Blue ceramics, clay pottery, handmade leather goods, woven rugs, icons, embroidered linen and finely wrought gold jewellery fill shops in all the tourist centres. In addition to crafted objects there's also wild herbs, olive oil, Cretan wine, jellies, cheese, olives and other edibles.

Most of the products displayed in the ubiquitous souvenir stores are mass-produced. Although they can still be good value, it's worthwhile to seek out special shops that offer authentic Cretan items. Of all the large towns, you'll find the best selection of crafts in Hania.

Maybe it's the beauty of the city's architecture that has inspired artisans, but you'll find the island's most artful leather, jewellery and rugs in the streets behind the harbour.

Rethymno and Agios Nikolaos have a few good craft places but you have to plough through miles of souvenir shops. As the island's capital and richest city, Iraklio has more high-end stores for clothing, appliances and records but fewer souvenir and crafts shops.

Several villages in the interior are known for their crafts. You can get good buys on linen in Anogia and Kritsa while spending a pleasant afternoon tooling around the countryside.

Antiques
It is illegal to buy, sell, possess or export any antiquity in Greece (see Customs earlier in this chapter). However, there are antiques and 'antiques'; a lot of items only a century or two old are regarded as junk, rather than

part of the national heritage. These items include handmade furniture and odds and ends from rural areas, ecclesiastical ornaments from churches and items brought back from far-flung lands.

Good hunting grounds for this 'junk' are Monastiraki and the flea market in Athens, and the Piraeus market held on Sunday morning.

Ceramics

You will see ceramic objects of every shape and size – functional and ornamental – for sale throughout Crete.

The shiny dark blue glaze of Cretan ceramics is easily distinguishable from the lighter mat finish of other Greek ceramics.

The glaze should be hard enough not to scratch under the blade of a knife; a glazed bottom is the best sign of machine-made pottery.

There are a lot of places selling plaster copies of statues, busts, grave stelae and so on.

Leather Work

The leather is hard rather than supple but reasonably priced nonetheless; durable bags, wallets, shoes and boots are best bought on 'Leather Lane' in Hania.

Jewellery

You'll find more idiosyncratic pieces in silver than gold. Look for replicas of Minoan objects such as the Phaestos disk, which are well crafted and available only in Crete.

Bags

Tagari bags are woven wool bags – often brightly coloured – which hang from the shoulder by a rope. Minus the rope, they make attractive cushion covers.

Getting There & Away

For most visitors, getting to Crete means getting first to mainland Greece, usually Athens.

AIR (INTERNATIONAL)
Most travellers arrive in Crete by air, the cheapest and quickest way to get there.

Airports & Airlines
There are three airports on Crete: Iraklio, Hania and Sitia. Iraklio's Nikos Kazantzakis Airport is the largest and the point-of-entry for most travellers arriving on the island. There's no shortage of direct charter flights between Iraklio and the UK and Europe, but very few direct scheduled flights; most flights to the island change at Athens or Thessaloniki. Athens' dilapidated airport, Ellinikon, is 9km south of the city. There are two main terminals: West for all Olympic Airways flights, and East for all other flights. The airport's old military terminal is dusted off for charter flights in peak season. Buses 19 and 91 connect the East and West terminals.

Buying Tickets
If you are flying to Greece from outside Europe, the plane ticket will probably be the most expensive item in your travel budget, and buying it can be an intimidating business. There will be a multitude of airlines and travel agents hoping to separate you from your money, so take time to research the options. Start early – some of the cheapest tickets must be bought months in advance, and popular flights tend to sell out early.

Charter Flights
Charter flight tickets are for seats left vacant on flights which have been block-booked by package companies. Tickets are cheap but conditions apply on charter flights to Greece. A ticket must be accompanied by an accommodation booking. This is normally circumvented by travel agents issuing accommodation vouchers which are not meant to be used – even if the hotel named on the voucher actually exists. The law requiring accommodation bookings was introduced in the 1980s to prevent budget travellers flying to Greece on cheap charter flights and sleeping rough on beaches or in parks. It hasn't worked.

The main catch for travellers taking charter flights involves visits to Turkey. If you fly to Greece with a return ticket on a charter flight, you will forfeit the return portion if you visit Turkey. Greece is one of several popular charter destination countries which have banded together to discourage tourists from leaving the destination country during the duration of the ticket. The countries involved want to ensure people don't flit off somewhere else to spend their tourist cash. The result is that if you front up at the airport for your return charter flight with a Turkish stamp in your passport, you will be forced to buy another ticket.

This does not apply if you take a day excursion into Turkey, because the Turkish immigration officials will not stamp your passport. Neither does it apply to regular or excursion-fare flights.

Charter flight tickets are valid for up to four weeks, and usually have a minimum-stay requirement of at least three days. Sometimes it's worth buying a charter return even if you think you want to stay for longer than four weeks. The tickets can be so cheap that you can afford to throw away the return portion.

The travel section of major newspapers is the place to look for cheap charter deals. More information on charter flights is given later in this chapter under specific point-of-origin headings.

Courier Flights
Another budget option (sometimes even cheaper than a charter flight) is a courier flight. This deal entails accompanying freight or a parcel that will be collected at the destination. The drawbacks are that your

Air Travel Glossary

Cancellation Penalties If you have to cancel or change a discounted ticket, there are often heavy penalties involved; insurance can sometimes be taken out against these penalties. Some airlines impose penalties on regular tickets as well, particularly against 'no-show' passengers.

Courier Fares Businesses often need to send urgent documents or freight securely and quickly. Courier companies hire people to accompany the package through customs and, in return, offer a discount ticket which is sometimes a phenomenal bargain. However, you may have to surrender all your baggage allowance and take only carry-on luggage.

Full Fares Airlines traditionally offer 1st class (coded F), business class (coded J) and economy class (coded Y) tickets. These days there are so many promotional and discounted fares available that few passengers pay full economy fare.

Lost Tickets If you lose your airline ticket an airline will usually treat it like a travellers cheque and, after inquiries, issue you with another one. Legally, however, an airline is entitled to treat it like cash and if you lose it then it's gone forever. Take good care of your tickets.

Onward Tickets An entry requirement for many countries is that you have a ticket out of the country. If you're unsure of your next move, the easiest solution is to buy the cheapest onward ticket to a neighbouring country or a ticket from a reliable airline which can later be refunded if you do not use it.

Open-Jaw Tickets These are return tickets where you fly out to one place but return from another. If available, this can save you backtracking to your arrival point.

Overbooking Since every flight has some passengers who fail to show up, airlines often book more passengers than they have seats. Usually excess passengers make up for the no-shows, but occasionally somebody gets 'bumped' onto the next available flight. Guess who it is most likely to be? The passengers who check in late.

Promotional Fares These are officially discounted fares, available from travel agencies or direct from the airline.

Reconfirmation If you don't reconfirm your flight at least 72 hours prior to departure, the airline may delete your name from the passenger list. Ring to find out if your airline requires reconfirmation.

Restrictions Discounted tickets often have various restrictions on them – such as needing to be paid for in advance and incurring a penalty to be altered. Others are restrictions on the minimum and maximum period you must be away.

Round-the-World Tickets RTW tickets give you a limited period (usually a year) in which to circumnavigate the globe. You can go anywhere the carrying airlines go, as long as you don't backtrack. The number of stopovers or total number of separate flights is decided before you set off and they usually cost a bit more than a basic return flight.

Transferred Tickets Airline tickets cannot be transferred from one person to another. Travellers sometimes try to sell the return half of their ticket, but officials can ask you to prove that you are the person named on the ticket. On an international flight tickets are compared with passports.

Travel Periods Ticket prices vary with the time of year. There is a low (off-peak) season and a high (peak) season, and often a low-shoulder season and a high-shoulder season as well. Usually the fare depends on your outward flight – if you depart in the high season and return in the low season, you pay the high-season fare.

time away may be limited to one or two weeks, your luggage is usually restricted to hand luggage (the parcel or freight you carry comes out of your luggage allowance), and you may have to be a resident of the country that operates the courier service and apply for an interview before you'll be taken on.

Travel Agents

Many of the larger travel agents use the travel pages of national newspapers and magazines to promote their special deals. Before you make a decision, there are a number of questions you need to ask about the ticket. Find out the airline, the route, the duration of the journey, the stopovers allowed, any restrictions on the ticket and – above all – the price. Ask whether the fare quoted includes all taxes and other possible inclusions.

You may discover when you start ringing around that those impossibly cheap flights, charter or otherwise, are not available, but the agency just happens to know of another one that 'costs a bit more'. Or the agent may claim to have the last two seats available to Greece for the whole of July, which they will hold for a maximum of two hours only. Don't panic – keep ringing around.

If you are flying to Greece from the USA, South-East Asia or the UK, you will probably find the cheapest flights are being advertised by obscure agencies whose names haven't yet reached the telephone directory – the proverbial bucket shops. Many such firms are honest and solvent, but there are a few rogues who will take your money and disappear, only to reopen elsewhere a month or two later under a new name. If you feel suspicious about a firm, don't give them all the money at once – leave a small deposit and pay the balance when you get the ticket. If they insist on cash in advance, go somewhere else or be prepared to take a big risk. Once you have booked the flight with the agency, ring the airline to check you have a confirmed booking.

It can be easier on the nerves to pay a bit more for the security of a better-known travel agent. Firms such as STA Travel, with offices worldwide, Council Travel in the USA or Travel CUTS in Canada offer good prices to Europe (including Greece), and are unlikely to disappear overnight.

The fares quoted in this book are intended as a guide only. They are approximate and are based on the rates advertised by travel agents at the time of writing.

Travel Insurance

The kind of cover you get depends on your insurance and type of ticket, so ask both your insurer and your ticket-issuing agency to explain where you stand. Ticket loss is usually covered.

Travellers with Special Needs

If you've broken a leg, require a special diet, are travelling in a wheelchair, are taking a baby, or have some other special need, let the airline staff know as soon as possible – preferably when booking your ticket. Check that your request has been registered when you reconfirm your booking (at least 72 hours before departure) and again when you check in at the airport.

Departure Tax

There is an airport tax of 6800 dr on all international departures from Greece. This is paid when you buy a ticket, not at the airport.

The USA

The North Atlantic is the world's busiest long-haul air corridor, and the flight options to Europe – including Greece – are bewildering. Microsoft's popular Expedia.com Web site at www.expedia.msn.com gives a good overview of the possibilities. Other sites worth checking out are the ITN (www.itn.net) and Travelocity (www.travelocity.com) sites.

Low season prices from New York to Athens can be as low as US$390 return but rise to US$944 in high season.

Canada

Olympic Airways has two flights weekly from Toronto to Athens via Montreal. There are no direct flights from Vancouver, but there are connecting flights via Toronto, Amsterdam, Frankfurt and London on

Canadian Airlines, KLM, Lufthansa and British Airways.

Low season prices from Toronto to Athens run at about C$1129 and rise to about C$1908 in high season.

Australia

Olympic Airways has two flights weekly from Sydney and Melbourne to Athens. Return fares are normally priced from about A$1799 in low season to A$2199 in high season.

New Zealand

There are no direct flights from New Zealand to Athens. There are connecting flights via Sydney, Melbourne, Bangkok and Singapore on Olympic Airways, United Airlines, Qantas Airways, Thai Airways and Singapore Airlines.

The UK

British Airways, Olympic Airways, and Virgin Atlantic operate daily flights between London and Athens. Pricing is very competitive, with all three offering return tickets for around UK£200 in high season, plus tax. Prices are for midweek departures; weekend departures cost UK£40 more.

Cronus Airlines (☎ 020-7580 3500) flies the London-Athens route five times a week for £210, and offers connections to Iraklio for UK£242. Greek newcomer Air Manos (☎ 171-216 8040) offers a weekly direct flight to Iraklio for UK£89 in the off season and UK£129 in the high season. Olympic Airways has direct London-Thessaloniki flights four times a week. Most scheduled flights from London leave from Heathrow.

Campus Travel
    (☎ 020-7730 3402) 52 Grosvenor Gardens, London SW1; www.campustravel.co.uk
Council Travel
    (☎ 020-7287 3337) 28A Poland St, London W1V 3DB; www.counciltravel.com
STA Travel
    (☎ 020-7361 6161) 86 Old Brompton Rd, London SW7; www.statravel.co.uk
Trailfinders
    (☎ 020-7937 5400) 215 Kensington High St, London W8

Listings publications such as *Time Out*, the Sunday papers, the *Evening Standard* and *Exchange & Mart* carry advertisements for cheap fares.

The *Yellow Pages* is worth scanning for travel agents' ads, and look out for the free magazines and newspapers widely available in London, especially *TNT*, *Footloose*, *Southern Cross* and *LAM* – you can pick them up outside the main train and tube stations and backpacker haunts.

Continental Europe

Athens is linked to every major city in Europe by either Olympic Airways or the flag carrier of each country.

France

Air France (☎ 0802-802 802) and Olympic Airways (☎ 01-42 65 92 42) have at least four Paris-Athens flights daily between them. Expect to pay from 2950FF to 3300FF in high season, dropping to about 2100FF at other times.

Cronus Airlines (☎ 01-47 42 56 77) flies Paris-Iraklio or Paris-Hania four times weekly stopping at Athens for 1650FF low season and 2220FF high season.

Olympic Airways also has three flights weekly to Athens from Marseille.

Reliable travel agents include:

Air Sud
    (☎ 01-40 41 66 66) 18 Rue du Pont-Neuf, 75001 Paris
Atsaro
    (☎ 01-42 60 98 98) 9 Rue de l'Echelle, 75001 Paris
Bleu Blanc
    (☎ 01-40 21 31 31) 53 Avenue de la République, 75011 Paris
Héliades
    (☎ 01-53 27 28 21) 24-27 Rue Basfroi, 75011 Paris
La Grece Autrement
    (☎ 01-44 41 69 95) 72 Boulevard Saint Michel, 75006 Paris
Nouvelles Frontieres
    (☎ 08-03 33 33) 87 Boulevard de Grenelle, 75015 Paris
Planete Havas
    (☎ 01-53 29 40 00) 26 Avenue de l'Opéra, 75001 Paris

Germany

Air Greece has three flights a week from Iraklio to Stuttgart and four flights a week to Cologne in the summer, stopping at Thessaloniki. Iraklio is linked by Lufthansa to Frankfurt with a direct flight on Saturday and Sunday.

Atlas Reisewelt has offices throughout Germany and is a good place to start checking prices.

The Netherlands

KLM-associate Transavia has direct flights between Amsterdam and Iraklio on Monday and Friday.

Reliable travel agents in Amsterdam include:

Budget Air
 (☎ 020-627 12 51) Rokin 34
NBBS Reizen
 (☎ 020-624 09 89) Rokin 66

If you're travelling from Athens to Europe, budget fares to a host of European cities are widely advertised by the travel agents around Syntagma. Following are some typical one-way fares (not including airport tax):

destination	one way fare (dr)
Amsterdam	57,500
Copenhagen	59,500
Frankfurt	55,000
Geneva	54,000
Hamburg	52,000
Madrid	73,000
Milan	48,000
Munich	55,000
Paris	55,500
Rome	42,000
Zurich	53,500

Turkey

Olympic Airways and Turkish Airlines share the Istanbul-Athens route, with at least one flight a day each. The full fare is US$250 one way.

Olympic Airways also flies twice weekly between Istanbul and Thessaloniki (US$190). Students qualify for a 50% discount on both routes.

Cyprus

Olympic Airways and Cyprus Airways share the Cyprus-Greece routes. Both airlines have three flights daily from Larnaca to Athens, and there are five flights weekly to Thessaloniki. Cyprus Airways also flies from Paphos to Athens once a week in winter, and twice a week in summer.

AIR (DOMESTIC)

If you are flying to Crete on a scheduled flight, chances are you'll arrive in Athens (or possibly Thessaloniki) and then take a domestic flight to your final destination. The domestic portion is incorporated into your ticket by your travel agent.

Airlines

The vast majority of domestic flights are handled by the country's much-maligned national carrier, Olympic Airways, together with its offshoot, Olympic Aviation.

Olympic Airways has offices wherever there are flights, as well as in other major towns. The head office in Athens (☎ 01-966 6666) is at Leoforos Syngrou 96, and its Web site is at www.olympic-airways.gr. Tickets can be purchased at the airport, from Olympic Airways offices or any travel agent.

Olympic offers a 25% student discount on domestic flights, but only if the flight is part of an international journey.

Olympic lost its monopoly on domestic routes in 1993. It took a while for any serious opposition to emerge, but there are now three established competitors on the scene and newcomers appearing all the time.

This Crete-based airline, Air Greece, was the first newcomer to show any sign of permanence. It has been around since 1995, offering a cheaper alternative to Olympic on some of the major routes. It also offers youth discounts (under 26).

Discount and package specialist Air Manos which offers some very cheap flight and accommodation packages, and has a reputation for good service. Its Web site is at www.manos.co.uk provides information on flights and packages.

Cronus Airlines (☎ 01-995 6400, fax 01-995 6405) is another traveller-friendly company that has quickly established itself on the local scene. It offers discounts for students and for travellers aged over the 60, and special rates for advance purchase. Its Web site, www.cronus.gr, has for more information on routes and fares.

Aegean Air is the latest addition to the line-up of airlines in Greece. It flies between Athens, Hania, Iraklio and Rhodes.

Forward planning is advisable as these domestic flights to Crete can be packed in high season

This information is for flights from mid-June to late September. Outside these months, the number of flights to the islands drops considerably. Prices are for one-way fares and include domestic airport tax of 3400 dr paid as part of the ticket

Hania

Olympic Airways have at least four flights a day from Hania to Athens (19,800 dr for the afternoon flights and 13,400 dr for the late evening flight).

Olympic Airways also has two flights a week to Thessaloniki (29,900 dr).

Air Greece has daily flights from Hania to Athens (20,400 dr).

Air Manos flies from Athens to Hania. It offers some very cheap flight and accommodation packages.

From Hania, Aegean Air has two daily flights to Athens (16,500 dr) and one to Thessaloniki (28,100 dr).

Iraklio

From Iraklio's Nikos Kazantzakis airport, Olympic Airways has at least six flights a day (21,900 dr) to Athens; three a week to Thessaloniki (29,900 dr); four a week to Rhodes (21,900 dr); and, two a week to Santorini (15,400 dr).

Air Greece has four flights a day from Iraklio to Athens (20,400 dr), two daily to Thessaloniki (29,400 dr) and three weekly to Rhodes in the summer (23,400 dr).

Cronus Airlines flies Athens-Iraklio twice a day and Iraklio-Thessaloniki and Rhodes-Thessaloniki once a day.

Aegean Air has three daily flights from Iraklio's Nikos Kazantzakis Airport to Athens

(18,500 dr) and one daily flight to Thessaloniki (29,700 dr).

Domestic Departure Tax

The airport tax for domestic flights is 3400 dr, paid as part of the ticket. All prices quoted in this book include this tax.

Domestic Baggage Allowance

The free-baggage allowance on domestic flights is 15kg. However, this does not apply when the domestic flight is part of an international journey. The international free-baggage allowance of 20kg is then extended to the domestic sector. This allowance applies to all tickets for domestic travel sold and issued outside Greece.

LAND
Turkey

Bus The Hellenic Railways Organisation (OSE) operates Athens-Istanbul buses (22 hours) daily except Wednesday, leaving the Peloponnese train station in Athens at 7 pm and travelling via Thessaloniki and Alexandroupolis.

One-way fares are 21,800 dr from Athens, 14,300 dr from Thessaloniki and 5600 dr from Alexandroupolis. Students qualify for a 15% discount and children under 12 travel for half-fare. See the Getting There & Away sections for each city for information on where to buy tickets.

Train There are daily trains between Athens and Istanbul (19,000 dr) via Thessaloniki (13,000 dr) and Alexandroupolis (6350 dr).

The service is incredibly slow and the train gets uncomfortably crowded. There are often delays at the border and the journey can take much longer than the supposed 22 hours.

Car & Motorcycle If you're travelling between Greece and Turkey by private vehicle, the crossing points are at Kipi, 43km north-east of Alexandroupolis, and at Kastanies, 139km north-east of Alexandroupolis. Kipi is more convenient if you're heading for Istanbul, but the route through Kastanies goes via the fascinating towns of

Soufli and Didymotiho, in Greece, and Edirne (ancient Adrianople) in Turkey.

Bulgaria
Bus The OSE operates two Athens-Sofia buses (15 hours, 13,400 dr) daily except Monday, leaving at 7 am and 5 pm. It also operates Thessaloniki-Sofia buses (7½ hours, 5600 dr, three daily).

Train There is an Athens-Sofia train daily (18 hours, 10,330 dr) via Thessaloniki (nine hours, 6700 dr).

Car & Motorcycle The Bulgarian border crossing is at Promahonas, 145km northeast of Thessaloniki and 50km from Serres.

Albania
Bus There is a daily OSE bus between Athens and Tirana (12,600 dr) via Ioannina and Gjirokastra. The bus departs Athens (Larisis train station) at 7 pm arriving in Tirana the following day at 5 pm. It leaves Ioannina at 7.30 am and passes through Gjirokastra at 10.30 am. On the return trip, the bus departs Tirana at 7 am. There are buses from Thessaloniki to Korça (Korytsa in Greek) daily at 8 am. The fare is 6600 dr.

Car & Motorcycle There are two crossing points between Greece and Albania. The main one is at Kakavia, 60km north-west of Ioannina; the other is at Krystallopigi, north-west of Kastoria.

Former Yugoslav Republic of Macedonia
Train There are Thessaloniki-Skopje trains (three hours, 4200 dr, two daily), which cross the border between Idomeni and Gevgelija. It leaves Thessaloniki at 6 am and 5.30 pm. Both trains continue to the Serbian capital of Belgrade (12 hours, 11,500 dr). The 5.30 pm service goes all the way to Budapest (21 hours, 20,000 dr).

Car & Motorcycle There are two border crossings between Greece and FYROM. One is at Evzoni, 68km north of Thessaloniki. This is the main highway to Skopje which

continues to Belgrade. The other border crossing is at Niki, 16km north of Florina.

Western Europe
Overland travel between Western Europe and Greece is almost a thing of the past. Airfares are so cheap that land transport cannot compete. Travelling from the UK to Greece through Europe means crossing various borders, so check whether any visas are required before setting out.

Bus There are no bus services to Greece from the UK, nor from anywhere else in northern Europe.

Train Unless you have a Eurail pass or are aged under 26 and eligible for a discounted fare, travelling to Greece by train is prohibitively expensive. For example, the full one-way/return fare from London to Athens is UK£265/521, including the Eurostar service from London to Paris. In order to get to Crete, you'll need to take a bus to Piraeus and then a boat to Crete.

There are special buses that operate 24 hours a day to Piraeus. Bus No 040 leaves from the corner of Syntagma and Filellinon, and No 049 leaves from the Omonia end of Athinas. The buses run every 20 minutes from 6 am to midnight, and then hourly. All these services cost a flat rate of 120 dr. Tickets can be bought from ticket kiosks and periptera.

Car & Motorcycle Before the troubles in the former Yugoslavia began, most motorists driving from the UK to Greece opted for the direct route: Ostend, Brussels, Salzburg and then down the Yugoslav highway through Zagreb, Belgrade and Skopje and crossing the border to Evzoni.

SEA
Ferry
Ferries come in all shapes and sizes, from the giant 'superferries' that work the major routes to the small, ageing open ferries that chug around the backwaters. In winter, services to some of the smaller islands are fairly skeletal. Services start to pick up

again from April onwards, and by July and August there are countless services crisscrossing the Aegean.

Routes The hub of Greece's ferry network is Piraeus, the port of Athens. Ferries leave here for the Cyclades, Dodecanese, the North-Eastern Aegean Islands, Saronic Gulf Islands and Crete. Note that there are two departure points for Crete. Ferries for Iraklio leave from the western end of Akti Kondyli, but ferries for other Cretan ports occasionally dock there as well. It's a long way to the other departure point for Crete on Akti Miaouli, so check where to find your boat when you buy your ticket.

Schedules Ferry timetables change from year to year and season to season, and ferries are subject to delays and cancellations at short notice due to bad weather, strikes or boats simply conking out. No timetable is infallible, but the comprehensive weekly list of departures from Piraeus put out by the EOT in Athens is as accurate as humanly possible. The people to go to for the most up-to-date ferry information are the local port police *(limenarheio)*, whose offices are usually on or near the quay side.

There's a lot of information about ferry services on the Internet. Try the Web site at www.ferries.gr with its useful search program and links.

Many of the larger ferry companies now have their own sites, including ANEK (www.anek.gr) and Minoan Lines (www.minoan.gr).

Throughout the year there is at least one ferry a day from a mainland port to the major island in each group, and during the high season (from June to mid-September) there are considerably more. Ferries sailing from one island group to another are not so frequent, and if you're going to travel in this way you'll need to plan carefully, otherwise you may end up having to backtrack to Piraeus.

Travelling time can vary considerably from one ferry to another, depending on the ship and the route it takes. Before buying your ticket, check how many stops the boat is going to make, and its estimated arrival time.

Costs Prices are fixed by the government, and are determined by the distance travelled rather than by the facilities of a particular boat. There can be big differences in the size, comfort and facilities of boats offering rival services on a given route, but the fares will be the same. Small differences in price you may find at ticket agencies are the result of some agents sacrificing part of the commission to qualify as a 'discount service'. The discount is seldom more than 50 dr.

Classes The large ferries usually have four classes: 1st-class has air-con cabins and a posh lounge and restaurant; 2nd-class has smaller cabins and sometimes a separate lounge; tourist class gives you a berth in a shared four-berth cabin; and 3rd (deck) class gives you access to a room with 'airline seats', a restaurant, a lounge/bar and, of course, the deck.

Deck class remains an economical way to travel, while a 1st-class ticket can cost almost as much as flying on some routes. Children under four travel for free, while children between four and 10 pay half fare. Full fares apply for children over 10. Unless you state otherwise when purchasing a ticket, you will automatically be given deck class. Prices quoted in this book are for deck class as this is what most tourists opt for.

Ticket Purchase Ferries are prone to delays and cancellations in bad weather, so it's best not to buy a ticket until it has been confirmed that the ferry is operating. If you need to reserve a car space, you may need to pay in advance. If the service is cancelled, you can transfer your ticket to the next available service with that company.

Agencies selling tickets line the waterfront of most ports, but rarely is there one that sells tickets for every boat, and often an agency is reluctant to give you information about a boat it does not sell tickets for. This means you have to check the timetables displayed outside each agency to find out which ferry is next to depart – or ask the port police. In high season, a number of boats may be due at a port at around the same time, so it is not beyond the realms of possibility that you might get on the wrong boat. The crucial thing to look out for is the name of the boat; this will be printed in your ticket, and in large English letters on the side of the vessel.

If for some reason you haven't purchased a ticket from an agency, makeshift ticket tables are put up beside a ferry about an hour before departure. Tickets can also be purchased on board the ship after it has sailed. If you are waiting at the quay side for a delayed ferry, don't lose patience and wander off. Ferry boats, once they turn up, can demonstrate amazing alacrity – blink and you may miss the boat.

Ferry Travel Once on board, the fun really begins. It can be absolute chaos in high season. No matter how many passengers are already on the ferry, more will be crammed on. Bewildered, black-shrouded grannies are steered through the crowd by teenage grandchildren, children get separated from parents, people stumble over backpacks, dogs get excited and bark – and everyone rushes to grab a seat. As well as birds in cages and cats in baskets there is almost always at least one truck of livestock on board – usually sheep, goats or cattle, vociferously making their presence known.

Greeks travelling deck class usually make a beeline for the indoor lounge/snack bar, while tourists make for the deck where they can sunbathe.

Some ferry companies have allegedly attempted to capitalise on this natural division by telling backpackers and non-Greeks that they are barred from the deck-class saloon and indoor-seating area, directing them instead to the sun deck. There is no such thing as 'deck only' class on domestic ferries, although there is on international ferries.

You'll need strong nerves and lungs to withstand the lounge/snack bar, though. You can reckon on at least two TVs turned up full blast, tuned to different channels and crackling furiously from in-

terference. A couple of other people will have ghetto blasters pumping out heavy metal, and everyone will be engaged in loud conversation.

Smoke-laden air adds the final touch to this delightful ambience. Unlike other public transport in Greece, smoking is not prohibited on ferries.

On overnight trips, backpackers usually sleep on deck in their sleeping bags – you can also roll out your bag between the 'airline seats'.

If you don't have a sleeping bag, claim an 'airline seat' as soon as you board. Leave your luggage on it – as long as you don't leave any valuables in it. The noise on board usually dies down around midnight so you should be able to snatch a few hours sleep.

The food sold at ferry snack bars ranges from mediocre to inedible, and the choice is limited to packets of biscuits, sandwiches, very greasy pizzas and cheese pies.

Most large ferries also have a self-service restaurant where the food is OK and reasonably priced, with main courses starting at around 1500 dr. If you are budgeting, have special dietary requirements, or are at all fussy about what you eat, take food with you.

Greek Mainland & Islands

There are no international connections by sea to Crete but there are international connections to Athens and Thessaloniki on mainland Greece, and to Greek islands, such as Rhodes, which are all connected by boat to Crete.

The main ferry port on Crete is at Iraklio with daily ferries to/from the port of Athens, Piraeus. Hania and Rethymno also have daily ferries to/from Athens. Iraklio also serves many other destinations throughout the Greek Islands.

Hydrofoil In addition to the ferry services, there is a daily hydrofoil service between Iraklio and Santorini (2¾ hours, 7200 dr) that runs in the summer and is operated by Speed Lines of Santorini.

Domestic Ferry Schedules

departure city	arrival city	boats per week	duration	fares (dr)
Iraklio	Piraeus	daily	10 hours	7000
Iraklio	Santorini	three	4 hours	3700
Iraklio	Paros	three	8½ hours	5200
Iraklio	Naxos	two	6¼ hours	5200
Iraklio	Tinos	one	8¾ hours	6300
Iraklio	Syros	one	8½ hours	5600
Iraklio	Volos	one	17½ hours	10,000
Iraklio	Rhodes	three	11 hours	6400
Iraklio	Karpathos	three	6½ hours	4200
Iraklio	Thessaloniki	three	13 hours	12,100
Iraklio	Kasos	one	6 hours	4200
Iraklio	Skiathos	two	15½ hours	9900
Sitia	Piraeus	three	14¾ hours	7600
Sitia	Agios Nikolaos	three	1½ hours	1600
Sitia	Milos	two	9½ hours	5200
Sitia	Kasos	two	2½ hours	2600
Sitia	Karpathos	two	4¼ hours	3400
Sitia	Halki	one	5½ hours	4000
Sitia	Rhodes	one	10½ hours	6000
Kastelli-Kissamos	Githio	two	7 hours	5100
Kastelli-Kissamos	Kythira	two	4 hours	4200
Kastelli-Kissamos	Antikithira	two	2 hours	2100
Rethymno	Piraeus	daily	10 hours	7000
Hania	Piraeus	daily	9 hours	5900

Note that Agios Nikolaos and Sitia share the same ferry schedule.

Turkey

There are three ferries daily from Rhodes to Marmaris in Turkey between April and October and less frequent services in winter. Prices vary, so shop around. There are also daily hydrofoils to Marmaris (weather permitting) from April to October for 10,000/14,000 dr one-way/return plus Turkish port tax. Tickets for ferries to Turkey must be bought a day in advance. You will almost certainly be asked to turn in your passport before the trip but don't worry, you'll get it back before you board the boat. Port tax for departures to Turkey is 3000 dr.

Italy

There are ferries to Greece from the Italian ports of Ancona, Bari, Brindisi, Trieste and Venice but all arrive in Patras. In order to get to Crete you can take any train or bus to Athens and then Piraeus for a boat to Crete. There are buses from Patras to Athens (three hours, 3500 dr) every 30 minutes, with the last at 9.45 pm. There are nine trains a day to Athens. Four are slow trains (4½ hours, 1580 dr) and five are express intercity trains (3½ hours, 2980 dr). The last intercity train leaves at 6 pm, and the last slow train leaves at 8 pm.

Most of the ferry companies have their own Web sites, including:

Adriatica	www.adriatica.it
ANEK Lines	www.anek.gr
Hellenic Mediterranean Lines	www.hml.it
Minoan Lines	www.minoan.gr
Strintzis	www.strintzis.gr
Superfast	www.superfast.com
Ventouris	www.ventouris.gr

The following ferry services are for high season (July and August), and prices are for one-way deck class. Deck class on these services means exactly that. If you want a reclining, aircraft-type seat, you'll be up for another 10 to 15% on top of the listed fares. Most companies offer discounts for return travel. Prices are about 30% less in the low season.

Ancona to Patras This route has become increasingly popular in recent years. There can be up to three boats daily in summer, and at least one a day year-round.

Superfast Ferries (☎ 71-20 28 05) provides the fastest and most convenient service, but it's also the most expensive. It has boats daily (20 hours, L148,000). Minoan Lines (☎ 71-20 17 08) has ferries to Patras (20 hours, L124,000) via Igoumenitsa (15 hours) daily except Tuesday. ANEK Lines (☎ 71-20 59 99) runs two direct boats weekly (24 hours, L115,000) and three via Igoumenitsa (34 hours). Strintzis (☎ 71-20 10 68) sails direct to Patras (23 hours, L96,000) three times weekly, twice via Igoumenitsa and Corfu.

Bari to Corfu, Igoumenitsa & Patras Superfast Ferries (☎ 80-52 11 416) operates daily to Patras (15 hours, L88,000) via Igoumenitsa (9½ hours). Marlines (☎ 80-52 31 824) has daily boats to Igoumenitsa (12 hours, L70,000), while Ventouris (☎ 80 521 7118) goes to Igoumenitsa (13½ hours, L65,000) via Corfu.

Brindisi to Corfu, Igoumenitsa & Patras The route from Brindisi to Patras (18 hours) via Corfu (nine hours) and Igoumenitsa (10 hours) is the cheapest and most popular of the various Adriatic crossings. There can be up to five boats daily in high season.

Companies operating ferries from Brindisi are: Adriatica di Navigazione (☎ 831-52 38 25), Corso Garibaldi 85-87, and on the 1st floor of the stazione marittima, where you must go to check in; Five Star Lines (☎ 831-52 48 69), represented by Angela Gioia Agenzia Marittima, Via F Consiglio 55; Fragline (☎ 831-59 01 96), Corso Garibaldi 88; Hellenic Mediterranean Lines (☎ 831-52 85 31), Corso Garibaldi 8; and Med Link Lines (☎ 831-52 76 67), represented by Discovery Shipping, Corso Garibaldi 49.

Adriatica and Hellenic Mediterranean are the most expensive at around L100,000 for deck class passage to Corfu (7½ hours), Igoumenitsa (nine hours) or Patras (15½ hours), but they are the best. They are also the only lines which accept Eurail passes. You will still have to pay port tax and a high-season loading in summer – usually about L15,000.

If you want to use your Eurail pass, it is important to reserve some weeks in advance, particularly in summer. Even with a booking, you must still go to the Adriatica or Hellenic Mediterranean embarkation office in the stazione marittima to have your ticket checked.

The cheapest crossing is with Five Star Lines, which charges L46,000 to either Igoumenitsa (7½ hours) or Patras (15½ hours). Med Link charges L62,000 to Igoumenitsa and L65,000 to Patras, while Fragline charges L68,000 to Corfu and Igoumenitsa. Fares for cars range from L65,500 to L120,000 in the high season, depending on the line.

From 1 July to 19 September, Italian Ferries (☎ 831-59 03 05), Corso Garibaldi 96, operates a daily high-speed catamaran to Corfu (3¼ hours, L154,000) leaving Brindisi at 2 pm. The service continues to Paxi (4¾ hours, L190,000 dr).

Trieste to Patras ANEK Lines (☎ 40-30 28 88), Stazione Marittima di Trieste, has three boats weekly to Patras travelling via Igoumenitsa. The trip takes 37 hours and costs L106,000 for deck class.

Venice to Patras Minoan Lines (☎ 41-27 12 345), Magazzino 17, Santa Marta, has boats from Venice to Patras (40 hours, L132,000). All services go via Corfu and Igoumenitsa, and from mid-May until late September two boats weekly call at Kefallonia.

Plying his trade – street cobbler mending shoes in Iraklio.

A street vendor selling donuts, breads and pastries in Rethymno.

Many Cretans still use traditional forms of transport.

Cafe tables line the old port of Rethymno.

Take your pick of local olives at Hania's food market.

Seafood market stall on 1866 Street in Iraklio.

Vegetables for sale in Rethymno.

Warning

The information in this chapter is particularly vulnerable to change: prices for international travel are volatile, routes are introduced and cancelled, schedules change, special deals come and go, and rules and visa requirements are amended. Airlines and governments seem to take a perverse pleasure in making price structures and regulations as complicated as possible. You should check directly with the airline or a travel agent to make sure you understand how a fare (and ticket you may buy) works. In addition, the travel industry is highly competitive and there are many lurks and perks.

The upshot of this is that you should get opinions, quotes and advice from as many airlines and travel agents as possible before you part with your hard-earned cash. The details given in this chapter should be regarded as pointers and are not a substitute for your own careful, up-to-date research.

Cyprus & Israel

Two companies ply the route between Piraeus and the Israeli port of Haifa, via Lemesos on Cyprus. These boats also stop at Rhodes and various other Greek islands.

During July and August, Salamis Lines leaves Haifa at 8 pm on Sunday and Lemesos at 4 pm on Monday, reaching Rhodes at noon on Tuesday, Tinos at 6 am on Wednesday, and Piraeus at 3 pm. The return service departs Piraeus at 7 pm on Thursday, and stops at Patmos on the way to Rhodes, Lemesos and Haifa.

For the rest of the year, the boat leaves Haifa at 8 pm on Monday and skips Tinos.

Bookings in Haifa are handled by Rosenfeld Shipping (☎ 04-861 3670), 104 Ha'Atzmaut St, and in Lemesos by Salamis Tours (☎ 05-355 555), Salamis House, 28 October Ave.

Poseidon Lines operates a similar service. In July and August, it sails from Haifa at 8 pm on Thursday and Lemesos at 1 pm on Friday, and then calls at Rhodes, Santorini and Tinos on the way to Piraeus. It leaves Piraeus at 7 pm on Monday, stopping at Santorini and Patmos on the way to Rhodes, Lemesos and Cyprus.

It operates virtually the same timetable for the rest of the year, but stops only at Rhodes and Lemesos. Bookings in Haifa are handled by Caspi Travel (☎ 04-867 4444), 76 Ha'Atzmaut St, and in Lemesos by Poseidon Lines Cyprus (☎ 05-745 666), 124 Franklin Roosevelt St.

Both lines charge the same. Deck-class fares from Haifa are US$101 to Rhodes and US$106 to Piraeus. Fares from Lemesos are US$68 to Rhodes and US$72 to Piraeus. If you want a seat you'll be up for an extra US$10 more, while the cheapest shared cabins cost an extra US$30.

You'll find the latest information on these services on the Internet: www.ferries.gr for Poseidon Lines, and www.viamare.com/salamis for Salamis Lines.

Yacht

Despite the disparaging remarks among backpackers, yachting is *the* way to see the Greek Islands. Nothing beats the peace and serenity of sailing the open sea, and the freedom of being able to visit remote and uninhabited islands.

The free EOT booklet *Sailing the Greek Seas*, although long overdue for an update, contains lots of information about weather conditions, weather bulletins, entry and exit regulations, entry and exit ports and guidebooks for yachties.

You can pick up the booklet at any GNTO/EOT office either abroad or in Greece.

The Internet is the place to look for the latest information. The Hellenic Yachting Server site at www.na-biznet.com.gr/sail has general information on sailing around the islands, and lots of links.

The sailing season lasts from April until October. The best time to go depends on where you are going. The most popular time is between July and September, which ties in with the high season for tourism in general.

Unfortunately, it also happens to be the time of year when the *meltemi* is at its strongest.

The meltemi is a northerly wind that affects the Aegean throughout the summer. It starts off as a mild wind in May and June, and strengthens as the weather hots up – often blowing from a clear blue sky. In August and September, it can blow at gale force for days on end.

If your budget won't cover buying a yacht there are several other options open to you. You can hire a bare boat (a yacht without a crew) if two crew members have a sailing certificate. Prices start at US$1300 per week for a 28-footer that will sleep six. It's an option only if two crew members have a sailing certificate; otherwise you can hire a skipper for an extra $100 per day.

Most of the hire companies are based in and around Athens. They include:

Aegean Tourism
 (☎ 01-346 6229, fax 342 2121) Kadmias 8, Athens; www.aegeantours.com
Alpha Yachting
 (☎ 01-968 0486, fax 968 0488, email mano @otenet.gr) Poseidonos 67; Glyfada
Ghiolman Yachts & Travel
 (☎ 01-323 3696, fax 322 3251, email ghiol man@travelling.gr) Filellinon 7, Athens
Hellenic Charters
 (☎/fax 01-988 5592, email hctsa@ath.forth net.gr) Poseidonos 66, Alimos
Kostis Yachting
 (☎ 01-895 0657, fax 895 0995) Epaminonda 61, Glyfada, www.kostis-yachting.com

Vernicos Yachts
 (☎ 01-985 0122, fax 985 0120) Poseidonos 11, Alimos, www.vernicos.gr

There are many more yacht charter companies operating in Greece; the EOT can provide addresses.

ORGANISED TOURS

The vast majority (80%) of travellers who decide to head for Crete opt for a package holiday.

Flight/accommodation packages can be a remarkably good deal, costing far less than what you would pay if you booked your air fare and hotel room separately.

The best deals can often pop up at the last-minute as tour operators struggle to fill charter flights and block-booked hotel rooms.

Most of the offerings are for large resorts along the northern coast.

For a less industrialised vacation experience, you can try one of the following companies:

Pure Crete (☎ 0181-760 0879) 79 George Street, Croydon, Surrey CRO 1LD
Simply Crete (☎ 0181-994 4462) Chiswick Gate,598-608 Chiswick High Road, London W4 5RT
Greek Islands Club (☎ 020-8232 9780)
Greek Options (☎ 020-7233 5233)
Diktynna Travel (☎ 0821-41 458, fax 43 930, email sales@diktynna-travel.gr) 6 Agiou Markou & Kanevaro, 73100 Hania, Greece
Island Holidays (☎ 0176-477 0107)

Getting Around

BUS

Crete is an easy place to travel around thanks to a comprehensive public transport system. A four lane national highway skirts the north coast from Hania in the west to Agios Nikolaos in the east, and is being extended further west to Kastelli-Kissamos. There are frequent buses linking all the major northern towns from Kastelli-Kissamos to Sitia. Less frequent buses operate between the north coast towns and resorts and places of interest on the south coast, via the mountain villages of the interior. Fares are fixed by the government, and are very reasonable by European standards.

Buses are operated by regional collectives known as KTEL (Koino Tamio Eispraxeon Leoforion). Every prefecture has its own KTEL, which operates local services within the prefecture and services to the main towns of other prefectures. A useful site is www.ktel.org which has schedules for all the island's buses.

Larger towns usually have a central, covered bus station with seating, waiting rooms, toilets, and a snack bar selling pies, cakes and coffee. Big cities like Iraklio have several bus stations, each serving different regions. In small towns and villages the 'bus station' may be no more than a bus stop outside a *kafeneio* or taverna which doubles as a booking office. Most booking offices have timetables in both Greek and Roman script. The timetables give both the departure and return times – useful if you are making a day trip. Times are listed using the 24-hour-clock system.

Regular and reliable buses link the major northern towns from Kastelli-Kissamos to Sitia. These buses are generally in good shape and some are even air-conditioned. Buses do not have toilets on board and they don't have refreshments available, so make sure you are prepared on both counts. Smoking is prohibited on all buses in Greece; only the chain-smoking drivers dare to ignore the no smoking signs.

Most buses use the northern highway but there are at least one or two buses each day that use the old roads. The trip is more scenic but takes much longer so ask before you buy the ticket. In major towns it's best to buy your ticket at the station to make sure you have a seat but if you board at a stop along the way you buy the ticket from the driver. When you buy a bus ticket, you will be given a seat number (look on the ticket). The seat number is indicated on the back of each seat of the bus, not on the back of the seat in front; this causes confusion among Greeks and tourists alike. Keep the ticket: it'll be checked a few times en route. The bus stations in major towns keep long opening hours and are a good source of information

The schedules below are for the high season 1999; services between the main cities on the north coast decline by about 20% in winter, but services to outlying towns and villages can decline by as much as 50%.

CAR & MOTORCYCLE

Crete is plenty big enough to warrant having your own vehicle which makes it possible to visit smaller, more out-of-the-way places. Roads have improved enormously in recent years but in many parts of the island, particularly in the south, you'll still find unpaved roads that are only suitable for jeeps. Few people bother to bring their own vehicle from Europe; there are plenty of places to hire both cars and motorcycles.

If you explore the island by car or scooter, prepare to spend a fair amount of time poring over maps, since country roads are often unmarked. Road signs, when they exist, are usually marked in Greek and Latin letters except in remote locations. Even when written in Latin letters, the spelling of place names can vary wildly from the names on your map or in this book. Invest in a good map (Road Editions publishes the most accurate island map) but even the best maps don't cover all the side roads.

Bus Schedules and Costs

From Iraklio

to	duration (hours)	fare (dr)	frequency (daily)
Agia Galini	2¼	1500	8
Agia Pelagia	¾	650	7
Agios Nikolaos	1½	1400	half-hourly
Anoghia	1	750	5
Arhanes	½	340	15
Dikteon Cave	2	1400	2
Hania	3	2900	half-hourly
Hersonisos	¾	600	half-hourly
Ierapetra	2½	2100	8
Malia	1	750	half-hourly
Matala	2	1500	8
Phaestos	1½	1250	10
Rethymno	1½	1550	half-hourly
Sitia	3¼	2850	5

From Hania

to	duration (hours)	fare (dr)	frequency (daily)
Hora Sfakion	2	1400	3
Kastelli-Kissamos	1	900	15
Lakki	1	600	4
Moni AgiasTriadas	½	400	3
Omalos (for Samaria gorge)	1	1250	4
Paleohora	2	1450	3
Rethymno	1	1500	half-hourly
Sougia	2	1400	1
Stavros	½	300	6

From Rethymno

to	duration (hours)	fare (dr)	frequency (daily)
Agia Galini	1½	1300	4
Hania	1	1350	half-hourly
Iraklio	1½	1550	hourly
Omalos	2	2750	1
Plakias	1	950	4
Moni Arkadiou	½	500	3
Preveli	1	950	2
Hora Sfakion	2	1450	1

From Agios Nikolaos

to	duration (hours)	fare (dr)	frequency (daily)
Elounda	½	230	20
Kritsa	¼	230	12
Ierapetra	1	750	8
Iraklio	1½	1400	half-hourly
Istron	½	280	11
Lassithi plateau	3	1900	1
Sitia	1½	1500	6

Almost all islands are served by car ferries, but they are expensive. For example, the price for a small vehicle from Piraeus to Crete (Hania or Iraklio) is 19,610 dr; the charge for a large motorbike is about the same as the price of a 3rd-class passenger ticket.

In general, petrol in Greece is expensive, and the farther you get from a major city the more it costs. Prices vary from petrol station to petrol station. Super can be found as cheaply as 199 dr per litre at big city discount places, but 225 dr to 235 dr is the normal range. You may pay closer to 245 dr per litre on the islands. The price range for unleaded available everywhere – is from 200 dr to 225 dr per litre. Diesel costs about 170 dr per litre.

See the Documents section in the Facts for the Visitor chapter for information on licence requirements.

See the Useful Organisations section in the Facts for the Visitor chapter for information about the Greek automobile club (ELPA).

Road Rules

Few would be surprised to learn that Greece has one of the highest road fatality rates in Europe – it's a good place to practise your defensive driving skills! Overtaking is the biggest cause of accidents, so as a visitor you should familiarise yourself with the rules of the road. Driving in the major cities is a nightmare of erratic one-way streets and irregularly enforced parking rules. Cars are not towed but parking tickets can be expensive. Parking for the handicapped is a rarity.

In Greece, as throughout Continental Europe, you drive on the right and overtake on the left. Highways and major roads are divided into four lanes so you should drive near but not in the right lane, and pull into the right lane to allow the car behind you to pass. Other regulations are that seatbelts must be worn in front and back seats, and you must travel with a first-aid kit, fire extinguisher and warning triangle. Carrying cans of petrol is banned. Outside built-up areas, traffic on a main road has right of way at intersections. In towns, vehicles coming from the right have right of way. Motorcyclists driving bikes of 50cc or more must wear helmets.

Offences and fines include:

* Speed Limits (Cars) – 120km/h on highways, 90km/h on other roads and 50km/h in built-up areas. Drivers exceeding the speed limit by 20% are liable for a fine of 20,000 dr; and by 40%, 50,000 dr.
* Speed Limits (Motorcycles) – 70km/h (up to 100cc), 90km/h (above 100cc).
* Drink Driving – A blood alcohol limit of 0.05% will incur a fine of 50,000 dr, and over 0.08% is a criminal offence.
* Illegal overtaking – 100,000 dr
* Going through a red light – 100,000 dr
* Driving without a seat belt – 50,000 dr
* Motorcyclist not wearing a helmet – 50,000 dr
* Wrong way down one-way street – 50,000 dr
* Illegal parking – 10,000 dr

The police can issue traffic fines, but payment cannot be made on the spot – you will be told where to pay. If you are involved in an accident and no-one is hurt, the police will not be required to write a report, but it is advisable to go to a nearby police station and explain what happened. A police report may be required for insurance purposes. If an accident involves injury, a driver who does not stop and does not inform the police may face a prison sentence.

Warning If you are planning to use a motorcycle or moped, check that your travel insurance covers you for injury resulting from a motorbike accident. Many insurance companies don't offer this cover, so check the fine print!

Signs of Trouble One reason for the scarcity of road signs on Crete is that they tend to get shot up. On an island where most adult men have a firearm, road signs make tempting targets for would-be marksmen. After a few hits by a rifle or .45 Magnum, piecing together the name on the sign is about as easy as deciphering Linear A.

Rental

Car Hiring a car in Crete is more expensive than in other European countries but the

Driving Distances

From Hania to:

Rethymno	78 km
Souda	6.5 km
Vrisses	33 km
Kastelli-Kissamos	42 km
Sougia	70 km
Hora Sfakion	73 km
Paleohora	77 km
Falassarna	55 km
Frangokastello	82 km
Vamos	26 km

From Rethymno to:

Iraklio	78 km
Spili	30 km
Moni Preveli	37 km
Anogia	54 km
Agia Galini	62 km
Argiroupolis	25 km
Plakias	41 km

From Iraklio to:

Agios Nikolaos	69 km
Knossos	5 km
Tilissos	14 km
Arhanes	16 km
Hersonisos	26 km
Malia	37 km
Gortyn	45 km
Phaestos	63 km
Agia Triada	66 km
Matala	70 km
Fodele	29 km
Dikteon Cave	70 km

From Agios Nikolaos to:

Sitia	73 km
Kritsa	11 km
Elounda	12 km
Ierapetra	36 km
Dikteon Cave	48 km
Moni Toplou	94 km
Kato Zakros	115 km
Lato	13 km
Vai	100 km
Itanos	100 km

prices have come down recently due to an increasingly competitive environment. It pays to shop around especially if you'll be renting a car for a week or more. Although major international companies such as Hertz, Budget and Europcar have offices in most towns you'll usually get a better deal if you rent from a local company.

High-season weekly rates with unlimited mileage from a major company start at about 110,000 dr for the smallest models, such as a 900cc Fiat Panda. The rate drops to about 90,000 dr per week in winter. The many local companies are normally more open to negotiation, especially if business is slow. Their advertised rates are about 25% cheaper than those offered by the multinationals. To these prices VAT of 18% must be added. Then there are the optional extras, such as a collision damage waiver of 3300 dr per day (more for larger models), without which you will be liable for the first 1,500,000 dr of the repair bill (much more for larger models). Other costs include a theft waiver of at least 1000 dr per day and personal accident insurance. It all adds up to an expensive exercise. Some companies offer much cheaper pre-booked and prepaid rates.

If you want to take a hire car onto a ferry, you will need advance written authorisation from the hire company. Unless you pay with a credit card, most hire companies will require a minimum deposit of 20,000 dr per day.

The minimum driving age in Greece is 18 years old, but most car-hire firms require you to be at least 23 years old, although some will rent to 21 year olds.

See the Getting Around section of the relevant cities for details of car rental outlets.

Motorcycle Extreme caution should be exercised when travelling by motorcycle. Roads change without warning from smooth and paved to cracked and pothole-ridden. Watch your speed. Greece is not the best place to initiate yourself into the world of motorcycling: many tourists have accidents every year. Experienced motorcyclists will find a lightweight enduro motorcycle between 400 and 600cc ideal for negotiating Crete's roads.

Mopeds and motorcycles are available for hire wherever there are tourists to rent them. In many cases their maintenance has been minimal, so check the machine thoroughly before you hire it – especially the brakes: you'll need them! When you rent a moped, tell the shop where you'll be going to ensure that your vehicle has enough power to get you up Crete's steep interior hills.

Motorbikes are a cheap way to travel around. Rates range from 2000 dr to 4000 dr per day for a moped or 50cc motorbike to 6000 dr per day for a 250cc motorbike. Out of season these prices drop considerably, so use your bargaining skills. By October it is sometimes possible to hire a moped for as little as 1500 dr per day.

Most motorcycle hirers include third party insurance in the price, but it is wise to check this. This insurance will not include medical expenses.

Taxi

Taxis are widely available in Crete except in remote villages, and are relatively cheap by European standards. Large towns have taxi stands that post a list of taxi prices to outlying destinations, which removes any anxiety about over-charging. Otherwise you pay what's on the meter. You can negotiate with taxis to take you sightseeing for the day using the following prices as a guide: Flagfall is 200 dr followed by 62 dr per km (120 dr per km outside town or between midnight and 5 am). There's a 300 dr surcharge when the taxi is hired at the airport and a 150 dr surcharge if the taxi is hired at a bus station or port. Each piece of luggage weighing more than 10kg carries a surcharge of 50 dr, and there's a surcharge of 300 dr for radio taxis. Grey rural taxis do not have meters, so you should always settle on a price before you get in.

If your destination is at the end of a bumpy, unpaved road you'll pay considerably more – if you can find a taxi to take you there at all.

If you have a complaint about a taxi driver, take the cab number and report your complaint to the tourist police. Taxi drivers in Crete are, on the whole, friendly, helpful and honest.

Official Taxi Fares	
From Iraklio to:	
Agios Nikolaos	9700 dr
Elounda	11,000 dr
Hania	20,000 dr
Hersonisos	4500 dr
Ierapetra	15,000 dr
Knossos	1500 dr
Matala	11,700 dr
Rethymno	12,000 dr
Sitia	19,500 dr
From Kastelli-Kissamos to:	
Falassarna	2000 dr
Hania	5000 dr
Iraklio	22,000 dr
Paleohora	6000 dr

BICYCLE

Cycling has not caught on in Crete, which isn't surprising considering the hilly terrain. Tourists are beginning to cycle in Crete, but you'll need strong leg muscles. You can hire bicycles in most tourist places, but they are not as widely available as cars and motorbikes. Prices range from 1000 dr to 3000 dr per day, depending on the type and age of the bike. Bicycles are carried free on ferries.

HITCHING

Hitching is never entirely safe in any country in the world, and we don't recommend it. Travellers who decide to hitch should understand that they are taking a small but potentially serious risk. People who do choose to hitch will be safer if they travel in pairs and should let someone know where they are planning to go. Greece has a reputation for being a relatively safe place for women to hitch, but it is still unwise to do it alone. It's better for women to hitch with a companion, preferably a male one.

Some parts of Crete are much better for hitching than others. Getting out of major cities tends to be hard work; hitching is much easier in remote areas. On country roads, it is not unknown for someone to stop and ask if you want a lift even if you haven't stuck a thumb out. You can't afford to be fussy about the mode of transport – it may be a tractor or a spluttering old truck.

WALKING

Unless you have come to Crete just to lie on a beach, the chances are you will do quite a bit of walking. You don't have to be a trekker to start clocking up the kilometres. The narrow, stepped streets of many towns and villages can only be explored on foot, and visiting the archaeological sites involves a fair amount of legwork.

See the What to Bring, Health and Trekking sections in the Facts for the Visitor chapter for more information about walking.

BOAT
Ferry

In addition to the large ferries which ply between the large mainland ports and island groups, there are smaller boats linking the towns along the south coast, some of which are only accessible by sea.

In summer, there are daily boats from Paleohora to Hora Sfakion via Agia Roumeli, Sougia and Loutro that offer wonderful coastal views. Although the schedules change from year to year, there are usually two to three boats a day between Hora Sfakion and Agia Roumeli and one boat a day from Hora Sfakion to Paleohora. There are also three boats a week in the summer between Paleohora and Gavdos Island and a weekly boat between Sougia and Gavdos Island.

There are also tourist boats connecting port cities with offshore islands. In the past these boats were always *caiques* – sturdy old fishing boats – but gradually these are being replaced by new, purpose-built boats, which are usually called express or excursion boats. Although it may be possible to negotiate with fishermen for trips on the caiques, it is illegal for fishing boats to take on passengers.

Some of the more popular excursions include Ierapetra to Hrysi Island, Agios Nikolaos to Spinalonga, and Kastelli-Kissamos to Gramvousa Peninsula.

Taxi Boat

Most southern port cities have taxi boats – small speedboats which operate like taxis, transporting people to places that are difficult to get to by land. Some owners charge a set price for each person, others charge a flat rate for the boat, and this cost is divided by the number of passengers. Either way, prices are usually quite reasonable.

LOCAL TRANSPORT
To/From the Airports

Olympic Airways operates buses to a few domestic airports (see individual entries in the appropriate chapters). Where the service exists, buses leave the airline office about 1½ hours before departure. In many places, the only way to get to the airport is by taxi. Check-in is an hour before departure for domestic flights.

Bus

Local city buses operating from Iraklio, Rethymno, and Hania are designed to take people back and forth from the city suburbs and are not really practical for getting around the cities themselves. They are cheap and reliable if not terribly comfortable. The procedure for buying tickets for local buses is covered in the Getting Around section for each city.

ORGANISED TOURS

Whether you want to see the island by boat, bus, jeep, bicycle, foot or on horseback, there's an organised tour for you. Organised tours can take you to otherwise inaccessible spots without having to hassle with buses, maps, bad roads, poorly marked roads, boat rentals or taxi drivers. The guide may provide you with fascinating insights into local culture and is right there to answer questions. The disadvantages are that you are locked into a pre-scheduled itinerary and, if you have limited time, there may not be a tour going to your destination on the days when you are available.

Most agencies have a tour schedule – Monday to the Samaria Gorge, Tuesday to Knossos etc. In large towns such as Hania, Agios Nikolaos, Iraklio or Rethymno travel agencies selling tours are abundant but they usually operate through one tour operator who provides the transport and guide. Price-shopping is useless since the prices are set by the tour operator. Most agencies take children up to 4-years-old free and give a 50% reduction to children between 5 and 15-years-old.

One of the most popular tours is to the Samaria Gorge, a trip you can arrange from almost any place on the island. The price ranges from 4500 dr to 9500 dr depending on your starting point, but it does not include the admission fee to the gorge or the boat trip from Agia Roumeli to Hora Sfakion. Most agencies also offer a Samaria Gorge 'easy way' for a few thousand drachma less that takes you from Agia Roumeli to the 'iron gates'. Unfortunately the route to the famous rock slabs is mostly hot and boring but you will get a taste of the gorge's majesty.

The Minoan Palace of Knossos is another tour favourite but taking a tour makes little sense if you're staying in Iraklio. From Hania or Agios Nikolaos the tour will cost 7000 dr to 7500 dr and includes a guide, transport and some free time for shopping and lunch in Iraklio. Admission to the site is not included.

Jeep safaris are a popular option if you're looking to get far off the beaten track. Although expensive (12,000 dr to 16,000 dr)

you can reach delightfully out-of-the-way villages and sights. If the agency is sending out a procession of jeeps however, your main sight will be the dust from the vehicle ahead of you. Jeep safaris generally include lunch in a local taverna.

Depending on your location you may be able to take tours to the Dikteon Cave on the Lassithi Plateau as well as the towns, sights and beaches of Crete. There are also various village tours that lean heavily on shopping during the day and dinner/folk dancing shows at night. These tours can be worthwhile, especially if you have more money than time, but they can get crowded in the summer. Boat tours that include swimming operate from the harbours of Hania, Rethymno, and Agios Nikolaos as well as many south coast beaches. These tours can also get crowded but, unless you have your own boat, an organised tour is the only way to see remote beaches and islands.

Organised Treks
Trekking Hellas (☎ 01-325 0853, fax 33 4548) Filellinon 7, Athens 105 57, specialises in treks and other adventure activities for small groups. They offer two week-long treks that cover central and western Crete. See the Hania, Agios Nikolaos and Rethymno chapters for more information about organised treks.

Hania

Hania is the largest town in western Crete and the capital of its prefecture. This part of the island has some of Crete's most spectacular sights including the Samaria Gorge, the Lefka Ori Mountains and Mount Gingilos in the rugged interior. The rocky southern coast is dotted with laid-back beach communities such as Paleohora, Sougia, Loutro and Hora Sfakion, and the nearly deserted west has two of Crete's finest beaches – Falassarna in the northern corner and Elafonisi in the southern corner. Near the town of Hania is the Akrotiri Peninsula with several interesting monasteries and a few beach resorts.

The prefecture is divided into five provinces: Sfakia that extends from the Lefka Ori mountain range to the coast; Kydonia which includes the town of Hania; Kissamos which covers the western third of the prefecture; Selino in the south-western corner; and Apokoronas in the east. Each province is unique, so from mountain climbing, gorge-trekking, and scuba diving to lazing on the beach and exploring Venetian architecture you'll always have something to do.

Kydonia Province

Kydonia includes Hania and the Akrotiri Peninsula and is western Crete's most populous province with 93,460 inhabitants. The coastline is highly developed, especially the stretch west of Hania, but it's possible to find more isolated spots on the Akrotiri Peninsula. The most outstanding geographical feature in this region is Souda Bay, the largest natural harbour of the Mediterranean, which is now used as a naval base.

HANIA Χανιά
☎ 0821 • postcode 731 00 • pop 65,000
Hania is Crete's most evocative city with a wealth of buildings from its former Venetian and Turkish overlords scattered throughout its narrow, stone streets. Don't be discouraged by the carapace of modern develop-

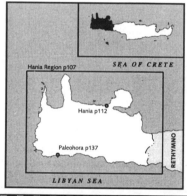

HIGHLIGHTS

- Trekking the spectacular Samaria Gorge
- Wandering the narrow streets of Hania's Venetian Quarter
- Relaxing on beaches such as Elafonisi and Frangokastello
- Taking in the ornate facades of the Akrotiri Peninsula's monasteries

ment that presses around the Old Town. Remnants of Venetian walls still border a web of atmospheric streets that tumble onto a magnificent harbour. The Venetian townhouses along the harbourside promenade have been restored and converted into *domatia*, restaurants, cafes and shops.

The massive fortifications built by the Venetians are still impressive. The best preserved section is the western wall, running from the fortress to Promahonas Hill. It was built in 1538 as part of a defense system when the Turks were looking to expand their real estate holdings in the Mediterranean. The engineer, Michele Sanmichele, also designed Iraklio's defences. The lighthouse at the entrance to the harbour looks in

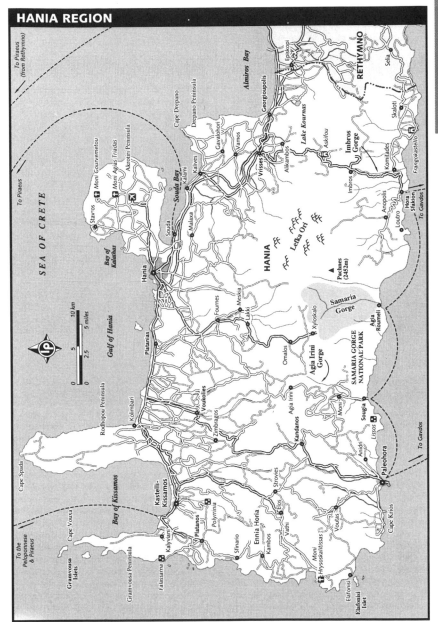

HANIA REGION

To Piraeus (from Rethymno)

To Piraeus

SEA OF CRETE

To the Peloponnese & Piraeus

Gramvousa Islets

Cape Vouxi

Gramvousa Peninsula

Cape Spada

Rodhopou Peninsula

Kolimbari

Bay of Kissamos

Falassarna

Kalyviani

Kastelli-Kissamos

Platanos

Polyrinia

Sinario

Ennia Horia

Kambos

Vathi

Moni Hrysoskalitissas

Elafonisi Islet

Voulas

Strovles

Elos

Moni

Kandanos

Zimbragos

Voukolies

Platanias

Bay of Kalathas

Stavros

Moni Gourvernetou

Moni Agias Triadas

Akrotiri Peninsula

Souda

Souda Bay

Kalami

Malaxa

Hania

Gulf of Hania

Fournes

Meskla

Laki

Omalos

Agia Irini

Andri

Agia Irini Gorge

Moni

Sougia

Lissos

Paleohora

Cape Knos

To Gavdos

SAMARIA GORGE NATIONAL PARK

Agia Roumeli

Samaria Gorge

Xyloskalo

HANIA

Lefka Ori

Pachnes (2452m)

Anopolis

Loutro

Hora Sfakion

To Gavdos

Imbros

Imbros Gorge

Komitades

Frangokastello

Askifou

Alikambos

Vrisses

Vamos

Gavalohori

Kalives

Drepano Peninsula

Cape Drepano

Georgioupolis

Lake Kournas

Almiros Bay

Episkopi

RETHYMNO

Sellia

Skaloti

10 km

5 miles

0   2.5   5

need of tender loving care these days, but makes a fine silhouette against the sky, especially at sunset.

Hania's war-torn history has left it with only a few impressive monuments but the city wears its scars proudly. Walk along Zambeliou, Theotokopoulou and Angelou streets in the old quarter and you'll come across roofless Venetian buildings turned into gracious outdoor restaurants. Many of the timber houses that date from Turkish rule have been restored. Even during the height of the tourist season when the buildings are festooned with technicolour beach towels and similar claptrap, Hania retains the exoticism of a city caught between East and West.

Hania is famous for its wonderful old Venetian quarter but there's lots more to discover in Crete's second city and former capital. Hania has a lively tradition of artisanship making it a great shopping city, and the inner harbour is ideal for relaxing in a cafe and watching the passing promenade. The covered food market was modelled after the one in Marseilles and presents a colourful panoply of Cretan products. To escape the crowds, take a stroll around the Splantzia quarter, a delightful tangle of narrow streets and little *plateias*, or head out to the beach. Nea Hora is the town beach, just west of the fortress, but the water is not particularly clean. For better swimming, keep heading west and you'll come to Oasis Beach which becomes Kalamaki Beach after about 5km.

Boats to Hania dock at Souda, about 7km south-east of town. There are frequent buses to Hania (240 dr) as well as taxis (2000 dr).

History

Neolithic people first settled on Kastelli Hill east of the port in Hania Harbour and were followed by the early Minoans who arrived around 2200 BC and founded a settlement known as Kydonia. Great seamen, the Minoans built a harbour and Kydonia became an important port. Little excavation work has been done, but the finding of clay tablets with Linear B script has led archaeologists to believe that Kydonia was both a palace and an important town, and is buried under the modern city of Hania.

Kydonia met the same fiery fate as most other Minoan settlements in 1450 BC, but soon re-emerged as a force. Although little has been excavated that dates from the millennium preceding the Roman conquest in 69 BC, the town was mentioned a few times by classical Greek writers as an important city. When the Romans stormed Crete, the town put up a heroic but futile resistance.

It continued to flourish under the Romans with Kastelli Hill serving as the Roman Acropolis. Its prosperity continued during the early Christian years and it became the seat of a bishopric.

Not much is known about the early Byzantine years (around 330 AD) through to the beginning of Venetian rule in 1204. It appears that the Byzantines recognised the port's strategic importance and built a fortress here out of the remains of ancient Kydonia. It is possible that the name Hania dates from this period.

Although the Venetians bought Crete from Boniface Monferatico in 1204, they failed to consolidate their control over Hania and lost it in 1266 to the Genoese. When the Venetians finally wrested this important harbour town from the Genoese in 1290 they made sure that they wouldn't lose it again. They invested considerable time and money in fortifying Hania, constructing massive walls around the town. The first walls were built in the 14th century around Kastelli Hill, and in the 16th century the Venetians walled the entire town as a defence against the pirates that were plaguing the Cretan coast.

By the 17th century pirates were not the problem – Turks were the problem. The growing menace from the east threatened all of Venetian rule and the Turks conquered Hania in 1645 after a gruelling two month siege, giving them a foothold on the island. The Turks made Hania the seat of the Turkish Pasha, and turned the churches into mosques. Turkish rule lasted until 1898 during which time the architectural style of the town changed, becoming more Oriental with wooden walls and latticed windows.

The Great Powers made Hania the island capital in 1898 and it remained so until 1971, when the administration was

Linear B

The methodical decipherment of the Linear B script by English architect and part-time linguist Michael Ventris was the first tangible evidence that the Greek language had a recorded history longer than any scholar had previously believed. The decipherment demonstrated that the language disguised by these mysterious scribblings was an archaic form of Greek 500 years older than the Ionic Greek used by Homer.

Linear B was written on clay tablets that lay undisturbed for centuries until they were unearthed at Knossos in Crete. Further clay tablets were unearthed later on the mainland at Mycenae, Tiryns and Pylos in the Peloponnese and at Thebes in Boeotia.

The clay tablets consisted of about 90 different signs date from the 14th to 13th century BC. Little of the social and political life of these times can be deduced from the tablets, though there is enough to give a glimpse of a fairly complex and well-organised commercial structure.

For linguists, the script did not provide a detailed image of the actual language spoken, since the symbols were used primarily as syllabic clusters designed to give an approximation of the pronunciation of the underlying language. Typically, the syllabic cluster 'A-re-ka-sa-da-ra' is the woman's name Alexandra, but the exact pronunciation remains unknown.

Importantly, what is clear is that the language is undeniably Greek, thus giving the modern-day Greek language the second-longest recorded written history, after Chinese. The language of an earlier script, Linear A, remains to this day undeciphered. It is believed to be of either Anatolian or Semitic origin, though even this remains pure conjecture.

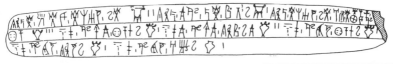

transferred to Iraklio. The WWII Battle of Crete largely took place on the coast west of Hania and the city was nearly destroyed by the German bombardment which was followed by a fire. Fortunately, enough remains so that Hania is still characterised as Crete's most beautiful city.

Orientation

The station for local buses is on Kydonias, two blocks south-west of Plateia 1866, one of the city's main squares. From Plateia 1866 to the Venetian Port is a short walk north down Halidon. The main hotel area is to the left as you face the harbour, where Akti Kountourioti leads around to the old fortress on the headland. The headland separates the Venetian Port from the crowded town beach in the quarter called Nea Hora. Zambeliou, which dissects Halidon just before the harbour, was once Hania's main

thoroughfare. It's a narrow, winding street, lined with craft shops, hotels and tavernas.

Information

Tourist Offices Hania's EOT (☎ 92 943, fax 92 624) is at Kriari 40, close to Plateia 1866. It is well-organised and considerably more helpful than most. Opening hours are 7.30 am to 2.30 pm weekdays. The tourist police (☎ 53 333) are at Irakliou 23. To get there, follow Apokoronou about 500m out of town to where it becomes Irakliou. The tourist police are open 7.30 am to 2.30 pm Monday to Friday.

Money The National Bank of Greece on the corner of Tzanakaki and Gianari, and the Credit Bank at the junction of Halidon and Skalidi have 24-hour automatic exchange machines. There are numerous places to change money outside banking hours. Most are willing to negotiate the amount of commission, so check around.

Post & Communications The central post office is at Tzanakaki 3. It is open 7.30 am to 8 pm Monday to Friday, and 7.30 am to 2 pm Saturday. The OTE is next door at Tzanakaki 5. Opening times are 7.30 am to 10 pm daily.

Internet access Internet access is available at Vranas Studios (☎ 58 618) on Ag Deka (see Places to Stay). The cost is 1000 dr per half hour and it's open 9 am to 11 pm daily.

Travel Agencies Tellus Travel (☎/fax 91 500) at Halidon 108 is centrally located and rents cars, changes money, arranges air and boat tickets and sells excursions. It's open 9 am to 7 pm Monday to Friday.

Bookshops The George Chaicalis Bookshop, on Plateia Venizelou, sells English-language newspapers, books and maps.

Laundry The town has two laundrettes: Laundry Fidias, at Sarpaki 6; and another at Ag Deka 18. The price is 1800 dr to wash and dry about 6kg of clothes.

Left Luggage Luggage can be stored at the main bus station on Plateia 1866 for 400 dr per day.

Things to See
Hania's **Archaeological Museum** (☎ 90 334), Halidon 21, is housed in the 16th-century Venetian Church of San Francisco that became a mosque under the Turks, a movie theatre in 1913, and a munitions depot for the Germans during WWII. The Turkish fountain in the grounds is a relic from the building's days as a mosque. The museum houses a well-displayed collection of finds from western Crete dating from the Neolithic to the Roman era. To the left as you enter the museum you'll see artefacts from 3400 BC to 1200 BC. Notice especially the tablets with Linear A script. Next you'll see vases from the Geometric era (1000-700 BC). From the Hellenistic and Roman exhibits the

---

Turkish Women in Hania

Turkish houses are distinguished by timber awnings jutting out from the building on the first and second floors. During the time of Turkish rule it was believed that Muslim women needed to be 'protected' from the rapacious glances of men and thus they were kept imprisoned in the house. The timber protrusions allowed women to gaze out onto the street without being seen by any men passing below.

---

statue of Diana is particularly impressive. In the same section there are vases, idols, and jewellery excavated from western Crete. Before leaving the museum, stop in the courtyard and notice the marble fountain decorated with lions' heads from the Venetian period. The museum is open 8 am to 4.30 pm Tuesday to Sunday. Admission is 500 dr.

The **Naval Museum** (☎ 44 156) has an interesting collection of model ships, naval instruments, paintings and photographs, including a picture of the old Venetian town. It is open 10 am to 4 pm daily. Admission is 500 dr. The museum is housed in the fortress on the headland.

Hania's interesting **Folklore Museum** (☎ 90 816), Halidon 46B, contains a selection of crafts and implements including weavings with traditional designs. It is open 9 am to 3 pm and 6 pm to 9 pm Monday to Friday. Admission is 500 dr.

The **Historical Museum and Archives**, on Sfakianaki 20, traces Crete's war-torn history with a series of exhibits focusing on the struggle against the Turks. There are also a few exhibits relating to the German occupation and a small folklore collection. The museum is open 9 am to 1 pm Monday to Friday. Admission is free.

Trekking & Mountain Climbing
Alpin Travel (☎ 53 309), in the complex at Bonaili 11-19, offers many trekking programs. The owner, George Antonakakis, helps run Hania's chapter of the EOS (☎ 44 647), at Tzanakaki 90, and is the guy to talk to for information about serious climbing in

A Walking Tour of Hania's Old Quarter

Begin the tour at the covered **food market**, which makes all other food markets look like stalls at a church bazaar. Unfortunately, the central bastion of the city wall had to be demolished to make way for this fine cruciform creation. It was built in 1911 and modelled after the market at Marseilles. It now contains over 70 food stores and there's a small park behind it.

Go around behind the food market to Tsouderon. Take a look at the **minaret**, one of only two left in Hania. There is a crescent moon at the top of the spire and you can see the curtain rails that shielded the *muezzin* from the sun. Turn left on Tsouderon and it turns into **Skridlof** with its rows of leather shops.

You'll come to Halidon, Hania's main shopping and most touristy street. Across the street is **Promahonas Hill** which is the best preserved section of the massive **Venetian fortifications** begun in 1538 by engineer Michele Sanmichele, who also designed Iraklio's defences.

Turn right on Halidon and you'll come to the **Folklore Museum** and then **Archaeological Museum** on your left. Grab a bite to eat at Cafe Eaterie Ekstra. Continue on to Plateia Venizelou with the **Mosque of the Janissaries** on the right. Built in 1645, the mosque is the oldest Ottoman building in Crete although the outer domes were only constructed around 1880. It is no longer in use as a mosque but has served various administrative functions over the years. Retrace your steps and stroll along the inner harbour. At the end of the harbour is the **Naval Museum**. You'll have a great view of the **lighthouse** sitting at the entrance to the harbour which is the most visible of the Venetian monuments. Go around the promontory and turn left up Theotokopoulou. This was a prosperous area in later years of Turkish rule housing many prosperous Christian families. The architecture is a mixture of Venetian mansions and **Turkish houses** such as you'll see on Ritsou street.

Turn left at Theofanous and notice the **Renieri Mansion** on the right which has a superb 17th-century Venetian gateway inside of which is Renieri's private chapel. Retrace your steps and turn left at Zambeliou, a charming street of Venetian facades. The side streets surrounding Zambeliou made up the former Jewish quarter of Hania under the Venetians.

Make a left on Halidon to Plateia Venizelou and then a right on Kanevaro. Remains of the site of **ancient Kydonia** can be seen at the junction of Kanevaro and Kandanoleu. The Venetians first settled here and it was this part of town that bore the brunt of the bombing in WWII. Continuing along Kanevaro and making a left on Arholeon you'll come to the **Venetian Arsenal**, which has now become cafes and exhibition spaces. Make a right on Kallergon and you'll come to Splantzia, the Turkish quarter. Wandering the old streets of this neighbourhood makes a pleasant end to your tour.

---

the Lefka Ori. George can provide information on Greece's mountain refuges, the E4 trail, and climbing and trekking in Crete in general. Alpin Travel is open 9 am to 2 pm weekdays and after 7 pm sometimes in the evening. Trekking Plan (☎ 0821-60 861), in Agia Marina on the main road next to the Santa Marina Hotel, offers treks to the Agia Irini Gorge, the Imbros Gorge and climbs of Mt Gingilos, among other destinations for about 7000 dr. They also offer treks to Omalos and the Lefka Ori for 12,000 dr.

Mountain Biking
Trekking Plan (see earlier) offers a full program of mountain bike tours at varying levels of difficulty for prices that begin at 8000 dr.

Scuba Diving
Blue Adventures Diving (☎ 40 608, fax 40 608), Daskalogianni 69, offers a PADI certification course for 10,5000 dr and dives around Hania for 17,000 dr including equipment.

Horse Riding

In Tersanos on the Akrotiri Peninsula, the Horseriding Club (☎ 39 966) offers lessons or trail rides for 4000 dr.

They also provide a half-day monastery ride (4½ hours) across Akrotiri which costs 12,000 dr for a minimum of two persons. English saddles are available.

If you'd like to stay, studios, including breakfast, dinner and a few hours riding per day, are available for 66,000 dr per person per week.

Rooms are also available for 6000/8000 dr a night for singles/ doubles.

Children's Activities

If your five-year-old has lost interest in Venetian architecture before the end of the first street, the place to head is the public garden between Tzanakaki and Dimokratias.

There's a playground, a small zoo with a resident *kri kri* and a children's resource centre that has a small selection of books in English.

Organised Tours

Historian Tony Fennymore (☎ 87 139) is a wealth of information about Hania's history

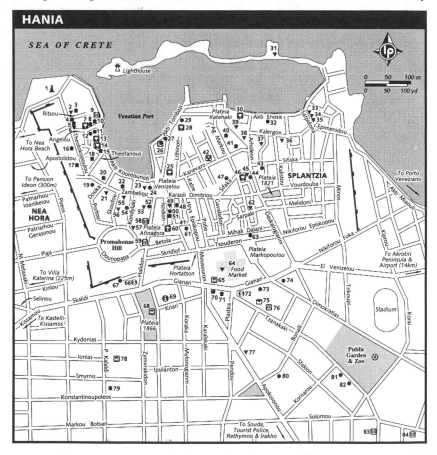

and culture. From April to July and September to October his two-hour walking tours (3500 dr) begin at the 'Hand' monument on Plateia Talo at the bottom of Theotokopoulou. He also runs various guided minibus tours around the region.

There are a number of boat trips which run from Hania and take you to the nearby island of Agia Theodori and the east coast of Hania Bay. The tours include swimming and snorkelling.

One good company is Stavros Cruises (☎ 094 914 045) that offers full day cruises from Hania for 6000 dr; children under 10 travel free.

Special Events
In addition to the religious and historical events that are celebrated throughout the island, the town of Hania commemorates the Battle of Crete with athletic competitions, folk dancing and ceremonial events during the last week of May.

Places to Stay
Hania's Venetian quarter is chock-full of family-run hotels and pensions housed in restored Venetian buildings.

The western end of the harbour is a good place to look but it can be noisy at night. Most hotels in town are open all year. Resorts can be found along the strip of beach that runs west of the town centre.

Places to Stay – Budget
Camping The nearest campsite is *Hania Camping* (☎ *31 138*), 3km west of town on the beach. The site is shaded and has a restaurant, bar and minimarket. Take a Kalamaki Beach bus (every 20 minutes) from the south-east corner of Plateia 1866 and ask to be let off at the campsite.

HANIA

PLACES TO STAY
3 Pension Lena
4 Pension Nora
5 Hotel Palazzo
8 Pension Theresa
10 Maria Rooms
15 Amfora Hotel
16 Apartments Anastasia
17 Rooms to Rent Irini
18 Casa Delfino
20 Nostos Pension
22 George's Pension
40 Monastiri Pension
41 Kasteli
48 Vranas Studios
51 Rooms Aphrodite
71 Hotel Kydon
79 Diana Rooms

PLACES TO EAT
2 Mano Cafe
6 Adiexodo
21 Tamam
23 Cafe-Eaterie Ekstra
31 Fortezza Restaurant & Bar
33 Apostolis Taverna
34 Hippopotamus
35 Dyo Lux
36 Cafe Crete
37 Doloma Restaurant
38 Kariatis
39 To Karnagio

45 Anaplous
49 Tholos
53 Suki Yaki
55 Tsikoydadiko
56 Synagogi
57 Ela
62 Well of the Turk
64 Market Tavernas
77 Bougatsa Hanion

OTHER
7 Fagotto Jazz Bar
13 Angelico Cafe
14 Street Club
24 George Chaicalis Bookshop
25 Point Music Bar
27 The Antiques Gallery
28 Ariadne
30 Four Seasons
43 Apostolos Pahtikos
44 Blue Adventure Diving Centre
46 Rudi's Bierhaus
47 Oinohoos
50 Laundrette
52 Ideon Antron
54 Mount Athos
61 Laundrette
65 Buses to Souda
66 Credit Bank
67 The Game

68 Buses to Western Beaches
69 EOT
70 Studio 2000
72 National Bank of Greece
73 ANEK Lines
74 Minoan Lines
75 Post Office
76 OTE
78 Bus Station
80 Alpin Travel
81 Olympic Airways
82 EOS
83 War Museum of Chania
84 Historical Museum and Archives

THINGS TO SEE
1 Hand Monument
9 Naval Museum
11 Top Hanas Carpet Shop
12 Carmela's Ceramic Shop
19 Roka Carpets
26 Mosque of the Janissaries
29 Hania District Association of Handicrafts Showroom
32 Venetian Arsenal
42 Ancient Kydonia
58 Archaeological Museum
59 Folklore Museum
60 Orthodox Cathedral
63 Minaret

Domatia If it's character you're after, you can't do better than *George's Pension* (☎ 88 715, Zambeliou 30), in a 600-year-old house dotted with antique furniture where singles/doubles with shared bathroom cost 3500/6000 dr. *Rooms to Rent Irini* (☎ 93 909, Theotokopoulou 9) has clean, simply furnished doubles with private bathroom for 7000 dr. Three storeys of antique-furnished rooms in a creaky old house make *Pension Theresa* (☎/fax 92 798, Angelou 2) the most atmospheric pension in Hania. Even if you don't snag a room with a view, there's always the stunning vista from the rooftop terrace. Rooms are 6000/9000 dr.

Located in a restored Turkish building, *Pension Nora* (☎/fax 72 225, Theotokopoulou 60) has large rooms attractively outfitted with Cretan rugs, iron lamps and wooden furniture. The composer Mikis Theodorakis reputedly lodged in one of them when he was a soldier. In an unusual arrangement, each room has its own locked toilet/shower cubicle in the hall. Rooms are 6500/10,000 dr with this version of private bathroom. Nearby is the friendly *Pension Lena* (☎ 86 860, Ritsou 3) which has rooms for 7000/9000 dr in an old Turkish building.

Monastiri Pension (☎ 54 776, Ag Markou 18) has a great setting right next to the ruins of the Moni Santa Maria de Miracolioco in the heart of the old kastelli. Rooms are simple with shared bathrooms but some have a sea view. There's a convenient communal kitchen for preparing meals. Double rooms are fair value at 6000 dr with shared bathroom. If you want to hop straight out of bed and onto an early morning bus bound for the Samaria Gorge, the best rooms around the bus station are at *Diana Rooms* (☎ 97 888, P Kalaïdi 33). The light, airy and clean rooms are 5000/7000 dr with private bathrooms. At the stylish *Apartments Anastasia* (☎ 46 582, Theotokopoulou 21) well-equipped studios cost 10,000 dr. *Rooms Aphrodite* (☎ 57 602, Ag Deka 10) has two-person apartments for 8000 dr, and double rooms with shared facilities for 5000 dr. *Villa Katerina* (☎ 95 183 or 98 940, Selinou 78) has a range of rooms starting with attractively furnished doubles for 8000 dr. *Akasti*

Hotel (☎ 31 352, fax 33 101), on Kalamaki, is a new hotel which offers simple but large rooms with telephones, fridges and balconies across the road from tiny swimming coves. The roof-terrace bar/ dining room has a view of the sea and there are stores nearby to pick up supplies. Any local bus to Kalamaki will drop you in front of the hotel. Rooms are 5000/8000 dr except in August when prices are 50% higher.

Places to Stay – Mid-Range

Mixing Venetian style and modern fixtures, *Nostos Pension* (☎ 94 740, fax 54 502, Zambeliou 42-46) is a 600-year-old building which has been modelled into classy split-level rooms/units, all with kitchen and bathroom. Try to get a room in front for the view of the harbour. Rooms are 12,000/ 18,000 dr.

Just outside the old town, on a pedestrian street at the western end of the old harbour, *Hotel Palazzo* (☎ 93 227, fax 93 229, Theotokopoulou 54) is a restored mansion with wrought iron balconies and wooden shutters. The pine-floored rooms have air-con, fridges, safes and telephones, but there's no elevator. Prices are 9000/11,000 dr.

Vranas Studios (☎/fax 58 618, Ag Deka 10) is on a lively pedestrian street and has spacious, immaculately-maintained studios with kitchenettes. All rooms have polished wooden floors, balconies, TV and telephones and you can have air-con for a supplement. Prices are 17,000 dr for August; figure on at least 40% less any other time. On the quieter, eastern end of the harbour, *Kastelli* (☎ 57 057, fax 45 314, Kanevaro 39) has rooms for 8000/9000 dr and renovated apartments with high ceilings, white walls and pine floors, for 16,000 dr to 20,000 dr depending on size. There's no TV or telephone, but some rooms have attractive views.

Places to Stay – Top End

Porto Veneziano (☎ 27 100, fax 27 105, email portoven@otenet.gr) on Akti Enosseos at the harbour's eastern edge, is a stylish and comfortable hotel offering large rooms with TV, telephone and air-con. The light fresh decoration is cheerful and there's an interior garden for relaxing. Prices are

18,000/24,000 dr and include a buffet breakfast. Information on the hotel can be found at www.aegean.ch/hotels/portoven/portoven.

Amfora Hotel (☎/fax 93 224/226, Parados Theotokopolou 2) is Hania's most historically evocative hotel. It is located in an immaculately restored Venetian mansion with rooms around a courtyard. There's no elevator and no air-con but the rooms are elegantly decorated and some have views of the harbour. Front rooms can be noisy in the summer. Rooms are 16,000/20,000 dr including buffet breakfast.

Kydon Hotel (☎ 52 280, fax 51 790, email kydon@cha.forthnet.gr, Plateia Venizelou) is slick, modern and comfortable. The carpeted rooms are soundproof and have satellite TV, fridges, safes, hairdryers and modem ports. There's air-con on demand plus free parking. Prices are 28,000/33,000 dr including buffet breakfast.

Casa Delfino (☎ 93 098, fax 96 500, email casadel@cha.forthnet.gr, Theofanous 7), a modernised 17th-century mansion, features a splendid courtyard of traditionally patterned cobblestones and 19 individually decorated suites. All have air-con, satellite TV, telephones, hair dryers, minibars and safes. Some suites have jacuzzis and business travellers will appreciate the modem ports. Doubles are 35,000 dr and a huge palatial split-level apartment, which sleeps up to four people, costs 66,000 dr including buffet breakfast.

Nea Hora The best feature of *Danaos (☎ 96 021, fax 96 022)*, on Akti Papanikoli in Nea Hora, a rather bland, modern hotel, is its location across the road from Nea Hora Beach. The functional rooms have balconies and telephones. Prices are 14,000/16,000 dr for an inside/seaview room.

The well-kept *Pension Ideon (☎ 70 132/133)*, on Patriarhou Ioanikeiou one block in from the beach, is a friendly place charging 6000/10,000 dr.

The modern *Rooms Stelisia (☎ 75 785, Akti Papanikoli 3)* has a taverna downstairs and simple, pleasant rooms with balconies and air-con for 8000/12,000 dr.

Places to Eat
Dining along Hania's scenic harbour has an undeniable appeal and the restaurants aren't bad, but the price-quality ratio is low. The best Cretan tavernas are housed in roofless Venetian ruins scattered in the streets of Splantzia and the Old Town. Halidon is a good place to grab a snack.

Places to Eat – Budget
The two restaurants in the *food market* are good places to seek out traditional cuisine. Their prices are almost identical. You can get a solid chunk of swordfish with chips for 1200 dr. More adventurous eaters can tuck into a bowl of garlic-laden snail and potato casserole for 1100 dr.

For a treat try the excellent *bougatsa tyri* (filo pastry filled with local myzithra cheese) at *Bougatsa Hanion (Apokoronou 37)*. A slice costs 500 dr and comes sprinkled with a little sugar. *Mano Cafe (Theotokopoulou 62)* is a tiny place and has very little seating, but offers good value breakfasts and snacks. It's open 8 am to midnight daily.

Doloma Restaurant (Kalergon 8), an unpretentious restaurant, is half-hidden amid the vines and foliage that surround the outdoor terrace. It's a relaxed spot to escape the crowds and the traditional cooking is faultless. It's open 7.30 pm to 1 am Monday to Saturday.

Places to Eat – Mid-Range
To Karnagio (Plateia Katehaki 8) is on every Hanian's short list of favourite restaurants. Its sprawling outdoor terrace near the harbour makes it appealing to tourists but it has not sacrificed one whit of authenticity. It's open noon to 1 am daily. *Cafe Eaterie Ekstra (Zambeliou 8)* is a friendly, casual eatery located right in the heart of Hania's bustling old town but the cooking is a modern take on traditional Cretan dishes. There are good-value set price menus and the unusual salads are excellent. It's open 8 am to 10 pm daily. *Well of the Turk Restaurant & Bar (Sarpaki 1)* occupies a former steam bath from the 19th century. Notice the carved relief of Istanbul on the marble fountain. Owned by a British woman, the restaurant

features mouth-watering Middle Eastern specialties. It's open 6.30 pm to midnight Wednesday to Monday.

With four crumbling walls and no roof, *Anaplous (Sifaka 34)* has nevertheless achieved a surprising stylishness with a few strategically placed urns and some potted plants. A subdued crowd comes here for traditional Cretan dishes and the occasional guitar playing. It's open 7 pm to 1 am daily.

In the quieter eastern harbour, *Apostolis Taverna (Enoseos 6)* is a good address for fish and Cretan dishes. Service is friendly and efficient, there's a good wine list and you get a view over the harbour. It's open noon to midnight daily.

All the usual suspects of Mexican cuisine are present and accounted for at *Hippopotamus (Sarpidona 6)*. A relaxed hang-out, it attracts an assortment of young, scruffy types that come for the ever-playing Latin music as well as the food. It's open noon to midnight daily.

Locals find most Old Town restaurants too touristy but *Tamam (Zambeliou 49)* has inspired a loyal following among the trendy set. Housed in old Turkish baths, this atmospheric place presents a superb array of vegetarian specialties. It's open 7.30 pm to 1 am daily. Dating from the 14th century, the building of *Ela (Kondylaki 47)* was first a soap factory, then a school, distillery and cheese-processing plant. Now it serves up a well-executed array of Cretan specialties while local musicians create a lively ambience on summer evenings. It's open noon to 1 am daily. The building dates from the 14th century and looks it but its crumbling roofless walls create a strangely beautiful interior.

The fish dishes are good but the speciality at *Tholos (Agia Deka 36)* is meat. The restaurant prides itself on its cooked-to-order steaks and tender baby veal. It's open noon to midnight daily May to October.

Tsikoydadiko (Zambeliou 31) has all the trappings of a tourist trap including a tout outside ready to hook all passers-by and the dreaded 'international' food. Despite all that, the kitchen turns out honest Cretan cooking and the roofless plant-filled interior is a delight. It's open noon to midnight

daily. The back-to-basics cuisine at *Adiexodo (Theotokopoulou 59)* provides a richly satisfying meal. Locals come here for the food and the live music on summer nights, packing the tables inside and outside on the narrow pedestrian street. It's open noon to 3 pm and then 7 pm to midnight daily.

You may hear the strains of Italian opera emanating from *Kariatis (Katehaki 12)* even before you come to the wide outdoor patio. The Greek dishes are standard but the pizza and pastas are well above average. It's open from noon to 3 pm and then 6 pm to midnight daily.

Places to Eat – Top End

Most people consider *Akrogiali (Akti Papanikoli 20, Nea Hora)* the best seafood restaurant in Hania. The fish is so fresh it's practically wiggling on the plate and the accompaniments are superb. The light airy restaurant opens onto the seafront road giving you a great view of the sunset. It's open 7 pm to midnight Monday to Saturday. The rustic decor at *Katofli (Akti Papanikoli 13, Nea Hora)* makes a pleasant backdrop for excellent seafood. Try the *kakavia* (fish soup) and wash it down with one of the restaurant's good local wines. It's open noon to 3 pm and then 7 pm to midnight daily.

Suki Yaki (Halidon 28), an elaborate Chinese-Thai restaurant, offers an intriguing change from Cretan food. The menu is varied and you can eat in the courtyard under an ancient plane tree. There's also an extensive wine list of local and imported wines. It's open noon to midnight daily in the heart of the old Turkish district of Splantzia.

Entertainment

Cafes/Bars Funky rock and roll joints play the dominant role in Hania's nightlife scene but there are also some cosy spots for jazz, light rock and Cretan music. When Hanians want to party the night away in a disco, they're likely to head out to Platanias, a coastal resort about 11km west of Hania.

Café Crete (Kalergon 22) is a rough-and-ready joint with a decorative scheme that relies on saws, pots, old sewing machines and animal heads, but it's the best place in Hania to hear live Cretan music. If they don't bring their own lyra, locals will reach for the instruments that line the walls once they've had a couple of drinks. Beware the *kamakia*. It's open 6 pm to 1 am daily.

In the middle of busy, touristy Halidon, **Ideon Antron** *(Halidon 26)* offers a more sophisticated atmosphere with discreet music and a garden seating. It's open noon to midnight daily.

Black-and-white photographs of jazz greats line the walls of **Fagotto Jazz Bar** *(Angelou 16)*. It's housed in a restored Venetian building and offers the smooth sounds of jazz and light rock. Sometimes there's a live jazz group in summer. It's open 7 pm to 2 am nightly.

Point Music Bar *(Sourmeli 2)* is a good rock bar for those allergic to techno. When the interior gets steamy you can cool off on the 1st floor balcony overlooking the harbour. It's open 9.30 pm to 2 am nightly.

On the waterfront, **Angelico Café** *(Koutourioti 54)* plays rock music at a volume that renders conversation possible only for lip readers but you can escape to the outdoor terrace. It's open 8 am to 1 am daily.

The cave-like interior of **Street Club** *(Akti Kountourioti 51)* on the harbour is filled with the sounds of soul and Latin music. Sundays at noon a guest DJ arrives to play the most recently released tracks. It's open 11 am to 1 am daily.

Formerly a disco, **Ariadne** *(Akti Tombazi 2)* has taken on a sleek new look and now uses its excellent sound system to play a variety of music. Usually there's jazz early in the evening and rock later on. There's a wide range of beverages on offer and some mezedes. It's open 10 am to 1 am daily.

Fortezza *(Old Harbour)*, a cafe/bar/restaurant installed in the old Venetian ramparts, is the best place in town for a sunset drink. A free barge takes you across the water from the bottom of Sarpidona to the sea wall wrapping around the harbour. From the rooftop bar, there's a splendid view of the Venetian harbour. It's open 10 am to 1 am daily April to October.

Four Seasons *(Akti Tombazi 29)*, a rock bar on the harbour, attracts a fashionable group of young Hanians. The harbourside terrace is always full and the atmosphere is friendly. It's open 10 am to 1 am daily.

If Che Guevara was alive and in Hania, he'd feel at home in this 'alternative cafe', **Dyo Lux** *(Sarpidona 8)*. The music is Latin American, there's plenty of reading material of a counter-cultural nature strewn about, and the cosy seating is perfect for plotting revolutions. It's open 10 am to midnight daily.

Austrian Rudi Riegler packs **Rudi's Bierhaus** *(Sifaka 26)*, a tiny bar with fine Belgian *guezes* and *krieks* as well as other excellent beers. He also serves some of the best mezedes in town. It's open 6 pm to midnight Monday to Saturday.

Housed in a roofless Venetian building that was once a synagogue, **Synagogi** *(Skoufo 15)* serves up fresh fruit juices, coffee, drinks and snacks. The stone and wooden interior is stunning and there's a good selection of rock music playing in the background.

Discos Most people head out to the sizzling nightlife at Platanias but if you want to party in town, take the first narrow passage on Halidon next to the Hania Exchange Bank and you'll come to Hania's main disco, **The Game**, which is located just off Halidon. The crowd runs from 18 to 21 and the music is deep house and techno. It's open midnight to 5 am nightly.

Shopping

Hania offers the best combination of souvenir hunting and shopping for crafts on the island. The main street is Halidon, which is impossible to avoid since it connects the inner town with the harbour.

There are no great shops on Halidon but there are several international bookshops and newsstands. The streets in the immediate vicinity of Halidon are very touristy, offering souvenirs, photo supplies, postcards and the like. El Venizelou along the harbour has the odd gem hidden among the cafes. Zambeliou, Theotokopoulou and Angelou in the inner harbour are where the smaller, more interesting shops are. Skridlof is 'leather lane' with good quality handmade boots, sandals and bags. Whether or not you are self-catering you should at least feast your eyes on Hania's magnificent covered food market; north of Gianari between Plateia Hortatson and Plateia Markopoulou it makes all other food markets look like stalls at a church bazaar.

There's also an outdoor market Saturday mornings from 7 am to 7 pm on Minoos street where you can pick up fruits, vegetables, local products and cheap clothes.

Carmela's Ceramic Shop (Angelou 7) produces ceramics using ancient techniques and also displays unusual jewellery handcrafted by young Greek artisans.

You can watch Mihailis weave his wondrous rugs on a 400-year-old loom at Roka Carpets (Zambeliou 61) using methods that have remained essentially unchanged since Minoan times. Prices begin at 8000 dr for a small rug. Top Hanas Carpet Shop (Angelou 3) specialises in old Cretan *kilims* (flatwoven rugs) that were traditional dowry gifts; prices start at 30,000 dr.

The embroidery, weaving and ceramics are well-executed at Hania District Association of Handicrafts Showroom (Akti Tombazi 15) but the sculptures of Greek mythological figures are unusually fine. At The Antiques Gallery (Akti Tobazi 1) next to the Mosque of the Janissaries, most of the stuff is too bulky to tuck into your suitcase, but, in addition to framed paintings and old furniture, there are more unusual odds and ends dating to Turkish occupation.

Apostolos Pahtikos (Sifaka 14) has been making traditional Cretan knives since he was 13. You can watch him work as he matches the blade to the carefully carved handle. The owner at Oinohoos (Sifaka 39) has amassed a fine selection of Greek and Cretan wines, displayed in an appropriately refined shop along with wine implements.

Mount Athos (Kondylaki 12) offers handmade icons but the best deals are had on the handmade chess sets using figures from Greek mythology. Catering to Cretan tastes for both popular and folk music, Studio 2000 (Plateia Agoras 15) is a good place to pick up a wide range of cassettes or CDs.

Getting There & Away

Air Olympic Airways has at least four flights a day to Athens which cost 19,800 dr for the afternoon flights and 13,400 dr for the late evening flight. There are also two flights a week to Thessaloniki (29,900 dr). The Olympic Airways office (☎ 57 701) is at Tzanakaki 88. Air Greece also has daily flights to Athens for about the same price. Aegean Airlines has two daily flights to Athens (16,500 dr) and one to Thessaloniki (28,100 dr). Their office (☎ 63 366) is at the airport. The airport is on the Akrotiri Peninsula, 14km from Hania.

Bus Buses depart from Hania's bus station for the following destinations:

Destination	Duration	Fare	Frequency
Iraklio	2½ hours	2900 dr	half-hourly
Hora Sfakion	2 hours	1400 dr	3 a day
Kastelli-Kissamos	1 hour	900 dr	15 a day
Lakki	1 hour	600 dr	4 a day
Moni Agias Triadas	30 mins	400 dr	3 a day
Omalos (for Samaria Gorge)	1 hour	1250 dr	4 a day
Paleohora	2 hours	1450 dr	3 a day
Rethymno	1 hour	1500 dr	half-hourly
Sougia	2 hours	1400 dr	1 a day
Stavros	30 mins	300 dr	6 a day

Ferry Ferries for Hania dock at Souda, about 7km east of town. There is at least one ferry a day for the 10 hour trip to/from Piraeus. ANEK has a boat nightly at 8.30 pm for 5900 dr. The ANEK office (☎ 27 500) is opposite the food market. Souda's port police can be contacted on ☎ 89 240.

Getting Around

To/From the Airport There is no airport bus and a taxi to the airport from the town centre costs about 3000 dr.

Bus Local buses (blue) leave for the port of Souda from outside the food market; buses for the western beaches leave from the main bus station on Plateia 1866.

Car, Motorcycle & Bicycle Hania's car hire outlets include Avis (☎ 50 510), Tzanakaki 58; Budget (☎ 92 778), Karïskaki 39; and Europrent (☎ 40 810 or 27 810), Halidon 87. Most motorcycle hire outlets are on Halidon.

AGIA MARINA

The coastline west of Hania is a non-stop strip of hotels, domatia, souvenir shops, travel agencies, minimarkets and restaurants. This is not the place to come if you're looking for a quiet, relaxing vacation, but the nightlife is good and there are plenty of banks, travel agencies, and car rental outlets along the main road. At about 9km from Hania you will enter the town of Agia Marina which has many domatia on the main road.

The best accommodation in town is *Ilianthos Village Apartments* (☎ 60 667, fax 60 721, email nikos@sov.cha.forth fnet/gr) which is a large resort on a wide stretch of beach. It has a swimming pool, air-con, children's facilities and is wheelchair accessible. It has rooms for 17,000/23,000 dr. There's also *Santa Marina* (☎ 68 570, fax 68 571) in the centre of town near a sandy beach which has rooms for 13,000/18,000dr. *Haris Hotel* (☎ 68 816, fax 68 393) is a small hotel on the beach with air-conditioning and a swimming pool. It has rooms for 14,000/20,000 dr. For a good feed try *Maria's Restaurant* on the eastern edge of town which serves Cretan and Mediterranean food on a plant-filled terrace. For nightlife, Patatrak Club is popular with the local crowd as much for the medieval decor as for its selection of Greek songs and its location right on the beach.

PLATANIAS

The next town west is Platanias which also has a busy main strip and an old town that sprawls over a steep hill on the south side of the road. The streets of the old town are picturesque but touristy; there are great views from the top. At the centre of town along the main road is a large square dominated by *Diogenis* restaurant next to a large supermarket. Banks and travel agencies are clus-

tered around the main square. For domatia try *Lola's* (☎ 68 345), close to the beach and over a snack bar, rooms cost 5000/6000 dr. There's also the hotel *Filoxenia* (☎ 48 502) which is next to *Anna's Apartments* (☎ 68 758), both of which have rooms for 8000/10,000 dr. The best hotel in town is the luxurious resort *Louis Creta Princess* (☎ 62 702, fax 62 406, email malemebeach@ cha.fourthnet.gr) which has a swimming pool, air-conditioning, tennis courts and a water sports centre right on the beach. It has rooms for 20,000/25,000 dr. Further inland, 200m from the beach is *Aegean Palace Hotel* (☎ 62 668, fax 62 647) which has air-conditioned rooms with sea view, suites with private swimming pools, an Olympic size swimming pool, children's pool, tennis courts, racquetball courts, sauna and fitness centre. Rooms cost 25,000/32,000 dr. The best restaurant in the area is *Mylos* on the main road. Even if the food wasn't as good as it is, it would be worth dining here for the setting alone. The centrepiece of the restaurant is an old flour mill beside a pool loaded with geese. The surrounding dining rooms are lush with plants, flowers, trees and vines leaving you with the sense of dining in the country rather than busy Platanias.

The nightlife in Platanias is its main attraction. From morning breakfasts to late night cocktails and dancing, *Splendid Cocktail & Dancing Bar* does a brisk business, especially at night when the interior is wall-to-wall with locals and visitors. It's open 9 am to 1 am April to October. *Utopia*, a relaxed cocktail bar attracts people of all ages who enjoy music from the 1960s, 1970s and 1980s. It's open 7 pm to 2 am.

GERANI

The next resort stretch is Gerani which is little more than a stretch of hotels, domatia, tavernas and souvenir shops, although it gets more deserted on the western end. The best hotel in town is *Creta Paradise Hotel* (☎ 61 315, fax 61 134, email cretpar@ sail.vaca tion.fourthnet.gr) which has a swimming pool, tennis courts, children's playground and is on the beach. It has rooms for 25,000/ 32,000 dr. On a more modest

HANIA

The Good Oil

The olive has been part of life in the eastern Mediterranean since the beginnings of civilisation. Olive cultivation can be traced back about 6000 years. It was the farmers of the Levant (modern Syria and Lebanon) who first spotted the potential of the wild European olive (*Olea europaea*) – a sparse, thorny tree that was common in the region. These farmers began the process of selection that led to the more compact, thornless, oil-rich varieties that now dominate the Mediterranean.

Whereas most Westerners think of olive oil as being just a cooking oil, to the people of the ancient Mediterranean civilisations it was very much more. It was almost inseparable from civilised life itself. As well as being an important foodstuff, it was burned in lamps to provide light, it could be used as a lubricant and it was blended with essences to produce fragrant oils.

The Minoans were among the first to grow wealthy on the olive, and western Crete remains an important olive-growing area, specialising in high-quality salad oils. The region's show piece, Kolymvari cooperative, markets its extra-virgin oil in both the USA (*Athena* brand) and Britain (*Kydonia* brand).

Locals will tell you that the finest oil is produced from trees grown on the rocky soils of the Akrotiri Peninsula, west of Hania. The oil that is prized above all others, however, is *agourelaio*, meaning unripe, which is pressed from green olives.

Few trees outlive the olive. Some of the fantastically gnarled and twisted olive trees that dot the countryside of western Crete are more than 1000 years old. The tree known as *dekaoktoura*, in the mountain village of Anisaraki – near Kandanos on the road from Hania to Paleohora – is claimed to be more than 1500 years old.

Many of these older trees are being cut down to make way for improved varieties. The wood is burnt in potters' kilns and provides woodturners with the raw material to produce the ultimate salad bowl for connoisseurs. The dense yellow-brown timber has a beautiful swirling grain.

LPP

---

level there is **Alfa** (☎ *73 571*) which has rooms for 6000/9000 dr.

Getting There & Away
Buses between Hania and Kastelli-Kissamos stop in Platanias, Gerani and Agia Marina.

AKROTIRI PENINSULA
The Akrotiri (ak-**tee**-ree) Peninsula, to the east of Hania, is a barren, hilly stretch of rock covered with scrub. There are a few coastal resorts, Hania's airport and a naval base on Souda Bay. There are few buses and the roads meander about making it a difficult region to explore. It's a good place to

escape the crowds, however, and the peninsula contains a few interesting monasteries.

Monasteries
If you haven't yet had your fill of Cretan monasteries, there are three on the Akrotiri Peninsula. The impressive 17th-century **Moni Agias Triadas** was founded by the Venetian monks Jeremiah and Laurentio Giancarolo. The brothers were converts to the Orthodox faith. There was a religious school here in the 19th century and it is still an active monastery with an excellent library. The church is worth visiting for its altar piece as well as its Venetian-influenced

HANIA

domed facade. The monastery is known for its excellent wine, *Agiotriathitiko*. The monastery is open 6 am to 2 pm and then 5 to 7 pm daily. Entry is 300 dr. The 16th-century **Moni Gourvernetou** (Our Lady of the Angels) is 4km north of Moni Agias Triada, at the end of an extremely poor road only suitable for 4WD. The monastery may date as far back as the 11th century at a time when an inland sanctuary was an attractive refuge from coastal pirates. The building itself is disappointingly plain but the church inside has an ornate sculptured Venetian facade. It's open 8 am to 12.30 pm and then 4.30 to 7.30 pm daily and there is no admission fee. This monastery is also still in use.

From Moni Gourvernetou, it's a 15 minute walk on the path leading down to the coast to the ruins of **Moni Katholiko**. The monastery, which has been in disuse for many centuries is dedicated to St John the Hermit who lived in the cave behind the ruins. There's a small pond near the entrance to the cave whose water is believed to be holy. On the feast day of St John (7 October), there's a festival here that begins with a vigil the previous evening. His grave is at the end of a cave at the bottom of a rock staircase. There are three buses a day (except Sunday) to Moni Agias Triadas from Hania (400 dr).

STAVROS
☎ 0821

The village of Stavros is little more than a scattering of houses and a few hotels located behind Stavros Cove. The cove is a narrow strip of sandy beach dominated by a mammoth rockshelf that served as a backdrop for a scene in the movie *Zorba the Greek*. Unfortunately there is no accommodation near the beach but there are a few hotels and domatia on the rocky outpost about a kilometre west of the beach. You could try *Villa Elena Apartments* (☎ 39 480) which has a swimming pool and apartments for 15,000 dr, or the nearby *Blue Beach* (☎ 39 404) which has rooms for about the same price and is on a rocky cove. There's also *Vlami's Villas* (☎ 74 427) which is a small hotel with a swimming pool overlooking the sea. *Rea Hotel* (☎ 39 001, fax 39 541) offers a swim-

ming pool, sauna, fitness room, children's pool and playground and babysitting service. Air-conditioned rooms are 10,000/14,000 dr.

Getting There & Away
There are six buses a day from Hania (45 minutes, 700 dr). If you're coming by car from Hania follow signs to the airport and then signs to Stavros.

KALATHAS
Kalathas is a tiny beach resort that closes down completely in the winter. In the summer the two sandy beaches lined by pine trees can fill up, but Kalathas remains a pretty place to spend the day.

If you'd like to stay overnight there's *Georgie's Blue Apartments* (☎ 64 080) at the entrance to town with studios for 10,000 dr and *Water Lily Apartments* (☎ 64 755) also at the entrance to the town. You could also try *Apollon Villa* (☎ 64 565) which has doubles/triples for 6000/9000 dr, or *Area* (☎ 69 002), a small hotel of only ten rooms with rooms for 5000/8000 dr. *Esplanade Apartments* (☎ 64 253, fax 69 810) is an attractive two-storey structure with a swimming pool that has studios for 12,000 dr.

Getting There & Away
Buses from Hania to Stavros stop at Kalathas.

SOUDA BAY
The harbour of Souda is one of Crete's largest and the port of entry if you come to Hania by ferry. The Venetians built a castle at the entrance of Souda Bay which they held onto until 1715, even though the Turks had already seized the rest of the island. It is now the site of an unpopular US naval base which provokes frequent demonstrations from Hania residents.

SOUDA
☎ 0821 • pop 5531

The town of Souda is uninteresting but may be unavoidable if you arrive or leave Hania by ferry. The town sprang up 130 years ago under the Turks but little remains from that period. There are a wealth of services

HANIA

including travel agencies, banks and stores although accommodation and dining opportunities are limited.

Orientation & Information

The main street of Souda is 3 Septemvrious which runs parallel to the harbour. The harbour opens onto a large square with travel agencies and cafes. The Bank of Greece is on the square and has an ATM. At the port is a 24hr exchange machine. Also on the main square is Gelasakis Travel Centre which changes money, handles air and boat tickets and rents cars. It's open 7.30 am to 9 pm daily. The post office is on 3 Septemvrious about 100m right from the main square. The OTE is on the same street about 20m right from the main square.

Places to Stay & Eat

Right across from the main square is *Hotel Parthenon* (☎ *89 245*) which has doubles for 7000 dr. There's also a taverna downstairs that serves souvlaki.

Getting There & Away

Souda is about 7km east of Hania. There are frequent buses to Hania (240 dr) that meet the ferries. There are also taxis (2000 dr).

AROUND SOUDA

About 1km west of Souda, there is an immaculate **military cemetery**, where about 1500 British, Australian and New Zealand soldiers who lost their lives in the Battle of Crete are buried. Beautifully situated at the water's edge, the rows of white headstones make a moving tribute to the heroic defenders of Crete. The buses to Souda port that depart from outside the Hania food market on Gianari can drop you at the cemetery. If you're coming by car from Hania make a left at Inka supermarket and turn right after the *Paloma* restaurant which serves decent Cretan food on a shady terrace overlooking a beautiful cove.

Apokoronas Province

This north-eastern corner of Hania prefecture contains some of its more interesting sights, such as the island's only freshwater lake, Lake Kournas and beach resorts such as Kalives, Almirida and Georgioupolis which are more intimate towns than the resorts that spread west of Hania along the coast. There's also the restored village of Vamos and the Turkish fortress at Aptera as well as off-the-beaten-track villages such as Plaka and Gavalohori.

GEORGIOUPOLIS
☎ 0825 • pop 608

Although it is no longer the traveller's secret getaway that it once was, Georgioupolis retains the flavour of an old town by the sea. Its most attractive feature is the eucalyptus trees lining the residential streets that fan out from the main square.

Located at the junction of the Almiros River and the sea, Georgioupolis is a nesting area for the endangered loggerhead sea turtle as well as hordes of mosquitoes in the summer. Georgioupolis was named after Prince George, High Commissioner of Crete from 1898 to 1906, who had a hunting lodge here. In classical times it was known as Amphimalla and was the port of ancient Lappa.

Orientation & Information

The main street leads from the highway to the centre of town and contains a number of

The Legend of the Lake

Once upon a time there was no lake, just a village whose inhabitants fell out of favour with God. To set an example for others, God decided to turn the village into a lake and its naughty inhabitants into seaweed. Only the virtuous and beautiful daughter of a priest was spared. God turned her into a fairy and her tears fed the waters of the lake. Every morning she emerges from the lake combing her long hair and from her golden cup scatters seeds to feed the living things of the lake.

travel agencies, tavernas and services. Geo Travel (☎ 61 370), on the far side of the main square, is a good place to change money and rent wheels. It's open 8 am to 1 pm and to 4 to 9 pm daily March to November. There's an ATM at the Hania Exchange Bank which is on the main road into town before the main central square. There's no post office or OTE but there is Internet access at Alchemist Gift Shop (☎ 61 732, email alchemist@otenet.gr), which costs 900 dr for 25 minutes and is open 8 am to 10 pm daily March to November. It's on the left side of the main road coming into town. There are two beaches, a long narrow stretch of beach south of town and a smaller beach to the north of the river.

Things to Do
The marshes surrounding the riverbed are known for its wildlife, especially egrets and kingfishers which migrate into the area in April. At the foot of the main street there's Yellowboat which rents pedalboats and canoes to go up the river where you can see turtles, fish, birds and ducks. Rental costs 2000 dr an hour per person.

Places to Stay
On the main road entering town *Hotel Nikolas* (☎ 61 375, fax 61 011) has doubles attractively furnished in pine for 10,000 dr including breakfast. At the bottom of the main road, turn right and you'll come to *Apartments Sofia* (☎ 61 325), a tidy white building with blue balconies overlooking the sea. Studios cost 10,000 dr.

Also to the right of the main road is *Andy's Rooms* (☎ 61 394) which provides mosquito nets for guests. Double rooms with a fridge are 9000 dr and studios range from 11,000 dr to 15,000 dr.

Across the street is *Zorba's Rooms* (☎ 61 381, fax 61 018) which has rooms for about the same price and a taverna downstairs. To the left of the main road is *Egeon* (☎ 61 161) which has doubles for 10,000 dr and studios with fridge for 11,000 dr. The friendly owner, Polly, has installed ceiling fans and screened windows in the rooms. Nearby is *Kristina Rooms and Studios* (☎ 61 165),

which has well-maintained doubles for 8000 dr with a kitchenette and ceiling fans. South of the town centre along the beach is *Hotel Gorgona* (☎ 61 341) which is a quiet place with three floors of large rooms surrounded by flowering plants and palm trees.

Rooms are 7000/8000 dr with an extra 1000 dr for breakfast. Also near the beach is *Nirvana Studios* (☎ 61 609) which has air-conditioned studios for 15,000 dr. For more luxury try *Pilot Beach Hotel* (☎ 61 002, fax 61 397, email pilot@otenet.gr) on the beach outside of town, with air-conditioning, tennis courts and a swimming pool for 21,000/28,000 dr.

Outside Georgioupolis in nearby Kavros there is another luxury resort, *Eliros Beach* (☎ 61 103, fax 61 213), which has a swimming pool, tennis courts, children's playground and air-conditioned rooms for 16,000/25,000 dr. Nearby is *Kournas Village Hotel* (☎/fax 61 416/417/418) which has beautifully furnished rooms, a swimming pool, children's pool, playground, fitness centre, sauna and tennis courts on the beach. Rooms are 16,000/25,000 dr.

On a more modest scale there is *Akti Manos* (☎ 61 221, fax 61 205), a small hotel which has basic rooms on the beach and a swimming pool for 10,000/15,000 dr. *Mare Monte Beach Hotel* (☎ 61 390, fax 61 274), on a wide stretch of sand, has a swimming pool and air-con for 10,000/15,000 dr.

Places to Eat
The best meal in town can be had at *Poseidon Restaurant* which is signposted down a narrow alley to the left as you come into the town on the main road. The chef is happy to explain the different varieties of fish on the menu, all of which are fresh and excellent. It's open 6pm to midnight daily March to November. *O Fanis* overlooks the river and also serves good seafood. *Edem Cocktail Bar and Restaurant* stretches along the beach and has a large swimming pool open to the public.

Entertainment
There's a lively bar scene in Georgioupolis. *Sunset Tavern* on the main square is a

popular place for a drink and *Georgioupolis Beach Hotel* presents live Cretan music from 8.30 pm nightly in the summer. There are three discos – *Time* which is across the river, *Phenomenon* on the main road and *Nembo* on the main square.

Getting There & Away
Buses between Hania and Rethymno stop on the highway outside Georgioupolis.

LAKE KOURNAS
Lake Kournas is 4km inland from Georgioupolis and is a lovely, restful place to pass an afternoon. It is about 1.5km in diameter and 45m deep, fed by underground springs. There's a narrow sandy strip around the lake, but no beaches as such and you can only walk two thirds of the way around the lake. The crystal-clear water is great for swimming and changes colour according to the season and time of day. You can rent pedalboats and canoes for 2000 dr an hour and visit the turtles, crabs, fish and snakes that make the lake their home.

There are a number of tavernas around the lake and a few simple places to stay. Try *The Beautiful Lake* (☎ 61 665) which has rooms with private bath for 5000 dr. On a hill overlooking the lake there's *Nice View Apartments & Studio* (☎ 61 315) which has rooms with spectacular views for 7000/9000 dr.

There are a number of pleasant places to grab a meal including the taverna bar, *Relax,* which is off the main road on the way to the lake and has a pleasant shady terrace. There's also *Loumoulou* near the stop for the tourist train and *Limmi* at the turn off for the lake.

The lake is below **Kournas Village** which is a steep 5km up a hill overlooking the lake. It's a traditional village of white-washed stone houses and a couple of kafeneia. There's no place to stay but you can get a delicious meal of roasted meat and Cretan specialities at *Taverna Kanarina* at the end of the village.

As you enter the village there's an excellent ceramics shop, run by friendly Kostas Tsakalakis, which sells exquisite vases and dishes at reasonable prices.

Getting There & Away
There's a tourist train that runs from Georgioupolis to Lake Kournas in the summer, but no other public transport.

KALIVES
☎ 0825 • pop 175
Originally a farming village, Kalives has now become a good sized resort. Located 18km east of Hania on Souda Bay, Kalives is popular with Greeks on holiday as well as international guests. The town is spread out along both sides of the main road and boasts a long sandy beach as well as an appealingly low-key small town ambience.

Orientation & Information
All services are located along the main road. The post office and the OTE are on the main road and there's a bank. The sandy beach stretches from the centre of town east to the Kalives Beach Hotel. West of the town centre the coast is rockier and most of the domatia are located at this end. Kalives Travel Agency (☎ 31 473) is in the centre of town and is a good place to rent cars, change money, find accommodation and book excursions throughout the region. It's open 8.30 am to 1.30 pm and then 5.30 to 10 pm daily April to October.

Places to Stay & Eat
There are some domatia at the western end of town. Try *Maria* (☎ 31 519), which has small rooms with a kitchenette, balcony and seaview for 5000/7900 dr. Most people stay at the luxurious *Kalives Beach Hotel* (☎ 31 825, fax 31 134) at the eastern end of town which has a fully equipped spa, an indoor and outdoor pool and air-conditioned rooms. It's open from April to October and costs 18,000/20,000 dr. For a good meal on the seaside there's *Provira Taverna* which has a fixed price daily meal for 1800 dr including wine. Stop in at *The Old Bakery* in the centre of town for scrumptious cakes and home-made breads and biscuits.

Getting There & Away
There are four buses (two on weekends) daily to Kalives from Hania (45 minutes, 500dr).

AROUND KALIVES
Almirida
The village of Almirida lies 4km east of Kalives but it is considerably less developed and there's the remains of an early Christian basilica at the western end of town. It's a popular spot for windsurfing because of its long, exposed beach. There's only one road through town that runs along the beach.

There's no post office or bank, but Flisvos Tours (☎/fax 32 213), on the main road, will change money, rent cars, scooters and mountain bikes and is a good source of information. It's open 8 am to 2 pm and then 5 to 9.30 pm daily March to November. The best hotel in town is *Hotel Dimitra (☎ 31 956)* which has a pool, tennis courts and excellent food. Rooms are 17,000/22,000 dr including breakfast. On a more modest level there's *Rooms for Rent Renata (☎ 31 381)* at the eastern end of town which has rooms for 4000/5000 dr. The beach road is lined with tavernas, *Psaros* has excellent fish and is open noon to midnight daily. There's a water sports centre (☎ 32 062) outside Hotel Dimitra where you can windsurf or rent a kayak for 3000 dr an hour, or a catamaran for 6000 dr an hour.

Plaka
If you have your own wheels it's a pretty drive up to the village of Plaka. The winding lanes and low-rise white buildings are a world away from the tourist bustle along the coast. With elderly men dozing in kafeneia and a main square shaded by eucalyptus trees, Plaka offers a glimpse of a traditional Cretan farming village. Scenes from *Zorba the Greek* were filmed in the main square.

Signs at the entrance direct you to *Studios Koukourous (☎ 31 145, fax 31 879)*. The owner Eva Papadomanolakas has gone to a lot of trouble to create a typically Cretan atmosphere for her guests and has decorated her place with a variety of tropical plants and flowers. There's also a roof garden with panoramic views over the coast. Studios with kitchenettes cost 9000 dr.

Aptera
The ruins of the ancient city of Aptera, about 3km west of Kalives, are spread out over two hills that loom over Souda Bay. Founded in the 7th century BC, Aptera was one of the most important city-states of western Crete and was continuously inhabited until it was destroyed by an earthquake in the 7th century AD.

It came back to life with the Byzantine reconquest of Crete in the 10th century and became the seat of a bishopric. In the 12th century, the monastery of St John the Theologian was established; the reconstructed monastery is the centre of the site.

The site is still being excavated but you can see Roman cisterns, a 2nd-century-BC Greek temple and massive defensive walls. At the western end there's a Turkish fortress, built in 1872, with a panoramic view of Souda Bay. The fortress was built at a time when the Cretans were in an almost constant state of insurrection as part of a large Turkish fortress-building program. Notice the 'Wall of the Inscriptions' which was probably part of a public building and was excavated in 1862 by French archaeologists. The Greek Ministry of Culture is continuing to restore the site, installing signs and paths. The visitor's centre is next to the car park adjacent to the monastery. It's open 8 am to 2.30 pm Tuesday to Sunday, and distributes a helpful brochure and map in English. There are no cafes or snack bars at the site but a few tavernas on the way up there. There's no public transport to the site.

VAMOS
☎ 0825 • pop 618
The 12th-century village of Vamos, 26km south-east of Hania, was the capital of the Sfakia province from 1867 to 1913 and was the scene of a revolt against Turkish rule in 1896. It is now the capital of the Apokoronas province. In 1995 a group of villagers banded together to preserve the traditional way of life of Vamos. They persuaded the EU to fund a renovation project to showcase the crafts and products of the region and develop a new kind of tourism in Crete. They restored the old stone buildings of the village using traditional materials and crafts and turned them into guest houses. They opened stores and cafes where visitors

could taste regional products and staged periodic exhibitions and musical evenings.

Orientation & Information

As you approach on the main road from Hania you'll see the taverna, Bloumosifi's Cistern, on the right. The OTE is about 20m up on the right and the post office is on Mariakaki, off to the right. The village square is 50m up from Bloumosifi's Cistern. The tourist office (☎/fax 23 100) is between the taverna and the main square, on the left. Opening hours are unreliable but if it is open you can change money, rent cars and book excursions here. Their Web site can be found at www.travel-greece.com/crete/xania/vamos.

Places to Stay & Eat

The apartments at *Bloumosifi's Cistern* are in old stone cottages and contain kitchens, fireplaces and TVs. The cottages are decorated with traditional furniture and fabrics. Most can accommodate up to four people but there's one two-bedroom cottage that accommodates up to seven people. Prices are 25,000 dr to 45,000 dr depending on size. In addition to the guest cottages, Bloumosifi's Cistern serves typical Cretan dishes, and has a cafe, *Liakoto*, that is also an art gallery. You can buy Cretan products at *Mirovolo Wine Store & General Store.*

Getting There & Away

There's a daily bus to Vamos from Hania (45 minutes, 600 dr).

AROUND VAMOS

The village of **Gavalohori**, 25km south-east of Hania, makes a pleasant stop if you're exploring the region. The main attraction is the **Folklore Museum** which is located in a renovated building constructed during Venetian rule and then extended by the Turks. The main architectural feature is the stone arches which divides the ground floor of the house into bedrooms, kitchen, a room for a wine press and a storage room. The exhibits are well-labelled in English and include examples of pottery, weaving, woodcarving, stonecutting and other Cretan crafts. Notice

examples of *Capaneli*, which is intricately, worked silk lace. There is also a historical section of the museum which documents Cretan struggles for independence. The museum is unreliably open 9 am to 8 pm daily and costs 500 dr.

Another highlight of a visit to Gavalohori is the **Women's Cooperative** which sells examples of handicrafts made by local women. It's not cheap (you'll pay 25,000 dr for a lace collar) but the quality is excellent. The store is unreliably open 9 am to 8 pm daily. The cooperative is on the main square; signs direct you to the nearby Folklore Museum and Byzantine wells, Venetian arches and Roman tombs about 1.5km above the village.

There are several tavernas around the main square and, if you're interested in staying, the *Gavalohori Cultural Society* (☎ 22 038) may be able to arrange a studio.

VRISSES
☎ 0825

Most travellers just pass through Vrisses, 30km south-east from Hania, on their way to or from the south coast but this cool, pleasant town deserves more time. There's not much to do here but the rivers Voutakas and Vrysanos run through the centre of town watering the giant plane trees along the banks. When the coast is sweltering you can cool off in the shade in one of the riverside tavernas under the trees. Vrisses is a market town for the region's agricultural products and is a relatively new town, dating back to 1925.

Orientation & Information

Buses stop at the crossroads in the town centre which is marked by a monument commemorating Cretan independence. Following the main street right across the river takes you to tavernas, stores, a supermarket and the National Bank of Greece which has an ATM. Following the main street left, you'll come to the post office and OTE about 100m up the road.

Places to Stay & Eat

The only domatia in town is *Spiridakis* (☎ 51 206) which is in the centre of town and has large studios for 10,000 dr. *Taverna Progoulis* has average food but tables under the trees along the river. At the crossroads in the town centre, *Vrisses Way* is a modest establishment that serves excellent *giro*, pitas and yoghurt with honey which is a speciality of the town.

Getting There & Away
There are three buses daily from Hania to Hora Sfakion that stop at Vrisses (30 minutes, 400 dr).

ASKIFOU
☎ 0825 • pop 377
The road south from Vrisses takes you across the war-torn plain of Askifou which was the scene of one of the most furious battles of the Cretan revolt of 1821. The Sfakiot forces triumphed over the Turks in a bloody battle that is still recounted in local songs. More than a century later the plain was the scene of more strife as Allied troops retreated across the plateau towards their evacuation point in Hora Sfakion. The central town of the region is Askifou which stretches out on either side of a hill. The post office is at the top of the hill with a mini market and several tavernas that rent rooms for 5000 dr. Try *Taverna Askifou* (☎ 95 291) or *Geronimos* (☎ 95 211) next to the bakery.

As you drive through Askifou, one sign after another directs you to the '**military museum**' (☎ 95 289), which turns out to be the gun and military odds and ends collection of Georgios Hatzidakis. The Sfakian is eager to show you around his collection which includes various artefacts from wars of the 20th century. In theory it's open 8 am to 7 pm Monday to Saturday. Admission is free.

IMBROS GORGE
The Imbros Gorge, 57km south-east of Hania, is less travelled than its illustrious sister at Samaria but just as beautiful. Cypresses, holm-oaks, fig and almond trees gradually thin to just cypresses and Jerusalem sage deep within the gorge. The narrowest width of the ravine is 2m while the walls of rock reach 300m. At only 8km the Imbros walk is also much easier on the feet.

Imbros Gorge

Like most Sfakian gorges, the Imbros Gorge sheltered Sfakian rebels during the Turkish occupation. The Sfakians knew how to take advantage of their mountainous terrain which made them effective fighters against the Turks. In 1941, 12,000 Allied survivors of the Battle of Crete were led to the coast through the Imbros Gorge and were under attack most of the way.

You can begin in the south at the village of Komitades but most people begin in the little mountain village of Imbros. Both places are used to gorge-hikers and have plenty of minimarkets and tavernas to fuel up. There's nowhere to stay in Imbros village but there are a few domatia in Komitades. If you start from Imbros you'll find the well-marked entrance to the gorge next to a taverna, just outside Imbros village on the road to Hora Sfakion. The track is easy to follow as it traces the streambed past rockslides and caves. The gorge path ends at the village of Komitades, from which you can either walk or take a taxi to Hora Sfakion (5km).

Getting There & Away
There are three daily buses from Hania to Hora Sfakion that stop at Imbros village (1½ hours, 1100 dr). Buses from Hora Sfakion to Hania stop at Komitades or take a taxi for about 2000 dr. The gorge is open daily all year. There is no admission fee.

Sfakia Province

The province of Sfakia extends from the Omalos Plateau down to the southern coast and includes the Lefka Ori Mountains with the spectacular Samaria Gorge. It is Crete's most mountainous region and the most culturally interesting. Sfakia was the centre of resistance during the island's long centuries of domination by foreign powers, its steep ravines and hills making effective hideaways for Cretan revolutionaries. The Sfakian people are renowned for their fighting spirit

Cretan Theology

Sfakians have a reputation throughout Crete for thievery, especially of livestock and crops. Stealing sheep is such a part of Sfakian culture that shepherds steal as much for sport as for any financial gain. In fact, Sfakian pilfering of each other's property is the cause of most of the vendettas that have decimated the region and is the inspiration for the following joke:

According to other Cretans, God gave orange groves to the Hania people, wheat to the people on the Messara Plain, vineyards to Kissamos and olive groves to eastern Crete. When it came time to provide for Sfakia, God only gave the Sfakians stones and rocks. But when the people demanded to know how they might survive on such barren land, God reportedly answered, "Just look around you! All over Crete on the fine, fertile plains farmers are working and cultivating produce – all for your benefit!"

which, sadly, has turned against each other in the form of murderous family vendettas that have depopulated many of the region's villages.

Road to Omalos

The road from Hania to the beginning of the Samaria (Sa-ma-**ria**) Gorge is one of the most spectacular routes in Crete. It heads through orange groves to the village of Fournes; there is not much there except stores. A left fork leads to **Meskla**, twisting and turning along a gorge offering beautiful views. Although the bottom part of the town is not particularly attractive with boarded-up buildings, the road becomes more scenic as it winds uphill to the modern, multi-coloured **Church of the Panagia**. Next to it is a 14th-century chapel built on the foundations of a 6th-century basilica that might have been built on an even earlier Temple of Aphrodite. At the entrance to the town a sign directs you to the **Chapel of Metamorphosis Sotirou** (Transfiguration of the Saviour) which contains 14th-century frescoes.

The fresco of the Transfiguration on the south wall is particularly impressive. There is nowhere to stay in Meskla but there is a **kafeneio** on the right as you enter the town. The main road continues to the village of **Lakki** (La-kee), 24km from Hania. This unspoilt village in the Lefka Ori affords stunning views wherever you look. The village was a centre of resistance during the uprising against the Turks, and in WWII. *Kri-Kri Restaurant & Rooms* (☎ 0821-67 316) has comfortable rooms for 4000/5000 dr with shared bathroom, and serves good value meals. Across the street is *Rooms for Rent Nikolas* (☎ 0821-67 232) which has rooms for about the same price. Both have magnificent views over the valley.

OMALOS
☎ 0825

Most tourists only hurry through Omalos, 36km south of Hania, on their way to the Samaria Gorge but this plateau-town deserves more. The air is bracingly cool in comparison to the steamy coast in the summer and there are some great mountain walks in the area. After the morning Samaria rush, there's hardly anyone on the plateau except goats and shepherds.

Orientation & Information

Omalos is little more than a few hotels on either side of the main road that cuts through the plateau. There is no bank, post office, OTE or travel agency and the village is practically deserted in the winter. The town is about 4km before the entrance to the Samaria Gorge.

Places to Stay & Eat

Most Omalos hotels are only open when the Samaria Gorge is open. *Hotel Neos Omalos* (☎ 67 269, fax 67 190) is the poshest hotel with comfortable modern rooms that include satellite TV and cost 7000 dr for a double. *Elliniko* (☎ 67 169) is the nearest to the Samaria Gorge and has simple double rooms for 6000 dr. *Hotel Exari* (☎ 67 180) is somewhat run down and has simple rooms for 5000 dr but you'd be better off at *Samaria* (☎ 67 168) for the same

Hania's lighthouse provides an impressive reminder of the town's Venetian past.

Ready for the day ahead – Frangokastello Beach.

The small seaside village of Loutro is only accessible by boat or foot.

Boats moored in Hania harbour.

NEIL SETCHFIELD

Arched doorway in the traditional style in Agriroupolis.

TREVOR CREIGHTON

Wildflowers often add
colour to Cretan homes.

DIANA MAYFIELD

A colourful doorway to
Hania's Venetian past.

JON DAVISON

Hania's waterfront with Lefka Ori in the background.

JOHN ELK III

Colourful doors in Hania.

DIANA MAYFIELD

Lunch anyone? A typical cafe scene in quiet Loutro.

View from the top: the Samaria Gorge is Europe's largest and most spectacular.

Six hours to go: the trek down into the Samaria Gorge begins with the steep staircase at Xyloskalo.

A Byzantine church sits within the Lefka Ori mountain range.

The small village of Lakki in the Lefka Ori affords stunning views whichever way you turn.

price. *Hotel Gigilos* (☎ *67 181*) is the friendliest hotel in Omalos and has rooms for 5000/6000 dr. All hotels except Neos Omalos and Exari have restaurants that do a bustling business serving breakfast to hikers and are open at meal times the rest of the day.

The EOS (Greek Mountaineering Club) maintains *Kallergi Hut* (☎ *74 560)* located in the hills between Omalos and the Samaria Gorge. It has 45 beds, electricity (but no hot water) and makes a good base for exploring Mt Gingilos and surrounding peaks.

Getting There & Away

There are four daily buses to Omalos from Hania (1 hour, 1250 dr)

SAMARIA GORGE

Φαράγγι της Σαμαριάς

A visit to this stupendous gorge is an experience to remember. You'll descend the gorge enveloped in the scent of pine until you reach the riverbed. Along the way you might see owls, eagles or vultures. If you're extremely lucky you might spot the *lammergeier* (bearded vulture), harrier eagle or golden eagle – all endangered species. The gorge's inaccessibility has saved it from the twin evils of Cretan wildlife – timber cutting and livestock grazing. As a result, the gorge is teeming with life. There's an incredible number of wildflowers, at their best in April and May. Watch for rare peonies that flourish in the dampness of the gorge. The gorge is home to the *zouridha* (Cretan polecat) and the kri-kri, a wild goat that survives in the wild only here and on the islet of Kri-Kri. The gorge was made a national park in 1962 to save the kri-kri from extinction but you're unlikely to see one of these timid animals.

At 18km, Samaria is supposedly the longest gorge in Europe. Beginning just below the Omalos Plateau, it was carved out by the river that flows between the Lefka Ori and Mt Volakias. The best way to see the gorge is on a trek but bear in mind that you won't be alone. The gorge attracts several thousand visitors a day in July and August making it uncomfortably crowded at times.

Be aware, also, that the trek is not easy and can be especially intensive in hot weather.

The trek from Xyloskalo to Agia Roumeli takes around six hours. Early in the season it's sometimes necessary to wade through the stream. Later, as the flow drops, it's possible to use rocks as stepping stones.

An early start helps to avoid the worst of the crowds, but during July and August even the early bus from Hania to the top of the gorge can be packed.

The trek begins at Xyloskalo, the steep wooden staircase that gives access to the Samaria Gorge. The towering wall of rock on the right is **Mt Gingilos**. You'll descend swiftly – about a kilometre in the first two kilometres of the walk. There are springs of fresh mountain water and several portable toilets en route. The route levels out after the **Chapel of Agios Nikolaos** on the right and you'll be amid pines and cypresses. The gorge is wide and open until you reach the abandoned village of Samaria, whose inhabitants were relocated when the gorge became a national park. The warden's office is in the abandoned village and just south is a **small church** dedicated to Saint Maria of Egypt, after whom the gorge is named. The walk becomes rockier, the path twists and turns and the scenery becomes more spectacular as the rock walls rise majestically on either side. The path narrows until, at the 12km mark, the walls are only 3.5m apart – the famous **Iron Gates**. After a few more kilometres you'll reach the almost abandoned village of Old Agia Roumeli where there are stands selling overpriced drinks. The last kilometre is the dullest, but finally you arrive at the small resort of **Agia Roumeli**, where you can grab some lunch at the Kri Kri restaurant or wade into the sparkling sea.

The gorge is open most years from May 1 until mid-October. The opening date depends on the amount of water in the gorge. Visiting hours are 6 am to 4 pm every day, and there's an entry fee of 1200 dr. Hold on to your ticket since it will be collected at the end of your hike in order to help wardens keep track of the people in the gorge. Swimming and spending the night in the gorge is forbidden. There's a small museum at the entrance to the gorge with exhibits relating to the ecology of the gorge. It's interesting if you have time to spare, but hardly essential. It's open 9 am to 2 pm daily March to November. Admission is 200 dr. There's also a snack bar and souvenir shop at the entrance to the gorge.

What to Bring
Sensible footwear is essential for walking on the uneven ground covered by sharp stones. Trainers will do but hiking shoes are even better. You'll also need a hat and sunscreen. There's no need to take water. While it's inadvisable to drink water from the main stream, there are plenty of springs along the way spurting delicious cool water straight from the rock. There is nowhere to buy food, so bring something to snack on.

Getting There & Away
There are excursions to the Samaria Gorge from every sizeable town and resort in Crete. Most travel agents have two excursions: 'Samaria Gorge Long Way' and 'Samaria Gorge Easy Way'. The first comprises the regular trek from the Omalos Plateau to Agia Roumeli; the second starts at Agia Roumeli and takes you as far as the Iron Gates. Although undoubtedly an easier hike, you miss the best part of the gorge which lies near the top.

Obviously it's cheaper to trek the Samaria Gorge under your own steam. Hania is the most convenient base. There are buses to Xyloskalo (one hour, 1250 dr) at 6.15, 7.30 and 8.30 am and 1.45 pm. If you intend to stay on the south coast ask for a one-way ticket (750 dr), otherwise you'll automatically be sold a return. There's also a direct bus to Xyloskalo from Paleohora (1½ hours, 1400 dr) at 6 am.

HORA SFAKION Χώρα Σφακίων
☎ 0825 • postcode 730 01 • pop 366
Hora Sfakion (Ho-ra Sfa-ki-on) is the small coastal port where the hordes of walkers from the Samaria Gorge spill off the boat and onto the bus. As such, in high season it can seem like Piccadilly Circus at rush hour. Most people pause only long enough

to catch the next bus out but the town makes a relaxing stay for a few days. Under Venetian and Turkish rule Hora Sfakion was an important maritime centre and, as capital of the Sfakia region, the nucleus of the Cretan struggle for independence. The Turks inflicted severe reprisals on the town's inhabitants for their rebelliousness in the 19th century and the town fell into an economic slump that lasted until the arrival of tourism several decades ago. Hora Sfakion played a prominent role during WWII when thousands of Allied troops were evacuated by sea from the town after the Battle of Crete.

Orientation & Information
The ferry quay is at the western side of the harbour. Buses leave from the square on the eastern side. The post office and OTE are on the square, and the police station overlooks it. There is no tourist office and no tourist police. You can change money on the main square at the Travellers Service Centre. Sfakia Tours (☎ 91 130) is next to the post office and is a good source of information; they can change money, rent cars and find accommodation. There is no parking in town but a large car park immediately outside of town.

Places to Stay & Eat
There are a number of hotels and domatia in town that provide reasonably good value. The best accommodation is *Livikon* (☎ 91 211) on the waterfront, which has large, brightly decorated rooms with stone floors and sea views for 9000/11,500 dr in the high season. *Hotel Stavros* (☎ 91 220), up the steps at the western end of the port, has clean rooms with bathroom for 5000/5500 dr. Don't expect a warm welcome though. *Hotel Samaria* (☎ 91 261), on the waterfront, has rooms with bathroom for 4000/6000 dr. *Hotel Xenia* (☎ 91 202/206), close to the ferry docks, is one of the few places where this government-run chain has come up with the goods. It has spacious rooms with a fridge overlooking the sea from 9000/12,000 dr including breakfast. Nearby is *Alkyon* (☎ 91 180) which has modern rooms of white walls and pine furniture for 7000/8500 dr. The cheapest rooms are at

Sofia Rooms (☎ *91 213)*, which has rooms with shared bath for 4500/5000 dr. The adjoining hotels Samaria and Livikon have a *taverna* downstairs that has a good selection of vegetarian dishes. The road that runs inland from the main square has a *bakery* and a *supermarket*.

Things to See & Do
There are two beaches in town, the town beach in front of the promenade and another less crowded beach at the town's western end. Ask at Hotel Xenia about boat and jeep excursions. They also run a day trip to Gavdos Island for 14,000 dr on a fast boat.

Getting There & Away
Bus There are four buses a day from Hora Sfakion to Hania (two hours, 1400 dr). In summer only there are two daily buses to Plakias (1¼ hours, 1150 dr) via Frangokastello, leaving at 11.30 am and 5.30 pm and one to Rethymno (two hours, '1700 dr) at 7.30 pm.

Boat In summer there are daily boats from Hora Sfakion to Paleohora (three hours, 3500 dr) via Loutro, Agia Roumeli and Sougia. The boat leaves at 12.30 pm. There are also three or four boats a day to Agia Roumeli (one hour, 1500 dr) via Loutro (30 minutes, 500 dr). From 1 June there are boats to Gavdos Island on Saturday and Sunday leaving at 9.30 am and returning at 4 pm (2650 dr).

FRANGOKASTELLO
Φραγγοκάστελλο
☎ 0825
Frangokastello, 82km south-east of Hania, boasts the finest stretch of beach on the south coast as well as a crumbling fort, a small town, an eventful history and even ghosts. The wide, white sand beaches are nearly deserted and slope gradually into shallow warm water making them ideal for kids. Development has been kept to a minimum with most hotels set back from the shore to leave the natural beauty intact.

The best beach is beneath the 14th-century fortress built by the Venetians to protect the coast from pirates and help the Venetians deal with chronically rebellious Hora Sfakion 14km to the east. The Sfakian region continued to pose problems for the Turkish occupiers several centuries later. The legendary Sfakian patriot Ioannis Daskalogiannis led a disastrous rebellion against the Turks in 1770 and was persuaded to surrender himself to the Turks at the Frangokastello Fortress. He was flayed alive. On May 17 1828, 385 Cretan rebels, led by Hadzi Mihalis Dalanis, made a heroic last stand at the fortress in one of the bloodiest battles of the Cretan struggle for independence. About 800 Turks were killed along with Dalanis and the Cretan rebels.

The bloodshed gave rise to the legend of the Drosoulites. On the anniversary of the decisive battle, or in late May around dawn, it's said that a procession of ghostly figures materialises around the fort and marches to the sea. The phenomenon has been verified by a number of independent observers. Although locals believe the figures are the ghosts of slaughtered rebels, others theorise that it may be an optical illusion created by certain atmospheric conditions and that the figures may be a reflection of camels or soldiers in the Libyan Desert.

Orientation & Information
There's no actual town centre in Frangokastello, just a series of domatia, tavernas and residences that stretch on either side of the main road from Hora Sfakion to the fortress which marks the end of the settlement. There's no bank, post office or OTE, but Castello Travel Agency (☎ 92 068) behind the supermarket is a good source of information; they find accommodation, handle air and boat tickets, change money and arrange car rentals. The bus stop is only about 40m west of the fortress.

Places to Stay & Eat
Stavris Rooms (☎ *92 250)* is on the right as you enter the town from Hora Sfakion and has rooms/studios for 6000/9000 dr. The rooms have balconies and sea views but it's about a kilometre walk to the minimarket and 2km before the fortress. *Vrahos Rooms*

& Apartments (☎ 92 019) is also on the right as you enter town and has a taverna downstairs. Four-person apartments cost 10,000 dr. *Blue Sky Apartments (☎ 92 095)* is set back from the beach and is on the left as you enter town. Apartments that sleep six cost 15,000 dr. *Corali Rooms to Rent (☎ 92 033)* is conveniently located near the fortress and a minimarket. Rooms cost 5000/7000 dr. Nearby is *Artemis Rooms (☎ 92 096)* which has large doubles overlooking the beach, with a fridge for 6000 dr. *Oasis (☎ 92 136)* has studios and rooms overlooking the beach about a kilometre before the fortress. Double rooms/studios cost 7000/10,000 dr. *Fata Morgana (☎ 92 074)* is a taverna with rooms to rent near the fortress. Rooms cost 5000/7000 dr.

Restaurant Kriti is a beautifully designed multi-level structure across from the fortress, elaborately outfitted with several terraces and a forest of potted plants. Meals are expensive (count on spending 3000 dr) but excellent and there's a daily happy hour at 7 pm where drinks are half price. It's open noon to midnight daily April to November.

Getting There & Away
In summer only, there are two daily buses from Hora Sfakion to Plakias (1¼ hours, 1150 dr) via Frangokastello. From Hania there's a daily afternoon bus (2½ hrs, 1750 dr) and there is a daily bus from Rethymno (1¼ hrs, 1550 dr). A taxi from Hora Sfakion costs about 3000 dr.

LOUTRO Λουτρό
☎ 0825 • pop 52
The small but rapidly expanding fishing village of Loutro (Loo-**tro**) lies between Agia Roumeli and Hora Sfakion. The town is little more than a crescent of houses and domatia bordering a narrow beach. It's a pleasant, lazy resort that is never overwhelmed with visitors although it can get busy in July and August.

Loutro is the only natural harbour on the south coast of Crete and is only accessible by boat or on foot. Its advantageous geographical position was appreciated in ancient times when it was the port for Phoenix

and Anopolis. According to legend, St Paul was on his way to Loutro when he encountered a storm that blew him off course past Gavdos Island and on to eventual shipwreck in Malta.

Orientation & Information
There's no bank, post office or OTE but there are many places to change money at the western end of the beach. The boat from Hora Sfakion docks in the centre of the beach but the boat from Agia Roumeli docks at the far western end in front of the Sifis Hotel. You can buy boat tickets at a stall on the beach that is open an hour before each departure.

Things to See & Do
Loutro is a good base for boat excursions along the south coast. There are two excursion boats a week to Gavdos Island that cost 14,000 dr including food and soft drinks. There are also excursion boats that do a 'sunset cruise' and a 'dolphin sightseeing cruise' for 4000 dr. Hotel Porto Loutro is a good source of information for boat schedules and there's a stall in front where you can rent canoes for 700 dr an hour or 2000 dr a day. Taxi boats leave from in front of Hotel Porto Loutro, charging 4000 dr to Sweet Water Beach and 7000 dr to Hora Sfakion.

Loutro is also a good base for walks. It's a half hour walk west to **Phoenix** (or Finix), an important settlement for the Romans and Byzantines now a cluster of stark, white houses set against rust-coloured cliffs on a narrow cove.

To get there, go past Sofia Rooms, bear left, go through a wooden fence and follow signs to the E4 European footpath. The path takes you over a plain and past a Turkish castle before descending to Phoenix. Loutro's liveliest bar, Labyrinth, is also along the path and has live music on weekends.

From Phoenix, the path continues over cliffs and hills to **Likkos**, a wide cove with three tavernas clustered at the eastern end. Barren cliffs loom over a wide shadeless beach with caves and rocks on either end. The next cove is **Marmara Beach**. It's a long, hot walk from Likkos (over an hour)

HANIA

which is why most people come on excursion boats from Hora Sfakion.

An extremely steep path leads up from Loutro to the village of **Anopolis** which was the scene of Daskalogiannis' great rebellion against the Turks. Now it is a tranquil and traditional mountain village that gets few visitors. Alternatively, you can save yourself the walk by taking the Hania-Skaloti bus which calls in at Anopolis en route. The bus leaves Hania at 2 pm and returns the following morning, calling in at Anopolis at 7 am.

From Loutro it's a moderate hour long walk along a coastal path to the celebrated **Sweet Water Beach** named after freshwater springs which seep from the rocks. Freelance campers spend months at a time here. Even if you don't feel inclined to join them, you won't be able to resist a swim in the translucent sea. There is a taverna on the western end of the beach that sells drinks and snacks and rents sun umbrellas.

Places to Stay & Eat

The *Sifis Hotel* (☎ 91 346) has pretty, well-kept rooms all with sea views. It's open April to October; rooms cost 7000/8500 dr and breakfast is an extra 1200 dr. The comfortable *Hotel Porto Loutro* (☎ 91 433) has doubles with private bathroom for 9000 dr. At the top of town *Apartments Niki* (☎ 91 265) has beautifully furnished four-person studios with beamed ceilings and stone floors for 12,000 dr a night.

You could also try *Restaurant and Rent Rooms Ilios* (☎ 91 160) at the eastern end of the beach, which has rooms for 6000 dr. *Rooms Sofia* (☎ 91 354) are over a mini-market one street in from the beach; rooms are 4000/4500 dr. The beachfront is lined with *tavernas* that maintain reasonably good standards.

Getting There & Away

Loutro is on the main Paleohora-Hora Sfakion boat route. From April to October there are three boats a day from Hora Sfakion (500 dr), three boats from Agia Roumeli (850 dr), and one boat a day from Paleohora (2500 dr).

AGIA ROUMELI Αγία Ρούμελη
☎ 0825 • pop 36

Agia Roumeli is a shadeless, rather bleak town of houses that are too new and streets that are too neatly laid out to make an interesting stroll. The town has little going for it but a wide pebbly beach that looks pretty good if you've just trekked 18km over pointed rocks. After the afternoon crush of gorge-trekkers has left there's not much to do here except hang-out in one of the many, many tavernas in town.

Orientation & Information

Most travellers just pass through Agia Roumeli waiting to catch the boat to Hora Sfakion. The boat ticket office is a small concrete structure near the beach. There's no post office or OTE and no travel agencies.

Places to Stay & Eat

There are many domatia but the best hotel is *Hotel Agia Roumeli* (☎ 91 232) at the far western end of town on the beach, where rooms are 6000/8000 dr with private bathroom. Many have balconies overlooking the sea. Also on the beach is *Hotel Farangi* (☎ 91 325) where you'll pay 5000 dr for a single or double. Nearby is the friendly and homey *Oasis* (☎ 91 391) which has simple rooms with private bath for 4000 dr. The only establishment in town with air-con is *Hotel-Restaurant Kri-Kri* (☎ 91 089) which has rooms with air-conditioning for 9000 dr and rooms without air-conditioning for 7000 dr. The restaurant is also very good or you could eat at *The Gorge*, a popular taverna. It's open 11 am to 11 pm daily April to November.

Getting There & Away

During the months the gorge is open to walkers, there are frequent boats leaving Agia Roumeli. There are three boats a day to Hora Sfakion (one hour, 1500 dr) via Loutro (30 minutes, 850 dr). It connects with the bus back to Hania, leaving you in Hora Sfakion just long enough to spend a few drachma. There's also a boat from Agia Roumeli to Paleohora (2100 dr) at 4.45 pm, calling at Sougia (950 dr).

Selino Province

Tucked into the south-western corner of the Hania prefecture, Selino is a pretty agricultural region with spectacular views over the sea and a wealth of little villages notable for their Byzantine churches. The district was named after the 'Kastello Selino' fortress built by the Venetians in Paleohora in the 13th century. The village of Kandanos is the capital of the province and contains two Byzantine churches. Kadros, 9km away, has churches with particularly fine Byzantine frescoes. Kandanos was a centre of resistance against the Germans in WWII and as a result most of the village was demolished and most of its inhabitants massacred. Most tourists head to the lovely calm beach resorts of Paleohora and Sougia from which there are many interesting walks and boat trips you can take to explore the region.

SOUGIA Σούγια
☎ 0823 • pop 50

It's surprising that Sougia hasn't yet been commandeered by the package tour crowd. With a wide curve of sand and pebble beach and a shady tree-lined coastal road, Sougia's tranquillity has been preserved only because it lies at the foot of a narrow, twisting road that would deter most tour buses.

The name Sougia derives from the word 'sis' which means pig and refers to the pig rearing that had been the mainstay of the town's economy. The ancient part of the town was on the western side and flourished under the Romans and Byzantines when it was the port of Elyros, an important inland city (now disappeared).

There was a 6th-century basilica at the western end of the village that contained a fine mosaic floor that is now in the Hania Archaeological Museum.

Orientation & Information
If you arrive by boat, walk about 150m along the coast to the town centre. If you arrive by bus, the bus will drop you on the coastal road in front of the Santa Irene Hotel. The only other road intersects the coastal road by the Santa Irene Hotel and runs north to the Agia Irini Gorge and Hania. Sougia doesn't have a post office, OTE or bank, but you can change money at several places, including Polifimos Travel (☎ 51 022), which is open 9 am to 1 pm and 4.30 to 10 pm March to October, and Roxana's Office (☎ 51 362) which is open 8.30 am to 11 pm April to October. Both are just off the coastal road on the road to Hania.

Organised Tours
Roxana Travel offers a trip to Lissos by taxi boat for 5000 dr, to Tripiti for 8000 dr, and to Pikilassos for 9000 dr. All prices are for a one-way trip.

Places to Stay
There's no camp site, but the eastern end of the long, pebbled beach is popular with free-lance campers. It seems almost every building in Sougia is a domatia or pension. The smartest accommodation is *Santa Irene Hotel* (☎ 51 342, fax 51 181), which has studios for 8000/12,000 dr. Air-conditioning costs 2000 dr extra. *Rooms Maria* (☎ 51 337) is a block further east on the coast and has clean, white rooms with private bath for 5000/7000 dr in August, 1000 dr less the rest of the summer. Next door is the equally attractive *Rooms Ririka* (☎ 51 167) also with rooms overlooking the sea for about the same price. Inland, on the road to Hania, *Aretouca Rooms to Rent* (☎ 51 178) has lovely rooms with wood-panelled ceilings and balconies for 7000/8000 dr. *Pension Galini* (☎/fax 51 488) next door, has beautiful rooms with private bathroom for 5000/6000/7000 dr and studios for 8000 dr.

Places to Eat
Restaurants line the waterfront and there are more on the main street. *Kyma*, on the seafront as you enter town, has a good selection of ready-made food. It's open 8 am to midnight daily April to November. *Taverna Rebetiko*, on the road to Hania, has an extensive menu including such Cretan dishes as *boureki* and stuffed zucchini flowers. It's open noon to midnight daily April to October.

Getting There & Away

There's a daily bus from Hania to Sougia (2½ hours, 1400 dr) at 1.30 pm. Buses from Sougia to Hania leave at 7 am. Sougia is on the Paleohora-Hora Sfakion boat route.

AROUND SOUGIA

Sougia is at the mouth of the pretty **Agia Irini Gorge**, 12km north of Sougia, which may not be as fashionable as the Samaria Gorge walk but is less crowded and less gruelling. The gorge is 7km long and is carpeted with oleander and chestnut trees and is redolent with the odours of rosemary, sage and thyme. You'll see the entrance to the gorge on the right side if you're travelling from Sougia. You'll cross a streambed before coming to olive groves but many trees were destroyed in a massive fire in 1994. The path follows a dried out riverbed bordered by caves carved into the large rocks. There are a number of rest stops along the way and many tranquil places to sit and admire the scenery.

Paleohora travel agents offer guided walks through the gorge for 4500 dr. It's easy enough to organise independently – just catch the Omalos bus from Paleohora or the Hania bus from Sougia, and get off at Agia Irini.

The ruins of ancient **Lissos** are 1½ hours away on the coastal path to Paleohora (see boxed text 'Paleohora-Sougia Coastal Walk'). Lissos arose under the Dorians, flourished under the Byzantines and was destroyed by the Saracens in the 9th century. It was part of a league of city-states, led by ancient Gortyn, and minted their own gold coins inscribed with the word 'Lission'. At one time there was a reservoir, a theatre and hot springs but these have not yet been excavated. Most of what you see dates from the 1st through 3rd centuries BC when Lissos was known for its curative springs. The 3rd-century-BC Temple of Asklepion was built next to one of the curative springs and named after the Greek god of healing Asclepius.

Excavations here uncovered a headless statue of Asclepius along with 20 other statue fragments now in the Hania Archaeological Museum. You can still see the mar-

ble altar-base that supported the statue next to the pit in which sacrifices were placed. The other notable feature of Lissos is the mosaic floor of multi-coloured stones intricately arranged in beautiful geometric shapes and images of birds. On the way down to the sea there are traces of Roman ruins and on the western slopes of the valley are unusual barrel-vaulted tombs.

Nearby are the ruins of two early Christian basilicas – **Agios Kirkos** and the **Panagia** – dating from the 13th century.

PALEOHORA

Παλαιοχωρα

☎ 0823 • pop 2150

Paleohora (Pal-ee-o-**hor**-a) was discovered by hippies back in the 60s and from then on its days as a tranquil fishing village were numbered. The resort operators have not gone way over the top – yet. The place retains a certain laid-back feel. It is also the only beach resort on Crete which does not go into total hibernation in winter.

The little town lies on a narrow peninsula with a long, curving sandy beach exposed to the wind on one side and a sheltered pebbly beach on the other. On summer evenings the main street is closed to traffic and the tavernas move onto the road. The most picturesque part of Paleohora is the narrow streets huddled around the castle.

Orientation

Paleohora's main street, El Venizelou, runs north-south. Walking south along El Venizelou from the bus stop, several streets lead off left to the Pebble Beach. There's an attractive seafront promenade that runs along the beach which is the centre of Paleohora's activity in the early evening. Boats leave from the old harbour at the southern end of this beach. At the southern end of El Venizelou, a right turn onto Kontekaki leads to the tamarisk-shaded Sandy Beach.

Information

The municipal tourist office (☎ 41 507) is in the town hall on El Venizelou. It is open 10 am to 1 pm and 6 to 9 pm Wednesday to Monday May to October. The National Bank

HANIA

of Greece is on El Venizelou and has an ATM. The post office is on the road that skirts the Sandy Beach. The OTE is on the west side of El Venizelou, just north of Kontekaki. Internet access is provided at PC Corner (☎ 42 422). There's a laundry on El Venizelou next to Notos Rentals. Interkreta Tourism and Travel (☎ 41 393, fax 41 050) on Kontekaki sells boat tickets and excursions and is a good source of information. It's open 9 am to 1 pm and 4 to 9 pm daily.

Things to See & Do

It's worth clambering up the ruins of the 13th-century **Venetian castle** for the splendid view of the sea and mountains. The castle was built by the Venetians in the 13th century as a defensive fortress from which the Venetians could keep an eye on the south-western coast from its commanding position on top of a hill. There's not much left of the fortress however, as it was destroyed by the Venetians, the Turks, the pirate Barbarossa in the 16th century, and later the Germans during WWII.

From Paleohora, a six-hour walk along a scenic coastal path leads to **Sougia**, passing the ancient site of **Lissos**. (See boxed text, 'Paleohora-Sougia Coastal Walk')

Paleohora is known for its excellent **windsurfing** which is the best on the island. Winds blow most strongly on the Sandy Beach and usually peak in the late morning and early afternoon. Westwind Windsurfing

Club (☎ 094 681 9777) near the Pal Beach Hotel rents equipment but you must buy an annual membership of 60 dr and then pay 50 dr a week for unlimited sailing.

Places to Stay

Camping Paleohora (☎ 41 225/120) is 1.5km north-east of the town, near the Pebble Beach. The camp site has a taverna but no minimarket.

Homestay Anonymous (☎ 41 509 or 42 098) is a great place for backpackers, with clean, simply furnished rooms set around a small, beautiful garden. Singles/doubles/triples with shared bathroom cost 3500/4500/5000 dr, and there is a communal kitchen. The owner, Manolis, is an amiable young guy who speaks good English and is full of useful information for travellers. To get there, walk south along El Venizelou from the bus stop and turn right at the town hall. Follow the road as it veers right, the rooms are on the left.

Oriental Bay Rooms (☎ 41 076) occupies the large modern building at the northern end of the pebble beach. The owner, Thalia, is a very cheerful woman and the immaculate rooms with private bathroom and ceiling fans are good value at 5000/7000 dr. There's also a shaded terrace-restaurant overlooking the sea that serves decent meals.

Dream Rooms (☎ 41 112) is aptly named for the large, excellently maintained rooms

Paleohora-Sougia Coastal Walk

From the town centre of Paleohora, follow signs to the camping grounds to the north-east. Turn right at the intersection with the road to Anidri and soon you'll be following the coastal path marked as the E4 European Footpath. After a couple of kilometres, the path climbs steeply for a beautiful view back to Paleohora. You'll pass **Anidri Beach** and several inviting **coves** where people may be getting an all-over tan. Take a dip because the path soon turns inland to pass over **Cape Flomes**. You'll walk along a plateau carpeted with brush that leads toward the coast and some breathtaking views over the Libyan Sea. Soon you'll reach the Minoan site of **Lissos**. After Lissos the path takes you through a pine forest and then a **gorge** bedecked with oleander and outfitted with some perfect picnic spots. The road ends at Sougia Harbour. Since the walk is nearly shadeless it's important to take several litres of water and sunscreen. If you come June through August, it's best to start at sunrise in order to get to Sougia before the heat of the day clamps down.

HANIA

PALEOHORA

PLACES TO STAY	20	Cretan Traditional	7	Bus Stop
2 Poseidon Pension		Sweet Cafe	10	National Bank
8 Oriental Bay Rooms	21	Restaurant Small Garden		of Greece
9 Dream Rooms	23	Pizzeria Nikki	13	Town Hall & EOT
12 Homestay Anonymous	25	Third Eye	14	Periptero
24 Dictamo	29	Caravello	15	Notos Rentals
26 Pal Beach			16	Laundry
30 Spamados Rooms		OTHER	17	Nostos Night Club
31 Kostas Rooms	1	Notos Rentals	18	Police Station
	3	Post Office	19	OTE
PLACES TO EAT	4	Westwind Windsurfing	22	Interkreta Tourism
11 Dionysos Taverna	5	Supermarket	27	PC Corner
	6	Outdoor Cinema	28	Port Police

To Hania

To Paleohora Disco
& Camping
Paleohora (1.5km)

School

Sandy

Beach

El Venizelou

Pebble
Beach

To Sougia,
Agia Roumeli
& Cavdos Island

Kontekaki

Old
Harbour

Quay

Einai Yrela

MEDITERRANEAN
SEA

Venetian
Castle

0   50   100 m
0   50   100 yd

with balconies overlooking the sea. Rooms with private bath are 6000/8000 dr. ***Spamandos Rooms*** (☎ 41 197), in the old quarter, has spotless, nicely furnished doubles/triples with private bathroom for 7000/8000 dr. To get there walk south along Einai Yrela take the first left after the Pelican taverna and then the first right. After 60m turn left and the rooms are on the right.

Nearby, ***Kostas Rooms*** (☎/fax 41 248) offers simple attractive rooms with ceiling fans, private baths, fridge and sea views for 3500/5000 dr. Out of season, it's worth looking for a deal at one of the places

offering self-catering apartments along the Sandy Beach on the other side of town.

Poseidon Pension (☎ 41 374/115) has cosy rooms for 5000/6000 dr with private bathroom, and studios for 7000/9000 dr.

Dictamo (☎ 41 569, fax 41 581) is an attractive two-storey hotel wrapped around a central courtyard with large, nicely furnished rooms for 8000/10,000 dr.

The most expensive hotel in town is ***Pal Beach*** (☎ 41 512, fax 41 578) with rooms for 11,500/16,000 dr. The occasional bursts of air-conditioning still do not make the rooms worth the price.

HANIA

Places to Eat

There are some good eateries. *Restaurant Small Garden*, in the street behind the OTE, is a fine little taverna and does a good job on old favourites like fried aubergine (800 dr). It's open noon to midnight daily. The very popular *Dionysos Taverna*, on El Venizelou, is a bit more expensive but also serves tasty food. It has a roomy interior and a few tables outside under the trees. It's open 7 pm to 1 am daily March to October. *Pizzeria Niki*, just off Kontehaki, serves superior pizzas cooked in a wood-fired oven and served on a spacious outdoor terrace. It's open 6.30 pm to midnight daily April to October. Vegetarians have a treat in store at the *Third Eye*, near the Sandy Beach. The menu includes curries and a range of Asian dishes, all at very reasonable prices. You can eat well and enjoy a beer for less than 2000 dr. Unfortunately the place is closed in winter. It's open 6 pm to midnight daily March to November. *Caravello* has a prime position overlooking the old harbour and offers a full array of fresh seafood. It's open 11 am to midnight daily April to November. Wherever you dine, round your meal off with a delicious dessert from *Cretan Traditional Sweet Café* almost opposite Restaurant Small Garden. It's open 8 am to 11 pm daily.

Few tourists make it to the town of Grammeno which leaves this exceptional *Taverna Grammeno* to the locals. Among the Cretan specialties on offer is a delicious rabbit stewed in *myzithra* (sheep's milk cheese) and stuffed zucchini flowers. Head west out of Paleohora along the coast road 5km west of Paleohora and you'll see the restaurant on the right. It's open 7 pm to 1 am daily April to October.

Entertainment

Most visitors to Paleohora spend at least one evening at the well-signposted *outdoor cinema*. Another option for a night out is *Paleohora Disco*, next to Camping Paleohora 1.5km north of town. If you've seen the movie and don't fancy the trek to the disco, try *Nostos Night Club* right in town, between El Venizelou and the Old Harbour.

Getting There & Away

Bus In summer there are three buses a day to Hania (two hours, 1450 dr); in winter there are two. In summer, this service goes via Omalos (1½ hours, 1250 dr) to cash in on the Samaria Gorge trade.

Boat In summer there are daily ferries from Paleohora to Hora Sfakion (three hours, 3700 dr) via Sougia (one hour, 950 dr), Agia Roumeli (two hours, 2100 dr) and Loutro (2½ hours, 2850 dr). The ferry leaves Paleohora at 9.30 am, and returns from Hora Sfakion at 12.30 pm. There's also a boat three times a week in the summer to Gavdos (four hours, 3000 dr) that leaves Paleohora at 8.30 am. Tickets for all of these boats can be bought at Interkreta Tourism & Travel (☎ 41 393/888, fax 41 050), Kontekaki 4.

Getting Around

Car, Motorcycle & Bicycle All three can be hired from Notos Rentals (☎ 42 110) on El Venizelou and by the Sandy Beach.

Excursion Boat The M/B *Elafonisos* gets cranked into action in mid-April ferrying people to the west coast beach of Elafonisi (one hour, 1300 dr). The service builds up from three times a week to daily in June through September. Travel agents around town offer excursions to ancient Lissos (6500 dr) and dolphin-watching trips (3500 dr).

AROUND PALEOHORA

The village of **Anidri** is 5km north-east of Paleohora and contains the Church of Agios Georgios with 14th-century frescoes by the local master, Pagomenos. The founding fathers of the village were two brothers from Hora Sfakion fleeing from a murderous vendetta which is why most villagers have the same surname.

The village is accessible by foot from Paleohora. Take the road that goes past the camping grounds and follow the paved road that forks off to the left, which is bordered by steep rocks. As you enter the village you'll see a sign directing you to the Anidri Gorge. After a few hundred metres on a footpath you'll see an overgrown path on the left.

What To Wear?

Cretans have a long tradition of welcoming foreigners, which has made them tolerant of different customs. Although Greek women are unlikely to go topless, in most places topless sunbathing is allowed. The few south coast beaches where it is frowned upon post signs to that effect. Although naturism is not widely practised and officially is not allowed, you'll find a sprinkling of naturists on the far ends of remote beaches or in secluded coves. Nude beaches change from year to year. Sometimes a taverna suddenly springs up on a popular naturist beach and the naturists disappear only to turn up on another distant cove. Beaches that are currently popular with naturists include Kommos near Matala, Sweet Water Beach, the south end of the sandy beach in Paleohora and the east end of the pebbly beach at Sougia. Glyka Nera, close to Loutro is an old standby as is Orthi Ammos 1km east of Frangokastello. Diktikos west of Lendas is the most reliable of Crete's nude beaches.

Red markers direct you to the gorge. After walking along the dried-out riverbed, signs direct you to the wide, deserted Anidri Beach at the end of the gorge. You can take a different path back to Paleohora following the E4 European footpath markers that take you along the coastal cliffs.

GAVDOS ISLAND Νήσος Γαύδος
☎ 0149 • pop 50

Gavdos Island (**Gav**-dos), in the Libyan Sea, 65km from Paleohora, is the most southerly place in Europe. Archaeological excavations indicate habitation as far back as the Neolithic period. In the Greco-Roman era Gavdos Island belonged to the city of Gortyn when it was known as Clauda. There was a Roman settlement on the north-west corner of the island. On his way from Kali Limenes to Rome, St Paul encountered a fierce storm which blew him off course past Gavdos Island and ended up shipwrecked on Malta, instead of a landing on Phoenix (or Finix). Under the Byzantines Gavdos Island was the seat of bishopric, but when the Arabs conquered Crete in the 9th century the island became a pirates nest.

A severe water shortage has limited development of the island. Rain water washes into the sea and the Greek government has had to fund projects drilling for groundwater. Visitors need to be aware that water is scarce; forget about long showers, or any showers at all in some places. Electricity is also limited since it comes from generators that are widespread but often shut down at night because of the noise.

The capital of the island is Kastri in the centre of Gavdos which is where you'll find the only post office, OTE, doctor and police officer. The best beach is Sarakinikos, in the north-east corner, which has a wide swathe of sand and several tavernas on the side. There's also another excellent beach, Agios Ioannis, on the northern tip, which has a scraggly summer settlement of campers. There are some wonderful beaches on the north coast such as Potamos and Pirgos which you can reach by foot from Kastri if you follow the footpath leading north from Ambelos. There are no hotels but several of the locals let rooms, and there are tavernas. There is no official camp site but camping freelance may be tolerated. Fishermen from Gavdos Island take tourists to the remote, uninhabited island of Gavdopoula. The best source of information about the island is Interkreta Tourism & Travel in Paleohora.

Getting There & Away

A small post boat operates between Paleohora and Gavdos on Monday and Thursday all year, weather permitting. It leaves Paleohora at 8.30 am and takes about four hours (3000 dr).

In summer there's also a Tuesday boat. The boats turn around from Gavdos almost immediately. There's also two boats a week from Hora Sfakion to Gavdos (2650 dr) and a weekly boat from Sougia (2300 dr).

HANIA

Kissamos Province

The Kissamos region in the far west is a wild, rugged land that attracts few tourists. Villages and towns are few and far between and even the spectacular beaches of Elafonisi and Falassarna are surprisingly under-developed. The largest town and capital of the province is Kastelli-Kissamos, usually referred to simply as Kissamos. West of Kissamos is the beautiful and deserted Gramvousa Peninsula, most of which is accessible only by boat. East of Kissamos is the Rodhopou Peninsula with the small resort of Kolimbari and several interesting villages and churches that are only accessible if you have your own wheels.

KASTELLI-KISSAMOS

Καστέλλι-Κίσσαμος
☎ 0822 • pop 3000

If you find yourself in the north coast town of Kastelli-Kissamos, you've probably arrived by ferry from the Peloponnese or Kythira. The most remarkable part of Kastelli-Kissamos is its unremarkableness. It's simply a quiet town of mostly elderly residents that neither expects nor attracts much tourism.

In antiquity, its name was Kissamos, the main town of the province of the same name. When the Venetians came along and built a castle here, the place became known as Kastelli. The name persisted until 1966 when authorities decided that too many people were confusing this Kastelli with Crete's other Kastelli, 40km south-east of Iraklio. The official name reverted to Kissamos, and that's what appears on bus and shipping schedules. Local people still prefer Kastelli, and many books and maps agree with them. An alternative that is emerging is to combine the two into Kastelli-Kissamos, which leaves no room for misunderstanding.

Ancient Kissamos was a harbour for the important city-state of Polyrrinia 7km inland. Vestiges of Roman buildings have been unearthed but most of the ancient city lies under the modern town of Kissamos and cannot be excavated. Kissamos achieved independence in the third century AD and then became the seat of a bishopric under the Byzantines. It was occupied by the Saracens in the 9th century and flourished under the Venetians.

Orientation & Information

The port is 3km west of town. In summer a bus meets the boats, otherwise a taxi costs 800 dr. The bus station is just below the square, Plateia Kissamos, and the main street, Skalidi, runs east from Plateia Kissamos. The post office is on the main road. Signs from the bus station direct you through an alley on the right of Skalidi which takes you to the post office. Turn right at the post office and you'll come to the National Bank of Greece which is on the central square. Turn left at the post office and the OTE office is opposite you about 50m along the main road. There is also a string of pensions and tavernas along the sea below the bus station. Kastelli-Kissamos has no tourist office but Horeftakis Tours (☎ 23 250) on Skalidi is a good source of information.

Places to Stay

Camping There are three camp sites to choose from. *Camping Kissamos* (☎ 23 444/322), close to the city centre, is convenient for the huge supermarket next door and for the bus station, but not much else. It's got great views of the olive-processing plant next door. Signs direct you there from the city centre.

A much better choice is *Camping Mithimna* (☎ 31 444/445), 6km west of town. It's an excellent shady site near the best stretch of beach. Facilities include a restaurant, bar and shop. It charges 900 dr per person and 600 dr per tent. It also has rooms to rent nearby. Getting there involves either a 4km walk along the beach, or a bus trip to the village of Drapania – from where it's a pleasant 15-minute walk through olive groves to the site. *Camping Nopigia* (☎ 31 111) is another good site, 2km west of Camping Mithimna. The only drawback is that the beach is no good for swimming, but it makes up for that with a swimming pool.

Domatia One of the best deals in town is *Koutsounakis Rooms* (☎ 23 753 or 22 064) adjacent to the bus station. The spotless rooms are 4000/5500 dr with private bathroom. Opposite, the C-class *Argo Rooms for Rent (☎ 23 563/322)*, on Plateia Teloniou, has spacious rooms for 5000/7000 dr with private bathroom. From the central square, walk down to the seafront, turn left, and you will come to the rooms on the left. On the beach, *Mandy's Apartments (☎ 22 830, fax 22 825)* is a white stucco house of studios with balconies and views of the sea. Studios cost 12,000 dr.

Hotels The C-class *Hotel Kissamos (☎ 22 086)*, west of the bus station on the north side of the main road, is in an uninspiring location across from an auto body shop but has rooms with private bathroom for 5500/7700 dr, including breakfast. *Hotel Castelli (☎ 22 140)* has similar prices. *Hotel Peli (☎ 23 223)* is a freshly renovated hotel on the waterfront about 500m west of town with rooms for 7000/10,000 dr. Also right on the sea is *Holiday Bay Hotel (☎ 23 488)* with rooms for about the same price.

Places to Eat
Papadakis Taverna, opposite the Argo Rooms for Rent, has a good setting overlooking the beach and serves well-prepared food. It's open 11 am to midnight daily. For local colour go to the no-frills *Restaurant Macedonas*, just west of Plateia Kissamos, where an excellent meal of crisply fried whitebait and Greek salad costs 1800 dr. It's open noon to 10 pm daily. Another good place is the *Stork,* west of the bus station, which has a good selection of daily specials, and is open noon to midnight Monday to Saturday.

Getting There & Away
Bus There are 13 buses a day to Hania (one hour, 900 dr), where you can change for Rethymno and Iraklio; and two buses a day for Falassarna (600 dr) at 10 am and 5.30 pm.

Ferry Golden Ferries Maritime operates the F/B *Maria* on a route that takes in Antikythira (two hours, 2100 dr), Kythira (four hours, 4200 dr), and Gythio (seven hours,

5100 dr). It leaves Kastelli-Kissamos at 2.30 pm Monday and Thursday. Both the Miras agent, Horeftakis Tours (☎ 23 250), and the ANEK Office (☎ 22 009 or 24 030) are on the right side of Skalidi, east of Plateia Kissamos.

Getting Around
Motorcycles can be hired from Motor Fun (☎ 23 400) on Plateia Kissamos and cars can be hired from Hermes (☎ 22 980) on Skalidi.

AROUND KASTELLI-KISSAMOS
The ruins of the ancient city of **Polyrrinia** (Pol-ee-ren-**ee**-a) lie 7km south of Kastelli-Kissamos, above the village of Ano Paleokastro (sometimes called Polyrrinia). It's a steep climb to the ruins but the views are stunning and the region is blanketed with wildflowers in spring. The city was founded by the Dorians in the 6th century BC and was constantly at war with the Kydonians from Hania. Coins from the period depict the warrior-goddess Athena who was evidently revered by the war-like Polyrrinians.

Unlike their rivals the Kidonians, Polyrrinia did not resist the Roman invasion and thus was spared destruction. It was the best fortified town in Crete and the administrative centre of western Crete from the Roman through to the Byzantine period. It was reoccupied by the Venetians who used it as a fortress. Many of the ruined structures date from the Roman period including an aqueduct built by Hadrian.

The most impressive feature of the site is the acropolis built by the Byzantines and Venetians. There's also a church built on the foundations of a Hellenistic temple from the 4th century BC. Notice also, near the aqueduct, a cave dedicated to the Nymphs that still contains the niches for the Nymphs statuettes.

Getting There & Away
It's a scenic walk from Kastelli-Kissamos to Polyrrinia. To reach the Polyrrinia road, walk east along Kastelli-Kissamos' main road, and turn right after the OTE. There are two buses daily in winter and a bus Monday, Wednesday, and Friday in summer (25 minutes, 400 dr).

THE RODHOPOU PENINSULA

The barren, rocky Rodhopou Peninsula has a few small villages clustered at the base of the peninsula but the rest is uninhabited. A paved road goes as far as Afrata but then becomes a dirt track that meanders through the peninsula. If you are travelling by foot, jeep or motorcycle you can reach the Diktynna Sanctuary at the end of the peninsula, but make sure you are well-supplied since there is not a drop of gasoline or water, or a morsel of food beyond Afrata.

KOLIMBARI

☎ 0824 • pop 151

Kolimbari, 23km west of Hania, is at the base of the Rodhopou Peninsula, and appeals to those seeking a quiet, relaxing vacation. Development is in its embryonic stage but that is changing fast as hotels and domatia arise to take advantage of the long pebbly beach. In addition to beach activities, Kolimbari is a good base for a walk to Moni Gonia.

Orientation & Information

The bus from Hania drops you off on the main road from which it is a 500m walk down to the beach settlement. At the bottom of the road you'll see a post office on the left; turn left and the OTE is about 100m further. There is no bank but you can change money and rent cars at Antilia Travel Agency (☎ 22 695) which is open 9 am to 7 pm Monday to Saturday April to November.

Places to Stay & Eat

On the way into town from the bus stop you will see *Rooms Lefka* (☎ 22 211) which has attractive rooms for 6000/7000 dr. The best choice along the beach is *Hotel Minerve* (☎ 22 485), which has large rooms with kitchenettes and balconies for 10,000 dr. They also have two-bedroom apartments for 14,000 dr.

Kolimbari is a good place to sample local fish. In the centre of town are *Diktina* and *Argedina*, across the street from each other, which offer fresh fish for about 9000 dr a kilo. They are open 6 pm to midnight Monday to Saturday. Along the beach, try *Taverna Arhontika* for Cretan taverna spe-cialities. There's also a mini market near the bus stop for self-catering.

Getting There & Away

Buses from Hania to Kastelli-Kissamos stop at Kolimbari (40 minutes, 550 dr).

Moni Gonia

Moni Gonia was founded in 1618. Although the 17th-century monastery church was damaged by the Turks in 1645, it was rebuilt in 1662 and extended in the 19th century. The monastery houses a unique collection of icons dating from the 17th and 18th centuries. Some are in the church while others are in the monastery museum. The most valuable icon is that of Agios Nikolaos, painted in 1637 by Palaiokapas, which perfectly exemplifies the Cretan school of icon painting that flourished in the 17th century under Venetian rule. The monastery is open 8 am to 12.30 pm and 4 to 8 pm Monday to Friday; 4 to 8 pm on Saturday. There is no admission charge. It's easy to reach from Kolimbari. Take the beach road north from the town centre for about 500m.

Diktynna

Right on the tip of the Rodhopou Peninsula is the remains of a temple to the Cretan goddess Diktynna, the most important religious sanctuary in the region under the Romans. Diktynna was the goddess of hunting and she was worshipped fervently in western Crete. According to legend her name derives from the word *diktyon* which means 'net'. Supposedly it was a fisherman's net that saved her when she leapt into the sea to avoid the amorous desires of King Minos. The temple dates to the 2nd century AD but it was probably built on the site of an earlier temple. After the collapse of the Roman Empire the temple was desecrated but you can see the temple's foundations and a sacrificial altar as well as Roman cisterns. If you're 'templed out' you can relax on a lovely sandy beach. Diktynna is only accessible by dirt road from Kolimbari but many travel agencies in Hania offer boat excursions to Diktynna for 6000 dr.

HANIA

FALASSARNA Φαλασάρνα
☎ 0822 • pop 24

Falassarna, 16km to the west of Kastelli-Kissamos, has been occupied at least since the 6th century BC but reached the height of its power in the 4th century BC. Although it was built next to the sea you will see that the town's ruins are about 400m away from the water because the western coast of Crete has risen over the centuries. The town owed its wealth to the agricultural produce derived from the fertile valley to the south. It was the west coast harbour for Polyrrinia but later became Polyrrinia's chief rival for dominance over western Crete. By the time of the Roman invasion of Crete in 67 BC, Falassarna had become a haven for pirates. Stone blocks excavated around the entrance to the old harbour indicate that the Romans may have tried to block off the harbour to prevent it from being used by pirates.

You can see the remains of the ancient city, but most people head to Falassarna for its superb beaches. The best beach is 3km of fine sand bordered by a few tavernas and hotels. In front of the ancient town there is a small pebbly beach and there is a third beach between the two of them.

Orientation & Information
Approaching Falassarna from the main road, the road forks to the north and to the south. The northern road takes you to the beaches that go on for several kilometres separated only by rocks. The beaches are shadeless but you can rent umbrellas and lounge chairs. Most of the hotels and domatia are at this end of town. The southern road takes you past a long strip of greenhouses and some goat pastures. You will also see signs to ancient Falassarna. There is no post office, OTE, tourist office or travel agency.

Things to See
The remains of the ancient city of Falassarna are the city's main attraction, although not much is visible. Signs direct you to the ancient city from the main road, following a dirt road at the end of the asphalt.

First you'll come to a large stone throne whose purpose has remained obscure. Further on there are the remains of the wall that once fortified the town and a small harbour. Notice the holes carved into the wall which were used to tie up boats. At the top of the hill there are the remains of the acropolis wall and a temple as well as four clay baths.

Places to Stay
There are numerous places for wild camping on Falassarna's beaches. At the northern end *Sunset Rent Rooms (☎ 41 204)* offers excellent value. There are five-person apartments for 12,000 dr and doubles with balconies and sea views for 6000 dr. The establishment is near the beach and has a taverna downstairs. Nearby is *Rooms Aquamarine (☎ 22 003)* which also offers double rooms with a view for about the same price. A little further from the beach is *Apartments Romantica (☎ 41 089)* which has studios and apartments for 7000 dr and 10,000 dr. On the way into town you'll pass *Rooms for Rent Panorama (☎ 41 336)* which has beautiful rooms for 7000/8000 dr and also a taverna that serves a full array of Cretan specialties as well as omelettes, burgers and spaghetti.

Getting There & Away
In summer there are two buses a day from Kastelli-Kissamos to Falassarna (600 dr) as well as two buses a day from Hania (1500 dr).

GRAMVOUSA PENINSULA
Χερσόνησος Γραμβούσα

North of Falassarna is the wild and remote Gramvousa Peninsula. There is a wide track, which eventually degenerates into a path, along the east coast side to the sandy beach of **Balos** on **Cape Tigani**, on the west side of the peninsula's narrow top. Behind the beach is Mt Geroskinos and offshore are two deserted islands, Agria (wild) and Imeri (tame) Gramvousa. The dirt road to Cape Tigani begins at the far end of the main street of Kalyviani and follows the eastern slope of Mt Geroskinos. The views are spectacular over the shoreline and the Rodhopou Peninsula. About 2km before

HANIA

the beach the dirt road becomes a path. One fork takes you to the beach while the other fork runs along the side of the mountain and eventually joins the beach path. The shadeless walk takes around three hours – wear a hat and take plenty of water.

The offshore island of Imeri Gramvousa was an important vantage point for the Venetians who built a fortress here to protect ships passing in front of the island on the way to and from Venice. It was considered an impregnable fort with a large cache of armaments. The Turks did not conquer Imeri Gramvousa along with the rest of Crete in 1645; the fort remained in Venetian hands along with their other forts, Souda and Spinalonga. Eventually the Venetians left and the fort fell into disuse until it was taken over in 1821 by Cretan revolutionaries who needed a base of operations in their war for independence. It later became a notorious base for piracy before the Turks got a hold of it again and used it to blockade the coast during the War of Independence. Local legend has it that the pirates amassed a fabulous fortune which they reportedly hid in caves around the island. Who knows? It could still be there today.

Getting There & Away

To reach Kalyviani, take a west-bound bus from Kastelli-Kissamos and ask to be let off at the turn-off to the right for the village of Kalyviani (5km from Kastelli-Kissamos). Kalyviani is a 2km walk from the main road.

X & K Maritime Company (☎ 24 344 or 23 650), in Kastelli-Kissamos ,runs a tour that takes in the Gramvousa Peninsula, which is inaccessible by car, and Imeri Gramvousa. White sand beaches, a climb to the top of the Venetian castle and the cove where Prince Charles and Diana reportedly honeymooned are also on the itinerary. It is open from 9.30 am Monday to Saturday April to October. The tour costs 5000 dr.

ELAFONISI Ελαφονήσι
☎ 0825

As one of the loveliest sand beaches in Crete it's easy to understand why people enthuse so much about Elafonisi, at the southern

extremity of Crete's west coast. The beach is long and wide and is separated from the Elafonisi Islet by about 50m of knee-deep water on its northern side. The clear, shallow water and fine white sand create the kind of tropical paradise not often found in the Mediterranean. There are a few snack bars on the beach near where the road ends and stalls to rent umbrellas and lounge chairs. The islet is marked by low dunes and a string of semi-secluded coves that attract a sprinkling of naturists. The beaches are popular with daytrippers but there are two small hotels and a pension on a bluff overlooking the main beach for those who want to luxuriate in the quiet that descends on Elafonisi in late afternoon. All have rooms for 5000/7000 dr with private bath and there is a mini market nearby. Try **Rooms Elafonissi** (*☎ 61 274*), which has an outdoor patio; **Rooms Elafonissos** (*☎ 61 294*) which has a taverna overlooking the sea from its commanding position on a bluff; or **Inahorion** (*☎ 61 111*).

There are two boats a day from Paleohora (one hour, 1140 dr) in summer, as well as daily buses from Hania (2½ hours, 1500 dr) and Kastelli-Kissamos (1½ hours, 900 dr). The buses leave Hania at 7.30 am and Kastelli-Kissamos at 8.30 am, and both depart from Elafonisi at 4 pm. The final 5km of road from Moni Hrysoskalitissas to the beach is unpaved.

MONI HRYSOSKALITISSAS
Μονή Χρυσοσκαλίτισσας

Moni Hrysoskalitissas (Mo-**nee** Hris-os-ka-**lee**-tiss-as), 5km north of Elafonisi, is inhabited by two nuns. It's a beautiful monastery perched on a rock high above the sea. Hrysoskalitissas means 'golden staircase' and the name derives from a legend which claims that one of the 90 steps leading up from the sea to the monastery is made of gold but you can only see it if you are pure in spirit.

The church is recent but the monastery is allegedly a thousand years old and may have been built on the site of a Minoan temple. There are tavernas and domatia in the vicinity. Buses to Elafonisi drop passengers here.

ENNIA HORIA Εννιά Χωριά
Ennia Horia (nine villages) is the name
given to the highly scenic mountainous region south of Kastelli-Kissamos, which is
renowned for its chestnut trees.

If you have your own transport you can
drive through the region en route to Moni
Hrysoskalitissas and Elafonisi or, with a
little back-tracking, to Paleohora.

Alternatively, you can take a circular
route, returning via the coast road.

Heading south from Kissamos you'll
pass through some of the lushest and most
fertile parts of the island. The scenery is unforgettable and you'll be far away from the
tourist track.

You'll first come to the village of **Voul-
garo** which has two Byzantine churches,
and then 3km further south the lovely village of **Topolia** with a cluster of whitewashed houses overhung with plants and
vines. There is a post office in the town centre, a couple of kafeneia and *Topolia Rooms*
(☎ 0822-51273), a new domatia with iron
balconies for 5000/6000 dr.

After Topolia the road skirts the edge of
the **Koutsomatados Ravine** bending and
twisting and affording dramatic views. Just
before the tunnel there is a *snack bar* on the
left which is a good place to fuel up and
take a photo of the ravine. Shortly you will
come to a cave, **Agia Sofia,** which dates
back to the Neolithic era. At the top of the
rock-cut stairs to the cave there's a taverna
with great views over the ravine. It's a spectacular drive to tiny **Koutsomatados** followed by the village of **Vlatos.** After the
village you'll see a turn-off on the right for
Milia.

A few years ago, the only two families
left in this isolated village managed to per-
suade the EU to help them reconstruct the
village in its original style using traditional
materials and furnishing it with Cretan antiques. The rebuilt *stone houses* are occasionally rented out to Cretans or tourists
who are looking for total isolation in a stunning mountain setting and don't mind the
lack of electricity. There's also a traditional
Cretan kitchen turning out scrumptious
dishes from the organic produce in the vil-

lage garden. The stone cottages rent for
13,000 dr and have modern bathrooms with
warm, solar-heated water. Call ☎ 0822-51
569 for reservations and information. The
rocky 5km road between Vlatos and Milia
is best suited to a jeep.

The road south from Vlatos passes
through chestnut trees which is the major
crop of the region. **Elos** is the region's
largest town and the centre of its chestnut
trade. In fact it stages a chestnut festival on
the third Sunday of October when sweets
made from chestnuts are eaten. The plane,
eucalyptus and chestnut trees around the
main square make Elos a cool and relaxing
stop. Behind the taverna on the main square
you'll see the remains of the aqueduct that
once brought water down from the mountains to power the mill. The only accommodation is *Taverna and Rent Rooms*
Kokolakis (☎ 0822-61 258) which has doubles for 5000 dr and scrumptious food in the
taverna.

Continuing south you'll pass the atmospheric village of **Pervolia** and then come to
Kefali with its 14th-century frescoed
church. The only place to stay and eat is
Taverna Polakis (☎ 0822-61 260) which
has rooms with views for 5000 dr. Taking
the coastal road from Kefali you will be
winding around cliffs with magnificent
coastal views unfolding after every bend in
the road.

Drive carefully because the road changes
abruptly from wide and paved to narrow
and unpaved. This is one of the most scenic
drives in Crete. You'll pass the little hamlet
of **Papadiana** driving along the gorge and
climbing into the mountains before coming
to **Amidagakofelli** which has beautiful
sweeping sea views from a bluff outside
town. About 50 minutes from Kefali you'll
come to **Kambos** a tiny village on the edge
of a gorge. It makes a good overnight stop
since you can hike down the gorge to the
beach.

For accommodation there is the new
Sunset Rooms (☎ 0822-41 128) with
freshly built rooms and a taverna and also
Hartzulakis Rent Rooms (☎ 0822-41 445).
Both have rooms for 4000/5000 dr. The

road then circles around the other side of the gorge cutting inland to **Sfinari**. The village stretches down to the beach which is marred by greenhouses on the northern end but has a gravelly cove on the southern end.

There are a lot of places for freelance camping. For accommodation try ***Rooms Nerida*** *(☎ 0822-41 105)* a two-storey building with lovely views. Rooms cost 5000/7000 dr. Opposite is ***Rooms for Rent Georgia*** *(☎ 0822-41 621)* which has rooms for the same price. Along the beach try the ***Taverna Dilina*** for good fresh fish. After Sfinari you'll get more coastal views before the road drops down to **Platanos**, a quiet tree-lined town of whitewashed houses and elderly residents.

You can stop for refreshments at the restaurant ***Ozaharias*** which serves local wine and fresh fish on an outdoor terrace under the trees. If you need a cash infusion there's an ATM on the right as you leave the town and across the street there's ***Rooms Castro*** *(☎ 0822-41 372)*.

Rethymno

Rethymno is Crete's most mountainous prefecture containing Mt Psiloritis in the east and bordered by the Lefka Ori in the west. Since most of the prefecture is composed of barren mountains and hills, only 537 sq km are cultivated out of the 1496 sq km in the prefecture. The rocky region is perfect for livestock which is the main occupation of Rethymno, although olives and olive oil are also produced.

The prefecture is divided into four provinces: Rethymno, with Rethymno town as its capital; Agios Vasileios, with its capital at Spili, the coastal resorts of Agia Galini and Plakias, as well as Moni Preveli; Amari with its capital at the town of the same name; and, Mylopotamos, with its capital at Perama, which includes the northern coastal resorts of Panormos and Bali, and the inland towns of Anogia and Zoniana, as well as the Ideon Cave.

RETHYMNO Ρέθυμνο

☎ 0831 • postcode 741 00 • pop 24,000
Rethymno (**Reth**-im-no) is Crete's third-largest town. The main attraction is the old Venetian-Ottoman quarter that occupies the headland beneath the massive Venetian *fortezza* (fortress).

The old quarter is a maze of narrow streets, graceful wood-balconied houses and ornate Venetian monuments, with minarets adding a touch of the Orient. Architectural similarities invite comparison with Hania, but Rethymno has a character of its own and boasts of being the most culturally aware city in Crete. The area occupies the headland north of Dimakopoulou, which runs from Plateia Vardinogianni on the west coast to Plateia Iroon on the east (becoming Gerakari en route).

A 16th-century fortress stands on Palekastro Hill, the site of the city's ancient acropolis. Many buildings once stood within its massive walls but now only a church and a mosque survive intact. The ramparts offer good views, while the site

HIGHLIGHTS

- Strolling the maze of narrow streets in Rethymno's Venetian quarter
- Exploring the unspoilt villages of the Amari Valley
- Cooling off by the water wheels of Agriroupolis
- Hitting the northern coastal resorts of Bali and Panormo

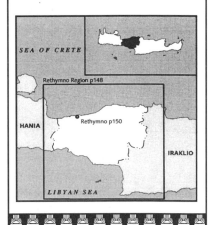

has lots of ruins to explore. Pride of place among the many vestiges of Venetian rule (from 1210-1645, when the Turks took over) goes to the Rimondi Fountain with its spouting lion heads, and the 16th-century Loggia. At the southern end of Ethnikis Antistaseos is the well-preserved Porto Guora (Great Gate), a remnant of the Venetian defensive wall.

History

The name Rethymno means 'stream of water' and evidence now found in the city's archaeological musuem indicates that the site of modern Rethymno has been occupied since Late Minoan times. In the 3rd

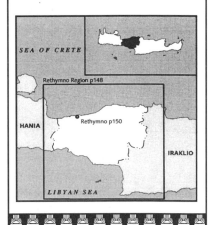

RETHYMNO

147

RETHYMNO

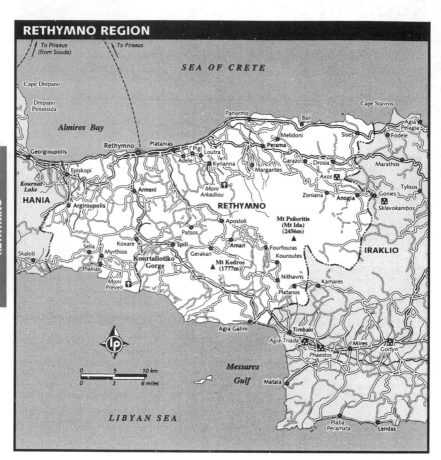

RETHYMNO REGION

and 4th centuries BC, 'Rithymna' emerged as an autonomous state of sufficient stature to issue its own coinage. Ancient Rithymna probably lay under Palekastro Hill but its remains have never been excavated, although Roman mosaics have been found underneath the modern town.

The town prospered once more under the Venetians, who ruled from 1210 until 1645, and made Rethymno into an important commercial centre based upon the export of wine and oil from the region. The town flourished artistically under the Venetians and became the seat of a Venetian Prefect.

The Venetians built a harbour, Mandraki, and began fortifying the town in the 16th century against the growing threat from the Turks. The best military architect of the era, Sammicheli designed thick outer walls of which only the Porto Guora survives. The walls did not stop the city from being sacked by the pirate Barbarossa in 1538.

The Venetians then built the massive fortress on the hill, that nevertheless was unable to withstand the Turkish assault of 1646, and collapsed after a 22 day siege. Rethymno was an important seat of government under the Turks but it was also a centre of resistance to Turkish rule. The Turks inflicted severe reprisals upon the town for its role in the uprising of 1821 but the resistance continued.

Turkish forces held the town until 1897, when it was taken by Russia as part of the occupation of Crete by the Great Powers. Rethymno became an artistic and intellectual centre after the arrival of a large number of refugees from Smyrna in 1923. The city has a campus of the University of Crete, attracting a student population that keeps the town alive outside the tourist season.

Orientation

The city's old quarter occupies the headland north of Dimakopoulou, which runs from Plateia Vardinogianni on the west coast to Plateia Iroon on the east (becoming Gerakari en route). Most of the good places to eat and sleep are to be found here, while banks and government services are just to the south on the edge of the new part of town.

The beach is on the eastern side of town, curving around from the delightful old Venetian harbour in the north. El Venizelou is the beachfront street. Curving parallel one block back is Arkadiou, the main commercial street. The old quarter's maze of twisting and curving streets make it an easy place to get lost, especially since street signs are a rarity.

Coming from the south, the best way to approach is through the Porto Guora onto Ethnikis Antistaseos. This busy shopping street leads to the Rimondi Fountain, the old quarter's best known landmark. The area around here is thick with cafes, restaurants and souvenir shops.

If you arrive in Rethymno by bus, you will be dropped at the new terminal at the western end of Igoumenou Gavril, about 600m west of the Porto Guora. To get into town, head east on Igoumenou Gavril back towards the town centre. A left turn at the far end of the Municipal Park will leave you facing the Porto Guora. If you arrive by ferry, the old quarter is as far away as the end of the quay. If you are driving into town

from the expressway, your final approach to the city centre is along Dimitrikaki from the south. The parking lot opposite the park is a convenient spot to stop and check things out.

Information

Tourist Offices Rethymno's municipal tourist office (☎ 29 148) is on the beach side of El Venizelou, opposite the junction with Kalergi. It's open 8 am to 8 pm Monday to Friday in summer and 8 am to 3 pm in winter. The tourist police (☎ 28 156) occupy the same building and are open from 7 am to 10 pm every day.

Money Banks are concentrated around the junction of Dimokratias and Pavlou Kountouriotou. The National Bank is on Dimokratias, on the far side of the square opposite the town hall. The Credit Bank (Pavlou Kountouriotou 29) and the National Mortgage Bank, next to the town hall, have 24-hour automatic exchange machines.

Post & Communications The OTE is at Kountouriotou 28, and the post office is a block south at Moatsou 21. In summer there is a mobile post office about 200m southeast of the tourist office on El Venizelou. You can check your email at Net c@fe (☎ 55 133) Venieri 2, which is open 10 am to 10 pm daily. Take Papandreou from El Venizelou east of Plateia Iroon and you'll find it behind the Elina Hotel.

Travel Agencies Ellotia Tours (☎ 24 533, fax 51 062, email elotia@ret.fourthnet.gr), at Arkadiou 161, is a helpful office that handles boat and plane tickets, changes money, rents cars and motor cycles and books excursions. It's open 9 am to 9 pm daily March to November.

Bookshops The International Press Bookshop (El Venizelou 81) stocks English novels, travel guides and history books. The bookshop at Souliou 43 stocks novels in English, books about Greece, tapes of Greek music and has a small second-hand section.

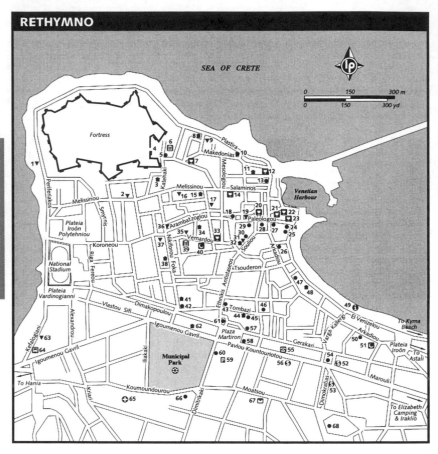

RETHYMNO

SEA OF CRETE

Fortress

Venetian
Harbour

Plateia
Iroön
Polytehniou

National
Stadium

Plateia
Vardinogianni

Municipal
Park

To Hania

To Kyma
Beach

To
Astali

To Elizabeth
Camping
& Iraklio

Laundry The Laundry Mat self-service laundry at Tombazi 45, next door to the youth hostel, charges 2500 dr for a wash and dry.

Things to See
The **Archaeological Museum** (☎ 29 975) is opposite the entrance to the fortress and was once a prison. The exhibits are well labelled in English and contain Neolithic tools, Minoan pottery excavated from nearby tombs, Mycenaean figurines and a 1st-century-AD relief of Aphrodite, as well as an important coin collection.

There are also some excellent examples of blown glass from the classical period. Various displays outline the history of archaeological excavations in the region. The museum is open 8.30 am to 3 pm Tuesday to Sunday. Admission is 500 dr.

Rethymno's excellent **Historical & Folk Art Museum** (Vernardou 30) gives an excellent overview of the region's rural lifestyle with a collection of old clothes, baskets, weavings and farm tools whose purpose would remain obscure if the exhibits were not so well labelled. It's open 10 am to 2 pm Monday to Saturday. Admission is 500 dr.

RETHYMNO

PLACES TO STAY
3   Pension Anna Rooms
8   Lefteris Papadakis
10   Hotel Ideon
11   Rooms to Rent Barbara
     Dolomaki
15   Hotel Fortezza
32   Olga's Pension
34   Hotel Veneto
38   Rent Rooms Garden
41   Rooms for Rent Anda
44   Youth Hostel
48   Rent Rooms Sea View
62   Park Hotel

PLACES TO EAT
1   Sunset Restaurant & Bar
2   Taverna Castro
9   Famagousta
16   Taverna Pontios
17   Avli
19   Taverna Kyria Maria
31   Stella's Kitchen
35   Old Town Taverna
36   O Psaras

37   Gounakis Restaurant & Bar
63   Fanari

OTHER
4   Entrance to Fortress
5   Theodonakis
6   Archaeological Museum
7   Notes
12   Club 252
13   Cretan Lines
14   Baja Club
18   Rimondi Fountain
20   Nitro
21   Metropolis/NYC
22   Fortezza Disco
23   Trapeza
24   International Press Bookshop
25   Paradise Dive Centre
26   Giorgios Galerakis
27   Xenia
28   Loggia
29   Motor Stavros
30   Bookshop
33   Figaro
39   Historical & Folk Art Museum

40   Neradjes Mosque
42   Katerina Karaoglani
43   Melissa
45   Laundry Mat
46   Happy Walker
47   Ellotia Travel
49   Municipal Tourist Office;
     Tourist Police
50   Xenia
51   Kara Musa Pasha Mosque
52   National Mortgage Bank
53   National Bank of Greece
54   Town Hall
55   OTE
56   Credit Bank
57   Supermarket
58   Allas Travel
59   Car Park
60   Thursday Market
61   Porto Guora
64   Bus Station
65   Hospital
66   Olympic Airways
67   Post Office
68   EOS

The main gate of Rethymno's 16th-century **Fortress** is opposite the Archaeological Museum on the eastern side of the fortress but there once were two other gates on the western and northern sides for the delivery of supplies and ammunition.

Barracks, the arsenal and storerooms were on the southern side, gunpowder was stored on the northern side and the centre once contained a cathedral which the Turks converted into a mosque. The ramparts offer good views of the town and the coast. The fortress is open 8 am to 8 pm every day. Admission is 800 dr.

Pride of place among the many vestiges of Venetian rule in the old quarter goes to the **Rimondi Fountain** with its spouting lion heads and Corinthian capitals, built first in 1588 and rebuilt in 1626 by Rimondi. Rethymno's other landmark is the 16th-century **Loggia**, once a meeting house for Venetian nobility.

At the southern end of Ethnikis Antistaseos is the well-preserved **Porto Guora** (Great Gate), a remnant of the defensive wall that was once topped with the symbol of Venice: the Lion of St Mark, now in the Archaeological Museum. Around the Porto Guora lies a network of old streets built by the Venetians and rebuilt by the Turks.

Other Turkish legacies in the old quarter include the **Kara Musa Pasha Mosque** which has a vaulted fountain and the **Neradjes Mosque**, which was converted from a Franciscan church in 1657. The minaret was built in 1890.

Trekking
The Happy Walker (☎ 52 920), Tombazi 56, runs a varied program of mountain walks in the region. Most walks start in the early morning when a minibus picks you up at the hotel and takes you to the beginning of your walk. The walks are usually about 14km along farm roads and donkey paths.

Favourite spots include the Bone Rapria Castle with a view of the Lefka Ori, Pikris, wild flowers around Kare, the ancient city of Eleftherna, the pottery village of Margarites and Moni Elias. Prices start at 6500 dr per person. The walks finish with lunch in a local taverna at a price of 2500 dr including wine and dessert.

Rethymno's chapter of the EOS (☎ 57 766) is at Dimokratias 12, and can give good advice on mountain climbing in the region.

Diving

The Paradise Dive Centre (☎ 53 258), El Venizelou 76, has activities and a PADI course for all grades of divers. There is also the Dolphin Diving Centre (☎ 71 703) at the Hotel Rethymno Mare that offers the same services.

Organised Tours

Lying in the centre of the Cretan coast, Rethymno is well placed for boat excursions. Along the harbour front there are several companies that offer boat trips. The most conspicuous is The Pirate (☎ 51 643, fax 24 729) which offers day-long swimming and fishing trips along the rocky indented coast on an old sailing schooner for 8900 dr (4450 dr for children under 12), including lunch. You could also try Zourbakis Cruises (☎ 57 032) on a modern sailboat, which offers five hours of sailing for 6000 dr. Dolphin Cruises (☎ 57 666) offers a day trip to Georgioupolis for 6000 dr (4000 dr children under 12).

Special Events

The city's main cultural event is the annual Renaissance Festival that runs during July and August, featuring dance, drama and films as well as art exhibitions. Some years there's a Wine Festival in mid-July held in the municipal park, that offers a good opportunity to sample local wine and cuisine for about 1000 dr. Ask the tourist office for details.

Places to Stay

Rethymno's accommodation scene has something for everyone. Because it's a dynamic, commercial centre, many hotels are open all year. Those who want to lounge around a resort will head east from the town centre to find an endless string of hotels. Within the town centre, there's an ample supply of restored mansions and friendly pensions to immerse yourself in the town's fascinating history. There are buses every half hour from Rethymno centre.

Camping The nearest camp site is *Elizabeth Camping* (☎ 28 694), near Myssiria beach 3km east of Rethymno. The site has a taverna, snack bar and minimarket. An Iraklio-bound bus can drop you at the site.

Hostels The *youth hostel (☎ 22 848, Tombazi 41)* is friendly and well run with beds for 1500 dr and free hot showers. Breakfast is available and there's a bar in the evening. There is no curfew and the place is open all year.

Domatia *Rooms for Rent Anda (☎ 23 479, Nikiforou Foka 33)* is a great choice if you have kids because it's just a short walk from Rethymno's municipal park. The prettily furnished rooms have private bathrooms but no other amenities, although the owner will gladly help you with anything you need. Singles/doubles are 9000/11,000 dr.

The friendly *Olga's Pension (☎ 28 665, Souliou 57)* is tucked away on the touristy but colourful Souliou. A network of terraces, all bursting with greenery, connects a wide range of rooms, some with bath and sea views and others without. Prices for singles/studios are 6000/10,000 dr.

Rooms to Rent Barbara Dolomaki (☎ 24 581, Thambergi 14) is a rambling pension in the middle of Rethymno's nightlife section which has comfortable rooms with and without kitchenettes. The rooms with kitchenettes are better value because they are larger and have recently been refurbished. Prices for doubles/studios are 10,000/11,000 dr.

Tranquillity is not the selling point at *Lefteris Papadakis Rooms (☎ 23 803, Plastira 26)*, but anyone who wants to be in the centre of Rethymno's nightlife has come to the right place. All rooms are pleasant but the front rooms have stunning sea views although they can be noisy at night. Rooms with private bathroom are 6500/7500 dr.

On a quiet street in Rethymno's old town, **Rent Rooms Garden** (☎ 28 586, Nikiforou Foka 82) is an impeccably maintained 600-year-old Venetian house retaining many of its original features including impressive doors and a gorgeous grape-arboured garden. The rooms are simple, comfortable and tasteful. Prices for doubles/triples are 10,000/15,000 dr with private bathroom.

Rent Rooms Sea View (☎ 51 981, fax 51 062, email elotia@ret.forthnet.gr, El Venizelou 45) is a delightful pension which has only six studio/apartments but each one is fresh and cheerful. The best part is that you're right across the street from the beach; the worst part is that the front rooms can be noisy at night. Prices are 5000/7000 dr with private bathroom.

Hotels – Mid-Range The *Hotel Fortezza* (☎ 55 551/552 or 23 828, fax 54 073, Melissinou 16) is an isle of calm in a busy neighbourhood. Housed in a refurbished old building in the heart of the old town, the tastefully furnished rooms have TVs, telephones and air-con on demand. After a day of roaming through Rethymno, it's pleasant to relax by the hotel swimming pool. Prices for singles/doubles/triples are 15,000/19,000/23,000 dr including buffet breakfast.

The only missing ingredient at **Park Hotel** (☎ 29 958, Igoumenou Gavril 9) is an elevator to take you to rooms that are spread over two floors. The rooms are comfortable with air-con, TV, telephone, sound-proofing and balconies offering a view of the municipal park. Prices are 11,000/14,000 dr which include breakfast.

To spare you the long walk to Rethymno's beach, the modern *Hotel Ideon* (☎ 28 667, fax 28 670, Plastira 10) provides you with a swimming pool. Other amenities in this polished establishment include rooms with air-con, safes, radios, telephones and balconies. Singles/doubles are 14,000/16,000 dr including buffet breakfast. The oldest part of *Hotel Veneto* (☎ 56 634, fax 56 635, email veneto@ interkriti.gr, Epimenidou 4) dates from the 15th century and it has preserved many of its traditional features without sacrificing modern comforts. The eye-catching rooms of polished wood floors and ceilings also have air-con, TVs, telephones, safes and kitchenettes. Rooms are 16,000/20,000 dr.

The *Astali* (☎ 24 721, fax 30 8310, Papandreou 1) is a new hotel east of Plateia Iroon and hasn't got around to installing TVs and telephones in the rooms but it hardly matters when the rooms are as spiffy and as modern as they are. The bathrooms are state of the art and there's air-con. Prices for rooms are 14,500/16,000 dr including buffet breakfast.

Hotels – Top End The *Kyma Beach* (☎ 55 503, fax 27 746, S. Venizelou 1) is a favourite with package tours largely because of its excellent location just across from the beach and within walking distance of the town centre. Most rooms have air-con, TV and telephone and there's a small pool. Prices include buffet breakfast.

Like all of Rethymno's luxury establishments, **Grecotel Creta Palace** (☎ 55 181, fax 54 085) is in Missira, 4km east of Rethymno, on the beach. There are two outdoor swimming pools and one indoor, a children's playground, tennis courts, a fitness club and all water sports facilities. The rooms have air-con on demand, TVs with international stations and telephones. Prices are 22,000/32,000 dr for a room.

Grecotel Porto Rethymno (☎ 50 432, fax 27 825, S.Venizelou 52A) is an A-class hotel on the beach about 1km east of the town centre and has a swimming pool and air-conditioned rooms for 25,000/32,000 dr.

The **Grecotel Rithymna Beach** (☎ 71 002, fax 71 668) is farther out of town but has a huge outdoor as well as an indoor pool, tennis courts, water sports centre and fitness room. Air-conditioned rooms are 25,000/35,000 dr.

Places to Eat

The waterfront along El Venizelou is lined with amazingly similar tourist restaurants staffed by fast-talking waiters desperately cajoling passers-by into eating at their establishments. The situation is much the same around the Venetian Harbour, except that the setting is better and the prices higher.

RETHYMNO

RETHYMNO

A Cretan Feast

Artichoke Omelette (4 persons)
Dice one large onion. Cut eight artichokes into quarters and fry them with the onions over low heat for five minutes with ¼ litre (one cup) of oil. Add two finely chopped tomatoes, salt and pepper. Gradually add ¼ litre (one cup) of water and boil for 15 minutes. Beat four eggs and pour over the vegetable mixture. Cook for two minutes over low heat.

Okra with Red Snapper (6 persons)
Fry 1 kilo (2.2 lbs) of okra and two large chopped onions in ¼ litre (one cup) of oil. Fry until soft and add salt and pepper to taste. Add three finely chopped tomatoes and cook for 15 minutes. Place in a large pan and spread 1 kilo (2.2 lbs) of red snapper on top of it. Put the pan in a pre-heated oven (180°C) and bake for 20 minutes.

Baked Halva (6 persons)
Sift ½ cup of flour with two teaspoons of baking powder and a pinch of salt. Add two cups of semolina and a cup of finely chopped nuts. Cream ¾ of a cup of butter or magarine with a cup of sugar and add three beaten eggs and grated lemon peel. Combine the mixtures well, then pour into a greased, 25cm (10-inch) square tin. Bake in a medium oven until golden. Boil three cups of water with three cups of sugar, add four cloves and ½ stick of cinnamon, then pour over the rest of the dessert. Leave it to stand until the cinnamon and clove mixture has been absorbed and serve without cream, warm or cold.

The most authentic places are in the web of side streets inland from the harbour. *Old Town Taverna (Vernardou 31)* is a good spot to come after an exploration of the Historical & Folk Art Museum right across the street. The traditional Cretan food is well prepared and there's a good value set-price menu with wine. It's open noon to 3 pm and 7 pm to midnight daily. *Taverna Pontios (Melissinou 34)* proves once again that some of the best Cretan food comes from places that look like upgraded street stalls. A convivial group of locals comes here for the delicious cheese-stuffed calamari among other dishes. It's open noon to 2.30 pm and 6 pm to midnight daily.

Gounakis Restaurant & Bar (Koroneou 6) is a fun place that is worth visiting for its food as much as for its music. The plain interior contains a small stage in back that attracts some of Rethymno's finest folk musicians and the cooking is delicious. It's open 8 pm to 1 am daily.

There's no better place in town than *Avli (Xanthoudidou 22)* for a romantic evening out. The food is superb and this former

Venetian villa has an idyllic enclosed garden for dining alfresco. It's open noon to 2.30 pm and 6 pm to midnight daily. *Famagousta (Plastira 6)* is a local favourite and has a large menu of Greek and international dishes but the best choices are the Cypriot specialties. Try the delicious lamb cooked in a clay oven or the meatballs with yogurt and pitta bread. It's open noon to 3 pm and 7 pm to midnight daily.

Let the tourists eat elbow to elbow on Venizelou street, *Sunset (☎ 23 943, Periferiakos)* is on the other side of the Venetian fortress where all is calm. You can feast on decent Cretan dishes while seated right along the water. Come at sunset, of course. It's open noon to midnight daily. The fish at *O Psaras (Arambatzoglou 69)*, an unpretentious taverna, is always fresh which is what makes O Psaras popular with locals and visitors alike. The tables are outside on an attractive square next to a church. It's open noon to midnight daily.

Stella's Kitchen (Souliou 55), a tiny, homey spot on one of Rethymno's oldest streets, serves up tasty snacks and a few

RETHYMNO

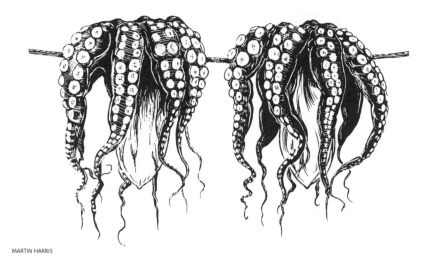

MARTIN HARRIS

Octopus drying: seafood features prominently on Cretan menus.

meals. It's a good bet for breakfast as well. There's only a couple of tables however, so you may have to take the food away. It's open 8 am to midnight daily. For authentic atmosphere try **Taverna Kyria Maria** *(Fotaki 22).* Wander inland down the little side streets to Kyria Maria, behind the Rimondi Fountain. This cosy, traditional taverna has outdoor seating under a leafy trellis with twittering birds. All meals end with a complimentary dessert and shot of raki. It's open 8 am to 1 am daily.

A little off the beaten track, **Taverna Castro** *(Melissinou 17)* often has space when others are full. The enclosed garden-terrace provides a soothing setting for decent Cretan dishes. It's open noon to midnight daily. Tourists rarely wander over this far west, but **Fanari** *(Kefalogiani 15)* is as typical a taverna as you're likely to find in Rethymno. The fish is fresh, carnivores will love the grilled steak and the home-made wine is surprisingly good. It's open noon to midnight daily.

When Rethymno couples and their kids, grandparents, cousins, aunts and nephews want to make a night of it, they'll head to the vast **Taverna Zisis** *(Mahis Kritis 17,* *Missiria),* 2km out of town on the old road to Iraklio. Vegetarians beware. Nearly all the dishes involve meat whether broiled, grilled, stewed or fried. It's open noon to 3 pm and 6 pm to midnight daily.

When locals from Rethymno are looking for a special meal, they'll pile into cars and drive to Atsipopoulo.

On the edge of this village you'll find **Kombos** *(Atsipopoulo)* a friendly taverna, which specialises in meaty meals. The lamb is good and, if you're up to it, try the *splinogardouba* (spleen). To get there, head west out of town and turn south on the road to Episkopi. You'll see the restaurant before entering the village. It's open 7 pm to 1 am daily.

Entertainment

The bar/cafes along El Venizelou fill up on summer evenings with pink-skinned tourists, dazed from the burning sun and nursing tropical drinks. The ambience is comfortable but soporific. Rethymno's livelier nightlife is concentrated in the streets around the Venetian harbour where a cluster of bars, clubs and discos create a carnivalesque atmosphere.

Did You Know?

- Greece has the lowest rate of alcoholism in Europe

- The miniature chapels you see by the side of the road are called 'ikonostassia' and are placed in spots where an accident happened

- Most Cretan names end in 'akis' because it is a diminutive (such as – ette) given by the Turks as a sign of disrespect to the people they ruled

- 100 years ago there were only 8km of paved roads on the entire island

- The Cretan version of the Spanish 'siesta' is called the 'ipnakos' and lasts from about 1.30 to 5 pm

- Sheep are considered a higher form of animal life than goats which is why only men are allowed to milk sheep while milking goats is left to women

There's not a lot of variety in the nightlife scene; most places are literally grabbing people off the street and cramming them onto the dance floor for a dose of techno and house but there are a few islands of calm amidst the uproar.

If you love drinking cheap wine and listening to live Cretan folk music, **Gounakis Restaurant & Bar** (Koroneou 6) is the place to go. There's music and impromptu dancing most nights. It's open 8 pm to 1 am nightly. In the heart of Rethymno's nightlife district, **Nitro Club** (Nearhou 26) is a crowded, friendly dance club with music programming that leans toward techno early in the evening and Greek music later on. It's open 10 pm to dawn nightly.

Fortezza Disco (Nearhou) is the town's showpiece disco. It's big and flashy with three bars, a laser show and a well-groomed international crowd that starts drifting in around midnight. It's open 11 pm to dawn nightly. Formerly a cinema, now a huge dance club, **Baja** (Salaminos) has hired an attractive multilingual staff in an effort to capture the tourist market. The pirate ship decor is good

hokey fun and the sounds are contemporary international. It's open 11 pm to dawn nightly.

Trapeza (Petihaki 2) is having its moment in the sun as Rethymno's trendiest hang-out. The crowd of young professionals that fills the club nightly may move on soon but right now this is where the actions is. It's open nightly from 9 pm to dawn. The DJ spins hits from the 60s at **Metropolis NYC** (Nearhou) for a crowd that comes to tank up on cocktails before hitting the discos. It's open 7 pm to dawn nightly. It may be getting passe, but **Delfini** on El Venizelou is still the only open-air disco in town and has an unbeatable location on the beach.

During the day, **Club 252** (Thambergi 1) is a great place to linger over a coffee. At night Rethymno's twenty-somethings polish themselves up to meet friends and soon-to-be-friends under the stars. It's open 10 am to 1 am daily.

Notes (Makedonias 1), a quiet bar/cafe with a polished wood bar, was opened by a musician who has an excellent selection of Greek music. It's a good place to escape the crowds along El Venizelou. It's open 10 am to midnight daily.

Housed in an ingeniously restored old building, **Figaro** (Venardou 21) is an atmospheric bar which attracts a subdued crowd for drinks, snacks and rock music. It's open noon to midnight daily.

Shopping

The shopping section of Rethymno is relatively compact and contains a wide assortment of stores selling everything from souvenirs to jewelled watches. The waterfront promenade of El Venizelou has plenty of souvenir shops sandwiched between the restaurants but you'll find higher quality merchandise, including jewellery shops, on Arkadiou.

Souliou is a narrow pedestrian street crammed with stores of every kind and makes a wonderful stroll. Don't miss the Thursday market on Dimitrikakis for fresh produce, clothing and odds and ends. The best thing about Giorgios Galerakis (Arkadiou 201) among the many on Arkadiou, is that the ornaments are made on site and you can visit the workshop.

A Cretan summer may make it difficult to think about leather outerwear but the suede and leather at Xenia (Arkadiou 32 and 265) is buttery soft and made into elegant ladies' suits, jackets and coats. It's open 8.30 am to 8 pm Monday to Saturday. Zaharias Theodorakis' workshop (Katehaki 4) turns out onyx bowls and goblets on the lathe at his small workshop. It's open 10 am to 8 pm Monday to Saturday.

Friendly Katerina Karaoglani (Katehaki 4) makes her pottery in the store. You'll find the standard blue-glazed Cretan ceramics of a better quality than the tourist shops deliver. It's open 10 am to 11 pm Monday to Saturday. In addition to handmade icons, Melissa (Ethnikis Antistaseos 23) sells candles, incense, oil lamps and other odorous substances. It's open 9 am to 8 pm Monday to Saturday.

Ilias Spontidakis' bookstore (Souliou 43) is jammed with novels in several languages as well as maps, guidebooks and cassettes of Cretan and Greek music. There's also a small second-hand section. It's open Monday to Saturday 10 am to 10 pm. In addition to foreign newspapers, you'll find a good selection of novels in English, travel guides and history books at the International Press Bookshop (El Venizelou 81). It's open Monday to Saturday 9 am to 10 pm.

Getting There & Away

Bus There are numerous services to both Hania (one hour, 1350 dr) and Iraklio (1½ hours, 1550 dr). There's a bus in each direction every half-hour in summer, every hour in winter. In summer there are also four buses a day to Plakias (one hour, 950 dr); four to Agia Galini (1½ hours, 1300 dr); three to Moni Arkadiou (30 minutes, 500 dr); one to Omalos (two hours, 2750 dr) and two to Preveli (950 dr). The morning bus to Plakias continues to Hora Sfakion (two hours, 1450 dr). Services to these destinations are greatly reduced in winter.

Ferry Cretan Lines (☎ 29 221) operates a daily ferry between Rethymno and Piraeus leaving Rethymno and Piraeus at 7.30 pm. Tickets are available from the company's office at Arkadiou 250. Deck-class tickets cost 7000 dr and a berth in a tourist-class cabin is 10,300 dr.

Getting Around

Car, Motorcycle & Bicycle Most of the car hire firms are grouped around Plateia Iroon.

Motor Stavros (☎ 22 858), at Paleologou 14, has a wide range of motorcycles and also rents bicycles.

Cire Perdue

The *cire perdue* (lost wax) method of casting bronze statues was pioneered by the Cretans in preclassical times. A wax original was made, with iron ducts placed at strategic points. These ducts were sufficiently long to project out of the clay mould which was then put around the wax. A pouring funnel was fitted into the clay mould at a suitable place. The cast was then heated so that the wax melted and ran out through the ducts. When all the wax had escaped, the ducts were removed and the holes were plugged. Molten bronze was then poured through the funnel. When the bronze had cooled the mould was carefully chipped away.

Advantages of the cire perdue method of casting include the high degree of detail that can be achieved, and the absence of joining lines on the bronze cast. The process is still used today for high-precision work.

The cire perdue method may have given rise to various legends including one which tells of Talos, a man made of bronze, who had one vein running from his neck to his leg. He was a servant of King Minos, and it was his duty was to help defend Crete. When the Argonauts arrived, he tried to repel them, but Medea, who had accompanied them, unplugged a pin in his ankle. He was drained of his colourless life-blood and died.

EPISKOPI

Episkopi, 23km south-west of Rethymno, is a pretty, traditional town of winding lanes and tiny houses, overlooking the valley. One main road runs through town with a smaller road running parallel to the main road. There is no OTE but there is a post office past the BP station on the right.

As a market centre for the region's produce Episkopi is busy and prosperous although most men and women are still clad in traditional black Cretan garb.

The town is a good place to experience Cretan life and attracts few tourists although there are a few domatia. Try *Loytraki* (π *61 677*) or *Rent Rooms Irene* (π *61 325*), both of which have rooms for 5000/6000 dr. From Monday to Friday there are two buses daily from Rethymno to Episkopi (30 minutes, 375 dr).

ARGIROUPOLIS
π 0831

When the summer heat becomes too intense even for the beach, you'll find a natural, outdoor air-conditioning system at Argiroupolis, 25km south-west from Rethymno. The lower village of this two-village town is a watery oasis formed by mountain springs that keep the temperature markedly cooler than the coast. Running through aqueducts, washing down walls, seeping from stones and pouring from spigots, the gushing springwater supplies the entire city of Rethymno.

Towering chestnut and plane trees and luxuriant vegetation create a shady, restful spot, perfect for lingering over lunch in one of the local tavernas.

Argiroupolis, is built on the remains of the ancient city of Lappa so there's also plenty to explore. The villagers maintain a traditional lifestyle, largely undisturbed by tourism but are proud of their heritage and eager to show you around.

History

Although legend has it that Agamemnon built Lappa, most likely it was founded by the Dorians. The inland city was safe from piracy and was bordered by a fertile valley in the north and protective mountains to the south and west. The city flourished but became a centre of resistance to rule from Knossos in the 3rd century BC along with the town of Lyttos.

When Lyttos was destroyed by Knossos in 220 BC its vanquished inhabitants took refuge in Lappa, which together with Polyrrinia succeeded in securing peace in western Crete with the help of Philip V of Macedonia. Lappa's gift for being on the right side of political struggles continued when it supported Octavian in his winning battle with Mark Antony. As Emperor, Octavian rewarded Lappa by erecting elaborate public buildings in the town. He built a reservoir in 27 BC that is still in use today and excavations have revealed a Roman floor mosaic, Roman baths and Roman tombs.

The city prospered until its destruction by the 9th-century Saracens and then enjoyed a second life under the Venetians who built villas and churches in this cool mountain hideaway. Archaeologists are continuing to excavate in the area and are turning up remnants of Lappa's history from its origins to its eventual destruction by the Saracens.

Most of the houses in the upper village date from the last years of Turkish domination but you'll find odds and ends from Roman to Byzantine rule.

Orientation & Information

The town is divided into two parts. The main square and old town is in the upper part, which is connected to the water wheels of lower Argiroupolis by a good paved road.

It's a steep 2km walk between the lower half and the upper half and many of the sights are scattered in and around the two sections. It's easier to explore Argiroupolis if you have your own wheels.

There is no post office, OTE, tourist office or travel agency but the Lappa Avocado Shop just off the main square is a good source of information on the town and will provide visitors with maps. You can change money here and pick up a supply of their excellent avocado-based creams and soaps.

Things to See
Upper Town The main square is marked by the 17th-century Venetian **Church of Agios Ioannis.** Passing through the stone archway opposite the church with the Lappa Avocado Shop on the left you will enter the old town where Roman remnants are scattered amid the Venetian and Turkish structures.

The main stone street will take you past a **Roman gate** on the left with the inscription 'Omnia Mundi Fumus et Umbra' (All Things in This World are Smoke and Shadow). In a few metres a narrow street to the right leads down to a 3rd-century-BC **marble water reservoir** with seven interior arches.

Returning to the main road and continuing in the same direction past grapevines and apricot trees you will see on the left a **Roman mosaic floor,** dating from the 1st century BC. With 7000 pieces in six colours, the well-preserved floor is a good example of design from the Geometric Period. The same road takes you back to the stone-arched entrance.

Lower Town The centre of the lower town is formed by a group of tavernas clustered around the tumbling springs. A path from the bottom of the town leads you to a **Roman bath** and a water-driven **wooden fulling machine** which was used to thicken cloth by moistening and beating it. Nearby is **St Mary's Church,** built on a temple to Neptune. Another path from the village centre takes you to the **St Nikolas Church** inside a cave, and **waterfalls.**

Other Sights North of the upper town a footpath on the right takes you about 50m to a **Roman Necropolis** with hundreds of tombs cut into the cliffs. The shady path leads on to a **plane tree** that is supposed to be 2000 years old and is so large that the path runs right through it. There are benches around the tree and mountain springs.

Places to Stay & Eat
Rooms Argiroupolis (☎ *81 281*) is about 500m uphill from the lower town, and has rooms for 5000/6000 dr with scenic views over the valley. In the upper town there is *Morpheus* (☎ *81 015*) and *Arhea Lappa* (☎ *81 004*), both of which have rooms for 5000/6000 dr. *Mikedakis* (☎ *81 225*) is a charming place half-buried behind trees and flowering bushes that offers spectacular views of the area from its balconies. Rooms are 5000/6000 dr. In the lower town, *Prasini Limni* is on the edge of a duck pond and *Agia Dinamis* is surrounded by waterfalls and fountains. Both offer good value meals.

Getting There & Away
From Monday to Friday there are two buses daily from Rethymno (40 min, 460 dr).

Amari Province

The Amari Province is the heartland of Crete and the repository of its culture. The province's capital at Amari is surrounded by some of the most tranquil and untouched villages on the island while the hills and valleys of Mt Psiloritis create breathtaking views.

From the legend of Zeus to the horrifying bloodbath at Moni Arkadiou, Crete's tormented history took shape under the shadow of the looming Mt Psiloritis now crisscrossed by shepherds' trails and goat tracks. You will need your own wheels to do justice to the province which is poorly served by public transportation, although there are three buses a day from Rethymno to Amari.

AMARI VALLEY Κοιλάδα Αμαρίου
If you have your own transport you may like to explore the enchanting Amari Valley, south-east of Rethymno, between Mts Psiloritis and Kedros. This region harbours around 40 well-watered, unspoilt villages set amid olive groves and almond and cherry trees. The valley begins at the picturesque village of **Apostoli,** 25km south-east of Rethymno. The turn-off for Apostoli is on the coast 3km east of Rethymno. The road forks at Apostoli and then joins up again 38km to

the south, making it possible to do a circular drive around the valley; alternatively, you can continue south to Agia Galini.

The road to **Apostoli** follows a wild and deserted gorge bordered by high cliffs and is spectacularly scenic. Apostoli makes a good rest stop; there's a taverna on the right side of the road that serves good chewy bread and has beautiful views over the valley, but there's no other place in Apostoli to pick up supplies. Taking the left fork from Apostoli you'll come to the village of **Thronos** with its Church of the Panagia constructed on the remains of an early Christian basilica. The 14th-century frescoes are faded but extraordinarily well-executed; the oldest are in the choir stalls. Ask at the kafenion next door for the key.

Returning to Apostoli continue along the main road south. The next town is **Agia Fotini** which is a larger town with a supermarket. The road twists and turns along the scenic valley before it comes to **Meronas**, a little village with big plane trees, and a fine Church of the Panagia. The oldest part of the church is the knave which was built in the 14th century. The southern side of the church with its elegant portal was added under the Venetians. The highlight of the church is the beautifully restored 14th-century frescoes.

The road continues south to **Gerakari**, known for its delicious cherries. Stop at Despina's Shop (☎ 0833-51 013) in the centre of town, which sells cherry brandy, cherries in syrup, and local cheeses. Her shop is a popular hang-out for the Gerakari ladies in the afternoon and she has rooms over the shop that she rents for 6000 dr. From Gerakari a new road continues on to Spili which affords sweeping views of the valley.

MT PSILORITIS

The imposing Mt Psiloritis, also known as Mt Ida, dominates the Amari Province and at 2456m is the highest mountain in Crete. The base of Mt Psiloritis is the Nida Plateau. The road leading up to the plateau

Cretan Superstitions

Dogs are treated so poorly in Crete that Cretans will name their dog after an enemy in order to have the pleasure of yelling at it. The contempt for dogs may stem from the belief that the hated Turks are reincarnated as dogs.

Saints Eyes are often missing from the frescoes in old churches, possibly because Cretans believed that if you took the plaster from a saint's eye and fed it to the object of an amorous passion, your love would be returned.

The fall of Constantinople to the Turks occurred on Tuesday 29 May 1453. Many Cretans still believe in **Unlucky Tuesday** and avoid transacting important business on that day.

Donkeys are treated even worse than dogs. Cretans have a variety of beliefs about donkeys – that they carry the souls of people sentenced to purgatory or that they may even house the devil himself. Donkeys possessed by the devil are called *Anaskelos* and can transform themselves into monstrous half-humans.

Baggy Trousers are worn as part of the traditional Cretan male dress. It is alleged that the trousers are baggy because of the Orthodox belief that the Saviour will literally be "born of man" that is, anally, and the trousers will facilitate this miraculous birth.

South Winds are said to be unlucky because Knossos was destroyed when a south wind was blowing.

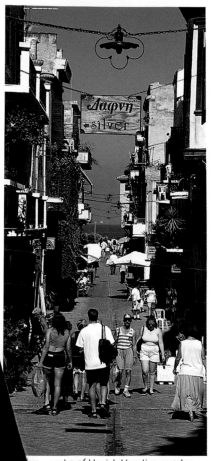

ou – centre of Hania's Venetian quarter.

Blue shutters colour a narrow Hania street.

the main architectural feature
enetian buildings.

DIANA MAYFIELD

Tourists are able to pick up a vast array of craft
in Hania's Venetian Quarter.

The almost deserted Cape Tigani and the rocky islet of Gramvousa in Crete's north-west provide a welcome respite from the crowded beaches of the island's northern coast.

The small port town of Hora Sfakion is a welcome sight for the hordes of walkers who [...] Samaria Gorge.

Ange[...]

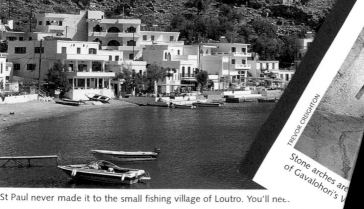

Stone arches are [...] of Gavalohori's V[...]

St Paul never made it to the small fishing village of Loutro. You'll nee[...]

Fishing boats moored in Rethymno harbour.

Night life – fishing boats provide a romantic backdrop for those eating along Rethymno's waterfront.

'Is that Zorba?' Getting about in the streets of Rethymno.

Locals playing backgammon outside a cafe in Rethymno.

Welcoming doorways abound in Rethymno's maze of narrow streets.

Harbour view of Agia Galini – a popular tourist base for Phaestos and Agia Triada.

is carpeted with wild flowers in the early spring and you'll notice many *mitata* (round stone shepherd's huts) along the way. Although traditionally used to make Crete's wonderful yogurts and cheeses, many of these huts have been abandoned to dogs and chickens. The mountain's historically important feature is the **Ideon Cave** the place where, according to legend, the god Zeus was reared. The cave may have been inhabited in the early Neolithic period but is now being excavated and is closed to visitors.

There are several routes to Timios Stavros, the summit of Mt Psiloritis and to the Ideon Cave but you need to be an experienced climber. The easiest route is to take the paved road south from Anogia to the point where it becomes a dirt track and then follow the signs. An alternative route from the west begins at the small village of **Kouroutes**, 5km south of Fourfouras on the edge of the Amari Valley. It's a 10km walk from Kouroutes to the EOS refuge on Mt Psiloritis. For information contact the Rethymno EOS (see the Rethymno section).

MONI ARKADIOU Μονη Αρκαδίου

This 16th-century monastery stands in attractive hill country 23km south-east of Rethymno. The most impressive building of the complex is the Venetian baroque church. Its striking facade has eight slender Corinthian columns and is topped by an ornate triple-belled tower. This facade features on the 100 dr note.

In November 1866 the Turks sent massive forces to quell insurrections which were gathering momentum throughout the island. Hundreds of men, women and children who had fled their villages used the monastery as a safe haven. When 2000 Turkish soldiers staged an attack on the building, rather than surrender, the Cretans set light to a store of gun powder. The explosion killed everyone, Turks included, except one small girl. This sole survivor lived to a ripe old age in a village nearby. A bust of this woman, and the abbot who lit the gun powder, stand outside the monastery.

The exterior of the monastery (which is still a working monastery) is coldly impressive but the Venetian church inside dates from 1587 and has a richly decorated Renaissance facade. On the right of the church a stairway leads to a small museum that commemorates the history of the monastery.

The monastery is open 8 am to 1 pm and 3.30 pm to 8 pm every day and entry is free. The small **museum** has an admission charge of 700 dr.

Getting There & Away

There are buses from Rethymno to the monastery (30 minutes, 500 dr) at 6 and 10.30 am, and 2.30 pm, returning at 7 am, noon and 4 pm.

Mylopotamos Province

The Mylopotamos Province has some of the more dramatic scenery in northern Crete. The coastline east of Rethymno is indented and pockmarked with watery caves and isolated coves that are only accessible by boat. The chief resorts along the north coast are Bali and Panormo. The hilly interior contains a scattering of villages and farming towns that are just beginning to attract some tourism. Within this region you will find some of Crete's most outstanding crafts, including the pottery at Margarites and the textiles at Anogia.

PANORMO

Panormo is one of the lesser known resorts on the northern coast despite the fact that it has a sandy beach and is easy to get to from Rethymno. It's a small village built on the site of an ancient settlement of which little is known. Coins found here indicate that the village flourished from the 1st to the 9th centuries AD when it was destroyed by the Saracens. There was once an early Christian basilica of Agia Sophia, probably built around the 6th century, and there are the ruins of a Genoese castle on the harbour.

RETHYMNO

RETHYMNO

Orientation & Information

The bus stop is on the main road outside of town. The post office is one block behind the remains of the Genoese castle. There is no bank or OTE.

Places to Stay

The best accommodation in town is the friendly *Panormo Beach Hotel (☎ 51 321)*, across the road from the beach, which has a pool in an interior garden and attractive studios with balconies for 10,000 dr. Nearby is *Lucy's Pension (☎ 51 212, fax 51 434)* which has rooms for 8000/10,000 dr. Also in town but closer to the main road is *Hotel Kirki (☎ 51 225, fax 51 013)* a B-class hotel with modern rooms for 10,000/12,000 dr.

Getting There & Away

Buses between Rethymno and Iraklio stop on the main road outside of town.

BALI
☎ 0834

Bali, 38km east of Rethymno, has one of the most stunning settings on the north coast. No less than five little coves are strung along the indented shore, marked by hills, promontories and narrow, sandy beaches. Helter-skelter development around the coast has marred the natural beauty of Bali and the narrow beaches can become crowded in the summer, but it's a great place to rent a boat to get the full effect of the dramatic landscape.

Orientation & Information

As you approach the resort from the main road you'll pass the Bali Paradise Beach Hotel which overlooks the first and largest cove, Paradise Beach. The next cove is Kyma Beach, followed by Bali Beach under the Bali Beach Hotel. There is a small beach along the port and the last beach on the strand is called Evita Beach. There is no bank or post office but you can change money at Racer Rent-a-Car on the left as you enter town or in one of the many travel agencies clustered around the coves. You can check your email at the Internet cafe/video games parlour (☎ 94 135) on the port.

Things to Do

There are a variety of water sports activities available in Bali. Diving Centre Hippocampos (☎ 94 193) is on the port and offers a 'discover scuba diving' dive for 16,000 dr and boat dives for 19,000 dr including equipment. Nearby is Water Sports Lefteris (☎ 94 102) which will rent you a pedal boat for 2000 dr an hour, a small canoe for 1500 dr an hour, a sailboat for 12,000 dr for two hours and a jet ski for 6000 dr for fifteen minutes. Lefteris also offers day-long and sunset cruises.

Places to Stay & Eat

The most luxurious hotel in town is the *Bali Paradise Beach (☎ 94 162, fax 94 255)* which has a swimming pool but no air-conditioning and rooms for 15,000/20,000 dr. There are also air-conditioned suites that run from 25,000 dr to 40,000 dr. Although it's an uninspiring concrete structure, most of the rooms have sea views and you are right over the beach. Near the *Bali Mare Hotel*, the *Talea Beach (☎ 94 297)* has a swimming pool and good value rooms for 10,000/15,000 dr.

The Bali Beach Hotel (☎ 94 210) is on top of a cliff overlooking a cove and has a swimming pool and rooms for 12,000/18,000 dr. *Evita Rent Rooms (☎ 94 250)*, overlooking the beach of the same name, has rooms with fridge for 8000/12,000 dr. *Apartments Ikonomakis (☎ 94 125)* is on a quiet street slightly inland from the port with rooms for 8000/12,000 dr. *Sunrise Apartments (☎ 94 267)* is a pleasant place offering apartments with a sea view for 10,000/15,000 dr.

There are a wealth of cafes and restaurants clustered along the coves. *Kyma Restaurant* on Kyma Beach serves good value meals in a pleasant setting. *Panorama* overlooking the port is another good choice.

Better than any establishment in Bali is *Mihalis* in Roumeli village, which is outstanding both in the quality of the cuisine and the authentically Cretan ambience.

It really gets going after midnight when Mihalis might bring out his guitar for a round of traditional Cretan tunes. To get there head to Panormo and at the junction, turn right following signs to Perama. Turn left after the bridge following signs to Roumeli. Mihalis is the only taverna in town. It's open 7 pm to 1 am daily.

Entertainment
The two most popular dance clubs in Bali are the *Highway Club* at the entrance to the town, which is an open-air space decorated as a tropical garden, *Volcano* at the top of the hill overlooking the church and *On The Rocks*, across from the church, which caters more to teenagers.

Getting There & Away
Buses between Iraklio and Rethymno drop you at the main road.

Getting Around
Racer Rent-a-Car (☎ 94 149, fax 94 249) has an office at the entrance to town and one at the port and offers a good deal on rentals.

MARGARITES
Known for its fine pottery, this tiny town is invaded by tour buses in the morning but it's a brief interlude. By the afternoon all is calm and you can enjoy wonderful views over the valley from the taverna terraces on the main square.

Orientation & Information
There is only one road that runs through town to the town square which is dominated by giant eucalyptus trees. The bus stop is in front of a taverna on the main square and you'll see many ceramics shops on the main street as well as the side streets. There is no bank, post office or travel agency.

Places to Stay & Eat
The only accommodation in town is the spiffy *Irini Apartments* (☎ 92 494) which has rooms with kitchenettes for 6000/8000 dr. Left of the main street, *Dionysio* is a good shop to buy ham, sausage and black-berry pies. Across the street is a cheese shop with big wheels of local cheese.

Getting There & Away
There are two buses daily Monday to Friday from Rethymno (30 minutes, 600 dr).

ANOGIA
☎ 0834
Anogia, 37km south-west of Iraklio, is a bucolic village perched on the foothills of Mt Psiloritis, which gives it a more temperate climate than you'll find on the coasts. Long known for its rebellious spirit, during WWII Anogia was a centre of resistance to the Germans, who massacred all the men in the village in retaliation for their role in sheltering Allied troops and aiding in the kidnap of General Kriepe. The town's renowned weaving industry was developed by the widows of the massacred men who were forced to support themselves the only way they could. Nowhere on Crete is the choice of weavings and embroidery as wide-ranging. Even though the town has become quite prosperous from cattle breeding, the women bring a deeply engrained sense of desperation to their sales pitches.

Orientation & Information
The town is spread out on a hillside with the textile shops in the lower half and most ac-commodation and businesses in the upper half. There's a bank, post office and OTE in the upper village but there is no ATM and no place to change money. Without your own transport you'll face a steep hike to see the upper portion of town.

Places to Stay & Eat
At the top of the hill is the best hotel in town, *Hotel Aristea* (☎ 31 459) which has simple but well-outfitted rooms for 6000/8000 dr. Views are great from the bal-conies. Downhill is *Rent Rooms Psiloritis* (☎ 31 194) which has simple, homey rooms for 6000 dr. Nearby is *Rent Rooms Arkadi* (☎ 31 099) which has comparable rooms at the same price. Farther down the hill is *Rooms Aris* (☎ 31 460, fax 31 058) which also has rooms for 5000/6000 dr. In the lower town the only accommodation is *Tav-erna and Rent Rooms Kitros* (☎ 31 429), which has double rooms for 6000 dr.

Prisini Folia is one of several tavernas in the lower village but it's particularly attrac-tive and serves decent Cretan food, al-though it can get overrun with tour buses.

RETHYMNO

Getting There & Away
There are five buses daily from Iraklio (one hour, 750 dr); and two buses daily Monday to Friday from Rethymno (1¼ hours, 1050 dr).

AROUND ANOGIA
The roads leading north-west from Anogia to the small commercial centre of Perama are stunning and pass through a series of cosy villages and bustling market towns along the foothills of Mt Psiloritis. The northern road takes you to the village of **Axos** with the kind of lazy Cretan ambience that has made it a popular stop for tour buses from Iraklio and Rethymno.

During the day the village is quiet but at night the few tavernas with open-air terraces host 'Cretan folklore evenings' for the tourists. Following this rural road you'll come next to the pretty, shady town of **Garazo** which has a couple of tavernas, a post office and a bank.

The route continues north and crosses the highway to arrive at **Melidoni** with a fascinating cave to explore. Over 300 villagers took refuge in the cave in 1824 from the Turkish army. When they refused orders to emerge, the Turks threw burning materials through a hole in the top of the cave and everyone was asphyxiated. After paying homage to the martyrs at a monument, you can wander through a series of chambers filled with stalactites and stalagmites.

The southern route from Anogia to Perama is equally scenic. The largest town in the region is **Zoniana**, where everyone seems to be dressed in black and driving pick-up trucks. Look for signs to the **Sendoni Cave**.

Whether named after a rebel or a robber according to local legend, Sendoni is the most spectacular cave on the island. Stalactites, stalagmites and strange rock formations make the visit an eerie experience. The front of the cave was a hideout for Greek fighters against the Turks but most of the large cave was undisturbed. Walkways make exploration easier but it's still important to watch your step.

Agios Vasileios Province

The Agios Vasileios Province begins at Armeni in the north and ends at the south coast. It is a region of gently rolling hills and pretty drives along good roads. As you near the coast the scenery becomes more dramatic and takes in marvellous views of the Libyan Sea. The capital of the province is Spili and the south includes the beach resorts of Agia Galini, Plakias and Moni Preveli.

Heading south from Rethymno, there is a turn-off to the right to the late Minoan **Cemetery of Armeni**, 2km before the modern village of Armeni. Some 200 tombs were carved into the rock between 1300 and 1150 BC in the midst of an oak forest. The curious feature of this cemetery is that there does not seem to have been any sizeable town nearby which would have accounted for so many tombs. Pottery, weapons and jewellery excavated from the tombs are now on display at the Archaeological Museum in Rethymno.

SPILI Σπήλι
☎ 0832 • postcode 740 53 • pop 700
Spili (**Spee**-lee) is a gorgeous mountain town with cobbled streets, rustic houses and plane trees. Its centrepiece is a unique Venetian fountain which spurts water from 19 lion heads.

Despite its distance from the coast, Spili is no longer an undiscovered hideaway. Tourist buses on their way to the south coast bring a fair amount of visitors to Spili during the day but in the evening the town belongs to the locals.

Orientation & Information
The post office and bank are on the main street. The OTE is up a side street, north of the central square. The bus stop is just south of the square.

Places to Stay & Eat
Green Hotel (☎ 22 225) across from the police station on the main street is a homey

place practically buried under plants and vines that also fill the interior. Attractive rooms with private bath are 5000/6000 dr.

Behind Green Hotel is **Heracles Rooms** (☎ *22 111, fax 22 411*) where sparkling, beautifully furnished rooms cost 5000/8000 dr with private bathroom.

Further along, on the left, **Costos Inn** (☎ *22 040/750*) has well-kept, ornate rooms with satellite TV, radio and the use of a washing machine. Doubles/triples with private bathroom cost 8000/9000 dr.

Another good choice is **Sunset Rooms** (☎ *22 306*) which has doubles for 5000 dr with private bath. **Taverna Stratidakis**, opposite Costos Inn, serves excellent trad itional Greek dishes. The specials of the day are in pots at the back of the room.

Getting There & Away

Spili is on the Rethymno-Agia Galini bus route.

AROUND SPILI

Most people come to the alluring little village of Patsos to visit the nearby **Church of Agios Antonios** in a cave above a picturesque gorge.

The cave was an important sanctuary for the Minoans and the Romans, and is still a pilgrimage destination on 17 January. You can drive here from Rethymno, or you can walk from Spili along a scenic 10km dirt track.

To reach the track, walk along 28 October, passing the lion fountain on your right. Turn right onto Vermopilan and ascend to the Spili-Gerakari road. Turn right here and eventually you will come to a sign for Gerakari. Take the dirt track to the left, and at the fork bear right. At the crossroads turn right, and continue on the main track for about one hour to a T-junction on the outskirts of Patsos. Turn left to get to the cave.

SPILI TO PLAKIAS

After the village of Koxare on the Plakias road, the road enters the dramatic **Kourtaliotis Gorge**. After Astomatis village there is a turn-off for Moni Preveli. The road continues through Lefkogia, then passes the turn-off for Myrthios (2km) and enters Plakias.

PLAKIAS Πλακιάς
☎ **0832 • postcode 740 602 • pop 100**

The south coast town of Plakias was once a tranquil fishing village before it became a retreat for adventurous backpackers. The package tour operators discovered the fine beaches and dramatic mountain backdrop in the 70's and Plakias became one of the larger resorts on the south coast. It's still not a bad place to visit outside peak season and there are some good walks.

Orientation & Information

It's easy to find your way around Plakias. One street skirts the long sandy beach and another runs parallel to it one block back. The bus stop is at the middle of the waterfront. The 30 minute path to Mythos begins just before the youth hostel. Plakias doesn't have a bank, but Monza Travel Agency (☎ 41 433 or 311 923), near the bus stop, offers currency exchange. Finikas Travel (☎ 31 785) is also a good source of information and rents cars. It's open 9 am to 7 pm daily. In summer there is a mobile post office on the waterfront.

Things to Do

Aegean Diving Shop (☎ 31 206) offers day-long scuba diving programs and a certification course as well as snorkelling trips. Plakias is an excellent base to explore the surrounding region since you don't have to walk very far out of town to find yourself in the middle of fields and greenery.

There are well-worn paths uphill to Myrthios overlooking the sea and to the scenic village of Sellia, the Moni Finikas, Lefkogia, and a lovely walk along the spectacular Kourtaliotis Gorge to Moni Preveli. A booklet of walks around Plakias is on sale at the minimarket by the bus stop (1200 dr).

There is a daily excursion boat, the *Venus Express*, that leaves at 10 am from April to October for a trip to Moni Preveli for 2500 dr return. For bookings ask at the supermarket across from Taverna Christo.

RETHYMNO

Places to Stay
Camping On the right of the main approach road to Plakias, *Camping Apollonia* (☎ *31 318)* has a restaurant, minimarket, bar and swimming pool. Rates are 900 dr per person and 600 dr per tent.

Hostel The excellent *youth hostel* is tucked away in the olive trees behind the town, 10 minutes walk from the bus stop – follow the yellow signs from the waterfront. Dorm beds are 1200 dr and hot showers are free. The hostel is open from 1 April until the end of October.

Domatia Next to the bus stop, *Morpheas Rent Rooms (☎ 31 583)* has light, airy and attractively furnished rooms. Prices are 7000/10,000 dr with private bathroom. There are some agreeable pensions tucked among the olive trees behind the town. *Pension Afrodite (☎ 31 266)* has spotless doubles/triples for 10,000/13,000 dr with private bathroom. Head inland at Monza Travel Agency, turn left at the T-junction and then take the first right and you will come to the pension on the left after 100m.

A right turn at the T-junction leads to *Studio Emilia (☎ 31 302)*, set back in the trees to the left after 100m. It charges 6000/7000 dr for large doubles/triples upstairs with private bathroom and access to a well-equipped communal kitchen; studios downstairs cost 8000 dr.

Pension Paligremnos (☎ 31 003) has a great position at the southern end of Plakias beach. Pleasant doubles with bathroom cost 6000 dr, and studio doubles are 7000 dr.

Hotels *Plakias Bay (☎ 31 315)* is a C-class hotel on the beach. Rooms are sparsely outfitted and cost 12,000/15,000 dr with breakfast. *Paleos Alianthos (☎ 31 851, fax 31 197)* is at the eastern end of the beach and has a pool and air-conditioned rooms for 15,000/20,000 dr. *Hotel Livykon (☎ 31 216, fax 31 271)* is on the seafront and has rooms for 12,000/15,000 dr.

Horizon Beach (☎ 31 476, fax 31 176) is right outside the town centre in a quiet location overlooking the beach and has rooms

for 11,000/14,000 dr. *Neo Alianthos Garden (☎ 31 280)* is at the entrance to town next to the road overlooking the sea. It's comfortably furnished in traditional Cretan style and has two pools. Rooms are 18,000/25,000 dr.

The *Kalypso Cretan Village (☎ 31 296)* is 5km east of Plakias along the road to Lefkogia and was the first nudist colony in Crete. It's a small village of 102 bungalows secreted in woods overlooking the sea. There is a pool, tennis courts and hotel boats take you to Damnoni beach and Plakias. Doubles are 35,000 dr including full board.

Places to Eat
Restaurant Ariadne, on the street opposite the mobile post office, is a popular place with reasonable prices.

One of the best waterfront tavernas is *Taverna Christos* with a romantic terrace overlooking the sea. It has a good choice of main dishes for around 1450 dr.

Nikos Souvlaki, just inland from Monza Travel Agency, is a good souvlaki place, where a monster mixed grill of gyros, souvlaki, sausage, hamburger and chips costs 1500 dr. On the western end of the beach try *Sunset* for an excellent array of local specialities. Next to the Plakias Beach Hotel, *Paligremnos* is also a good bet.

Entertainment
Plakias has a good nightlife scene in the summer. *Disco Meltemi* and *Disco Hexagon* are both popular and conveniently located in the town centre.

Getting There & Away
Plakias has good bus connections in summer, but virtually none in winter. A timetable is displayed at the bus stop. Summer services include four buses a day to Rethymno (one hour, 950 dr) and one to Hora Sfakion. In winter there are three buses a day to Rethymno, two at weekends. It's possible to get to Agia Galini from Plakias by catching a Rethymno bus to the Koxare junction (referred to as Bale on timetables) and waiting for a bus to Agia

Galini. This works best with the 11.30 pm bus from Plakias, linking with the 12.45 pm service from Rethymno to Agia Galini.

Getting Around

Odyssia (☎ 31 596), on the waterfront, has a large range of motorcycles and mountain bikes. Cars Allianthos (☎ 31 851) is a reliable car-hire outlet.

AROUND PLAKIAS

Myrthios Μύρθιος

This pleasant village is perched on a hillside overlooking Plakias and the surrounding coast. Apart from taking in the views, the main activity is walking, which you'll be doing a lot of unless you have your own transport.

Places to Stay & Eat There are a few domatia in the village, including the comfortable *Niki's Studios & Rooms* (☎ *31 593*), just below Restaurant Panorama. Rooms with private bathroom cost 3500/6000 dr, and a studio costs 8000 dr for two. *Restaurant Panorama* lives up to its name; it has great views. It also does good food, including vegetarian dishes and delicious desserts.

Moni Preveli Μονή Πρέβελη

The well-maintained Moni Preveli stands in splendid isolation high above the Libyan Sea. From the parking lot outside the monastery, there's a lookout with a panoramic view over the southern coast. It would be worthwhile making the trip for the view alone but the monastery itself has an interesting history. The origins of the monastery are unclear because most historical documents were lost in the many attacks inflicted upon it over the centuries. The year '1701' is carved on the monastery fountain but it may have been founded much earlier.

Like most of Crete's monasteries, it played a significant role in the islanders' rebellion against Turkish rule. It became a centre of resistance during 1866, causing the Turks to set fire to it and destroy surrounding crops. After the Battle of Crete, many Allied soldiers were sheltered here by

Abbot Agathangelos befo tion to Egypt. In retaliati plundered the monastery.

The monastery's **museum** contains a candelabra presented by grateful British soldiers after the war. Built in 1835, the church is worth a visit for the wonderful icon screen containing a gaily painted *Adam and Eve in Paradise* by the monk Mihail Prevelis.

From the road to the monastery, a track leads downhill to Preveli Beach. Entry to the monastery and museum costs 700 dr. It's open 8 am to 7 pm mid-March through May, and 8 am to 1.30 pm and 3.30 to 8 pm June to October.

Getting There & Away In summer there are two buses a day from Rethymno to Moni Preveli.

Preveli Beach Παραλία Πρέβελης

Preveli Beach, at the mouth of the Kourtaliotis Gorge, is one of Crete's most photographed beaches. The river Megalopotamos cuts the beach in half on its way into the Libyan Sea. It's fringed with oleander bushes and palm trees and is popular with freelance campers.

Walk up the palm-lined banks of the river and you'll come to cold, freshwater pools ideal for a swim. A steep path leads down to the beach from the road to Moni Preveli. You can get to Preveli from Plakias by boat in summer for 2500 dr return or by taxi boat from Agia Galini for 5000 dr return.

Beaches between Plakias & Preveli

Between Plakias and Preveli Beach there are several secluded coves popular with freelance campers and nudists. Some are within walking distance of Plakias, via Damnoni Beach. To reach them ascend the path behind the Plakias Bay Hotel. Just before the track starts to descend, turn right into an olive grove.

At the first T-junction turn left and at the second turn right. Where six tracks meet, take the one signposted to the beach. Walk to the end of Damnoni Beach and take the track to the right, which passes above the oves. Damnoni Beach itself is pleasant out of high season, despite being dominated by the giant Hapimag tourist complex.

AGIA GALINI Αγία Γαλη νη
☎ 0832 • postcode 740 56 • pop 600

Agia Galini (A-ya Ga-**lee**-nee) is another picturesque little town which has gone down the tubes due to an overdose of tourism. Before the advent of mass tourism Agia Galini was a port of the ancient town of Sybritos. At the turn of the century it was populated by families from nearby mountain villages who built a cluster of white houses around the harbour.

The late-19th-century town is the core of Agia Galini's appeal even though the shoulder to shoulder crowds at the height of the season obscure the town's undeniable charm. Still, it does boast 340 days of sunshine a year, and some places do remain open out of season.

It's a convenient base from which to visit Phaestos and Agia Triada, and although the town beach is more dirt than sand, there are boats to better beaches.

Orientation & Information
The bus station is at the top of Eleftheriou Venizelou, the main street, which is a continuation of the approach road. The central square, which overlooks the harbour, is downhill from the bus station. You'll walk past the post office on the way as well as a number of hotels and domatia, and the OTE is on the square. There is no bank but you can change money at Cretan Holidays (☎ 91 241) as well as many other places. There is a laundry just off the main square open 10 am to 2 pm and 5 to 10 pm daily. To find the beach take the rocky path leading left from the harbour.

Organised Tours
Monza Travel (☎ 91 278) offers boat excursions to Preveli for 5000 dr, a day-long fishing excursion for 7000 dr, and a boat trip to the lovely beach of Agios Pavlos for 3000 dr. Cretan Holidays offers minibus tours to Knossos for 9500 dr, a tour of south Crete that includes Zaros and Phaestos for 8000 dr and a tour of west Crete that includes Moni Arkadiou, Lake Kournas and Rethymno for 9000 dr.

Places to Stay
There is no shortage of places to stay in Agia Galini at every price level although you may have trouble finding the room of your dreams at the height of the season. The village is a popular destination for the package tour market and many of the hotels are pre-booked by tour operators. Still you will generally find that the price-quality ratio is quite high, and you can always bargain.

Camping *Agia Galini Camping (☎ 91 386/239)* is next to the beach, 2.5km east of the town. It is signposted from the Iraklio-Agia Galini road. The site is well-shaded and has a restaurant, snack bar and minimarket.

Domatia On the road to town *Areti (☎ 91 240)* has pleasant rooms with a private bath and balcony for 6000/10,000 dr. The nearby *Agapitos (☎ 91 164)* offers studios with fans for 6000/8000 dr and five-person apartments with a patio for 12,000 dr.

In the centre of town *Angelika (☎ 91 304)* is over a newspaper kiosk and has rooms with private bath and a balcony for 5000/6000 dr.

The only accommodation on the beach is *Stochos Rooms (☎ 91 433)*, where studios for two or three people cost 12,000/13,000 dr. *Candia Rooms (☎ 91 203)* has very basic rooms with bath for 3000/4000 dr. To get there take the first left opposite the post office.

Hotels The D-class *Hotel Selena (☎ 91 273)* has pleasant rooms for 10,000/12,000 dr with private bathroom. It's open all year. To reach the hotel, walk downhill from the bus station, turn left after the post office, take the second turning right and turn left at the steps.

On the right side of the main road is *Hotel Kissandros (☎/fax 91 406)*, a pretty, white building overhung with vines that has a roof garden and small rooms with sea views for 6000/7000 dr, including continental breakfast. On a quiet side street leading off the main road into town, the *Fevro* (☎ *91 275, fax 91 475)* has attractively furnished doubles for 17,000 dr, or 19,000 dr with air-conditioning.

Nearby is *Hotel Glaros (☎ 91 151, fax 91 159)* that has a pool and doubles with sea or mountain views for 15,000 dr. At the top of the hill leading into town is *El Greco (☎ 91 187, fax 91 491)* which is a new hotel that offers rooms with views of the sea for 13,000/16,000 dr.

Hotel Astoria (☎ 91 253, fax 91 153) often has rooms available when other places are booked. It's a sleek, modern hotel with air-conditioned rooms that have views of the sea or the mountains. Prices are 15,000/17,000 dr, including a small buffet breakfast.

Nearer to the beach is *Hotel Rea (☎ 91 390, fax 91 196)* which is a small, modern hotel that offers tidy rooms with white walls and pine floors for 6000/8000 dr. You will find it at the bottom of the main road on the right.

Places to Eat

Restaurant Megalonissis, near the bus stop, is one of the town's cheapest restaurants, if not the friendliest. It's open 9 am to midnight daily. *Medousa Taverna* in the town centre is owned by a German/Greek couple and presents a menu of specialties from both countries. It's open noon to 2 am daily April to October.

The upmarket *Acropol Taverna*, on Vasileos Ioannis, has an extensive menu of both Greek and international dishes. A meal for two with wine costs around 6000 dr. It's open 6.30 pm to midnight daily April to October.

La Strada pizzeria is on the first street left of the bus station and has excellent pizzas, pastas and risotto for about 2000 dr. It's open noon to 3 pm and 6 pm to midnight daily.

The most elaborate restaurant-bar is *Zorbas* at the end of the harbour which has three levels of comfortably furnished dining rooms with sea views and decent food. It's open 11 am to midnight daily. *Onar* overlooks the harbour and is a good place to come for breakfast, ice cream or cocktails. It's open 8 am to 1 am daily March to November.

At the end of the harbour near the beach, *Anikas* is a quiet cafe-bar, half buried behind flowering plants, that is popular with backpackers. It's open 9 am to 1 am daily. For self-catering there is a *supermarket* up the street from the bus station on the left side and a *bakery* down the street from the bus station on the right side.

Entertainment

Agia Galini's nightlife centres on Taverna Street. The most popular dance clubs are the *Jukebox Club*, *Paradise Club* and *Escape Club*, which are open after 11 pm nightly in the summer but weekends only in the winter. Jukebox plays Greek music after 2 am; Paradise has a rooftop garden-bar; and Escape Club plays 70s and 80s rock. Along the harbour, *Zorbas* is another popular venue.

Getting Around

Mano's Bike (☎ 91 551), opposite the post office, rents scooters and motorcycles, and Monza Travel (☎ 91 278) rents cars.

Getting There & Away

Bus The story is the same as at the other beach resorts: heaps of buses in summer, skeletal services in winter. In peak season there are eight buses a day to Iraklio (2½ hours, 1500 dr), four to Rethymno (1½ hours, 1300 dr), six to Matala (45 minutes, 600 dr) and six to Phaestos (40 minutes, 420 dr). You can get to Plakias by taking a Rethymno-bound bus and changing at Koxare (Bale).

Taxi Boat In summer there are daily taxi boats from the harbour to the beaches of Agios Giorgios and Agios Pavlos. These beaches, which are west of Agia Galini, are difficult to get to by land. Both are less crowded than, and far superior to, the Agia Galini beach.

RETHYMNO

Iraklio

The Iraklio region may not be Crete's most beautiful region but as the island's main point of entry for tourism it is undoubtedly the busiest. The twin poles of Cretan culture – mass tourism and Minoan archaeology – are amply represented in the region. The northern coast of Iraklio has surrendered lock, stock and barrel to package tourism. The eastern resorts of Malia and Hersonissos sum up for Cretans everything that is wrong with mass tourism. Yet behind the concrete sea-barrier of hotels lie the island's most fascinating archaeological sites strewn throughout the nearly deserted interior. Knossos, Phaestos, Agia Triada, Gortyn, and Malia are all within a day trip from Iraklio. The southern coast is quieter than the northern coast; Matala is fairly developed but Keratokambos and Arvi provide a more tranquil vacation experience.

IRAKLIO Ηραηλειο

☎ 081 • postcode 710 01 • pop 127,600

Hectic, noisy and traffic-ridden, Iraklio is mainly viewed as a grim necessity to be endured for the sake of archaeology. After the obligatory visit to the Archaeological Museum and Knossos, most visitors hurry away to more inviting spots.

Yet, as Crete's capital and Greece's 5th largest city, Iraklio manages to achieve a certain urban sophistication despite its poor infrastructure. The city is prosperous; many neighbourhoods have been rebuilt and there are enough drachmas around to support a thriving cafe scene and lively nightlife.

The Archaeological Museum and the palace at Knossos are a window into Minoan culture but Iraklio abounds in other reminders of its turbulent history. The 14th-century Venetian walls and fortress underscore the importance of Iraklio (then called Candia) to the Venetians and many monuments date from Venetian occupation. Notice Morosini Fountain, the Venetian Loggia and Agios Markos Church.

HIGHLIGHTS

• Exploring the ruins of the Minoan civilisation at Knossos and Phaestos

• Languishing on the long, sandy beaches of Matala, Kalamaki and Lendas on the south coast

• Indulging in the lively nightlife and cafe scene of the island's capital, Iraklio

• Enjoying the cool mountain air of Zaros

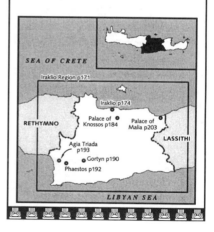

History

Iraklio is believed to have been settled since the Neolithic age. Under the Minoans it became the harbour of Knossos. Little is known about the intervening years but in 824 AD Iraklio was conquered by the Saracens and became known as Rabdh el Khandak (Castle of the Ditch), after the moat that surrounded their fortified town. It was reputedly the slave-trade capital of the eastern Mediterranean and the launching pad for the region's notorious pirates, who preyed upon unwary ships, looted them and sold the captive seamen into slavery.

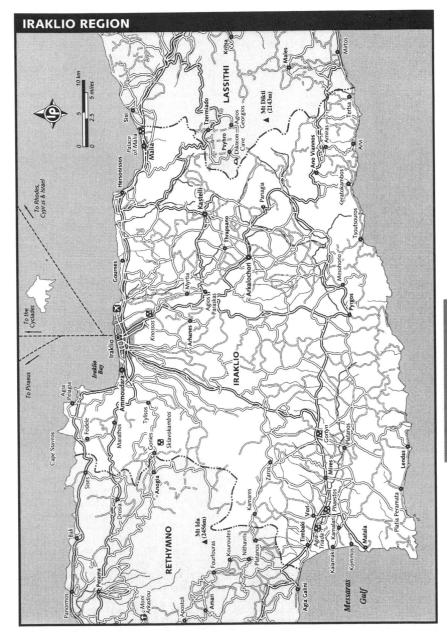

IRAKLIO REGION

IRAKLIO

Byzantine troops finally dislodged the Arabs after a siege which lasted almost a year in 961 AD. The Byzantine leader Nikiforas Fokas made a lasting impression upon the Arabs by chopping off the heads of his prisoners and throwing them over the walls of the fortress.

The city became known as Chandakas and remained the island's capital until Crete was sold to the Venetians in 1204. The Venetians also chose the city as the island's capital and named it Candia. The Venetians built magnificent public buildings and churches, and barricaded themselves inside the fortress when necessary to protect themselves against a rebellious populace.

Under the Venetians Candia became a centre for the arts and residence for painters such as Damaskinos and El Greco. When the Turks captured Constantinople the walls of the fortress where fortified and extended in anticipation of the growing Turkish menace. Although the Turks quickly overran the island in 1645 it took them 21 years to penetrate the walls of Candia.

Other European countries sent men and supplies from time to time but it was mainly the strength of the walls that kept the Turks at bay. Pounding the walls with cannons proved ineffective so the Turks finally resorted to bribery. They managed to pay a Venetian colonel to reveal the weak points in the wall and thus were able to capture it in 1669. Casualties were high on both sides; the Venetian defenders lost 30,000 men and the Turks lost 118,000 men.

Under the Turks the city became known as Megalo Kastro (Big Castle). A cloud of darkness descended upon the city under Turkish rule. Artistic life withered away and most Cretans fled or were massacred.

On August 25 1898 a Turkish mob massacred hundreds of Cretans, 17 British soldiers and the British Consul in Iraklio. Within weeks, a squadron of British ships steamed into Iraklio's harbour and ended Turkish rule on Crete forever.

Hania became the capital of independent Crete at the end of Turkish rule in 1898, but Candia's central location soon saw it emerge as the commercial centre. It was re-

A Bunch of Bull?

After King Minos' wife, Pasiphae, gave birth to the Minotaur, her lover, the bull, went wild and laid waste to the Cretan countryside. He was out of control, tearing up crops and stamping down orchard walls. Fortunately, help was at hand in the form of iron-man Heracles, the man who once killed a lion with his bare hands. His voyage to Crete to kill the bull was the seventh of his 12 mighty labours. Minos offered to help but Heracles would have none of it. As the monstrous animal belched flames and fumes, Heracles captured it single-handedly and took it away. The ancient Cretans were so grateful that they named Minos' port city after their superman. And that's how Iraklio (Iraklion, Heraklion) got its name.

named Iraklio and it resumed its position as administrative centre in 1971.

The city suffered badly in WWII, when most of the old Venetian and Turkish town was destroyed by bombing.

Orientation

Iraklio's two main squares are Plateia Venizelou and Plateia Eleftherias. Plateia Venizelou, instantly recognisable by its famous Morosini Fountain (better known as the Lion Fountain), is the heart of the city and the best place from which to familiarise yourself with the layout of Iraklio. The city's major intersection is a few steps south of the square. From here, 25 Avgoustou runs north-east to the harbour; Dikeosynis runs south-east to Plateia Eleftherias; Kalokerinou runs west to the Hania Gate; 1866 (the market street) runs south; and 1821 runs to the south-west. To reach Plateia Venizelou from the quay, turn right, walk along the waterfront and turn left onto 25 Avgoustou.

Iraklio has three intercity bus stations. Station A, on the waterfront between the quay and 25 Avgoustou, serves eastern

Crete. A special bus station which services Hania and Rethymno is opposite Station A. Station B, just beyond Hania Gate, serves Phaestos, Agia Galini and Matala. To reach the city centre from Station B walk through the Hania Gate and along Kalokerinou. For details on bus schedules, see the Iraklio Getting There & Away section.

Information

Tourist Offices EOT (☎ 22 8225/6081/ 8203, fax 22 6020) is just north of Plateia Eleftherias at Xanthoudidou 1. The staff at the information desk are very often work-experience students from a local tourism training college. They hand out maps and photocopied lists of ferry and bus schedules. Opening times are 8 am to 2 pm Monday to Friday. In high season they also open on Saturday and Sunday. The tourist police (☎ 28 3190), Dikeosynis 10, are open from 7 am to 11 pm.

Foreign Consulates Foreign consulates in Iraklio include:

Germany
    (☎ 22 6288), Zografou 7
Netherlands
    (☎ 34 6202), Avgoustou 23
UK
    (☎ 22 4012), Apalexandrou 16

Money Most of the city's banks are on 25 Avgoustou, including the National Bank of Greece at No 35. It has a 24-hour automatic exchange machine, as does the Credit Bank at No 94. American Express (☎ 24 6202 or 22 2303) is represented by Adamis Travel Bureau, 25 Avgoustou 23. Opening hours are 8 am to 2 pm Monday to Saturday. Thomas Cook (☎ 24 1108/9) is represented by Summerland Travel, Epimendou 30.

Post & Communications The central post office is on Plateia Daskalogianni. From Plateia Eleftherias go up Giannari and make a left on Zografou. Make a right on the first street in and you'll see the post office on your left. Opening hours are 7.30 am to 8 pm Monday to Friday; and 7.30 am to 2 pm on Saturday. In summer, there is a mobile post office at El Greco Park, just north of Plateia Venizelou, which is open 8 am to 6 pm, Monday to Friday and 8 am to 1.30 pm on Saturday. The OTE, on Theotokopoulou just north of El Greco Park, opens 7.30 am to 11 pm daily.

Email & Internet Access Istos Cyber Cafe (☎ 22 2120), at Malikouti 2, charges 1300 dr an hour to use their computers and also scans, prints, and faxes documents. There are a half-dozen computers with fast connections. It's open 9 am to 1 am daily. Polykentro Cyber Cafe (☎ 399 212), at Androgeo 4, is a large place, more conducive to lingering with a large bar area and backgammon. It costs 500 dr an hour to use the computers and it's open 9 am to 1 am daily.

Travel Agencies Prince Travel (☎ 28 2706), at 25 Avgoustou 30 is an excellent source of information on cheap flights. It's a friendly office that has a luggage storage and has tons of useful advice about Iraklio. It's open 9 am to 6pm Monday to Friday.

For the latest ferry schedules and all advice on boat transport go to Arabatzoglou (☎ 22 6697), at 25 Avgoustou 54. It's open 9 am to 7pm Monday to Friday.

Bookshops The huge Planet International Bookshop (☎ 28 1558) on the corner of Hortatson and Kidonias stocks most of the books recommended in this guide and has a large selection of Lonely Planet guides. It's open 8.30am to 2.30pm Monday, Wednesday, and Saturday and Tuesday, 8.30am to 2pm and 5.30 to 9pm Thursday, and Friday.

Laundry There are two self-service laundrettes: Laundry Washsalon, Handakos 18, and Wash-O-Mate, Mirabelou 25, near the Archaeological Museum. Both charge 2000 dr for a wash and dry.

Luggage Storage The left-luggage office at Bus Station A charges 300 dr per day and is open 6.30 am to 8 pm daily. Other options are Prince Travel (☎ 28 2706), at 25 Avgoustou 30, which also charges 500 dr,

IRAKLIO

SEA OF CRETE

Old Harbour

New Harbour

Quay

To Agios Nikolaos

El Greco Park

Plateia Venizelou

Plateia Eleftherias

Plateia Kornarou

Plateia Kiptiu

To Hania Gate, Bus Station B,
University Hospital at Voutes,
Rethymno & Hania

To Hotel
Galaxy
Sbokos &
Knossos

0   125   250 m
0   125   250 yd

Washsalon (see Laundry) which charges
450 dr and the youth hostel at Vyronos 5
which charges 500 dr.

Medical Services The new University
Hospital (☎ 39 2111) at Voutes, 5km south
of Iraklio, is the city's best equipped medical facility. The Apollonia Hospital (☎ 22
9713), inside the old walls on Mousourou,
is more convenient.

Things to See
Archaeological Museum This outstanding museum (☎ 22 6092) is second in size

and importance only to the National Archaeological Museum in Athens. If you are seriously interested in the Minoans you will want
more than one visit. Even a fairly superficial
perusal of the contents requires half a day.

The exhibits, arranged in chronological
order, include pottery, jewellery, figurines,
and sarcophagi as well as some famous
frescoes, mostly from Knossos and Agia
Triada. All testify to the remarkable imagination and advanced skills of the Minoans.
Unfortunately, the exhibits are not very
well-explained. If they were, there would be
no need to part with 2200 dr for a copy of

IRAKLIO

PLACES TO STAY
4 Hotel Kronos
8 Hotel Rea
9 Vergina Rooms
11 Atrion
13 Hotel Lena
14 Youth Hostel
18 Hotel Irini
20 Hotel Lato
21 Hotel Ilaira
28 Atlantis Hotel
35 Hotel Kastro
36 Hotel Mirabello
37 Youth Hostel
    (Rent Rooms Hellas)
50 Astoria Hotel
66 El Greco
74 Olympic

PLACES TO EAT
2 Taverna Kastella
3 Ippokampos Ouzeri
6 Garden of
   Deykaliola Taverna
10 Bexos
12 Tierra del Fuego
15 Vareladika Ouzeri
16 Katsina Ouzeri
30 Pagopeion
33 Aithrion
47 New China

48 Loukoulos
49 Giovanni Taverna
61 Ta Leontaria 1922
62 Loukoumades Cafe
69 Giakoumis Taverna
70 Restaurant Ionia
73 Bella Casa

OTHER
1 Venetian Fortress
5 Historical Museum
   of Crete
7 Jasmin
17 Prince Travel
19 Summerland
22 Buses to Hania & Rethymno
23 Buses to Knossos & Airport
24 Bus Station A
25 Privilege Club
26 Yacht Club
27 Istos Cyber Cafe
29 Wash-O-Mate
31 National Bank of
    Greece
32 Adamis Travel
    Bureau
34 OTE
38 Guernica
39 Laundry Washsalon
40 Planet International
    Bookshop

41 Take Five
42 Venetian Loggia
43 Buses to Knossos
44 St. Marco Church
45 Sousouro
46 Ideon Andron
51 EOT
52 Archaeological
    Museum
53 Battle of Crete
    Museum
54 DNA
55 Fougaro
56 Buses to Airport
57 EOS
58 Aktapika
59 Morosini Fountain
60 De Facto
63 Tourist Police
64 Spyros Valergos
65 Four Lions
67 Church of Agia Ekaterini
68 Agios Minos
    Cathedral
71 Post Office
72 Olympic Airways
75 Bembo Fountain
76 Apollonia Hospital
77 Kazantzakis' Tomb
78 Kazantzakis Open
    Air Theatre

the glossy illustrated guide by the museum's director.

Room 1 is devoted to the Neolithic and Early Minoan periods. Room 2 has a collection from the Middle Minoan period. Among the most fascinating exhibits are the tiny, glazed colour reliefs of Minoan houses from Knossos, called the 'town mosaic'.

Room 3 covers the same period with finds from Phaestos, including the famous **Phaestos Disc**. The symbols inscribed on this 16cm diameter disc have not been deciphered. Here also are the famous **Kamares pottery vases**, named after the sacred cave of Kamares where the pottery was first discovered. Case 40 contains fragments of 'eggshell ware', so called because of its fragility. The four large vases in case 43 were part of a royal banquet set. They are of exceptional quality and are some of the finest examples of Kamares pottery.

Exhibits in Room 4 are from the Middle Minoan period. Most striking is the 20cm black stone **Bull's Head**, which was a libation vessel. The bull has a fine head of curls, from which sprout horns of gold. The eyes of painted crystal are extremely lifelike. Also in this room are relics from a shrine at Knossos, including two fine **snake goddess** figurines. Snakes symbolised immortality for the Minoans.

Room 5 contains pottery, bronze figurines and seals. Other exhibits include vases imported from Egypt and some Linear A and B tablets. The Mycenaean Linear B script has been deciphered, and the inscriptions on the tablets displayed here have been translated as household or business accounts from the palace at Knossos.

Room 6 is devoted to finds from Minoan cemeteries. Especially intriguing are two small clay models of groups of figures which were found in a tholos tomb. One depicts four male dancers in a circle, their arms around each other's shoulders. The dancers may have been participating in a funeral ritual. The other model depicts two groups of three figures in a room flanked by two columns. Each group features two large seated figures, who are being offered libations by a smaller figure. It is not known whether the large figures represent gods or departed mortals. On a more grisly level, there is a display of the bones of a horse, which had been sacrificed as part of Minoan worship.

The finds in Room 7 include the beautiful bee pendant found at Malia. It's a remarkably fine piece of gold jewellery depicting two bees dropping honey into a comb. Also in this room are the three celebrated vases from Agia Triada. The **Harvester Vase**, of which only the top part remains, depicts a light-hearted scene of young farm workers returning from olive picking. The **Boxer Vase** shows Minoans indulging in two of their favourite pastimes – wrestling and bull grappling. The **Chieftain Cup** depicts a more cryptic scene: a chief holding a staff and three men carrying animal skins. Room 8 holds the finds from the palace at Zakros. Don't miss the gorgeous little crystal vase which was found in over 300 pieces and was painstakingly put together again by museum staff. Other exhibits include a beautiful elongated libation vessel decorated with shells and other marine life.

Room 10 covers the postpalatial period (1350-1100 BC) when the Minoan civilisation was in decline and being overtaken by the warrior-like Myceaneans. Nevertheless, there are still some fine exhibits, including a child (headless) on a swing in case 143.

Room 13 is devoted to Minoan sarcophagi. However, the most famous and spectacular of these, the **sarcophagus from Agia Triada**, is upstairs in Room 14 (the Hall of Frescoes). This stone coffin, painted with floral and abstract designs and ritual scenes, is regarded as one of the supreme examples of Minoan art.

The most famous of the Minoan frescoes are also displayed in Room 14. Frescoes from Knossos include the **Procession Fresco**, the **Griffin Fresco** (from the Throne Room), the **Dolphin Fresco** (from the Queen's Room) and the amazing **Bull-Leaping Fresco**, which depicts a seemingly double-jointed acrobat somersaulting on the back of a charging bull. Other frescoes here include the two lovely **Frescoes of the Lilies** from Amnisos and fragments of frescoes from Agia Triada. There are more frescoes in Rooms 15 and 16. In room 16 there is a large wooden model of Knossos.

The museum is on Xanthoudidou, just north of Plateia Eleftherias. Opening times are 8 am to 7 pm Tuesday to Sunday, and 12.30 to 7 pm Monday. It closes at 5 pm from the end of October to the start of April. Admission is 1500 dr.

Historical Museum of Crete This museum (☎ 28 3219) houses a fascinating range of bits and pieces from Crete's more recent past. The ground floor covers the period from Byzantine to Turkish rule, displaying plans, charts, photographs, ceramics and maps. On the 1st floor is the only El Greco painting on display in Crete. Other rooms contain fragments of 13th- and 14th-century frescoes, coins, jewellery, liturgical ornaments, and vestments and medieval pottery.

The 2nd floor has a reconstruction of the **library of author Nikos Kazantzakis** and displays letters, manuscripts and books. Another room is devoted to Emmanual Tsouderos, who was born in Rethymno and who was Prime Minister in 1941. Some dramatic photographs of a ruined Iraklio are displayed in the **Battle of Crete** section. There is an outstanding **folklore collection** on the 3rd floor.

The museum, which is just back from the western waterfront, is open 9 am to 5 pm Monday to Friday and 9 am to 2 pm Saturday in summer. In winter, it opens 9.30 am to 2.30 pm Monday to Saturday. Admission is 1000 dr.

Other Attractions Iraklio burst out of its city walls long ago but these massive fortifications, with seven bastions and four gates, are still very conspicuous, dwarfing the concrete structures of the 20th century. Venetians built the defences between 1462 and 1562. You can follow the walls around the heart of the city for views of Iraklio's neighbourhoods but it is not particularly scenic. The 16th-century **Rocca al Mare**, another Venetian fortress, stands at the end of the Old Harbour's jetty. The Venetian fortress stopped the Turks for 22 years and then became a Turkish prison for Cretan rebels. The exterior is most impressive with reliefs of the Lion of St Mark. The interior has 26 overly-restored rooms and good views from the top. The fortress (☎ 24 6211) is open 8 am to 6 pm Monday to Saturday, 10 am to 3 pm Sunday. Entry is 500 dr.

Several other notable vestiges from Venetian times survive in the city. Most famous is **Morosini Fountain** on Plateia Venizelou, which spurts water from four lions into eight ornate U-shaped marble troughs. The fountain, built in 1628, was commissioned by Francesco Morosini while he was governor of Crete. Opposite is the three-aisled 13th-century **Basilica of San Marco**. It has been reconstructed many times and is now an exhibition gallery. A little north of here is the attractively reconstructed 17th-century **Venetian Loggia**. It was a Venetian version of a gentleman's club; the male aristocracy came here to drink and gossip.

The delightful **Bembo Fountain**, at the southern end of 1866, is shown on local maps as the Turkish Fountain, but it was actually built by the Venetians in the 16th century. It was constructed from a hotchpotch of building materials including an ancient statue. The ornate edifice next to the fountain was added by the Turks, and now functions as a snack bar.

The former Church of Agia Ekaterini, next to Agios Minos Cathedral, is now a **museum** (☎ 28 8825) housing an impressive collection of icons. Most notable are the six icons painted by Mihail Damaskinos, the mentor of Domenikos Theotokopoulos (El Greco). It is open 9 am to 1:30 pm Monday to Saturday and also from 5 to 8 pm on Tuesday, Thursday and Friday afternoons. Admission is 500 dr.

The **Battle of Crete Museum**, on the corner of Doukos Dofor and Hatzidakj, chronicles this historic battle through photographs, letters, uniforms and weapons. It is open 9 am to 1 pm daily. Entrance is free.

You can pay homage to Crete's most acclaimed contemporary writer, Nikos Kazantzakis (1883-1957), by visiting his **tomb** at the Martinenga Bastion (the best-preserved bastion) in the southern part of town. The epitaph on his grave, 'I hope for nothing, I fear nothing, I am free', is taken from one of his works.

Special for kids

When the kids get tired of building sandcastles, Water City (☎ 781 316), 15km south-east of Iraklio, has 23 water slides, wave pools and an artificial river. In some slides, kids plunge from the heights while in others they emerge from a tube. It's open 10 am to 7 pm daily from April to September; admission is 4000 dr adults, 3000 dr children 4-12. There's no public transport. Drivers should take the main road east from Iraklio and turn south at Hani Kokini, following signs to the park.

Kritiki Farm (☎ 0897-51 546) is 34 km south-east of Iraklio near Potamies. This recreation of a typical Cretan farm may be a little tame for adults but kids are sure to appreciate the carriage rides, donkey rides and playground. There's also a sampling of farm animals to help city kids connect pork with pig. There is also a restaurant serving Cretan dishes. It's open 9 am to 7 pm daily from March to October. Admission is 1500 dr. Take the bus from Iraklio to Diktean Cave, and get off at Potamies (1 hour, 700 dr).

Places to Stay

As the island's capital and business centre, Iraklio's accommodation opportunities are weighted toward the needs of business travellers. Hotels tend to be bland but they are clustered in the centre of town, convenient to public transport. The closest beach resort to Iraklio is Amoudara, 2km west of town. You'll find the top end resorts stretching to Amoudara to the west and Hersonissos in the east. Hotels in town are open all year but most beach resorts are only open from March to November.

Places to Stay – Budget

Camping The nearest campsites are at Gouves and Hersonissos. *Camping Creta* (☎ 897-41 400, fax 41 400) is 16 km east of Iraklio along the main road to Agios Nikolaos and then 2 km left to the beach. The camping grounds are in a flat, shadeless area but there is a sand and pebble beach.

Camping Hersonissos (☎/fax 22 902) is 22 km east of Iraklio, 3 km before Hersonissos. The camping ground is on the sandy beach and features traditional style buildings.

Hostels Iraklio has two youth hostels. The former *youth hostel* (☎ 28 628, Vyronos 5), which was stripped of its official status, is a clean, well-run place, where a bed in a single-sex dorm costs 1500 dr and basic doubles/triples cost 4000/5000 dr.

Many people prefer the livelier atmosphere at *Rent Rooms Hellas* (☎ 28 8851, Handakos 24), a hostel which has a roof garden and a bar. Rates are 1800 dr for a dorm bed and 5200/6700/8200 dr for doubles/triples/quads.

Domatia There are few domatia in Iraklio and not enough cheap hotels to cope with the number of budget travellers who arrive in high season. One of the nicest low-priced places is the spiffy *Hotel Mirabello* (☎ 28 5052, Theotokopoulou 20) on a quiet street in the centre of town. The immaculate rooms cost 6500/8500 dr with shared bathroom, and 8000/10,000 dr with private bathroom. Try to get a room with a balcony.

Hotel Lena (☎ 22 3280; fax 24 826, Lahana 10) has basic singles/doubles with shared bathrooms for 6500/9000 dr, and doubles with private bathroom for 11,000 dr.

The pleasant *Vergina Rooms* (☎ 24 2739, Hortatson 32), is a pleasant, characterful turn-of-the-century house with a small courtyard and spacious high-ceilinged rooms. Doubles/triples/quads cost 5000/6500/8500 dr. Bathrooms are on the terrace and hot water is available upon request.

Hotel Rea, (☎ 22 3638) at the intersection of Hortatson and Kalimeraki, is clean, quiet and friendly. Singles/doubles with shared bathroom are 5000/6500 dr, while doubles/triples with private bathroom are 6500/8000 dr.

Places to Stay – Mid-Range

Hotel Kronos (☎ 282 240, fax 285 853, Venizelou 2) is as close to the sea as you can get in Iraklio without actually being in the sea. The large, twin-bedded rooms are in excellent condition with sparkling tile floors and white walls. All rooms have balconies, some with views of the sea and double-glazed windows to keep out traffic noise from the road below. Singles/doubles are 9000/12,000 dr in high season with an extra 1200 dr for breakfast.

Atrion Hotel (☎ 229 225, fax 223 292, Chronaki 9) is a business-like establishment with few concessions to frivolity. The large, well-furnished rooms have air-con on demand, TVs with international stations and modern bathrooms but the most attractive feature of the hotel is the enclosed garden-terrace. Singles/doubles are 18,500/21,600 dr. Prices include buffet breakfast.

Hotel Irini (☎ 226 561, fax 226 407, Idomeneos 4) is a modern establishment with 59 large, airy rooms with TV (local stations only), radio, telephone and air-con. Most of the Mediterranean-style rooms have balconies enlivened by plants and flowers. Prices are 13,500/18,000 dr for singles/doubles including breakfast. It's well-located in the centre of town and also has parking facilities. There's a taverna downstairs with long opening hours.

Hotel Kastro (☎ 284 185/285 020, fax 223 622, Theotokopoulou 22) has comfortable amenities including a great rooftop terrace with chairs for sunbathing. The rooms are large, contain telephones and have air-con. Some have balconies with corner views of the sea and/or TVs. Prices are 9000/12,000 dr for a single/double including breakfast.

The best feature of *Hotel Ilaira (☎ 227 103 or 227 125, fax 242 367, Ariadnis 1)* is the rooftop terrace with a panoramic view of the ports and fortress. The pleasant stucco and wood rooms have telephones and showers; some have TVs and others have small balconies with sea views. Singles/doubles are 10,000/14,000 dr.

Near Morosini Fountain, *El Greco (☎ 281 071, fax 281 072/1821/1824)* has a no-nonsense look. The large, bland lobby seems designed to discourage lingering and no one would accuse the hotel of over-decorating the rooms. The location is good, the rooms are in decent shape and some have TVs and air-con. Singles/doubles are 17,400 dr including breakfast. Air-con is an extra 2500 dr.

Although somewhat charm-impaired, the large, bland *Olympic (☎ 288 861, fax 222 512, email galaxyir@otenet.gr, Plateia Kornarou)* offers a sunny roof garden in a central location. The large rooms are in good condition and equipped with telephones. Prices are 21,000/18,000 dr and include breakfast.

Places to Stay – Top End

Although not in the town centre *Galaxy Hotel (☎ 238 812, fax 211 211, email galaxyir@otenet.gr, Demokratias 67)* offers a lot of amenities. There's a swimming pool large enough to swim laps, a sauna and very comfortable rooms with air-con on demand, TVs with international stations, telephones, hair dryers, safes and balconies. Singles/doubles are 22,000/30,000 dr.

Astoria Hotel(☎ 343 080, fax 229 078, email astoria@her.forthnet.gr, Plateia Eleftherias 11) is the businessperson's hotel of choice. It's in the thick of the action on Plateia Eleftherias, convenient to all public transport and equipped with a rooftop swimming pool. The luxurious rooms are outfitted with air-con on demand, hair dryers, cosmetic sets, TVs (international channels) and telephone. Singles/doubles cost 28,500/36,000 dr and include buffet breakfast.

Atlantis Hotel (☎ 22 9103/4023, fax 22 6265, Igias 2) is located on a quiet street near the harbour. This gleaming, modern hotel has an indoor swimming pool, health club, sauna and solarium. The rooms are spacious and well-appointed with air-con on demand, TV (no English-language stations), telephone, bathtubs, and double-glazed windows to ensure quiet. Prices of 24,000/34,000 dr for a single/double include buffet breakfast.

Hotel Lato (☎ 228 103, fax 240 350, email lato@her.forthnet.gr, Epimendou 15) was completely renovated in 1995, this sleek hotel overlooking the fortress offers excellent value. The comfortable rooms have air-con on demand, TVs with international stations, telephone, radio and balconies with views of the sea. There's also a conference room and parking facilities. Singles/doubles cost 22,700/ 28,500 dr including buffet breakfast.

Places to Eat

Iraklio has restaurants to suit all tastes and pockets from excellent fish tavernas to exotic international cuisine. The business-like temperament of the city also allows for a wider choice of formal dining options, unlike the rest of the island. Note that the majority of restaurants are closed on Sunday. You may be relegated to self-catering, looking for a hotel restaurant or heading to one of the fast-food outlets around the Morosini Fountain.

Places to Eat – Budget

Loukoumades Cafe (Dikeosynis 8) has the best *loukoumades* (honey-dipped fritters) in Iraklio. Workers, shopkeepers and business people drift in an out all day for their loukoumades fix but, on a scale of one to ten, the ambience is minus six. It's open 5 am to midnight daily.

IRAKLIO

The delicious cheese-filled bougatsa served at *Ta Leontaria*, on 1922, has a loyal following among Iraklio's older set who linger for hours over bougatsa, coffee and water, watching the crowds mill around the Morosini Fountain. It's open 7am to midnight daily.

Places to Eat – Mid-Range

Mexican food is trendy right now in Crete making *Tierra del Fuego (Theotokopoulou 26)* popular with a hip, young crowd. If you don't have your heart set on authenticity, you'll be amused by the Cretan versions of Mexican standards. It's open 8pm to midnight Monday to Saturday.

Ippokampos Ouzeri (Mitsotaki 2) is as good as taverna-style eating gets. The interior is attractively decorated with cooking pots but most people prefer to squeeze onto one of the sidewalk tables. Whether you opt for vegetarian mezedes or baked squid, you'll find the food fresh and savoury. As proof of its quality, the taverna is always packed.

Garden of Deykaliola Taverna (Kalokerinou 8) with its wicker chairs, red-checked tablecloths and plastic grapevines put diners in a cheery mood intensified by delicious food. After the tourists leave at around 11pm, the locals pile in, the owner takes out his accordion and the festivities commence. It's open 8pm to 4am Monday to Saturday.

Vareladika Ouzeri (Moni Agarathou 13) is cheerful place that has recently been taken over by a Greek-American couple who have spruced-up the interior while maintaining the ouzeri's tradition of serving simple, well-prepared Cretan dishes. Try the excellent sea-urchin salad. It's open noon to 2.30pm and 7pm to midnight Monday to Saturday.

Taverna Kastella (Sophokles Venizelou 3) has good food but a better setting. The taverna is right on the wharf offering a spectacular view of the Venetian fortress. Come at the end of the day and enjoy the sunset over an ouzo and *mezedes*. It's open 9.30am to 12.30am daily from March to November.

Katsina Ouzeri (Marineli 12) is an old neighbourhood favourite. Most people come

for the lamb and pork roasted in a brick oven or the excellent stewed goat. Portions are hearty and the atmosphere is convivial. It's open 7pm to 1am daily Tuesday to Sunday.

Bella Casa (Zografou 16) is set in a stunning turn-of-the-century villa with a small terrace-garden on the street. The stylish rooms are air-conditioned in the summer allowing you to savour a wide assortment of richly flavoured Greek and Italian dishes without working up a sweat. It's open noon to 5pm and 8pm to 1am Monday to Saturday. *Baxes (Gianni Chroaki 14)* was recently taken over by country folk. This simple restaurant offers Cretan special-occasion cooking. Lamb and goat are stewed for hours or roasted in a brick oven just the way Cretans would cook them. It's open 11am to 2am daily.

Theodosaki is lined with tavernas catering to the market on 1866 and *Giakoumis Taverna (Theodosaki 5-8)* is one of the best. There's a full menu of Cretan specialties and turnover is heavy which means that the dishes are freshly cooked. It's open noon to 3pm and 7 to 10pm Monday to Saturday.

Restaurant Ionia, at the intersection of Evans and Giannari, is the place for good Cretan home cooking. Choose your meal from the pots and pans of food on display, sit down and prepare to enjoy a scrumptious meal. It's open 7pm to midnight Monday to Saturday.

Places to Eat – Top End

When you're ready for a more formal dining experience head to *Aithrion*, on the corner of Almyrou and Arholeondos, an upscale restaurant that serves a full menu of well-prepared Greek specialties. Linen tablecloths and a grand piano set a romantic tone for a meal on the plant-filled terrace. It's open 7.30pm to 1am Monday to Saturday. Bookings are advisable on weekends, especially for later in the evening.

Giovanni Taverna (Korai 12) is a splendid place with two floors of large, airy rooms and, in summer, outdoor eating on a quiet pedestrian street. The food is a winning Mediterranean combination of Greek and Italian specialties, prepared with care and imagination. It's open noon to 2.30pm and 7.30pm to midnight Monday to Saturday. Bookings are advisable on weekend evenings.

Loukoulos (Korai 5) offers luscious Mediterranean specialties served on fine china and accompanied by soft classical music. You can either choose the elegant interior or dine on the outdoor terrace under a lemon tree. All the vegetables are organically grown and vegetarians are well cared for. It's open noon to 3pm and 7pm to midnight Monday to Saturday.

No city can call itself truly cosmopolitan without a Chinese restaurant and Iraklio is no exception. *New China (Korai 1)* has an extensive menu of competent Chinese dishes slightly altered to please local palates. There is a pleasant courtyard. It's open noon to 3pm and 7pm to midnight Monday to Saturday.

Entertainment

The best time to engage in cultural pursuits is during the Iraklio Summer Arts Festival which presents international guest orchestras and dance troupes as well as local talent. Concerts and stage productions are offered sporadically the rest of the year; the tourist office of Iraklio will have the latest schedules.

The main venue for Iraklio's cultural scene is *Nikos Kazantzakis Open Air Theatre* at Jesus Bastions. This immense open air theatre is the main site for Iraklio's Summer Arts Festival when musicians, actors and dancers perform under the stars. There are special events the rest of the year and, when not being used by live performers in the summer, it's used as an open-air cinema. The box office (☎ 242 977) is open 9am to 2.30pm and 6.30 to 9.30pm daily.

Iraklio has about half a dozen cinemas but the most centrally located is the *Astoria Cinema* on Plateia Eleftherias. It screens first-run movies in their original language which is usually English.

Cafes & Bars The bars and cafes around Plateia Venizelou are as hyped-up as the non-stop crowds milling around the Mo-

rosini Fountain. The pedestrian area of Korai and Perdikari is lined with stylish kafeneia that attract a before-disco crowd eager to see and be seen. The old buildings along Handakos street contain relaxed bar/cafes with cosy interiors and enclosed patios more suitable for conversation than people-watching.

Four Lions (Plateia Venizelou) has a restaurant downstairs and a rooftop bar that is a great perch to watch the goings on around the Morosini Fountain, directly below. A subdued crowd chats in comfortable chairs around a replica of the famous Four Lions Fountain. It's open noon to midnight daily.

Although busy all day, *De Facto (Kantanoleon 2)* is one of the most fashionable bars in town early in the evening when it offers ringside seats to the evening promenade around Morosini Fountain. It's also very gay-friendly. It's open noon to midnight daily.

Guernica (Apokoronou Kritis 2) boasts traditional decor and contemporary rock which mix well to create one of Iraklio's hippest bar-cafes. The terrace-garden of this rambling old building is a delight in summer and in winter you can warm up next to the fireplace. It's open 10 am to midnight daily .

Take Five (Arkoleontos 7) is an old favourite on the edge of El Greco Park that doesn't get going until after sundown when the outside tables fill up with a diverse crowd of regulars. It's a gay-friendly place, the music and ambience are low-key and it's open daily 10 am to midnight.

Jasmin (Handakos 45) is a friendly bar/cafe with a back terrace that specialises in herbal tea but also serves alcoholic beverages. The nightly DJs play rock and world music as well as techno. It's open noon to midnight daily.

Aktapika (Dedalou 2) is a large airy upscale place next to the Morosini Fountain that bustles day and night. It has a great balcony and is a good place to come early in the evening for people-watching. The DJ plays jazz, rock and world music. It's open 10am to 1am daily.

IRAKLIO

Pagopeion (The Ice Factory), on Plateia Agios Titou, is a former ice factory and the most original bar/restaurant on the island. There's almost too much to look at in this whimsical place but don't miss the surreal toilets. The restaurant serves dishes with names like 'Roll With Me, Baby' pasta and Arm Agadon peppers. At around 10pm a DJ comes to spin jazz, rock and techno. It's gay-friendly, and open from 8am to midnight daily.

On trendy Korai with its rows of postmodern kafeneia, *Ideon Antron* (*Perdikari 1*), is a throwback to the past. The stone interior with its shiny wood bar creates a relaxed, inviting place. It's open 10am to 1am daily.

Sousouro (Androgeo 9) has a quieter ambience than other places in the neighbourhood. Sit outside and watch the scene around Korai or retreat to the artsy interior where a pianist entertains most evenings. It's open 6pm to 1am daily. *Rebels*, at the intersection of Korai and Perdikari, was one of the pioneers in the neighbourhood and is the most obvious 'designer' bar. Marble-topped tables and hanging lamps with Japanese patterns create a decor that blends badly with the relentless techno pounding in the background.

Discos Iraklio has the smartest and most sophisticated discos on the island. The following venues open around midnight, close near dawn and devote the intervening hours to keeping a young crowd of clubbers in perpetual motion. The cover charge runs from 1500 dr to 2000 dr and includes a drink.

You may not want to buy real estate on Ikarou Avenue but this action-packed street serves up the wildest nightlife in town. The music is a contemporary mix of rock, techno and Greek. One or more of these venues is likely to be closed weeknights in the summer as the club scene moves to Ammoudara. There's *DNA* at No 11; *Politia, Fougaro, Kratitirio*, and *Vareladiko* at No 9; and *Silo Club* at No 24. Wear black.

There's also nightlife action near the harbour. Iraklio's smart set packs the recently refurbished *Privilege Club* (*Dukos Beaufort 7*), a dancing club that can easily hold 1000 people. Like many of Crete's dancing clubs, there's international music (rock, techno etc) until about 2am when the Greek music takes over. Next door is the *Yacht Club* (*Dukos Beaufort 9*) that attracts a smartly dressed assortment of young locals and visitors. The clubs vie to attract the chicest crowd.

Shopping

Iraklio is where the money is so it's a good place to pick up the latest Cretan fashions, replace a suitcase or shop for luxury goods. Dedalou is a pedestrian shopping street lined with some of the classier tourist shops but the market street, 1866, is a lot more fun. This narrow street is always packed (except on Saturday and Sunday when it is closed) and stalls spill over with sponges, herbs, fruits, vegetables, utensils, T-shirts, nuts, honey, shoes, and jewellery. Look for the ornate Cretan wedding loaves. These round loaves decorated with flower motifs are not meant to be eaten but they do make attractive kitchen decorations. For gold and silver jewellery, head to Kalokerinou or the busily commercial 25 Avgoustou. Kalokerinou is also a good street to buy embroidery, although you'll get better deals in Kritsa. There are no department stores in Iraklio. For leather goods try Tsihlakis at No 96 on 1821, which offers a wide selection of handbags and ladies shoes, some of which are handmade by local artisans. Spyros Valergos is a good stop on colourful 1866 street for ceramics, clothing, statues and icons.

Getting There & Away

Air – international Air Greece has three flights a week to Stuttgart and four flights a week to Cologne in the summer. Cronus Airlines has five flights a week to London and four flights a week to Paris in the summer. Their office (☎ 34 3366) is at 1821 10. KLM-associate Transavia flies direct between Amsterdam and Iraklio on Monday and Friday. Transavia is represented by Sbokos Tours (☎ 22 9712), Dimokratias 51.

Iraklio has lots of charter flights from all over Europe. Prince Travel (☎ 28 2706), 25 Avgoustou 30, advertises cheap last-minute tickets on these flights. Sample fares include London for 28,000 dr and Munich for 41,000 dr.

Air – domestic Olympic has at least six flights a day to Athens (21,900 dr) from Iraklio's Nikos Kazantzakis airport; three a week to Thessaloniki (29,900 dr); four a week to Rhodes (21,900 dr) and two a week to Santorini (15,400 dr). The Olympic Airways office (☎ 22 9191) is at Plateia Eleftherias 42.

Air Greece has four flights a day to Athens (20,400 dr), two daily to Thessaloniki (29,400 dr), and three weekly to Rhodes in the summer (23,400 dr). Their office (☎ 33 0729 or 33 0739) is at Ethnikis Antistaseos 67 (off the map).

Aegean Airlines has three daily flights to Athens (18,500 dr) and one daily flight to Thessaloniki (29,700 dr). Their office is at the airport (☎ 33 0475).

Bus There are buses every half-hour (hourly in winter) to Rethymno (1½ hours, 1550 dr) and Hania (3 hours, 2900 dr) from the Rethymno/Hania bus station opposite Bus Station A. Following is a list of other destinations from Bus Station A:

destination	duration	fare	frequency
Agia Pelagia	45 mins	650 dr	5 daily
Agios Nikolaos	1½ hours	1400 dr	half-hourly
Arhanes	30 mins	340 dr	15 daily
Hersonisos/ Malia	1 hour	750 dr	half-hourly
Ierapetra	2½ hours	2100 dr	7 daily
Lassithi plateau	2 hours	1400 dr	2 daily
Milatos	1½ hours	1000 dr	1 daily
Sitia	3½ hours	2850 dr	5 daily

Buses leave Bus Station B for:

Agia Galini	2½ hours	1500 dr	7 daily
Anogia	1 hour	750 dr	6 daily
Matala	2 hours	1500 dr	9 daily
Phaestos	2 hours	1250 dr	8 daily

Taxi There are long-distance taxis (☎ 21 0102) from Plateia Eleftherias, opposite the Astoria Hotel and Bus Station B, to all parts of Crete. Sample fares include Agios Nikolaos (9700 dr); Rethymno (12,000 dr); and Hania (20,000 dr).

Ferry Minoan Lines and ANEK both operate ferries every evening each way between Iraklio and Piraeus (10 hours). They depart from both Piraeus and Iraklio between 7.45 and 8 pm. Fares are 7000 dr deck class and 14,100 dr for cabins. The Minoan Lines' boats, the F/B *Nikos Kazantzakis* and the F/B *Knossos*, are more modern and more comfortable than their ANEK rivals. ANEK, though, is a better bet for deck-class travellers. It has dorm beds with plastic-covered mattresses, while Minoan Lines has only seats.

GA Ferries has three boats a week to Santorini (four hours, 3700 dr), continuing to Paros (8½ hours, 5200 dr) and Piraeus and stopping at Naxos. GA also has three ferries a week to Rhodes (11 hours, 6400 dr) via Karpathos (3800 dr). Minoan Lines runs three boats a week to Thessaloniki (12,100 dr) via Santorini, Paros, Volos, Tinos and the Sporades. The travel agencies on 25 Avgoustou are the place to get information and buy tickets. Iraklio's port police can be contacted on ☎ 24 4912.

Getting Around
To/From The Airport Bus No 1 goes to/from the airport every 15 minutes between 6 am and 1 am for 170 dr. It leaves the city from outside the Astoria Hotel on Plateia Eleftherias.

Bus Local bus No 2 goes to Knossos every 10 minutes from Bus Station A (20 minutes, 240 dr). It also stops on 25 Avgoustou and 1821.

Car & Motorcycle Most of Iraklio's car and motorcycle-hire outlets are on 25 Avgoustou. You'll get the best deal from local companies like Sun Rise (☎ 22 1609) at 25 Avgoustou 46, Loggeta Cars & Bikes (☎ 28 9462) at Plateia Kallergon 6, next to El

Greco Park, Motor Club (☎ 222 408), at Agglon Square 18 or Ritz Rent-A-Car at the Hotel Rea (see Places to Stay), which has discounts for hotel guests. The airport has a full range of car-rental companies including Hertz, Eurodollar and Europcar. Sun Rise also has a range of scooters and motorcycles.

Bicycle Mountain bicycles are able to be hired from Porto Club Travel Services (☎ 28 5264) Avgoustou 20.

KNOSSOS Κνωσσός

Knossos (k-nos-**os**), 5km from Iraklio, was the capital of Minoan Crete. Nowadays it's the island's major tourist attraction. The road leading up to the famous site is an uninspiring gauntlet of souvenir shops and fruit juice stands but the palace is magnificent. Thanks to a beautiful site surrounded by green hills and shaded by pine trees it is Crete's most evocative location.

The ruins of Knossos were uncovered in 1900 by the British archaeologist Sir Arthur Evans. Heinrich Schliemann, the legendary discoverer of ancient Troy, had had his eye on the spot (a low, flat-topped mound), believing an ancient city was buried there, but had been unable to strike a deal with the local landowner. Arthur Evans was a well-travelled journalist, museum curator and classicist with an interest in ancient scripts when he came across some ancient stones engraved with what appeared to be hieroglyphic writing.

Learning that the stones came from Crete, Evans set sail in 1894. Still thinking that the low, flat-topped mound that interested Schliemann might contain the key to his hieroglyphics, Evans acquired a share of the site which, significantly enough, gave him exclusive rights to the excavation. He returned five years later and began digging with a group of Cretan workmen.

The flat-topped mound was called Kephala and the vanished palace that it

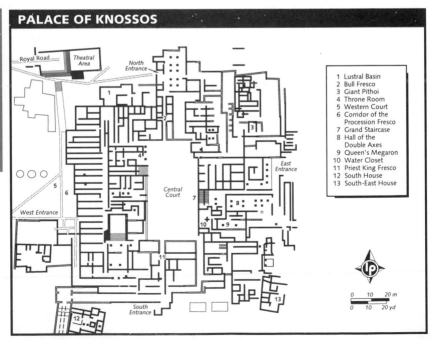

PALACE OF KNOSSOS

Royal Road · Theatrical Area · North Entrance · West Entrance · East Entrance · Central Court · South Entrance

1 Lustral Basin
2 Bull Fresco
3 Giant Pithoi
4 Throne Room
5 Western Court
6 Corridor of the Procession Fresco
7 Grand Staircase
8 Hall of the Double Axes
9 Queen's Megaron
10 Water Closet
11 Priest King Fresco
12 South House
13 South-East House

0   10   20 m
0   10   20 yd

IRAKLIO

contained emerged quickly. The first treasure to be unearthed was a fresco of a Minoan man followed by the discovery of the Throne Room. The archaeological world was stunned. Until he began his excavations no one had suspected that a civilisation of this maturity and sophistication had existed in Europe at the time of the great Pharaohs of Egypt. Some even speculated that it was the site of the lost city of Atlantis to which Plato referred many centuries later.

Evans was so enthralled by his discovery that he spent 35 years and £250,000 of his own money excavating and reconstructing sections of the palace. Some archaeologists have disparaged Evans' reconstruction, believing he sacrificed accuracy to his overly vivid imagination. Unlike other archaeological sites in Crete however, substantial reconstruction helps the visitor to visualise what the palace might have looked like at the peak of its glory. Evans maintained that he was obliged to rebuild columns and supports in reinforced concrete or the palace would have collapsed, but many archaeologists feel that the integrity of the site was irretrievably damaged. Most non-specialists maintain that Sir Arthur did a good job and that Knossos is a knockout. Without these reconstructions it would be impossible to visualise what a Minoan palace looked like.

You will need to spend about four hours at Knossos to explore it thoroughly. To beat the crowds and avoid the oppressive heat,

it's best to get there as soon as the site opens and visit the Throne Room first before the tour buses arrive. The cafe at the site is expensive – you'd do better to bring a picnic along. The site (☎ 23 1940) is open 8 am to 7 pm every day between April and October. In winter the site closes at 5 pm. Admission is 1500 dr.

History

The first palace at Knossos was built around 1900 BC but most of what you see dates from 1700 BC after the Old Palace was destroyed by an earthquake. It was then rebuilt to a grander and more sophisticated design. The palace was partially destroyed again sometime between 1500 and 1450 BC and inhabited for another 50 years before it was devastated once and for all by fire.

The New Palace was not erected helterskelter but carefully designed to meet the needs of a complex society. There were domestic quarters for the king or queen, residences for officials and priests, homes of common folk and burial grounds. Public reception rooms, shrines, workshops, treasuries and storerooms were built around a paved courtyard in a design so intricate that it may have been behind the legend of the Labyrinth and the Minotaur. (See Myth of the Minotaur boxed text.)

Until recently it was possible to enter the royal apartments, but in early 1997 it was decided to cordon this area off before it

IRAKLIO

The palace at Knossos is regarded as a masterpiece of Minoan civilisation.

LPP

The Myth of the Minotaur

King Minos of Crete invoked the wrath of Poseidon when he failed to sacrifice a magnificent white bull sent to him for that purpose. Poseidon's revenge was to cause Pasiphae, King Minos' wife, to fall in love with the animal.

In order to attract the bull, Pasiphae asked Daedalus, chief architect at Knossos and all-round handyman, to make her a hollow, wooden cow structure. When she concealed herself inside, the bull found her irresistible. The outcome of their bizarre association was the Minotaur: a hideous monster who was half-man and half-bull.

King Minos asked Daedalus to build a labyrinth in which to confine the Minotaur and demanded that Athens pay an annual tribute of seven youths and seven maidens to satisfy the monster's huge appetite.

Minos eventually found out that Daedalus had been instrumental in bringing about the union between his wife and the bull, and threw the architect and his son Icarus into the labyrinth. Daedalus made wings from feathers stuck together with wax and, wearing these, father and son made their getaway. As everyone knows, Icarus flew too close to the sun, the wax on his wings melted, and he plummeted into the sea off the island of Ikaria.

Athenians, meanwhile, were enraged by the tribute demanded by Minos. The Athenian hero, Theseus, vowed to kill the Minotaur and sailed off to Crete posing as one of the sacrificial youths. On arrival, he fell in love with Ariadne, the daughter of King Minos, and she promised to help him if he would take her away with him afterwards. She provided him with the ball of twine that he unwound on his way into the labyrinth and used to retrace his steps after slaying the monster. Theseus fled Crete with Ariadne. The two married, but Theseus abandoned Ariadne on the island of Naxos on his way back to Athens.

On his return to Athens, Theseus forgot to unfurl the white sail that he had promised to display to announce that he was still alive. This prompted his distraught father, Aegeus, to hurl himself to his death from the Acropolis. This, incidentally, is how the Aegean sea got its name.

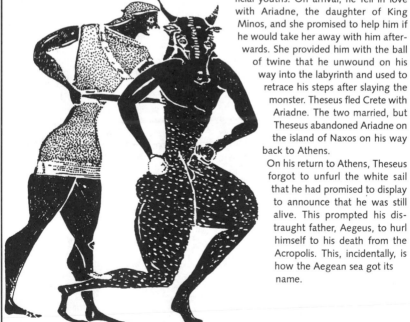

LPP

Theseus killing the Minotaur.

IRAKLIO

disappeared altogether under the continual pounding of feet. Extensive repairs are under way but it is unlikely to be open to the public again.

Exploring the Site

Numerous rooms, corridors, dogleg passages, staircases, nooks and crannies, prohibit a detailed walk description of the palace. However, Knossos is not a site where you'll be perplexed by heaps of rubble, trying to fathom whether you're looking at the Throne Room or a workshop. Thanks to Evans' reconstruction, the most significant parts of the complex are instantly recognisable (if not instantly found). On your wanders you will come across many of Evans' reconstructed columns. Most are painted deep brown-red with gold-trimmed black capitals. These, like all Minoan columns, taper at the bottom.

Strategically placed copies of Minoan frescoes help infuse the site with the artistic spirit of these remarkable people. The Minoan achievements in plumbing equal their achievements in painting; drains and pipes were carefully placed to avoid flooding, taking advantage of centrifugal force. It appears that at some points water ran uphill, demonstrating a mastery of the principle that water finds its own level. Also notice the placement of light wells and the relationship of rooms to passages, porches, light wells and verandas, which keep rooms cool in summer and warm in winter.

The usual entrance to the palace complex is across the Western Court and along the **Corridor of the Procession Fresco**. The fresco depicted a long line of people carrying gifts to present to the king; only fragments remain. A copy of one of these fragments, called the **Priest King Fresco**, can be seen to the south of the Central Court.

An alternative way to enter is to have a look at the Corridor of the Procession Fresco, then walk straight ahead to enter the site from the northern end. If you do this you will come to the **theatral area**, a series of steps whose function remains unknown. It could have been a theatre where spectators watched acrobatic and dance perform-

ances, or the place where people gathered to welcome important visitors arriving by the Royal Road.

The **Royal Road** leads off to the west. The road, Europe's first (Knossos has lots of firsts), was flanked by workshops and the houses of ordinary people. The **Lustral Basin** is also in this area. Evans speculated that this was where the Minoans performed a ritual cleansing with water before religious ceremonies.

Entering the **Central Court** from the north, you will pass the relief **Bull Fresco** which depicts a charging bull. Relief frescoes were made by moulding wet plaster, and then painting it while still wet.

Also worth seeking out in the northern section of the palace are the **giant pithoi**. Pithoi were ceramic jars used for storing olive oil, wine and grain. Evans found over 100 of these huge jars at Knossos (some were 2m high). The ropes used to move them inspired the raised patterns that adorn the jars.

Once you have reached the Central Court, which in Minoan times was surrounded by the high walls of the palace, you can begin exploring the most important rooms of the complex.

From the northern end of the west side of the palace, steps lead down to the **Throne Room**. This room is fenced off but you can still get a good view of it. The centrepiece, the simple, beautifully proportioned throne, is flanked by the **Griffin Fresco**. Griffins were mythical beasts regarded as sacred by the Minoans.

The room is thought to have been a shrine, and the throne the seat of a high priestess, rather than a king. Certainly, the room seems to have an aura of mysticism and reverence rather than pomp and ceremony. The Minoans did not worship their deities in great temples but in small shrines, and each palace had several.

On the 1st floor of this side of the palace is the section Evans called the **Piano Nobile**, for he believed the reception and state-rooms were here. A room at the northern end of this floor displays copies of some of the frescoes found at Knossos.

Returning to the Central Court, the impressive **grand staircase** leads from the middle of the eastern side of the palace to the royal apartments, which Evans called the Domestic Quarter. This section of the site is now cordoned off. Within the royal apartments is the **Hall of the Double Axes**. This was the king's megaron, a spacious double room in which the ruler both slept and carried out certain court duties. The room had a light well at one end and a balcony at the other to ensure air circulation.

The room takes its name from the double axe marks on its light well. These marks appear in many places at Knossos. The double axe *(labrys)* was a sacred symbol to the Minoans, and the origin of our word 'labyrinth'.

A passage leads from the Hall of the Double Axes to the **queen's megaron**. Above the door is a copy of the **Dolphin Fresco**, one of the most exquisite Minoan artworks. A blue floral design decorates the portal. Next to this room is the queen's bathroom, complete with terracotta bathtub and a **water closet**, touted as the first ever to work on the flush principle; water was poured down by hand.

Getting There & Away
Regular buses operate from Iraklio. See Iraklio's Getting Around section for details.

AMMOUDARA
Ammoudara lies about 4 km west of Iraklio and is the closest beach to the city. Long, sandy and wide, the beach is relatively uncrowded, making Ammoudara a good alternative place to stay if you want to escape big-city Iraklio. The discos and nightlife of Ammoudara lure tourists and residents of Iraklio alike during the summer.

Orientation
The town lies along the main road from Iraklio. The strip of hotels begins at Candia Maris in the east and ends at the hotel Dolphin Bay in the west. Although it may seem as though the beach is completely barricaded by hotels, in fact there are entrances next to the Agapi Beach hotel and the Candia Maris hotel.

Places to Stay
Ammoudara is dominated by large resort hotels but there are a few domatia scattered about. Across from the Candia Maris is *Rent Rooms* (☎ 250 723) with singles/doubles for 8000/10,000 dr. Nearby is *Hotel Sun* (☎ 251 790, fax 251 161) which has a small swimming pool and simple single/ double rooms for 10,000/12,000 dr. *Agapi Beach* (☎ 250 502, fax 258 731) is in the middle of the hotel strip right on the beach and has two outdoor swimming pools, three tennis courts, air-conditioning and a water sports centre. Singles/doubles are 29,000/ 48,000 dr in the high season and includes half-board.

The other deluxe hotel is *Candia Maris* (☎ 314 632, fax 250 669) which has a centre for thalassotherapy as well as an open air cinema, six tennis courts, air-con and a kindergarten that offers babysitting. Singles/ doubles are 57,800/66,000 dr in high season, including breakfast.

Places to Eat
The dining scene in Ammoudara is uninspiring but you could try *Golden Wheat Chinese Restaurant* which has crispy duck and fried noodles with shrimp at a reasonable price. It's open 6.30pm to midnight Monday through Saturday.

Discos
When the summer gets going in Iraklio, clubbers head west to Ammoudara Beach and beyond. *Bachalo* is the hottest disco in the region and generates high-voltage glamour on summer evenings. It's in Linoperamata, 2 km west of Ammoudara, and is open 11 pm to dawn daily from June to September.

In the centre of Ammoudara try *Banana Club* across the street from the Candia Maris hotel which has live music. *Barracuda Cafe* is a spacious bar right on the beach.

Getting There & Away
The No 6 bus from Iraklio stops in front of the Cretan Beach hotel and the Agapi Beach hotel in Ammoudara. By taxi it costs about 1000 dr.

South Central Iraklio Region

The highway that runs from Timpaki to Pirgos divides the northern portion of the Iraklio prefecture from the southern coastal resorts. Along the highway are busy commercial centres, such as Timpaki, Mires, Agia Deka and Pirgos that market the agricultural produce from the surrounding region. Although these towns hold little interest for tourists they do give a sense of the dynamism of the Cretan economy. Of more interest to travellers are the extraordinary archaeological sites of Phaestos, Agia Triada and Gortyn which trace almost 3000 years of ancient history from Minoans through the Romans to the early Christians.

When you get tired of poking around ancient ruins the south coast beaches of Matala, Kalamaki and Lendas beckon with long stretches of sandy beach. Further to the east are the more deserted beach towns of Arvi and Keratokambos and the lovely mountain town of Ano Viannos.

VORI

The pleasant unspoilt village of Vori, 2km east of Timpaki, is composed of a main square surrounded by winding streets of whitewashed houses. The main attraction here is the outstanding **Museum of Cretan Ethnology**, which provides a fascinating insight into traditional Cretan culture. The detailed explanations are in English, the first part of the exhibits deal with the herbs, flora and fauna that form the basis of the Cretan diet. There are descriptions about how snails, crabs and eels were gathered and eaten. Other exhibits include farm implements such as ploughs and grinding mills as well as beautiful weavings, wicker furniture, woodcarvings and musical instruments. The museum is well-signposted from the main road and is open 10 am to 6 pm daily in the summer, 9 am to 3 pm Monday to Friday, from November to March. Admission is 500 dr.

There are a few *tavernas* around the main square and *Pension Margarite* which is signposted 400m up from the museum.

MIRES
☎ 0892 • pop 3500

This busy market town is an inevitable stop if you're changing buses from Iraklio en route to the south coast. It's a good place to pick up supplies in the many stores lining the main street. There's a post office on the main street and the OTE is on the street immediately south of the bus station. Also around the bus station is the Commercial Bank of Greece with an ATM. If you have to stay overnight you'll find **Rent Rooms Gortys** (☎ 22 528) signposted 150m up from the bus station. There are 13 buses a day from Iraklio (1¼ hours, 1050 dr).

GORTYN Γόρτυν

The archaeological site of Gortyn (also called Gortina and Gortys), 46km southwest of Iraklio, is the largest in Crete and one of the most fascinating. There's little here from the Minoan period because Gortyn was little more than a subject town of powerful Phaestos until it began accumulating riches (mostly from piracy) under the Dorians. By the 5th century BC, it was as influential as Knossos. When Crete was under threat from the Romans the Gortynians cleverly made a pact with them and, when the Romans conquered the island in 67 BC, they made Gortyn the island's capital. The city blossomed under Roman administrators who endowed it with lavish public buildings such as a Praetorium, amphitheatre, public baths, music school and temples. Except for the 7th-century-BC Temple of the Pithian Apollo and the 7th-century-AD Church of Agios Titos, most of what you see in Gortyn dates from the Roman period. Gortyn's centuries of splendour came to an end in 824 AD when the Saracens raided the island and destroyed the city.

The vastness of the site indicates how important Gortyn city was to the Romans. The city sprawls over a square kilometre of plains, foothills and the summit of Agios Ioannis Mountain. As for most Roman cities, water was an important matter. The

IRAKLIO

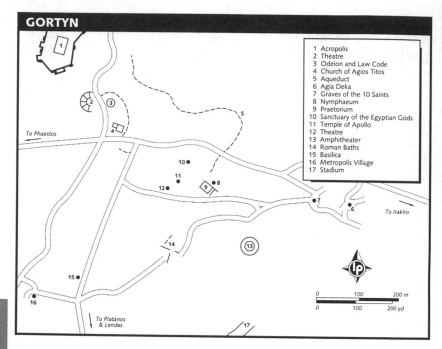

GORTYN

1 Acropolis
2 Theatre
3 Odeion and Law Code
4 Church of Agios Titos
5 Aqueduct
6 Agia Deka
7 Graves of the 10 Saints
8 Nymphaeum
9 Praetorium
10 Sanctuary of the Egyptian Gods
11 Temple of Apollo
12 Theatre
13 Amphitheater
14 Roman Baths
15 Basilica
16 Metropolis Village
17 Stadium

To Phaestos

To Iraklio

To Platanos & Lendas

Romans needed water for their elaborate systems of fountains and public baths. At one time there must have been ducts and an aqueduct that brought water from the springs of Votomos, 15 km away. There also must have been streets and a town square, but these have not been excavated.

Although Italian archaeologist Federico Halbherr first explored the site in the 1880s, excavations are still going on. There is a fenced area north of the main road with a large number of ruins outside the fenced area both north and south of the main road from Agia Deka. Beginning south of the main road you'll first come to **Temple of the Pythian Apollo** which was the main sanctuary of pre-Roman Gortyn. Built in the 7th century BC, the temple was expanded in the third century BC and converted into a Christian basilica in the 2nd century AD. Nearby is **Praetorium** which was the palace of the Roman governor of Crete, an administrative building with a

basilica and a private residence. Most of the ruins date from the 2nd century AD and were repaired in the 4th century. To the north is the 2nd century **Nymphaeum**, a public bath supplied by an aqueduct bringing water from Zaros. It was originally adorned with statues of nymphs. South of the nymphaeum is the **amphitheatre** which dates from the late 2nd century AD.

The most impressive monument within the fenced area is **Church of Agios Titos** which is the finest early Christian church in Crete. It was probably built on the site of an earlier church but this construction dates from the 6th century. The stone cruciform church has two small apses and contains three levels. The surviving apse provides a hint of the magnificence of this church many centuries ago. Nearby is the **Odeion** which was a theatre built around the 1st century BC. Behind the Odeion is a plane tree that, according to legend, served as a love nest for Zeus and Europa.

Iraklio's fortress – a safe haven for fishing boats.

Cretan anchor near Iraklio's harbour.

...as once one of Crete's most famous hippie hang-outs.

Beyond the Odeion is the star attraction – the stone tablets engraved with the 6th century BC **Laws of Gortyn**. The stone tablets containing the laws, written in 600 lines in a Dorian dialect, were the earliest law code in the Greek world. Ancient Cretans were preoccupied with the same issues that drive people into court today – marriage, divorce, transfers of property, inheritance and adoption as well as criminal offences. Dorian legal theories are interesting but the main value of these remarkable tablets is the insight they provide into the social organisation of pre-Roman Crete. It was an extremely hierarchical society, divided into slaves and several categories of free citizens, each of whom had strictly delineated rights and obligations.

It's a bit of a hike but it's worth visiting the **Acropolis** at the top of the hill in the north-west corner of the site. Following the road along the stream near the Odeion you will come to a gate beyond the theatre that marks the start of the path to the top. In addition to a birds-eye view of the entire site, the acropolis contains impressive sections of the pre-Roman ramparts.

The site (☎ 0892-31 144) is open 8 am to 6 pm daily. Admission is 800 dr. Buses to Phaestos stop at Gortyn.

PHAESTOS Φαιστός

The Minoan site of Phaestos (Fes-**tos**), 63km from Iraklio, was the second most important palace city of Minoan Crete. Of all the Minoan sites, Phaestos has the most awe-inspiring location, with all-embracing views of the Mesara Plain and Mt Psiloritis. The layout of the palace is identical to Knossos, with rooms arranged around a central court.

Pottery deposits indicate that the site was inhabited in the Neolithic era probably around 4000 BC when the first settlers established themselves on the slopes of nearby Kastri Hill. The first palace was built around 2000 BC and then destroyed in the earthquake that levelled so many Minoan palaces. The ruins were covered with a layer of lime and debris which formed the basis for a new palace that was begun

around 1700 BC. It too was destroyed in the catastrophe that befell the island in 1450 BC. In the intervening centuries Phaestos was the political and administrative centre of the Mesara Plain. Ancient texts refer to the palace's importance and note that it minted its own coins. Although Phaestos continued to be inhabited in later centuries, it fell into decline as Gortyn rose in importance. Under the Dorians Phaestos headed a league of cities that included Matala and Polyrrhinia in western Crete. The leagues battled continuously and Phaestos was defeated by Gortyn in the 2nd century BC.

Excavation of the site began in 1900 by Professor Federico Halbherr of the Italian School of Archaeology, which is continuing the excavation work. In contrast to Knossos, Phaestos has yielded very few frescoes; it seems the palace walls were mostly covered with a layer of white gypsum. Perhaps, with such inspiring views from the windows, the inhabitants didn't feel any need to decorate their walls. There has been no reconstruction of these ruins. The difficulty of visualising the structure of the palace is further compounded by the fact that the site includes remains of the Old Palace and the New Palace.

Exploring the Site

Past the ticket booth, the **Upper Court** which was used in both the old and new palaces contains remains of buildings from the Hellenistic era. A stairway leads down to the **Theatral Area** which was once the staging ground for performances. The seats are at the northern end and the southern end contains the **west facade of the Old Palace**. The 15m-wide **grand stairway** leads to the **Propylon** which was a porch. The steps of the stairway are thicker and higher in the middle to produce a more impressive effect. Below the Propylon are the **storerooms** which still contain pithoi storage urns. The square hall next to the storerooms is thought to have been an **office**, where tablets containing Linear A script were found beneath the floor in 1955. South of the storeroom a **corridor** led to the west side of the **Central Court**. South of the corridor

PHAESTOS

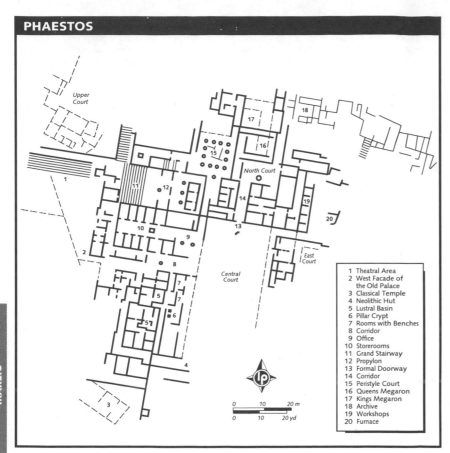

1	Theatral Area
2	West Facade of the Old Palace
3	Classical Temple
4	Neolithic Hut
5	Lustral Basin
6	Pillar Crypt
7	Rooms with Benches
8	Corridor
9	Office
10	Storerooms
11	Grand Stairway
12	Propylon
13	Formal Doorway
14	Corridor
15	Peristyle Court
16	Queens Megaron
17	Kings Megaron
18	Archive
19	Workshops
20	Furnace

Fishing boats moored in Iraklio's harbour with the skyline of the island's capital in the background.

Fortress walls rise out of the harbour in Iraklio.

Matala Beach w

is a **lustral basin**, rooms with benches and a **pillar crypt** similar to that at Knossos. The Central Court is the centrepiece of the palace, affording spectacular views of the surrounding area. It is extremely well-preserved and gives a good sense of the magnificence of the palace. Porticoes with columns and pillars once lined the long sides of the Central Court. Notice the **Neolithic hut** at the south-western corner of the Central Court. The best preserved parts of the palace complex are the reception rooms and private apartments to the north of the Central Court, where excavations continue. Enter through the **Formal Doorway** with half columns at either side, the lower parts of which are still *in situ*. The corridor leads to the north court; the **Peristyle Court**, which once had a paved veranda, is to the left of here. The royal apartments (**Queen's Megaron** and **King's Megaron**) are north-east of the Peristyle Court but they are currently fenced off. The celebrated Phaestos Disc was found in a building to the north of the palace. It now resides in Iraklio's Archaeological Museum. The site is open 8 am to 7 pm daily. Admission is 1200 dr.

The highlight of Iraklio's Rocca al Mare is its exterior relief of the Lion of St Mark.

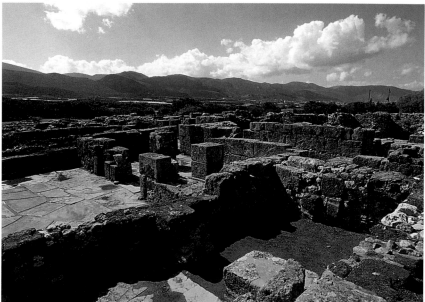

The Central Court of the Minoan site of Phaestos, near Iraklio.

Excavations of the Palace of Malia have uncovered exquisite Minoan artefacts.

The restoration of Knossos helps visitors understand how the Minoans lived 4000 years ago.

Getting There & Away

There are eight buses a day from Iraklio's Bus Station B to Phaestos (1½ hrs, 1250 dr), six from Agia Galini (40 minutes, 400 dr) and five from Matala (30 minutes, 300 dr). Services are halved in winter.

AGIA TRIADA Αγία Τριάδα

Agia Triada (ag-i-a tri-a-da) is a small Minoan site 3km west of Phaestos in an enchanting landscape surrounded by hills and orange groves. Like the site of Phaestos it appears that Agia Triada has been occupied since the Neolithic era.

Masterpieces of Minoan art such as the 'Harvester's Vase', the 'Boxer Vase' and the 'Chieftain's Cup', now in the Iraklio Archaeological Museum, were found here but the palace was clearly not as important as the palace at Phaestos. Its principal building was smaller than the other royal palaces although it was built to a similar design. This, and the opulence of the objects found at the site, indicate that it was a royal residence, possibly a summer palace of Phaestos' rulers.

After the entrance, you will first pass the ruins of a **Minoan House** before reaching

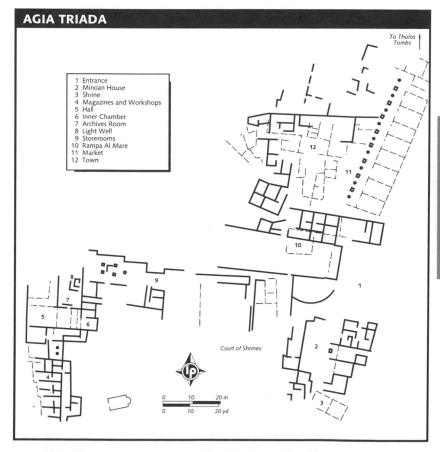

AGIA TRIADA

1 Entrance
2 Minoan House
3 Shrine
4 Magazines and Workshops
5 Hall
6 Inner Chamber
7 Archives Room
8 Light Well
9 Storerooms
10 Rampa Al Mare
11 Market
12 Town

To Tholos Tombs

Court of Shrines

0   10   20 m
0   10   20 yd

IRAKLIO

the **shrine** that dates from the early 14th century BC. It once contained a frescoed floor painted with octopus and dolphins. The floor is now in the Archaeological Museum of Iraklio. North-west of the shrine is a paved courtyard that Italian excavators called the **Court of Shrines**. Notice the **magazines and workshops** in the south-west wing of the palace; the 'Chieftain's Cup' was found in one of these rooms. North of the workshops you will come to a **hall** and then the **inner chamber** that contains a raised slab that might have supported a bed, indicating that these were the residential quarters. This part of the palace had rooms for entertainment and rooms for business. The **archives room** once contained over 200 sealstones, which were probably used to fasten documents, and a wall painting of the wild cat of Crete that is now in the Archaeological Museum of Iraklio. The **Rampa al Mare** ramp that runs beneath the north side of the palace is thought to have run down to the sea at one point. A path leads from the fenced site along the hillside to a Minoan **cemetery** that dates from around 2000 BC. There are two circular beehive tombs.

The site is open 8.30 am to 3 pm daily. Admission is 500 dr. The road to Agia Triada takes off to the right about 500m from Phaestos on the road to Matala. There is no public transport to the site.

MATALA Μάταλα
☎ 0892 • postcode 702 00 • pop 300
Matala (**ma**-ta-la), on the coast 11km south-west of Phaestos, was once one of Crete's best known hippie hang-outs. When you see the dozens of eerie caves speckling the rock slab on the beach's edge, you'll see why 60s hippies found it like groovy, man. The hippies turned the caves into a modern troglodyte city – moving ever higher up the cliff to avoid sporadic attempts by the local police to evict them. Joni Mitchell was among a number of hippies who lived in the caves; she wrote about the Matala moon in her song, *Carey*. The caves were originally Roman tombs cut out of the sandstone rock in the 1st century AD and have been used as

dwellings for many centuries. The soft rock allowed cave-dwellers to carve out windows, doors and beds.

The caves are all that remains of ancient Matala which probably served as a port for the great Minoan centre of Phaestos. Matala enjoyed a burst of activity under the Romans that lasted from 67BC until the Arab conquest in the 9th century. During those centuries Matala was the port for Gortyn. Excavations around Matala have revealed coins from Gortyn, vases and amphorae.

These days, Matala is a decidedly tacky tourist resort packed out in summer and bleak and deserted in winter. The turtles like it however. Matala and the area around it is a popular nesting ground for *Caretta Caretta* sea turtles. The Sea Turtle Protection Society has a booth near the car park. The sandy beach below the caves is one of Crete's best, and the resort is a convenient base from which to visit Phaestos and Agia Triada.

Orientation & Information
Matala's layout is easy to fathom. The bus stop is on the central square, one block back from the waterfront. There is a mobile post office just past the car park on the right as you enter the town. The OTE is beyond here in the beach car park. There is no tourist office but Monza Travel (☎ 45 757, fax 45 763) on the right as you enter town rent rooms, apartments, cars and bikes, change money and arrange for boat excursions. There is a laundry on the left as you enter town and a bookshop with English language books and newspapers next to the Hotel Zafiria.

Things to See & Do
Forget about museums, monuments, and archaeological sites. Matala is about the beach and the caves. The caves are fenced off by night but you can visit them from 8 am to 7 pm daily, June to September. It costs 500 dr. The beach is great for swimming and has pine trees along the edge which cast some shade. You can rent a lounge chair for 700 dr a day. If you feel more energetic, pedalboats cost 2500 dr an hour and canoes are 1000 dr an hour.

For a less crowded beach head to Kokkini Ammos (Red Beach). It's a 30 minute scramble south over the rocks and attracts a smattering of nudists. At the furthest end of town along the beach is a market street with woodcarvings, jewellery, ceramics and small fruit stands selling local products.

Places to Stay

Matala Community Camping (☎ 42 340) is a lovely, shady site just back from the beach. There is another *campsite (☎ 42 596)* near Komos Beach, about 4 km before Matala on the road from Phaestos.

There are several pleasant options in Matala proper. Walk back along the main road from the bus station and turn right at the Zafiria Hotel. This street is lined with budget accommodation.

One of the best options is *Fantastic Rooms to Rent (☎ 45 362)*, on the right. The pretty double/triple rooms cost 6000/7000 dr with private bathroom, telephone and fridge. *Pension Antonios (☎ 45 123/438)*, opposite, has attractively furnished singles/doubles/triples with bathrooms are 4000/6000/7000 dr, and double/triple apartments cost 8000/9000 dr.

On the same street you'll find *Silvia Rent Rooms (☎ 45 127)* that has doubles/triples for 5000/7000 dr. The C-class *Hotel Fragiskos (☎ 45 380/135)*, on the left as you head out of town, charges 8000/14,500 dr for singles/doubles with private bathroom. The hotel is somewhat bland but it has a swimming pool. Breakfast is an extra 1500 dr per day and air-conditioning is an extra 1500 dr a day.

On the right as you head out of town is *Hotel Europa (☎ 45 113)*, an attractive building of whitewashed walls and pine that has singles/doubles for 7000/8000 dr a day.

The sprawling *Hotel Zafiria (☎ 45 366, fax 45 747)* takes up a good portion of Matala's main road into town. At the hotel there is a spacious lobby-bar and rooms have balconies, sea views, and telephones. Singles/doubles are 7000/8500 dr including breakfast.

Places to Eat

Most of the restaurants in Matala are more notable for their seaside views than their cuisine which tends to be undistinguished. *Lions* is a popular hang-out right on the beach with pretty good food. You could also try *Two Brothers* and *Manolis*. For self-caterers, there's a minimarket across the street from the Hotel Zafiria.

Restaurant Mystical View, high above Komos Beach about 3km from Matala, has spectacular views over the Messara Gulf and Komos Beach and serves excellent Cretan specialties. The restaurant is signposted off the road to Phaestos and is open noon to midnight daily.

Getting There & Away

There are eight buses a day between Iraklio and Matala (two hours, 1500 dr), five a day between Matala and Phaestos, (30 minutes, 300 dr), eight a day between Mires and Matala (30 minutes, 300 dr) and six a day between Matala and Agia Galini (45 minutes, 600 dr).

AROUND MATALA

When Matala fills up in the summer, travellers head to **Pitsidia,** a sleepy little town 5km north-east of Matala. There's not much to do here except meet other travellers and book a horse riding tour from Melanouri Horse Farm (☎ 0892-45 040) which offers lessons and beach rides through the surrounding region. A full day tour is 12,000 dr. There is no post office or OTE. You can rent cars or motorcycles from Monza Travel Agency (☎ 0832-45 275). *Hotel Aretousa (☎ 0892-45 555)*, on the main road, has singles/doubles for 6000/7000 dr.

Also on the main road is *Rent Rooms Babis (☎ 0892-45 273)* which has a large taverna on the ground floor and rooms above. One kilometres west of Pitsidia is *Kommos Camping (☎ 0892-45 596, fax 45 250)* which is beautifully located next to the beach and has a swimming pool.

All buses to Matala stop in Pitsidia; the bus stop is in the centre of the town in front of Hotel Aretousa.

Three kilometres east of Pitsidia is the

small village of **Sivas**. It's a good alternative to Matala and has more character than Pitsidia. It is almost untouched by tourism although there are two domatia: **Rent Rooms Kunterbunt** (☎ 0892-42 649) and **Rent Rooms Lofos** (☎ 0892-42 605). There are signs to both places at the entrance to the town. There are a few kafeneia in the pleasant, shady square and an excellent ceramic shop. Vasilis Peios is the potter and you can see him working at the wheel turning out typical Cretan cups, vases and dishes. Buses from Miras to Matala stop just outside of the village.

KAMALARI
☎ 0892 • pop 339

Built on top of three hills, Kamalari provides a complete escape into traditional Cretan village life. Its proximity to Kalamaki Beach makes it attractive to visitors plus there's an important Minoan tomb just outside town. Since the town is only 2.5km west of Phaestos, it's a good base from which to explore the beaches and archaeological sites of the south coast.

Orientation & Information
There's no tourist office but in the centre of town Moto Auto Store (☎/fax 42 690) rents cars, motorcycles, rooms and apartments. It's open 8 am to 1 pm and 5 to 9 pm Monday to Saturday.

Things to See
The circular **Minoan Tomb** of Kamalari dates from 1900 BC and is extraordinarily well-preserved with stone walls still standing two metres high. Archaeologists believe that there were five small rooms outside the circular tomb that were used for burial rites. Clay models depicting the funerary rituals were unearthed by excavators and are now in the Archaeological Museum of Iraklio. The road to the tomb is clearly indicated at the entrance to Kamalari.

Places to Stay & Eat
Kamalari is becoming popular with travellers so there are a number of accommodation opportunities. At the entrance to the

town is **Pension Cula** (☎ 41 689) which has tidy rooms and a shady garden. Next door is **Studios Pelikanos** (☎ 42 690). Both have singles/doubles for 5000/6000 dr. **Apartments Ambeliotisa** (☎/fax 42 690, email ambeliostisa@nikitakis.mir.forthnet.gr) has furnished studios/apartments for 56,000/ 70,000 dr a week. The pink and white stucco building has a stone fireplace, veranda and an outdoor barbecue. **Taverna Milonas** has good Cretan food in the centre of town.

Getting There & Away
There is one morning bus daily from Iraklio via Mires (1½ hours, 1450 dr).

KALAMAKI
☎ 0892

The wide, sandy beach that stretches for many kilometres in either direction is Kalamaki's best feature, and makes for a beautiful walk. Located 2.5km south-west of Kamalari, tourism is in its embryonic stage in Kalamaki after the recent opening of a paved road all the way to the beach. The good news is that you won't feel crowded but, unfortunately, the beach is lined with a string of half-finished concrete structures. It's a quiet place to stay however, and the swimming is good.

Orientation & Information
There is one main road leading into the town square which is right behind the beach. There is no post office, tourist office, or OTE but Kalamaki Rent Motors (☎ 45 470) is a friendly, informative office that handles car and bike rentals, hotel reservations and air and boat tickets. It's in the main square and is open 9 am to 2 pm and 5 to 10 pm daily from Easter to October. Umbrellas and beach chairs are available for rent on the beach but most taverna lining the beachfront promenade offer them for free if you eat at their establishment.

Places to Stay & Eat
On the right when you enter the town you'll come to **Rooms Nefeli** (☎ 45 211) a brand new three-storey building which has singles/doubles for 7000/9000 dr. Nearby is

Pension Libyan Sea (☎/fax 45 180) which has simple but pleasant rooms for 8000 dr. *Kostas Rent Rooms (☎/fax 45 692)*, on the main square on top of a mini market and travel agency, has singles/doubles for 5000/7000 dr. Along the beach try *Rooms Psiloritis (☎ 45 693)* with singles/doubles at 6000/8000 dr. One of the most attractive places to stay in Kalamaki is *Pension Galini (☎ 45 042, fax 23 442)* which is about 100m from the sea. The spacious rooms with balconies are furnished in pine and some have fully equipped kitchens. There's also a roof top terrace with a view of the sea. Singles/doubles are 9000/11,000 dr.

On the central square *Taverna Avra* is a good breakfast spot, offering fresh juice and pastries. Along the beach try *Dilino* restaurant, *Restaurant Posidonas* and *Taverna Ilios* which offer Cretan specialties at fair prices.

Getting There & Away
There's one morning bus daily from Iraklio via Mires (2 hours, 1550 dr)

KOMMOS
The archaeological site of Kommos, 1km west of Pitsida along a beautiful beach, is still being excavated by American and Canadian archaeologists. Although the site is fenced off it's easy to get an idea of it from the outside. Kommos is believed to have been the port for Phaestos and contains a wealth of Minoan structures. It's even possible to spot the layout of the ancient town with its streets and courtyards, and the remains of workshops, dwellings and temples. Notice the Minoan road paved in limestone that leads from the southern section inland towards Phaestos; the ruts in the road from Minoan carts and a sewer on its northern side are still visible.

LENDAS
☎ 0892
The narrow pebbly beaches of Lendas would not be anyone's idea of an idyllic getaway, but the village that clings to the cliff over the beach has a pleasant view over the Libyan Sea. The demands of tourism

have expanded the original little village into a more sizeable town, but Lendas retains an appealing intimacy. Within walking distance there's an archaeological site and the Dytikos naturist beach.

Orientation & Information
As you enter town from the main road there's a left fork that takes you to the eastern car park and a right fork that takes you to the main square. The bus stops outside the eastern car park. In the main square you'll find Monza Travel Agency, an exchange place and a supermarket. There is no post office, bank or OTE. To get to Dytikos (often called Diskos) follow the main road west for a kilometre or the path alongside the coastal cliffs.

Things to See
The archaeological site of **Lebena** is right outside town. Lebena was a kind of health spa that the Romans visited for its therapeutic springs. Only two granite columns remain of a temple that dates from the 4th century BC. Next to the temple was a treasury with a mosaic floor that is still visible. Very little else is decipherable and the springs have been closed since the 1960s.

Places to Stay & Eat
The right fork from the main road takes you down to the restaurant and *Rent Rooms Zorbas (☎ 95 228)*. Apartments cost 8000 dr, rooms with a seaview are 5000 dr and those without are 4000 dr, all with private bathroom. Nearby is the taverna and *Rent Rooms El Greco (☎ 95 322)* which has singles/doubles for 5000/6500 dr all with private bathrooms and balconies with seaviews. Next to the main square is *Eva's Rooms (☎ 95 244)* with doubles for 4500 dr.

Getting There & Away
There's a daily afternoon bus from Iraklio (3 hours, 1600 dr)

ANO VIANNOS
☎ 0895 • pop 1400
Ano Viannos, 65km south of Iraklio, is a delightful village built on the southern flanks of

Mt Dikti. Steep, cobbled streets lead up from the main road to a thicket of lanes bedecked with flowers and overhung with trees. From the top of the village there are panoramic views over the region. The air is cooler than it is along the overheated coast and the village gets very little tourism which makes it a pleasant stop or overnight stay.

Orientation & Information
There is only one main road that passes through the village. The post office is next to the restored church and the Folklore Museum is on the western end of town. Signs from the town centre direct you up to the Agia Pelagia Church.

Things to See
The **Folklore Museum**, has a wealth of exhibits explaining traditional Cretan culture there are colourful costumes, musical instruments, wine and olive presses, weavings and a collection of farm implements. It's open 10 am to 2 pm daily. Admission is 500 dr.

The village's 14th-century **Church of Agia Pelagia** is a tiny structure. The interior walls, covered with luscious frescoes by Nikoforos Fokas, are in remarkably good condition.

The blues, rusts, oranges and greens of the frescoes create an otherworldly effect that perfectly suits the spiritual nature of their subjects. Follow signs from the main street but first ask in a kafeneia for the whereabouts of the key.

Places to Stay & Eat
Ano Viannos has one domatia. *Taverna & Rooms Lefkas* (☎ 22 719), opposite the large church, has basic singles/doubles for 3000/4000 dr with private bathroom. The rooms are over the taverna which has good Cretan specialties and a pleasant shady terrace.

Getting There & Away
Public transport is poor. There are two buses a week from Iraklio to Ano Viannos (2½ hours, 1900 dr) and two a week to Ierapetra (one hour, 800 dr) via Mirtos.

KERATOKAMBOS
☎ 0895
From Ano Viannos it's 13km south to the unspoilt village of Keratokambos, where there's a pleasant tree-lined beach and not much else. The one road that runs along the beach contains a few domatia and tavernas. The tranquillity of this tiny resort is its chief asset.

Orientation & Information
There's no bank, post office, OTE, car rental agency or any other reminder of the outside world.

Places to Stay & Eat
At the coast turn left to reach *Taverna & Rooms Thoinikas* (☎ 51 401), where singles/doubles with private bathroom cost 4000/6000 dr. *Taverna Nikitas* (☎ 51 477), by the sea in the town centre, offers delicious roast lamb and pork and has access to four-person apartments for 5000 dr. Ecologically sound and aesthetically pleasing, *Komis Studios* (☎ 51 390) offers 15 three-level apartments exquisitely decorated in a rustic style but with the comforts of air-con, telephone and TV. The units use wind and solar power; the sewage is treated biologically. Rooms cost 25,000 dr and are worth every bit of it. The excellent on-site restaurant uses local products. *Morning Star Taverna* is the best bet for vegetarians with tasty artichoke stew for 1000 dr. *Taverna Kriti* offers excellent fish dishes and *Taverna Thoinikas* specialises in grilled food.

Getting There & Away
There's no public transport available to Keratokambos.

ARVI
☎ 0895 • pop 300
The turn-off for Arvi is 3km east of Ano Viannos. Arvi is bigger than Keratokambos, but only gets visitors during July and August. Hemmed in by cliffs, Arvi is a suntrap where bananas grow in abundance. Like Keratokambos, it's a good place to escape the hectic summer resort scene.

Orientation & Information

The main street skirts a long sand and pebble beach. It's a 15-minute walk inland to Moni Agios Andronios, a 19th-century monastery on a hillside. There is no bank, post office or OTE in Arvi.

Places to Stay & Eat

Pension Kolibi (☎ 0895-71 250), in a quiet setting 1km west of Arvi, has immaculate doubles/triples with private bathroom for 6000/7000 dr.

Pension Gorgona (☎ 0895-71 353), on the main street, has pleasant doubles for 7500 dr with bathroom. Further west, *Hotel Ariadne* (☎ 0895-71 300) has well-kept singles/doubles for 7000/8000 dr with private bathroom. *Apartments Kyma* (☎ 0895-71 344) at the eastern end of the village has luxurious apartments for 8000 dr. *Kima Restaurant*, on the main street, serves hearty Greek fare and *Taverna Diktina* features vegetarian food.

Getting There & Away

There is no public transport to Arvi. With a 4WD the 10km coastal dirt road between Keratokambos and Arvi is accessible.

Central Iraklio Region

Although most travellers zip through the region that lies between Iraklio and the south coast, several sights make it well worth a stop, but you need your own wheels to explore the region. Mount Psiloritis lies to the west in the Rethymno region; its eastern slopes taper down to a series of high plateaux and deep caves. The most famous cave is the Ideon Andron which was either the birthplace of Zeus or his playground as a young child, depending on which legend you believe. There's not much to see in the cave and there are no paved roads, but if you have a motorcycle or a jeep, take the main road south from Anogia and follow the signs to the cave.

The main roads leading south from Iraklio pass through a series of bustling commercial towns and villages that see very few tourists. There are no hotels or domatia in this region. Arhanes makes a worthwhile stop and Zaros is a good base to explore the surrounding region.

ZAROS

☎ 0894 • pop 2,500

If the name rings a bell, it's probably because your litres of mineral water are labelled 'Zaros'. Known for its spring water and bottling plant, Zaros (46km south of Iraklio) is a traditional town where many men and women still wear black. Various excavations in the region indicate that the Minoans and the Romans settled here, lured by the abundant supply of fresh water. The spring water from Zaros also supplied the great Roman capital of Gortyn. Byzantine monasteries are nearly as abundant as the spring water. You can visit the monasteries of Vrondisi, Agios Nikolaos, Odigitria, Apezano and Kardiotissa; Hotel Idi has full details on treks to all the monasteries.

Orientation & Information

The business end of Zaros is at the southern entrance of the town. The post office and a supermarket are across the street from the police station. There's no OTE, but there is a phone in the minimarket, next to Libero pub. You can change money at the Hotel Idi.

Things to See & Do

The Zaros **bottling plant** is on the northern end of town past the Hotel Idi. They usually will allow you to take a look at the packaging and bottling operations inside. A short distance before the bottling plant you will come to a lovely shady park, **Votomos**, with a small lake and a children's playground, which makes a great picnic stop. If you have your own wheels the Byzantine monasteries and traditional villages that are tucked away in the hills are worth exploring. Take the road that leads west from Zaros and you'll see a sign directing you to **Moni Agios Nikolaos** which is at the mouth of the Agios Nikolaos Gorge. The monastery still houses several monks and the church contains some 14th-century paintings. A few kilometres beyond Moni Agios Nikolaos is the **Moni Vrondisi** which is notable for its 15th-century Venetian fountain. The monastery also has a church with excellent examples of early 14th-century frescoes from the Cretan School of Fresco Painting. The drive to the monasteries and beyond to the traditional mountain villages of Vorizia and Kamares is particularly scenic. Tracks along the way lead up into the mountains if you are in for further explorations. The E4 European Climbing Route runs through the Zaros region providing well-marked hiking trails.

Places to Stay & Eat
A couple of kilometres outside the town, *Hotel Idi (☎ 31 301, fax 31 51, email votomos@otenet.gr)* is surrounded by trees and greenery and makes for a restful escape from the crowds along the coast. The pleasant, traditional rooms cost 9300/13,700 dr for singles/doubles with air-con, including buffet breakfast. The hotel is open all year and has a swimming pool, tennis courts, and opportunities to hike in the surrounding hills. Close to the town centre is the homey *Studios Keramos (☎ 31 352)*. It's run by friendly Katarina who has decorated her cosy establishment with a display of Cretan crafts, weaving, baskets and pottery. The large studios cost 6000 dr and include a copious traditional Cretan breakfast.

Trout is the speciality at *Votomos*, a superb fish restaurant affiliated with the Hotel Idi. You'll see the trout gliding through a huge fresh water reserve so you'll know they're fresh. It's open 11 am to midnight daily from March to October and weekends only from November to February.

Getting There & Away
There are two afternoon buses daily from Iraklio (1 hour, 900 dr).

ARHANES
☎ 081 • pop 4000
Known for its excellent wine, Arhanes, 16km south of Iraklio, lies in the heart of Crete's principal grape-producing region.

The fertile basin of Arhanes has been settled since the Neolithic period. The ancient Minoans built a grand palace that was an administrative centre for the entire Arhanes basin. The palace was destroyed, rebuilt and destroyed again along with the other great Minoan palaces. The town came back to life under the Myceaneans flourishing until the Dorian conquest of Crete in 1100 BC. Today Arhanes is a quiet and obviously prosperous town with meticulously restored old houses and neatly laid out squares. The main reason to visit is for the excellent archaeological museum but there is no place to stay in town.

Orientation & Information
The bus stop is across the street from a restored church. Uphill from the bus stop and a right fork is another small square. Signs direct you to the post office, and the OTE is in a pastel building next to a taxi stand. Nearby is a small park surrounded by tavernas and a Creta Bank.

Things to See
Only scraps of the palace (signposted from the main road) remain but the **Archaeological Museum of Arhanes** has some interesting finds from the archaeological excavations that have been taking place for the last three decades in numerous sites around the region. The exhibits, including **larnakes** (coffins) and musical instruments from Fourni and the dagger from Anemospilia, are well displayed and extremely informative. The museum is open 8.30 am to 2.30 pm Wednesday to Monday and admission is 500dr.

Getting There & Away
There are buses hourly from Iraklio (30 minutes, 340 dr).

AROUND ARHANES
Vathypetro Villa is 5km south of Arhanes, and well-signposted from the town. Dating from 1600 BC the Minoan villa was probably the home of a prosperous Minoan noble. The villa complex included storerooms, where wine and oil presses, a weaving loom

Murder in the Temple

Human sacrifice is not commonly associated with the peace-loving Minoans but the evidence found at the site of Anemospilia suggested irrefutably otherwise. A simple three-room temple was excavated in the 1980s. To the immense surprise of the scientists they found a young man placed on an altar and trussed, with a huge sacrificial dagger amid the bones. The remains of two other skeletons nearby which were probably those of a priestess and an assistant, seemed to indicate that the boy's death was part of a sacrificial rite. The sacrifice was probably made just as the 1700 BC earthquake began, in a desperate attempt to appease the gods. The site is now fenced but the scenic drive there makes it worthwhile.

and a kiln were discovered. Although the doors to the rooms with the wine press and oil press are locked you can catch a glimpse of the tools through the barred windows. The site is open 8.30 am to 3 pm daily and there is no admission charge. There is no public transport to the site although several travel agencies in Iraklio include a visit as part of their tour itinerary.

From the bus stop in Arhanes follow signs up a steep trail to the Minoan burial grounds at **Fourni**. The round stone 'beehive tombs' form the most extensive Minoan cemetery in the island and date from about 2500 BC. One of the tombs contained the remains of a Minoan noble woman whose jewellery is on display in the Archaeological Museum of Iraklio.

North-Eastern Coast

Ever since the national road along the north coast opened in 1972, the coast between Iraklio and Malia has seen a frenzy of de-

velopment. A concrete wall of hotels, schnitzel outlets, and tacky souvenir shops lines every stretch of sandy beach here. There's not much here for individual travellers since the hotels deal almost exclusively with package tour operators who block-book hotel rooms many months in advance. The prices for individual travellers are relatively steep compared with the discounts package tourists receive and the service is likely to be indifferent for those without the clout of a tour operator behind them. The main centres here are Hersonissos and Malia. The Minoan palace at Malia is the only site of cultural interest.

MALIA

The township of Malia is a highly commercialised resort that developed in the 1970s because of its long sandy beach. It's crowded and noisy but there's plenty to do and it's within easy reach of the fascinating Minoan Palace of Malia.

Orientation & Information

The main road from Iraklio runs through Malia and divides the town into two parts. The north side of the road is packed with hotels, restaurants, travel agencies and nightlife, while the south side of the road leads up to the old town. The post office is near the main road at 28 Octovrou 2 and the OTE is uphill about 500m and signposted from the old town. There are plenty of places to change money on the main road. Charlie's Travel (☎ 33 834) is a good source of information and sells excursions to all destinations on the island.

Places to Stay & Eat

There are very few rooms available for individual travellers. One of the few reasonably priced places is *Sofia Rent Rooms* (☎ 31 873) which has doubles for 8000 dr. At the top of the old town is *Scorpios Apartments* (☎ 33 300) with studios for 10,000 dr. You could also try *Argo* (☎ 31 636) right on the main road which has doubles for 12,000 dr. *Espera* (☎ 31 086) in the old town has doubles for 15,000 dr and studios for 20,000 dr.

IRAKLIO

Mass Tourism

Although none of the resorts along the north-eastern coast would win any beauty contests, Hersonissos and Malia set a new standard of dreariness. In both resorts, the local population has retreated to pleasant little hill villages behind the main road and left the lower beachfront towns to wallow in sleazy commercialism. From frozen fish in the seaside restaurants to imported 'Cretan' ceramics and machine-made weavings in souvenir shops, nothing is authentic. Unlike the rest of the island, the music in bars and tavernas is either western or the most Westernised Greek music available. Don't understand Greek letters? Don't worry. You won't see a single one in Hersonissos and Malia. All signs are in Latin letters. Fish & chip stands, cafes with names like 'Cheers' and 'Union Jack', video bars playing British sitcoms seem designed to shield visitors from the horrible realisation that they are actually in a foreign country.

Although Hersonissos and Malia are often considered identical examples of atrocious overdevelopment, there are subtle differences between the two resorts. Both places chase bargain-hunting package tourists but Hersonissos has a few luxury hotels on the outskirts. The crowds are young in both towns but in Malia, you'll feel decrepit if you're over 22. Both places assume that you will consume copious quantities of alcohol. In Hersonissos you drink to get drunk, dance and wake up with a stranger while at Malia you drink to get drunk, fall down and wake up on the pavement. If that sounds good to you, you know where to go, but try to visit Crete someday.

IRAKLIO

Curiously enough you get better Indian food in Malia than you do Greek food. *Delight of India* is off the main road and has excellent chicken masala. Otherwise try *Romantic Raphael Restaurant* in the old town which has a good selection of Asian food.

Entertainment

Currently the most popular discos are *Disco Flash* and *Cloud Nine*. During the summer raves are held in the nearby stadium about every two weeks.

Getting There & Away

There are buses from Iraklio every 30 minutes (1 hour, 750 dr).

PALACE OF MALIA Μάλια

The Palace of Malia, 3km east of Malia, was built at about the same time as the two other great Minoan palaces at Phaestos and Knossos. The first palace was built around 1900 BC and rebuilt after the earthquake of 1700 BC. What you see is the remains of the newer palace from which many exquis-

ite artefacts from Minoan society were found. Excavation began in 1915 by Greek archaeologists and is being continued by French archaeologists. Because the ground plan has been well-preserved, it's an easy site to comprehend. The site (☎ 31 597) is open 8.30 am to 3 pm Tuesday to Sunday. Admission is 800 dr. Any bus going to/from Iraklio along the north coast can drop you at the site.

Exploring the Site

Entrance to the ruins is from the **West Court**. Head south through the **Magazines** and at the extreme southern end you'll come to the eight circular pits which archaeologists think were **grain silos**. To the east of the pits is the main entrance to the palace which leads to the southern end of the **Central Court**. Moving north-east you'll come to the **Kernos Stone**, a disc with 24 holes around its edge. Archaeologists have yet to ascertain its function, but it probably had a religious purpose. Adjacent is the **Grand Staircase** which might have led to a shrine. To the north is the **Pillar Corridor**

PALACE OF MALIA

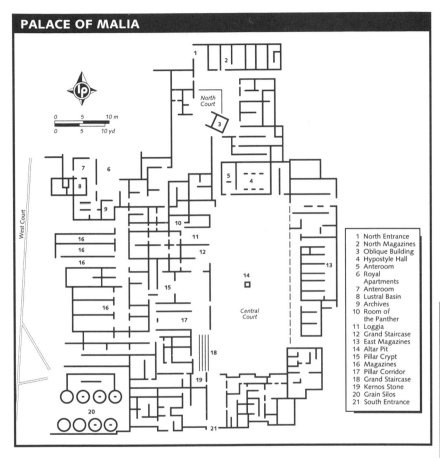

North Court

West Court

North
Court

Central
Court

0   5   10 m
0   5   10 yd

1 North Entrance
2 North Magazines
3 Oblique Building
4 Hypostyle Hall
5 Anteroom
6 Royal
   Apartments
7 Anteroom
8 Lustral Basin
9 Archives
10 Room of
   the Panther
11 Loggia
12 Grand Staircase
13 East Magazines
14 Altar Pit
15 Pillar Crypt
16 Magazines
17 Pillar Corridor
18 Grand Staircase
19 Kernos Stone
20 Grain Silos
21 South Entrance

IRAKLIO

with interconnecting rooms and next to it is the **Pillar Crypt** with the Minoan double-axe symbol engraved on the pillars. The impressive **Central Court** is 48m long and 22m wide and contains remains of the Minoan columns. Notice the pit in the exact centre of the courtyard, which may have been an altar.

At the north end of the west side of the court is the **Loggia**, which was probably used for ceremonial purposes. Next to the Loggia is the **Room of the Panther** in which a 17th-century-BC stone axe shaped like a panther was found. North-west are the **Royal Apartments** with a **Lustral Basin.** At the north end of the central court is the **Hypostyle Hall** with benches on the side indicating that it may have served as a kind of council chamber. Other rooms include the **archives room** in which tablets containing Linear A script were found. On your way out through the north entrance notice the pithoi in the **North Court.**

HERSONISSOS
☎ 0897

Hersonissos, 26km east of Iraklio, began its days as a small fishing village on a hill, but those days are long past. It is now a mecca to package tourism with a long coastal strip of neon-lit restaurants and look-alike hotels. The beach is sandy but packed with lounge chairs and umbrellas. There is always something to do in Hersonissos; there are plenty of excursions to all parts of the island and an action-packed nightclub scene.

Orientation & Information
The coastal road from Iraklio to Agios Nikolaos runs through a town called El Venizelou. Most travel agencies, banks and services are located along this road. The OTE office is north of El Venizelou and the post office is in the centre of town on Digeni Akriti. There is also a beachfront road of taverns, hotels and nightclubs. There is no tourist office but Hermes Rent a Bike (☎ 32 271) is a good source of information.

Uphill from the main road is the village of Koutoulafari which is touristy but retains some of the atmosphere of a traditional village.

Places to Stay & Eat
Most hotels only deal with groups, but you could try *Aquarius Apartments* (☎ 24 560) which has studios for 10,000 dr and apartments for 12,000 dr. *Hersonissos Hotel* (☎ 23 568) has rooms with balconies, sea-views, and air-conditioning for 30,000 dr. On the waterfront is *Palmera Hotel* (☎ 22 481) with doubles for 12,000 dr.

With almost 400 newly built bungalows, the vast *Royal Mare Village* (☎ 25 025, fax 21 664, email marketing@aldemar.gr) is more like a metropolis on the sea than a village. It has two children's pools, two outdoor pools, an indoor pool, tennis courts, water sports, a children's playground, fitness centre, volleyball and archery.

The most outstanding feature is the Thalasso Centre, the most modern and best-equipped water wonderland in Crete. Rooms start at 80,000 dr for a simple bungalow and go up to 250,000 dr for a suite with a private pool. Their Web site is at www.aldemar.gr.

There are plenty of restaurants in Hersonissos serving 'Cretan food' but none are more than mediocre. For a decent meal you would be better off eating at the restaurant of a luxury hotel.

Entertainment
Most people come to Hersonissos for the nightlife. As soon as the sun goes down, the bars fill up, the discos crank up their volume and the whole resort turns into one vast party.

Although the popular places change from year to year, you can usually rely on the *It Club* and *After Dark* on El Venizelou and *Camelot* on the beachfront road.

Getting There & Away
There are buses from Iraklio every 30 minutes (45 minutes, 600 dr).

Lassithi

Crete's easternmost prefecture, Lassithi receives far fewer visitors than the rest of the island. The southern coast extends from the village of Myrtos in the west to the commercial centre of Ierapetra and beyond to the lovely and untouched beaches of Xerokambos and Kato Zakros. The centre of the north coast is Sitia with the lovely palm-lined beach of Vai in the far east. The fertile region of the Lassithi Plateau in the west provides wonderful walks through quiet villages and fields to Dikteon Cave where Zeus was born. Archaeology buffs will enjoy the Palace of Zakros, an evocative Minoan site in the east next to Kato Zakros Beach.

AGIOS NIKOLAOS Αγιος Νικόλαος
☎ 0841 • postcode 721 00 • pop 9000
Agios Nikolaos, or 'Ag Nik' as it's familiarly known, emerged as a port for the city-state of Lato (see Ancient Lato later in the chapter) in the early Hellenic years when it was known as Lato-by-Kamara. The harbour assumed importance in the Greco-Roman period after the Romans put an end to the piracy that had plagued the northern coast.

The town continued to flourish in the early Christian years and in the 8th or 9th century the small Byzantine Church of Agio Nikolaos was built.

When the Venetians bought Crete in the 13th century, the Castel Mirabello was built on a hill overlooking the sea and a settlement arose below. The Castel was damaged in the earthquake of 1303 and was burned by pirates in 1537, before being rebuilt according to plans from the famous military architect Sammicheli. When the Venetians were forced to abandon the castel to the Turks in 1645 they blew it up, leaving it in ruins. There's no trace of the Venetian occupation except the name they gave to the surrounding gulf – Mirabello or 'beautiful view'.

The town was resettled in the mid-19th century by fleeing rebels from Sfakia and it

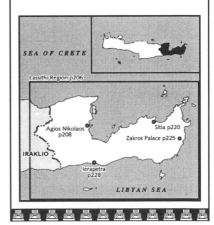

was later named capital of the Lassithi region. In the early 1960s, it became a chic hideaway for the likes of Jules Dassin and Walt Disney. By the end of the decade package tourists were arriving in force.

The beaches outside town are mediocre but the heart of the town is an irresistibly fetching conjunction of lake and harbour.

Even though the waterside has been shamelessly overbuilt with bars, shops and restaurants, the natural beauty of the setting hasn't been entirely extinguished.

Orientation
The town centre is Plateia Venizelou, 150m up Sofias Venizelou from the bus station. The most interesting part of town is around the picturesque Voulismeni Lake, 100m north of Plateia Venizelou. From the lake,

LASSITHI REGION

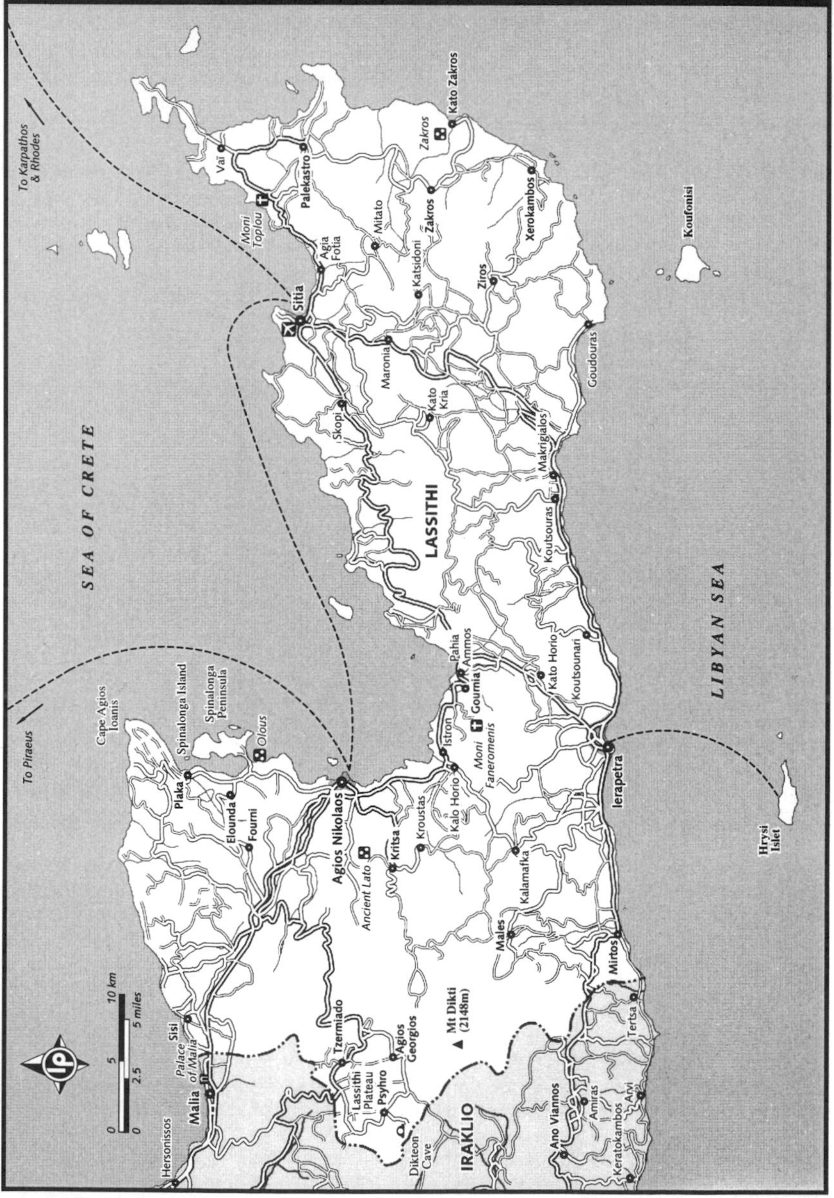

Mt Dikti (2148m)

LIBYAN SEA

SEA OF CRETE

To Karpathos & Rhodes

To Piraeus

LASSITHI

IRAKLIO

walk north-east along Koundourou, turn left at the bottom and you will come to a bridge that separates the lake from the harbour. The tourist office is at the far side of the bridge.

Information

The municipal tourist office (☎ 22 357, fax 82 354) is open 8 am to 9.30 pm daily from the beginning of April to mid-November. The tourist police (☎ 26 900, Kondogianni 34), are open 7.30 am to 2.30 pm daily.

The port police (☎ 22 312) are in the same building as the tourist office.

Money The National Bank of Greece on Plastira has a 24-hour automatic exchange machine. The tourist office also changes money.

Post & Communications The post office (28 Oktovriou 9), is open 7.30 am to 2 pm Monday to Friday. The OTE is on the corner of 25 Martiou and K Sfakianaki. It is open 7 am to 11 pm daily. Internet access is available at the pleasant Polychoros (☎ 24 876, email peripou@agn.forthnet.gr, Octovorou 28), open 9 am to 2 am daily.

Bookshop There is a well-stocked English-language bookshop at Koundourou 5 next to the bank.

Emergency Agios Nikolaos' general hospital (☎ 25 221) is between Lassithiou and Paleologou.

Things to See

The **folk museum**, next door to the tourist office, has a well-displayed collection of traditional handcrafts and costumes. It's open 10 am to 3 pm Sunday to Friday. Admission is 250 dr.

The **Archaeological Museum** (☎ 22 462), on Paleologou, is a modern building housing a large, well-displayed collection from eastern Crete. The exhibits are arranged in chronological order beginning with Neolithic finds from Mt Traostalos, north of Kato Zakros and early Minoan finds from Agia Fotia in the first room. Room II con-

tains the museum's highlight, *The Goddess of Myrtos*, a clay jug from 2500 BC found near Myrtos. Notice also gold jewellery, stone vases and stone tables with inscriptions in Linear A. Room III displays finds from the late Minoan period including pottery from Knossos, a marble chalice from Zakros and clay bathtubs decorated with birds and fish. Notice also a gold pin with an inscription in Linear A on the reverse side. Room IV is devoted to the late Minoan period with many finds from the Myrsini cemetery and a potter's wheel from Kritsa. Room V has pottery from Sitia and clay animals from Olous near Elounda. Room VI is a continuation of Room V and displays more pottery. The exhibits conclude in Room VII with glass and vases from the Greco-Roman period. The museum is open 8.30 am to 3 pm Tuesday to Sunday. Admission costs 500 dr.

The **Local Aquarium of Agios Nikolaos** (☎ 24 953), on Akti Koundourou, has interesting displays of fish and information about diving (including PADI courses) and snorkelling throughout Crete. It is open 10 am to 9 pm Monday to Saturday. Admission is 1300 dr.

Beaches The popularity of Agios Nikolaos has nothing to do with its beaches. The town beach, south of the bus station, and Kitro Platia Beach, north of the harbour, have more people than pebbles. Ammoudi Beach, on the road to Elounda, is equally uninspiring. The sandy beach at Almiros about a kilometre south of town is the best of the lot and tends to be less crowded than the others. There's little shade but you can rent umbrellas for 500 dr a day.

Voulismeni Lake The lake is the subject of many stories in relation to its depth and origins. The locals have given it various names, including Xepatomeni (bottomless), Voulismeni (sunken) and Vromolimni (dirty). The lake isn't bottomless – it's 64m deep. The 'dirty' tag came about because the lake used to be stagnant and gave off quite a pong in summer. This was

AGIOS NIKOLAOS

SEA OF CRETE

Ammoudi Beach

Voulismeni Lake

To Christina Pension, Minos
Beach Hotel & Bungalows
& Elounda

To Neapolis
& Iraklio

Quay

Port

Voulismeni
Lake

Kitroplatia
Beach

Plateia
Venizelou

To Miramare
Hotel, Kritsa,
Istron Beach,
Ierapetra,
Almiros Beach
& Sitia

PLACES TO STAY
2 Coral Hotel
5 Katerina Pension
6 Aphrodite Rooms
17 Hotel Panorama
19 Hotel Pergola
20 Mary Pension
35 Cronos Hotel
38 Green House
42 Hotel Elena
43 Apollon Hotel
44 Hotel Doxa
48 Hotel Mariella
49 Dias Hotel

PLACES TO EAT
8 Aouas Taverna
9 Avli
10 Pelagos
12 Taverna Pine Tree
13 Embassy Garden Restaurant
21 New Kow Loon
32 Restaurant du Lac
39 Sarri's Food
40 Taverna Itanos

OTHER
1 Local Aquarium
3 General Hospital
4 Archaeological Museum
7 Scooterland
11 Children's Playground
14 Folk Museum
15 Tourist Office
16 Lipstick Disco
18 Enplo
22 Santa Maria Bar
23 Royale Bar
24 Riffifi
25 Nostos
26 Kerazoza
27 Polychoros
28 Cafe du Lac
29 Manolis
30 OTE
31 Bookshop
33 Post Office
34 Olympic Airways
36 National Bank of Greece
37 Patsaki
41 Bus Station
45 Laundry
46 Supermarket
47 Tourist Police

rectified in 1867 when a canal was built linking it to the sea. The area around this picturesque lake is ringed with tavernas and cafes.

Activities
There is a diving centre, Creta's Happy Divers (☎ 82 546), in front of the Coral Hotel that offers boat dives and PADI certification courses.

Diexodos Adventure Unlimited (☎ 28 098) in Havania, north of Agios Nikolaos town offers cycling tours that take in the Lassithi Plateau for 1400 dr to 1600 dr.

They also have treks that include the archaeological site of Lato, the Dikta Summit and country villages for 1200 dr. All tours leave from Kritsa.

Organised Tours
Travel agencies in Agios Nikolaos offer coach outings to all Crete's top attractions. Nostos Tours (☎ 22 819), Koundourou 30, has boat trips to Spinalonga for 4000 dr, as well as guided tours of Phaestos and Matala (7500 dr); the Samaria Gorge (12,500 dr); and the Lassithi Plateau (7000 dr). It's open 8 am to 8 pm daily from March to November.

Special Events

In July and August Agios Nikolaos hosts the Lato Cultural Festival in various venues around town. There are concerts by local and international musicians, Cretan music played on traditional instruments, folk dancing, *mantinades* contests, theatre, art exhibits, literary evenings and swimming competitions. Ask at the tourist office for details. Agios Nikolaos also celebrates a Marine Week, the last week of June in even-numbered years with swimming, windsurfing and boat races as well as a fireworks display over the port.

Places to Stay

Agios Nikolaos receives few guests in the winter and most hotels close. The only establishments open all year are the Hotels Doxa and Dias. Once over the bridge, turn right and follow the road around the northern stretch of waterfront along the road to Elounda. Most of Agios Nikolaos' large and expensive hotels are along here. If you turn right at the bottom of Koundourou, without crossing the bridge, you will come to a stretch of waterfront with steps leading up to the right. These lead to the streets that have the highest concentration of small hotels and pensions.

Camping The nearest camp site to Agios Nikolaos is *Gournia Moon Camping (☎ 0842-93 24)*, near the Minoan site of Gournia. It has a swimming pool, restaurant, snack bar and minimarket. Buses to Sitia can drop you off outside.

Domatia *Green House (☎ 22 025, Modatsou 15)*, is a favourite with backpackers. It is ramshackle but clean, with a lush garden. Singles/doubles are 3000/4000 dr with shared bathroom. Breakfast is an additional 500 dr per person. Walk up Tavla (a continuation of Modatsou) from the bus station, and you'll find it on the right. *Aphrodite Rooms (☎ 28 058, Koritsas 27)*, has rooms for 3000/4000 dr with shared facilities and a tiny communal kitchen. At *Mary Pension (☎ 23 760, Evans 13)*, rooms with private bathroom cost 5000/6000 dr.

One of the best pensions in Agios Nikolaos is *Katerina Pension (☎ 22 766, Stratigou Koraka 33)* which is in an old house on a quiet, residential street. The enclosed garden is a delight and some rooms have their own balcony. Singles/doubles are 8000/10,000 dr.

Hotels – Budget The plant-filled lobby sets a homey tone for *Hotel Doxa (☎ 24 214, fax 24 614, Idomeneos 7)* that also boasts an attractive terrace for breakfast or drinks. Rooms are small but inviting and are equipped with telephones and balconies and cost 8000/10,000 dr.

A solid value in the centre of town, *Elena (Minoos 15)* offers large, airy rooms equipped with the basics but no extras. Everything is in working order but don't expect much in the way of decoration. *Hotel Pergola (☎ 28 152)* on Akti Themistokleous, has comfortable rooms with private bathroom for 5000/7000 dr.

The lobby isn't much in *Mariella Hotel (☎ 28 639, Latous 4)*, a small, family-run hotel, but the clean white rooms are cheerful and many have balconies. The hotel is conveniently located on a busy commercial street; front rooms can be noisy during the day but the area calms down at night when the action shifts to the bars around the port. Singles/doubles are 6000/7000 dr.

Dias Hotel (☎ 28 263/264, Latous 6), a small hotel in the town centre, is decorated in a traditional style and offers rooms with telephones, TVs, fridges and hair dryers. Some rooms have balconies. Doubles are 7000 dr without air-conditioning and 10,000 dr with air-conditioning. *Cronos Hotel (☎ 28 761, fax 22 217, Arkadiou 2)*, is in the centre of town in an ugly beige building but it has simple large rooms for 5000/7000 dr.

Hotels – Mid-Range On the edge of Ammoudi Beach, *Coral Hotel (☎ 28 363/367, fax 28 754)*, Akti Koundourou, is large and modern, offering comfortable rooms with TV and balconies. There's also a sauna, outdoor swimming pool and water sports centre. It has singles/doubles for 15,250/19,500 dr including buffet breakfast.

Hotel Panorama (☎ 28 890, fax 27 268) is named after the views it offers over Agios Nikolaos's harbour and bay. The hotel has recently been renovated to include air-con in its attractive, Mediterranean-style rooms. If you can't get a room with a balcony and sea view, you can console yourself with the view from the roof-garden. The hotel has singles/doubles with air-conditioning and a sea view for 7000/12,000 dr and singles/doubles without air-conditioning for 6000/10,000 dr. It's open from March to November.

Conveniently located in the centre of town near Kitroplatia Beach, *Apollon Hotel* (☎ 23 023, fax 28 939) is a large modern hotel that offers rooms with balconies, telephones, fridges and air-con. There's also a small pool and a game room with a pool table. Singles/doubles are 15,000/20,000 dr and include buffet breakfast. Their Web site is at www.forthnet.gr/internetcity/hotels/apollon.

Hotels – Top End *Minos Beach Hotel & Bungalows* (☎ 22 345/349, fax 22 548) on Agios Nikolaos, is a hotel-bungalow complex 2km north of Agios Nikolaos with everything a luxury-seeker could want. Although built in 1962 as the opening salvo in Agios Nikolaos' assault on global tourism, it has been scrupulously maintained and updated. The exquisitely decorated bungalows are on a rocky cove with a few sandy beaches; there's a pool and all conceivable water sports activities. Prices are 46,400/61,800 dr for a seaside bungalow including buffet breakfast. Their Web site is at www.forthnet.gr/internetcity/hotels/minosb/.

Nearby on a rocky promontory, is the luxury *Minos Palace* (☎ 23 801, fax 23 816). It has a swimming pool, tennis courts, water sports centre and air-conditioned singles/doubles for 40,000/55,000 dr. All regular local buses from Venizelou Square take you to the hotel strip on the way to Elounda.

About a kilometre south of the town centre, *Miramare Hotel* (☎ 23 875, fax 24 164, email mare@agn.forthnet.gr) has been attractively landscaped into a hillside. The skillfully decorated rooms are outfitted with

air-con on demand, satellite TV, fridges, telephones and balconies. Try to get a room near the top of the hill for the stunning views of the sea. There's a swimming pool, tennis courts and fitness centre. Prices are 21,000/28,000 dr for a singles/doubles, including buffet breakfast.

Places to Eat

Dining is not the strong point of Agios Nikolaos – possibly because there's not enough of a permanent population to support a thriving restaurant scene. Restaurants that are relegated to soaking up as much money as possible during the tourist season have no incentive to provide consistently good food to a discerning crowd of regulars. Voulesimeni Lake and the harbour area are full of passable but undistinguished restaurants. Most are open until past midnight feeding the nightbirds.

Not only is *Sarri's* (Kyprou 15) the best breakfast spot in town but it stays open until the wee hours serving up mouth-watering food to a neighbourhood crowd. Savouring a souvlaki in the shady courtyard is especially pleasant. It's open 8am to midnight daily. *Aouas Taverna* (Paleologou 50) is the kind of family-run place where your waiter may be a ten-year-old and the cook is her aunt. The interior is plain but the enclosed garden is refreshing and the mezedes are wonderful. Open noon to midnight daily. The decor at *New Kow Loon* (Pasifias 1) blares 'Chinese' with lots of red, gold and multi-coloured lights. The menu is large and the food is reasonably authentic. It makes a nice change of pace. Open noon to 3pm and 6pm to midnight daily.

Embassy Garden Restaurant (Kondilaki 5) is a friendly eatery that has a pleasant outdoor terrace and some interesting pasta dishes as well as the standard Cretan fare. It's open noon to midnight daily from March to November.

Technically an ouzeri, *Avli* (Georgiou 12) offers an outstanding selection of mezedes that make a meal in itself. Like many ouzeris, it's going upscale and also offers good-value meals in a garden setting. It's open 7pm to midnight daily.

For an excellent selection of fresh seafood, *Pelagos (Katehaki 10)*, in a beautifully restored old house, is generally considered the best restaurant in Agios Nikolaos. The elegance extends to the fine china and tranquil garden-dining area. It's open 7pm to midnight Monday to Saturday from March to October.

Taverna Itanos (Kyprou 1) is a vast place with beamed ceilings and stucco walls. It has a few tables on the sidewalk as well as comfortable banquettes. The solid Cretan food is displayed in a glass case and the house wine is more drinkable than most, it's open daily from 9am to 11pm.

Dining along scenic Voulismeni Lake is one of the great pleasures of Agios Nikolaos and *Taverna Pine Tree*, *(Paleogolou 18)* is a good choice. Make your selection from the glass display case inside and then relax in comfortable wicker chairs for a view of the lake. Open 8am to midnight daily.

Restaurant du Lac, on Voulismeni Lake, is known for its excellent seafood but there's a full array of Cretan fare on the menu as well as a flashy steak flambé. The restaurant offers good-value breakfasts and set-price menus. Open 8am to 1am daily from mid March to November.

Entertainment
You don't need a guide to find the nightlife in Agios Nikolaos – the nightlife will find you. This is a town that slumbers during the day and comes alive at night. As soon as the heat of the day passes, one by one the cafes and bars along the harbour open, by midnight the action is in full swing. Just head to the streets around the harbour and keep your eyes open for a place that appeals to you.

It's loud, crowded and overpriced but *Lipstick Disco*, on Akti Koudourou, is Agios Nikolaos' premier disco. In fact, it's the only disco. You'll see many foreigners but few locals. It's open 11 pm to dawn from April to October.

A perennial favourite, *Royale Bar (25 Martiou)* is known for its excellent cocktails and relentlessly upbeat mood. It's no place for a quiet conversation but a good place to meet other people. It's open from 6 pm to 2 am nightly.

Along the lively Agios Nikolaos harbour, *Rififi (25 Martiou 2)* provides a raucous good time to a late-night crowd. It's open 10 pm to dawn nightly from April to October. *Santa Maria Bar* on M. Sfakianaki, provides more of a local ambience than many other bars along the waterfront. There's no live music but the bar has a good selection of contemporary Greek popular music on disc. It's open 10 pm to 2 am nightly from April to October. *Cafe du Lac* on 28 Octovriou is a quiet place to take a breather from the frenzied harbour nightlife with a soothing view over Voulismeni Lake. The decor is modern. It's open 10 am to midnight daily.

On a bluff overlooking the harbour, *Enplo (Akti Koundourou 4)* is a subdued bar/cafe that is usually less crowded than the bars below. The music is 80s and 90s rock. It's open 10 am to midnight daily from March to November. *Rex 'Polycenter'* on M. Sfakianaki, is a 300-seat convention centre that doubles as a cinema, presenting first run movies.

Shopping
Years of experience with mass tourism has left a 'greatest quantity of goods for the greatest number' mentality in Agios Nikolaos. A certain crass commercialism persists even though the tackiest enterprises have migrated to Malia and Hersonissos. The rows of places selling identical souvenirs on Koundourou and 28 Oktovriou testify to the enduring desire to make a fast buck from package tourism. The offerings run the gamut from cheap Asian imports to luxury watches but the bulk of the stores offer mid-range ceramics, icons, beach gear, light cotton clothing and postcards.

In Maria Patsaki's eclectic store (K Sfakianaki 2), you'll find embroidery, rugs and antiques that are a cut above the average. It's open 8 am to 10 pm daily from March to October. Kerazoza (R Koundourou 42), means rainbow in the Cretan dialect and refers to the shop's focus on make-believe and illusion. The unusual items include handmade masks, marionettes and figurines derived from ancient Greek theatre. It's open 10 am to 10 pm daily from March to January. The English book selection at Anna Karteri (Koundourour 5), concentrates on best sellers and books about Crete and Greece with plenty of glossy photos. It's open 8 am to 10 pm Monday to Saturday. If the strange harmonies of Cretan and Greek music are bewitching you, you can find a good selection of tapes and CDs at Panagiotis Eydaimon Music Formula (Kontogianni 13). It's open 8 am to 9 pm Monday to Saturday from April to October; and 8 am to noon and 4 to 8 pm Monday to Saturday from November to March.

Getting There & Away
Bus Destinations of buses from Agios Nikolaos' bus station are:

Destination	Duration	Fare	Frequency
Elounda	20 mins	230 dr	20 daily
Kritsa	15 mins	230 dr	12 daily
Ierapetra	1 hour	750 dr	8 daily
Iraklio	1½ hours	1400 dr	half-hourly
Istron	30 mins	280 dr	11 daily
Lassithi Plateau	3 hours	1900 dr	1 daily
Sitia	1½ hours	1500 dr	6 daily

Ferry Agios Nikolaos has the same ferry schedule as Sitia. Ferry tickets can be bought from the Creta Travel Bureau among others.

Getting Around
You will find many car and motorcycle-hire outlets on the northern waterfront. Scooterland (☎ 26 340, Koundourou 10), has a huge range of scooters and motorcycles. Prices begin at 4000 dr a day for a scooter and go to 15,000 dr a day for a Kawasaki EN. You can rent mountain bikes from Manolis (☎ 24 940) down the street from the OTE office at Martiou 25. Prices begin at 2000 dr a day. Local buses run regularly from Almiros Beach to the Candia Park Hotel on the road to Elounda. The buses stop in front of the tourist office or in Plateia Venezilou; the maximum for a journey is 222 dr.

KRITSA Κριτσά
☎ 0841 • pop 2000
Kritsa village is a charmer from every angle. As you approach from below, the swathe of whitewashed houses terraced into the mountainside is strikingly photogenic. From the 600m-high village, there are sweeping views over the valley on one side and steep mountains on the other. The village is a carnival of colour with Kritsa's renowned weavings and embroidery draped and hung on every available surface. Even the busloads of tourists that swarm through the streets all summer haven't managed to dim Kritsa's allure. As in many Cretan villages, the men are in kafeneia while the women run the shops. When not hawking their merchandise, the women sit on stools with fingers flying over their fabric.

Agios Nikolaos to Sitia Driving Tour
The road from Agios Nikolaos to Sitia skirts along the indented north-eastern coast with splendid views over the sea to the left and the coastal mountains on the right. Follow the road east past the beach resort of Istron; in less than 10km you'll reach the Minoan site of Gournia. A bit farther on is the beach town of Pachia Amos. The road climbs into the mountains to Platanos with the taverna Panorama (it's name says it all) and picnic spots. A few kilometres past Platanos, there's a turn-off for the scenic, winding road to Mochlos. Return to the main road bordered with snow-white oleander, continue past Mirsini and through Mesa Mouliana, known for its wine and Hamezi. At the village of Skopi watch for the turn-off on the right to Moni Faneromenis which leads down a 5km road. After a visit to the monastery, head back to the main road and continue on to Sitia.

Although the designs have been bastardised to fit tourist tastes, it's still possible to search out the traditional geometric designs of Crete. Kritsa is also within easy reach of two other sights: the Church of Panagia Kera and the archaeological site of Lato.

Orientation & Information

One narrow street runs through Kritsa. There are no parking spaces, but there are car parks at the bottom and top of the town. The post office is near the bottom car park. There is no bank but there is an ATM halfway up the hill on the left.

Places to Stay & Eat

There's very little accommodation in Kritsa. *Rooms Argyro (☎ 51 174)* is a quiet, friendly place about a kilometre outside of town that has singles/doubles for 5000/7000 dr. *Rooms Kera (☎ 54 045)*, in the town, uphill from the bus stop offers basic rooms for 4000/5000 dr. *The Plane Tree* is a cool, restful place in the centre of town to grab a pizza or light meal to eat under a plane tree.

Getting There & Away

There are 12 buses a day from Agios Nikolaos to Kritsa (15 minutes, 230 dr).

AROUND KRITSA

The tiny triple-aisled **Church of Panagia Kera** is on the right 1km before Kritsa on the Agios Nikolaos road and contains the most outstanding Byzantine frescoes on Crete. The oldest part of the church is the central nave which is from the 13th century, but most of the frescoes date from the early to mid-14th century. The dome and nave are decorated with four gospel scenes: the Presentation, the Baptism, the Raising of Lazarus and the Entry into Jerusalem. On the west wall there's a portrayal of the Crucifixion and grimly realistic depictions of the Punishment of the Damned. The vault of the south aisle recounts the life of the Virgin and the north aisle is an elaborately worked out fresco of the Second Coming. Nearby is an enticing depiction of Paradise next to the Virgin, the Patriarchs, Abraham, Isaac and Jacob. Judgement Day is por-

trayed on the west end with the Archangel Michael trumpeting the Second Coming. Unfortunately the church is usually packed with tourists. It's open 8.30 am to 3 pm Monday to 8.30 am to 2 pm Friday and Saturday. Admission is 500 dr.

ANCIENT LATO Λατώ

The ancient city of Lato (la-**to**), 4km north of Kritsa, is one of Crete's few non-Minoan ancient sites. Lato was founded in the 7th century BC by the Dorians and at its height was one of the most powerful cities on Crete until it was destroyed in 200 BC. It sprawls over the slopes of two acropolises in a lonely mountain setting, commanding stunning views down to the Gulf of Mirabello.

The city's name derived from the goddess Leto whose union with Zeus produced Artemis and Apollo, both of whom were worshipped here. Lato is far less visited than Crete's Minoan sites. It's open 8.30 am to 3 pm Tuesday to Sunday. Entry is free.

Exploring the Site

The **city gate** is the entrance to the site and leads to a long, stepped street. The wall on the left contains two towers which were also residences. Follow the street to reach the **agora** built around the 4th century BC, which contained a cistern and a small rectangular sanctuary. Excavations of the temple revealed a number of 6th century BC figurines. The circle of stones behind the cistern was a threshing floor. The western side of the agora contains a **stoa** with stone benches. There are remains of a pebble mosaic nearby. A terrace above the south-east corner of the agora contains the remains of a **rectangular temple** probably built in the late 4th or early 3rd century BC. There is an inscription at the base of the temple statue but it is too damaged to be read. Between the two towers on the northern end of the agora there are steps which lead to the **prytaneion**, the administrative centre of the city-state. The centre of the prytaneion contained a hearth with a fire that burned day and night. On the east side of the prytaneion is a colonnaded court. Below the prytaneion is a semi-circular **theatre** which could seat about 350 people next to an **exedra** with a bench around the walls.

Getting There & Away

There are no buses to Lato. The road to the site is signposted to the right on the approach to Kritsa. But if you don't have your own transport, it's a pleasant walk through olive groves along this road.

GOURNIA Γουρνιά

The important Minoan site of Gournia (gour-**nya**) lies just off the coast road, 19km southeast of Agios Nikolaos. The ruins, which date from 1550 to 1450 BC, consist of a town overlooked by a small palace. Gournia's palace was far less ostentatious than the ones at Knossos and Phaestos; it was the residence of an overlord rather than a king. The town is a network of streets and stairways flanked by houses with walls up to 2m in height. Domestic, agricultural and trade implements found on the site indicate that Gournia was a thriving little community.

South of the palace is a large rectangular **court** which was connected to a network of paved stone streets. South of the palace is a large **stone slab** used for sacrificing bulls. The room to the west has a stone **kernos** ringed with 32 depressions and probably used for cult activity. North of the palace was a **Shrine of the Minoan Snake Goddess** which proved to be a rich trove of objects from the Postpalatial Period. Notice the storage rooms, workrooms, and dwellings

to the north and east of the site. The buildings were two-storey structures with the storage and workrooms in the basement and the living quarters on the first floors.

The site (☎ 0841-24 943) is open 8.30 am to 3 pm Tuesday to Sunday. Admission is 500 dr. Gournia is on the Sitia and Ierapetra bus routes from Agios Nikolaos. Buses can drop you at the site.

MONI FANEROMENIS

Μονή Φανερωμένης

Just 2km before Gournia, on the Agios Nikolaos-Sitia road, a 5km road leads off right to the late-Byzantine Moni Faneromenis. If you have your own transport, a visit to the monastery is worthwhile for the stunning views down to the coast and to see its 15th-century fresco of the Panagia.

SPINALONGA PENINSULA

Χερσόνησος Σπιναλόγκας

Just before Elounda (coming from Agios Nikolaos), a sign points right to **ancient Olous**, which was the port of Lato. The city stood on and around the narrow isthmus (now a causeway) which joined the southern end of the Spinalonga Peninsula to the mainland. Olous was a Minoan settlement that flourished from 3000 to 900 BC. Around 200 BC Olous entered into a treaty with the island of Rhodos as part of Rhodos Island's desire to control eastern Crete and put an end to the piracy that was ravaging the Aegean. Excavations indicate that Olous was an important trade centre with the eastern islands and minted its own currency. Little is known about Olous during the Greek, Roman and Byzantine eras but it appears that Olous was destroyed by the 9th-century Saracens.

The isthmus sank as a result of the earthquakes that have repeatedly devastated Crete. In 1897 the occupying French army dug a canal across the isthmus connecting Spinalonga Bay to the open sea. Most of the ruins lie beneath the water, and if you go snorkelling near the causeway you will see the remains of the walls and shipberths of the old city, although it's difficult to discern any recognisable structure. The shallow water around here appears to be paradise for sea urchins and the area is known for the many birds that nest here. The peninsula is a pleasant place to stroll – there is an early Christian mosaic near the causeway which was part of an early Christian basilica.

SPINALONGA ISLAND
Νήσος Σπιναλόγκα

Spinalonga Island lies just north of the Spinalonga Peninsula and was strategically important from antiquity to the Venetian era. The island's massive **fortress** was built by the Venetians in 1579 to protect the bays of Elounda and Mirabello. It was considered impregnable, withstood Turkish sieges for longer than any other Cretan stronghold but finally surrendered in 1715, some 30 years after the rest of Crete. The Turks used the island as a base for smuggling. Following the reunion of Crete with Greece, Spinalonga became a leper colony. The last leper died there in 1953 and the island has been uninhabited ever since. Spinalonga is still known among locals as 'the island of the living dead'.

The island is a fascinating place to explore. It has an aura that is both macabre and poignant.

The **cemetery**, with its open graves, is an especially strange place. Dead lepers came in three classes: those who saved up money from their government pension for a place in a concrete box; those whose funeral was paid for by relations and who therefore got a proper grave; and the destitute, whose remains were thrown into a charnel house.

Getting There & Away
There are regular excursion boats to the island from Agios Nikolaos and a boat every half-hour from the port in Elounda (2000 dr). Alternatively, you can negotiate with the fishermen in Elounda and Plaka (a fishing village 5km further north) to take you across.

The boats from Agios Nikolaos pass Bird Island and Kri-Kri Island, one of the last habitats of the *kri-kri*, Crete's wild goat. Both of these islands are designated wildlife sanctuaries and uninhabited.

ELOUNDA Ελούντα
☎ 0841 • postcode 720 53 • pop 1600
There are magnificent mountain and sea views along the 11km road from Agios Nikolaos to Elounda (el-**oon**-da). Although formerly a quiet fishing village, Elounda is now bristling with tourists and is only marginally calmer than Agios Nikolaos. The harbour is attractive, however, and there's a sheltered lagoon-like stretch of water formed by the Spinalonga Peninsula.

Near modern Elounda, about 500m towards Agios Nikolaos, a sign directs you past the remains of Venetian salt pans to the site of the Greco-Roman city-state of Olous, which lies on an isthmus that joins the Spinalonga Peninsula to mainland Crete.

Orientation & Information
Elounda's post office is opposite the bus stop. From the bus stop walk straight ahead to the clock tower and church which are on the central square. There is a small OTE office next to the church. The new municipal tourist office (☎ 42 464) is opposite the church and is open 8 am to 11 pm daily from June to October. They will help you find accommodation and change money. Olous Travel (☎ 41 324, fax 41 132) is in the centre of town and handles air and boat tickets, finds accommodation as well as booking organised tours and cruises. It is open 8 am to 9 pm daily from April to November. There is no tourist police, but there are two banks located near the Hotel Aristea.

Organised Tours
A number of boats from Elounda Harbour offer trips to Spinalonga as well as all-day swimming and fishing trips, and four-hour cruises that include a visit to the island of Spinalonga, swimming and a visit to the sunken city of Olous.

Places to Stay
There's some good accommodation around, but nothing particularly cheap. *Katerina Apartments* (☎ 41 484) at the entrance to the town, has well-equipped studios for 10,000 dr. *Hotel Aristea* (☎ 41 300) is in the town centre and has rooms with a sea view

for 7000/10,000 dr. *Hotel Sofia* (*☎ 41 482*), on the seafront 100m from the town centre, has pleasantly furnished two-room apartments with kitchen for 12,000 dr among its range of options.

Most of Elounda's finer hotels are on the beach road south of town on the way to Agios Nikolaos. Frequent local buses to and from Agios Nikolaos stop in front of all the hotels. *Horizon Hotel* (*☎ 41 895*) is about 1km south of town and offers singles/doubles with balconies and sea views for 8000/ 10,000 dr. *Grecotel Elounda Village* (*☎ 41 002, fax 41 278*) is the first of Elounda's resort hotels on the main road from Agios Nikolaos. It has a splendid outdoor swimming pool, water sports centre, tennis courts and air-conditioned singles/doubles for 25,000/35,000 dr.

One of the world's great luxury resorts, *Elounda Beach Hotel & Villas* (*☎ 41 412, fax 41 373, email elohotel@eloundabeach.gr*), located about 1.5km south of Elounda Village, is the place to go for pampering on a major scale. The rooms run the gamut from 'simple' affairs with fresh flowers, bathrobes, twice daily maid service, jacuzzis and TVs in the bathrooms to royal suites with a private indoor swimming pool, personal fitness trainer, butler, secretary and cook. There are also bungalows with a private outdoor swimming pool and platform on the sea. Prices are 131,800 dr for a double room and 500,000 dr for an executive suite with private swimming pool.

Next door and under the same management, Elounda Bay Palace (*☎ 41 502, fax 41 583, email bay@compulink.gr*) also offers a high standard of luxury with prices that begin at 91,000 dr for a room with sea view to 152,000 dr for bungalows on the waterfront. Their Web site is at www.compulink.gr/eloundabay.

The road north of Elounda on the way to Plaka also has a number of hotels. Just outside of town is the attractive *Pension Oasis* (*☎ 41 076, fax 41 128*) which has singles/doubles with fans and fridges for 10,000/13,000 dr. A little further on is *Kalypso* (*☎ 41 367*) which is on the beach

with a taverna downstairs. Singles/doubles are 8000/10,000 dr.

You could also try *Selena* (*☎ 41 525*), just outside of town and across the road from the sea and a small beach, which has singles/doubles for 8000/10,000 dr.

Places to Eat

Vritomaris in the square next to the harbour bills itself as the oldest fish taverna in the village, and offers an impressive collection of fresh fish. Another good choice for fish is *Nikos* which has outdoor tables under a canopy. *Poulis Restaurant* offers a good selection of fresh fish and Cretan dishes on a floating pontoon near Olous. For scrumptious pastries try *Aggela* opposite the church. *Marilena* is touristy but serves excellent mezedes, fish and lobster.

Entertainment

Currently the most popular night clubs are *Katafigio*, *Mylos* and *Lasers Disco* located south of the town centre next to the ancient city of Olous, open nightly in summer from midnight, but weekends only in winter. Katafigio is the most scenic place, built in a former carob processing plant with tables along the water. It plays live Greek music. In town *Eden Cafe* near the church is a spacious comfortable cafe/bar popular with the locals for its eclectic selection of discs.

Getting Around

Elounda Travel (*☎ 41 333, fax 41 433*) in the town centre rents cars, motorcycles and scooters.

Getting There & Away

There are 20 buses a day from Agios Nikolaos to Elounda (20 minutes, 230 dr).

Lassithi Plateau
Οροπέδιο Λασιθίου

☎ 0844 • postcode 720 52

The first view of the mountain-fringed Lassithi Plateau, laid out like an immense patchwork quilt, is stunning. The plateau,

900m above sea level, is a vast expanse of pear and apple orchards, almond trees and fields of crops, dotted by some 7000 windmills. These are not conventional stone windmills but slender metal constructions with white canvas sails, built under the Venetians to irrigate the land. Unfortunately the original windmills are no longer in continuous use but you may see a few examples outside tavernas or shops. There are 20 villages dotted around the periphery of the plateau, the largest of which is Tzermiado, with 1300 inhabitants, a bank, post office and OTE.

The plateau's rich soil has been cultivated since Minoan times. The inaccessibility of the region made it a hotbed of insurrection during Venetian and Turkish rule. Following an uprising in the 13th century, the Venetians drove out the inhabitants of Lassithi and destroyed their orchards. The plateau lay abandoned for 200 years.

DIKTEON CAVE Δικταίον Αντρον

Lassithi's major sight is the Dikteon Cave, just outside the village of **Psyhro** (psi-**hro**). Here, according to mythology, Rhea hid the newborn Zeus from Cronos, his offspring-gobbling father.

The cave, which has both stalactites and stalagmites, was excavated in 1900 by the British archaeologist David Hogarth. He found numerous votives indicating that the cave was a place of cult worship. These finds are housed in the Archaeological Museum in Iraklio.

The cave began to be used for cult worship in the middle Minoan period and continued, though less intensely, up to the first century AD. An altar for offerings and sacrifices was in the upper section of the cave. Stone tables inscribed with Linear A were found here along with bronze and clay religious figurines.

Two deities were worshipped in the cave: one god is, of course, Zeus symbolised by the double axe, and the other was a female deity variously referred to as Mother Gaia or Pantheme. Even the stalactites and stalagmites, often taking human or animal form, were worshipped.

There are two sections to the cave. To the north is the flat ante chamber which is 42m long, 19m wide and 6.5m high. The ground is strewn with boulders and there is a group of stalagmites. The main cave is on a north-south axis and is 38m wide, 85m long and 5 to 14m high. In the back on the left is a smaller chamber where it is alleged that Zeus was born. There is a larger hall on the right which is divided into two sections; the first section has small stone basins filled with water which Zeus allegedly drank from. In the second section there is a spectacular stalagmite which came to be known as the mantle of Zeus. The entire cave covers 2200 sq metres.

The moment you reach the parking area beneath the site, representatives from the Association of Cave Guides & Donkey Owners will be upon you. The cave guides want 2000 dr for a lantern-guided tour, while the donkey owners want the same to save you the 15-minute walk up to the cave. A guide is not essential, but a torch is. So are sensible shoes.

The path to the cave is pretty rough, and the cave itself is slippery. There is a car park outside the cave that costs 600 dr for a car and 100 dr for a bike. Opening times are 8 am to 4 pm. Admission is 800 dr.

TZERMIADO

Tzermiado is a sleepy town with dusty little streets lined with houses overgrown with vines and hanging plants. It's the largest and most important town on the Lassithi Plateau, however, and gets a fair amount of tourism from the tour buses going to the Dikteon Cave. There are a fair number of shops selling rugs and embroidered blouses, although not of a particularly high quality.

Orientation & Information

There is only one main road running through town that takes you past the town square.

The post office is on the town's main square and the bank and OTE are on a nearby street.

JOHN PENDLEBURY

From the centre of Tzermiado, there are signs to the Trapeza Cave, a Neolithic burial site excavated by the Indiana Jones of Cretan archaeology – John Pendlebury. Pendlebury was a protege of Sir Arthur Evans who, impressed by his brilliance and physical endurance, made him curator of Knossos.

In addition to his administrative duties, Pendlebury produced a layman's guide to Knossos (available in the site's bookstore) and tramped through Crete searching out other possible sites. He began excavations at Trapeza Cave and another site in 1936, but war interrupted his work four years later. Pendlebury immediately enlisted and was put in charge of coordinating the Cretan resistance. His knowledge of the countryside was put to good use as he hiked the hills in traditional Cretan dress with a rifle over his shoulder and a patch over his eye. Cretans loved him. During the Battle of Crete, Pendlebury fought heroically against the German parachutists, but was wounded. While waiting for a doctor in a house near Iraklio, German soldiers entered and shot him.

Places to Stay & Eat

On the left as you enter town you'll see *Hotel Kourites* (☎ 22 194) that has singles/doubles/triples available in a few nearby buildings for 6000/8000/9000 dr, breakfast included. There is free use of the hotel's bicycles. You can also rent singles/doubles from *Taverna Kri-Kri* (☎ 22 170) for 5000/6000 dr.

Getting There & Away

From Agios Nikolaos there's an afternoon bus to Tzermiado on Monday, Wednesday and Friday (1700 dr, 2 hrs) and a morning bus from Tzermiado to Agios Nikolaos also on Monday, Wednesday and Friday. From Iraklio there are two buses daily (except weekends) to Tzermiado (1200 dr, 1½ hr) and three daily buses except weekends) returning to Iraklio.

Walk from Tzermiado to Psyrho

This 90-minute walk from Tzermiado to Psyrho goes through the heart of the Lassithi Plateau, replete with fields of onions, wheat, cabbage, beans and kale. If you're lucky, the famous windmills will be unfurled and pumping water to irrigate the fields. Even if the windmills are idle, it's a lovely walk.

From Tzermiado's central square take the street with the Agricultural Bank and OTE. At the end, turn right, then take the first left onto a road which becomes a dirt track. Continue ahead for 1km, at the T-junction turn right, then veer right onto the surfaced road. At the crossroads, turn left onto a rough dirt track. Turn right at the second crossroads and you will see Psyhro in the distance to the left. Continue straight ahead for 1km; at the T-junction turn left. At the road turn left to reach Psyhro's central square. If you're hungry, you face the agonising choice between *Stavros* or *Platanos* tavernas – the only dining establishments in town. Continue straight ahead from the town square to reach the Dikteon Cave.

AGIOS GEORGIOS

Agios Georgios is a tiny town with a **folklore museum** that is an interesting place to while away an hour or so. It's open 10 am to 4 pm daily from June to September. Admission is 500 dr.

There are three accommodation options. *Hotel Rea* (☎ 31 209), opposite the school on the main street, has cosy rooms for 2500/5000 dr with shared bathroom. *Rent Rooms Maria*, nearby, has spacious stucco rooms decorated with weavings for 6000/8500/10,800 dr with private bathroom. The plant-filled enclosed garden is a pleasant place to relax. *Hotel Dias* (☎ 31 207), also on the main street, has pleasant rooms for 3000/4000 dr with shared bathroom. Both hotels have restaurants.

LASSITHI

Getting There & Away

Agios Georgios is on the bus routes from Iraklio and Agios Nikolaos to the Dikteon Cave.

PSHYRO

Psyhro, the village nearest the cave, has only one main street with a few tavernas and rooms, and plenty of souvenir shops. There is only one place to stay, the D-class *Zeus Hotel (☎ 31 284)*, where singles/doubles with private bathroom cost 6000/8000 dr and singles/doubles without bathroom cost 5000/7000 dr. On the main street, *Stavros* and *Platanos* tavernas serve similar fare at similar prices. Buses drop you at the end of the town from which it's about a kilometre walk uphill to the Dikteon Cave.

Getting There & Away

Public transportation to Psyhro is problematic if you don't have your own wheels. From Agios Nikolaos there's an afternoon bus to Lassithi on Monday, Wednesday and Friday (1900 dr, 2½ hrs) and a morning bus from Lassithi to Agios Nikolaos also on Monday, Wednesday and Friday. From Iraklio there are two buses daily (except weekends) to Lassithi (1400 dr, 2 hr) and three daily buses (except weekends) returning to Iraklio. All buses go through Tzermiado and Agios Georgios before terminating at Psyrho at the foot of the road leading to the Dikteon Cave.

North-Eastern Coast

SITIA Σητεία

☎ 0843 • postcode 72 30 • pop 80,000

Sitia (si-**tee**-a) is the perfect escape from the tourist frenzy that can grip most of the north coast in summer. You will not see shop after shop of cookie-cutter ceramics, waiters will not try to drag you into their restaurants and the menus are not translated into four languages. What you will see are

ordinary Cretans going about their business in an attractive mid-sized coastal town. The harbourside promenade is clear of taverna tables making it a lovely venue for an early evening stroll.

The bustling streets of the old town wind their way uphill from the harbour and the town's southern end is on a long, narrow stretch of sandy beach. Even at the height of the season, the town has a laid-back feel that is a refreshing antidote to the commercialism of Agios Nikolaos.

Archaeological excavations indicate that there were Neolithic settlements around Sitia and an important Minoan settlement at Petras, a kilometre east of the current town centre. There was a palace at the top of the hill containing a shrine and yielding vases, clay figurines and pithoi which are now on display in the Sitia Archaeological Museum. The settlement was destroyed and eventually abandoned after the earthquake of 1700 BC.

In the Greco-Roman era there was a town called Iteia in or around modern Sitia although its exact site has not yet been located. In Byzantine times Sitia became the seat of a bishopric which was eliminated by the Saracen conquest of Crete in the 9th century, but re-established in the 10th century. Under the Venetians, Sitia became the most important port in eastern Crete and was protected by massive walls.

Except for the birth of Crete's most important poet, Vitzentzos Kornaros, author of the *Erotokritos*, the 16th century was disastrous for Sitia. It was racked by a terrible earthquake in 1508 followed by destructive raids by the pirate Barbarossa that caused irreparable damage.

It is unclear whether the town was abandoned after 1538 but the population certainly dropped dramatically. The Turkish blockade of Sitia in 1648 was the death knell for the town.

The remaining inhabitants fled and the walls and buildings of the town were destroyed. It was not until the late 19th century when the Turks decided to make Sitia an administrative centre that the town gradually came back to life.

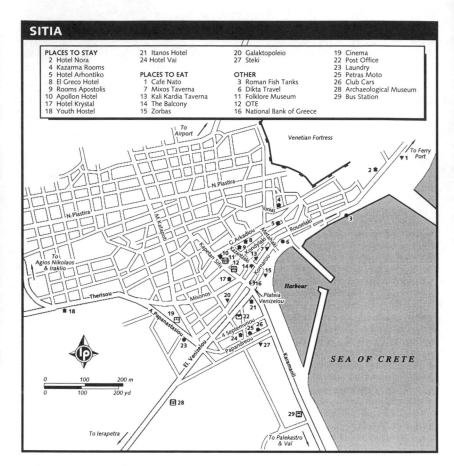

SITIA

PLACES TO STAY	21 Itanos Hotel	20 Galaktopoleio	19 Cinema
2 Hotel Nora	24 Hotel Vai	27 Steki	22 Post Office
4 Kazarma Rooms			23 Laundry
5 Hotel Arhontiko	PLACES TO EAT	OTHER	25 Petras Moto
8 El Greco Hotel	1 Cafe Nato	3 Roman Fish Tanks	26 Club Cars
9 Rooms Apostolis	7 Mixos Taverna	6 Dikta Travel	28 Archaeological Museum
10 Apollon Hotel	13 Kali Kardia Taverna	11 Folklore Museum	29 Bus Station
17 Hotel Krystal	14 The Balcony	12 OTE	
18 Youth Hostel	15 Zorbas	16 National Bank of Greece	

Orientation & Information

The bus station is at the southern end of Karamanli, which runs behind the bay. The town's main square, Plateia El Venizelou – recognisable by its palm trees and statue of a dying soldier – is at the northern end of Karamanli. The harbour near the square is for small boats. Ferries use the large quay, about 500m from Plateia Agnostou. There's no tourist office but Tzortzakis Travel (☎ 25 080), Kornarou 150, is a good source of information.

There are plenty of places to change money and plenty of ATMs. The National Bank of Greece on the main square has a 24-hour automatic exchange machine.

The post office is on Democritou; the OTE is on Kapetan Sifis, which runs uphill directly off Plateia Venizelou.

Things to See & Do

Sitia's **Archaeological Museum** (☎ 23 917) houses a well-displayed collection of local finds spanning from Neolithic to Roman times, with emphasis on the Minoan civilisation. One of the more interesting exhibits is the *Paleokastro Kouros* – a figure pieced together from fragments, composed of hippopotamus tusks and adorned with gold. The finds from the palace at Zakros are also interesting and include a wine press, a bronze saw, jars, cult objects and pots that are clearly scorched from the great fire that destroyed the palace. The most valuable objects in the museum are the Linear A tablets which reflect the palace's administrative function. The museum is on the left side of the road from Sitia to Ierapetra. It is open 8.30 am to 3 pm Tuesday to Sunday. Admission is 500 dr.

About 100m north of the pier are the remains of the **Roman fish tanks** that stored freshly caught fish until they were needed although only traces of them are still visible on the rock. Their position on the coast indicates that eastern Crete has sunk slightly over the centuries. Towering over the town is the fort or **kazarma** which was a garrison under the Venetians. They are the only remains of the wall that once protected the town. It is now used as an open-air theatre.

There is also a **folklore museum** that displays a fine collection of local weavings. It's open 9.30 am to 2.30 pm Tuesday to Sunday; admission is 500 dr.

Special Events

Sitia produces superior sultanas and the town holds a **Sultana Festival** in the last week of August, during which wine flows freely and Cretan dances are performed. Admission is 2500 dr, including local wine.

There is also the **Kornaria Festival** that runs from mid-July through August in which concerts, folk dancing and theatre productions are staged in the kazarma and other venues. Posters around town announce the events, some of which are free. For paying events look for a ticket kiosk in the main square.

Places to Stay

Hostels Sitia's *youth hostel* (☎ 22 693, *Therissou 4*), is on the road to Iraklio. It's a well-run hostel with hot showers and a communal kitchen and dining room. Dorm beds cost 1500 dr and doubles with shared bathroom are 3000 dr. Camping in the grounds costs 1000 dr per person.

Domatia The up-market domatia at *Rooms to Let Apostolis* (☎ 28 172, 22 993), Kazantzaki 27, have doubles with fridge for 7500 dr. Kazantzaki runs uphill from the waterfront, one street north of the OTE. Another attractive place is *Kazarma Rooms to Rent* (☎ 23 211, Ionias 10), where doubles with bathroom cost 8000 dr. There is a communal lounge and a well-equipped kitchen. The rooms are signposted from Patriarch Metahaki.

Hotels The D-class *Hotel Arhontiko* (☎ 28 172, 22 993, Kondylaki 16), is beautifully maintained and spotless. Singles/doubles are 5000/6000 dr with shared facilities. On summer evenings, the friendly owner enjoys sharing a bottle of raki with guests on the communal terrace. Kondylaki is two streets from the port.

The well-signposted *El Greco Hotel* (☎ 23 133, Arkadiou 13), has more character than the town's other C-class places. Comfortable rooms with private bathroom cost 7000/10,000 dr.

The B-class *Itanos Hotel* (☎ 22 900, fax 22 915), has a conspicuous location on the waterfront and a popular terrace restaurant. The comfortable rooms are outfitted with air-con on demand, satellite TV, balconies and sound-proofing for a tranquil night's sleep. Singles/doubles cost 9000/12,000 dr. Add another 1500 dr per person for breakfast at the hotel but there are plenty of cafes nearby. There are also special rooms for disabled travellers.

Hotel Nora (☎ 23 017, Rouselaki 31) is uphill from the town centre and has tidy rooms with telephone, TV and balconies for 6000/7000 dr. *Apollon Hotel* (☎ 28 155, fax 22 733, Kapetan Sifi 28) has extremely comfortable rooms with air-con on demand, TV and telephone for 10,750/13,200 dr. *Hotel Kristol* (☎ 22 284, fax 28 644, Kapetan Sifi 17) is a four-storey building with wrap-around balconies in the town centre that has modern rooms with air-con for 11,000/13,000 dr. *Hotel Vai* (☎ 22 528), at the intersection of Dimokritou and 4 Septemvriou, has bare and slightly worn but clean rooms for 6000/8400 dr.

Places to Eat

A string of tavernas along the quay side on El Venizelou offer an array of mezedes and speciality fish dishes at comparable prices. Inland, *Mixos Taverna* (*Kornarou 117*) has excellent charcoal-grilled souvlaki. Walk up Patriarch Metahaki from the waterfront, take the first left and the taverna is on the right.

Kali Kardia Taverna (*Foundalidhou 20*), is excellent value and popular with locals. Mezedes cost from 400 dr to 800 dr and main dishes from 1250 dr to 1800 dr. Walk up Kazantzaki from the waterfront, take the second right and the taverna is on the right. It's open daily from 10 am to midnight. *The Balcony* on the corner of Kazantzaki and Foundalidou provides the finest dining in Sitea with an extraordinarily creative menu that combines Greek, Italian and Mexican food. A meal for two with wine will cost about 12,000 dr. It's open noon to 3 pm and 6.30 pm to midnight daily.

Steki (Papandreou 13) is popular with the locals for its excellent selection of Cretan dishes at reasonable prices. A large plate of mixed mezedes costs 2500 dr. They make a wonderful Cretan spaghetti dish and numerous vegetarian specialities. It's open 11.30 am to midnight daily. *Cafe Nato*, on Rouselaki 20m further up from Hotel Nora, is a laid-back little taverna with outdoor tables that serves a variety of grilled meat, artisanal cheeses and good raki. It's open daily from noon to midnight. *Zorbas* on the harbour is a large, crowded and happy place that serves excellent seafood. It's open noon to midnight daily. *Galaktopoleio (Kornarou 33)* is a shop that specialises in fine sheep's milk products, including fresh milk, curdled milk, delicious yoghurt and cheese. It's open from 8 am to 12.30 pm and 5 to 7.30 pm Monday to Saturday.

Getting There & Away

Air Sitia's tiny airport has flights to Athens once a week for 23,100 dr.

The Olympic Airways agent is Tzortzakis Travel (☎ 25 080/090, Kornarou 150).

Bus There are six buses a day to Ierapetra (1½ hours, 1200 dr); five buses a day to Iraklio (3½ hours, 2850 dr) via Agios Nikolaos (1½ hours, 1500 dr); five to Vai (one hour, 600 dr); and two to Kato Zakros (one hour) via Palekastro and Zakros (one hour, 1000 dr). The buses to Vai and Kato Zakros run only between May and October; during the rest of the year, the Vai service terminates at Palekastro and the Kato Zakros service at Zakros.

Ferry The F/B *Vitsentzos Kornaros* leaves Sitia on Tuesday, Thursday and Sunday afternoons for Piraeus (14½ hours, 7600 dr in deck class) via Agios Nikolaos. The F/B *Georgios Express* leaves Sitia on Thursday and Saturday mornings for Karpathos (four hours, 3400 dr) and Kassos (six hours, 2600 dr) and Saturday mornings for Rhodes (6000 dr). Buy ferry tickets at Tzortzakis Travel Agency (☎ 22 631, 28 900, Kornarou 150).

Getting Around

To/From the Airport The airport (signposted) is 1km out of town. There is no airport bus; a taxi costs about 1000 dr.

Car & Motorcycle Car and motorcycle hire outlets are mostly on Papandreou and Itanou. Try Club Cars (☎ 25 104, fax 28 135, Papandreou 8).

PALEKASTRO
☎ 0843

Palekastro is a modern, rather bland town that is useful more as a base for exploring eastern Crete than as a destination in itself. It's situated in the midst of a rocky barren landscape but is within easy reach of the lovely Kouremenos Beach, Vai Beach and Moni Toplou. It's best to have your own wheels.

Orientation & Information

The main street, Karamanli, runs through town and forks to the right and left in the town centre. The bus stop is in the centre of town. There's no post office but there is a tourist office (☎ 61 546) combined with the OTE, that change money and are also a good source of information. It's open 9 am

While less ostentatious than Knossos and Phaestos, Gournia is still an important Minoan site.

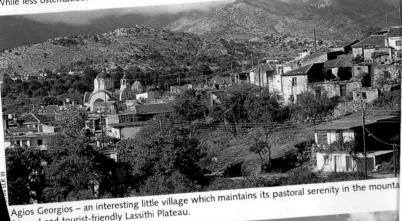
Agios Georgios – an interesting little village which maintains its pastoral serenity in the mounta[in]-fringed and tourist-friendly Lassithi Plateau.

[Ancien]t Dorian city of Lato sprawls over two acropolises.

to 10 pm Monday to Saturday from May to October. You can check your email at Kazamias Rent-a-car (☎ 61 093, Karamanli 20).

Places to Stay & Eat

The best accommodation in town is at *Hotel Hellas* (☎ 61 240) which has singles/doubles with air-con, TV and telephone and double-glazed windows for 6000/7000 dr. It's on the right fork from the town centre. Nearby is *Itanos Rooms* (☎ 61 205) which has basic but good rooms for 5000/6000 dr. *Rooms and Apartments Nikos* (☎ 61 480), near the Hotel Hellas, is on the left fork and has six-bed apartments with kitchens for 14,000 dr and double rooms for 6000 dr. *Evas Rooms* (☎ 61 388) is also a good choice with singles/doubles for 5000/6000 dr.

Two kilometres east of Palekastro on the road to Vai is *Castri Village Hotel Bungalows* (☎ 61 100, fax 61 249), an attractively designed establishment on the slope of a hill overlooking Kouremenos Beach. Fresh modern singles/doubles cost 7000/9000 dr and there's a swimming pool.

There are not a large number of tavernas in town and most do not open until the evening. *Restaurant Elena* next to the tourist office serves good Cretan cuisine and the Hotel Hellas and Itanos Rooms also have good restaurants.'

Entertainment

Design is a music and dance club on the eastern end of town as you are leaving Palekastro.

Getting There & Away

There are two buses a day from Sitia that stop at Palekastro (30 minutes, 600 dr) before continuing on to Kato Zakros and three buses a day from Sitia that stop at Palekastro on their way to Vai.

AROUND PALEKASTRO

The closest beach to Palekastro is **Kouremenos**, a nearly deserted pebble beach with good swimming and excellent windsurfing. You can rent boards from Kouremenos Windsurfing (☎ 093 751 7444). There are a few domatia. *Rooms Kouremenos Beach* (☎ 61 370), right on the beach, has six apartments sleeping four people each that cost 12,000 dr. Also on the beach, *Apartments Grandes* (☎ 61 496), a pretty place surrounded by a flower garden and trees, has apartments for about the same price.

There's also a Minoan **archaeological site** about a kilometre from Palekastro town. The site is still being excavated and most of it is closed to visitors but it's a pleasant walk getting there and you can still see the layout of the streets. Excavations have produced important finds such as Kamares ware, amphorae, soapstone lamps and pithoi.

MONI TOPLOU Μονή Τοπλού

The imposing Moni Toplou looks more like a fortress than a monastery – a necessity imposed by the dangers it faced at the time of its construction. The middle of the 15th century was marked by piracy, banditry and constant rebellions. The monks defended themselves with all the means at their disposal including a heavy gate, cannons (the name Toplou is Turkish for 'with a cannon'), and small holes for pouring boiling oil onto the heads of their attackers. Nevertheless, it was sacked by pirates in 1498, looted by the Knights of Malta in 1530, looted by the Turks in 1646 and captured by the Turks in 1821.

With the wealth and treasure that the monastery had accumulated, it's not surprising that it was a tempting target for looters and sackers. The star attraction is undoubtedly the icon *Lord Thou Art Great* by Koannis Kornaros. Each of the 61 small scenes painted on the icon is beautifully worked out and each is inspired by a phrase from the Orthodox prayer that begins 'Lord, Thou Art Great'. The icon is in the north aisle of the church along with 14th-century frescoes and an antique icon stand from 1770.

Moni Toplou had always been active in the cause for Cretan independence and paid a price for it. Under the Turkish occupation, its reputation for hiding rebels led to severe reprisals. During WWII many resistance leaders were sheltered in the monastery and operated an underground radio transmitter that led to the execution of Abbot Silignakis. The monastery is open from 9 am to 1 pm and 2 to 6 pm. It's a 3km walk from the Sitia-Palekastro road. Buses can drop you off at the junction.

VAI Βάι

The beach at Vai, on Crete's east coast 24km from Sitia, is famous for its palm forest. There are many stories about the origin of these palms including the theory that they sprouted from date pits spread by Roman legionaries relaxing on their way back from conquering Egypt. While these palms are closely related to the date, they are a separate species found only on Crete.

You'll need to arrive early to appreciate the setting, because the place gets packed out in July and August. It's possible to escape the worst of the ballyhoo – jet skis and all – by clambering over a rocky outcrop (to the right facing the sea) to a small secluded beach. Alternatively, there's a quiet beach over the hill in the other direction which is frequented by nudists. There are two tavernas at Vai but no accommodation.

The Vai Watersports & Scuba Centre (☎ 0843 61 070) is on the left side of the beach. You can dive for 10,000 dr including equipment or take a certification course for 100,000 dr.

If you're after more secluded beaches, head north for another 3km to the ancient Minoan site of **Itanos**. Although inhabited from about 1500 BC Itanos was clearly prosperous by the 7th century BC since it was an important trading post for exports to the Near East and Middle East. Its archrival was Praisos, near Ierapetra, and in 260 BC Itanos hosted a garrison of Egyptians to fortify its position against Praisos.

When Ierapetra destroyed Praisos 155 BC Itanos fought with Ierapetra as well and again received foreign help from Magnesia, a Roman city. The town was destroyed somewhere toward the end of the Byzantine era and may have been re-inhabited by the Venetians. It's difficult to discern any recognisable building in Itanos

but there are remains of two early Christian basilicas and a Hellenistic wall. The site is well-marked and next to swimming coves shaded by pine trees.

Getting There & Away
There are five buses a day to Vai from Sitia that stop at Palekastro (one hour, 600 dr).

ZAKROS Ζάκρος
☎ 0843
The village of Zakros, 45km south-east of Sitia, is the nearest permanent settlement to the east-coast Minoan site of Zakros, which is 7km away. Kato Zakros, next to the site, is a beautiful little seaside settlement that springs to life between March and October. If the weather is dry, there is a lovely two-hour walk from Zakros to Kato Zakros through a gorge, known as the Valley of the Dead due to the cave tombs dotted along the cliffs. The gorge emerges close to the Minoan site.

Places to Stay
Zakros has one hotel, the bleak C-class *Hotel Zakros* (☎ 93 379), where doubles with private bathroom are 5000 dr. Rooms in the back have great views over the gorge. Kato Zakros is a much better place to stay.

Getting There & Away
There are two buses a day to Zakros (via Palekastro) from Sitia (one hour, 1000 dr). They leave Sitia at 11 am and 2.30 pm and return at 12.30 and 4 pm. In summer, the buses continue to Kato Zakros. The Hotel Zakros offers guests free transport to Kato Zakros.

ZAKROS PALACE
A visit to Zakros Palace and Kato Zakros combines two of the best things about Crete – an intriguing archaeological site and a long stretch of under-populated beach. Although Zakros Palace was the last Minoan palace to have been discovered, the excavations proved remarkably fruitful.

The exquisite rock crystal vase and stone bull's head now in Iraklio's Archaeological Museum were found at Zakros Palace along

Looking over Agios Nikolaos towards the sea.

JON DAVISON

Scooters for hire: a great way to get around Agios Nikolaos.

NEIL SETCHFIELD

Shopping in Agios Nikolaos

...ing along scenic Voulismeni Lake is one of the great pleasures of Ag...

The ancie...

NEIL SETCHFIELD

LASSITHI

ZAKROS PALACE

1 Storeroom Block
2 Storerooms
3 Kitchen & Dining Room
4 Hall of Ceremonies
5 Light Well
6 Archive Room
7 Central Shrine
8 Lustral Basin
9 Treasury
10 Banquet Hall
11 King's Apartment
12 Queen's Apartment
13 Bathroom
14 Main Gate
15 Cistern Hall
16 Well Spring Chamber
17 Well
18 Work Rooms

North East Court

Central Court

0   15   30 m
0   15   30 yd

with a treasure-trove of Minoan antiquities. Ancient Zakros, the smallest of Crete's four palatial complexes, was a major port in Minoan times, trading with Egypt, Syria, Anatolia and Cyprus. The palace consisted of royal apartments, storerooms and workshops flanking a central courtyard but the ruins are not well-preserved and water levels have risen over the years so that some parts of the palace complex are submerged.

Exploring the site
If you enter the palace complex on the south side you will first come to **workshops** for

the palace. The **King's apartment** and **Queen's apartment** are to the right of the entrance. Next to the King's apartment is the **Cistern Hall** which once had a cistern in the centre surrounded by a colonnaded balustrade. Seven steps descended to the floor of the cistern which may have been a swimming pool, an aquarium or a pool for a sacred boat. To the left of the cistern room is the **Light Well** and then the **Central Court** which was the focal point of the whole palace. Notice the altar base in the north-west corner of the court; there was a well in the south-east corner of the court at the bottom of eight steps. When the site was excavated the well contained the preserved remains of olives that had been offered to the deities. Adjacent to the central court is the **Hall of Ceremonies** in which two rhytons were found. The room to the south is the **Banquet Hall** so named for the quantity of wine vases found there. To the north of the central court is the **kitchen**. The column bases probably supported the dining room above. To the west of the central court is another **light well** and to the left of the banquet hall is the **Lustral Basin** which once contained a magnificent marble amphora. The Lustral Basin served as a washroom for those entering the nearby **Central Shrine**. You can still see a ledge and a niche in the south wall for the ceremonial idols. Below the Lustral Basin is the **Treasury** which yielded nearly a hundred jars and rhytons. Next to the treasury is the **Archive Room** which once contained Linear A record tablets. Although there were hundreds of tablets, only the ones baked by the fire that destroyed the palace were preserved. North-east of the archives room is the **bathroom** with a cesspit.

The site is open from 8.30 am to 3 pm Tuesday to Sunday. Admission is 500 dr.

KATO ZAKROS

Little more than a long stretch of pebbly beach shaded by pine trees and bordered by a string of tavernas, Kato Zakros is about the most tranquil place to stay on Crete's south coast. Although there is the *Amnesia* bar for nightlife there is little to do here but relax on the beach and poke around the archaeological site. There is no bank, post office or OTE but you can change money at the tavernas and make phone calls from a kiosk.

Places to Stay

The several domatia in Kato Zakros fill up fast. If there are no rooms available you can camp on the beach.

Make sure you bring your own supplies since there are no stores in Kato Zakros. *Athena Rooms (☎ 93 458, 93 377)* has doubles with private bathroom for 8000 dr.

It is jointly owned with *Poseidon Rooms* which has singles/doubles for 5000/6000 dr with shared bathroom.

Taverna Akrogiali (☎ 93 316) is also on the beach and has rooms for 5000/6000 dr. *George's Villas (☎ 93 201/207)* has spotless, beautifully furnished rooms with private bathroom and terrace for 6000/7000 dr. The villas are in a verdant setting 500m along the old road to Zakros.

Nearby is *Ameles Rooms (☎ 93 020)* which has singles/doubles for 5000/6500 dr.

About 2km up the road is *Faragi Rooms (☎ 93 439/458)*, a pretty tree-shaded structure with rooms for 6000/7000 dr.

Getting There & Away

There are two buses a day to Zakros (via Palekastro) from Sitia (1 hour, 1000 dr). In summer, the buses continue to Kato Zakros.

South Coast

XEROKAMBOS

Xerokambos is an isolated idyllic spot with several kilometres of an almost deserted, wide sandy beach.

It lies at the foot of the Sitian Mountains which form a dramatic backdrop to the beach. The paved road stops several hundred metres before the beach and turns into a rocky track. There is no shade on the beach and just a few tavernas and half-finished buildings set back from the wide cove. The new road from Ziros offers a spectacular drive with many hairpin turns and the occasional goat herd ambling across the road. There are only a few places to stay.

Taverna Kastri and Rooms (☎ 0843-31 745) is a sleek, upmarket pension with rooms overlooking the beach. Singles/doubles cost 7000/9000 dr. *Apartments Eolos (0843-31 792)* has studios for 9000 dr on the north side of the beach.

Getting There & Away

There is no public transport to Xerokambos; the only road runs through the town of Ziros and zigzags across the mountains.

IERAPETRA Ιεράπετρα

☎ 0842 • postcode 722 00 • pop 11,000

Ierapetra is Crete's most southerly major town. It was an important city for the Dorians and the last city to fall to the Romans, who made it a major port of call in their conquest of Egypt. Despite its antiquity virtually nothing survives from the classical period.

The city languished under the Venetians, but they did build a small fortress at the western end of the harbour. In recent years agriculture has made the town wealthy enough to finance the restoration of the old town and the harbourside. The town attracts few tourists – after the tourist hype of Agios Nikolaos, the unpretentiousness of Ierapetra is refreshing.

Orientation & Information

The bus station is on Lasthenous, one street back from the beachfront north of the town centre. From the ticket office, turn right and after about 50m you'll come to a six-road intersection. There are signposts to the beach, via Patriarhou Metaxaki, and to the city centre, via the pedestrian mall section of Lasthenous.

The mall emerges after about 150m on to the central square of Plateia Eleftherias. To the north of the square is the National Bank of Greece.

The OTE is one block inland on Koraka. South of Plateia Eleftherias is Plateia Emmanual Kothri, where you'll find the post office at Stylianou Houta 3. You can check email at the cybercafe Orpheas (☎ 80 462, Kountouriotou 25).

There is no tourist office, but South Crete Tours (☎ 22 892, Lasthenous 36), opposite the bus station is a good source of information. It's open 8 am to 6 pm Monday to Friday.

There's a bookstore with English language books at Marcopoulou 71.

Things to See

Ierapetra's one-room **archaeological museum** is perfect for those with a short concentration span. It does have a good collection of headless classical statuary and a superb statue of the goddess of Demeter that dates from the 2nd century AD. Also notable is a *larnax* or clay coffin dating from around 1300 BC. The chest is decorated with 12 painted panels showing hunting scenes, an octopus and a chariot procession among others. It's at the intersection of Adrianou and Keraka.

Opening times are 8.30 am to 3 pm Tuesday to Sunday. Admission is free.

If you walk south along the waterfront from the central square you will come to the **fortress**, which was built in the early years of Venetian rule and strengthened by Francesco Morosini in 1626. It's in a pretty fragile state but you can visit it 8.30 am to 3 pm Tuesday to Sunday. Admission is free.

Inland from here is the labyrinthine old quarter, a delightful place to lose yourself for a while. Notice the **Turkish fountain**, the restored **Turkish mosque** with its minaret, and the old churches of **Agios Ioannis** and **Agios Georgios**.

Beaches Ierapetra has two beaches. The main town beach is near the harbour and the other one stretches east from the bottom of Patriarhou Metaxaki. Both have coarse, grey sand.

Special Events

Ierapetra's Kyrvia Festival runs from July through August and includes concerts, plays and art exhibits. Brochures are available in hotels and at the town hall. Some of the bands are free but tickets to top name concerts cost 1500 dr to 5000 dr. An all inclusive ticket costs about 10,000 dr

Places to Stay

Camping The nearest camp site to Ierapetra is *Koutsounari Camping* (☎ 61 213) 7km east of Ierapetra at Koutsounari. It has a restaurant, snack bar and minimarket. Ierapetra-Sitia buses pass the site.

Hotels-Budget Most of the places to stay are either near the bus station or in the old quarter. *Hotel Coral* (☎ 22 846, Katzonovatsi 14) has well-kept singles/doubles for 3000/5000 dr with private bathroom. The

LASSITHI

IERAPETRA

PLACES TO STAY
4 Four Seasons
5 Cretan Villa Hotel
8 Astron Hotel
9 Katerina Hotel
10 Hotel Cosmo
12 Hotel El Greco
27 Hotel Coral

PLACES TO EAT
6 Odeion
16 Veteranos
28 Taverna Napoleon
29 Taverna Babi's

OTHER
1 Saturday Street Market
2 South Crete Tours
3 Bus Station
7 Waikiki Cafe/Bar
11 Cafe Orpheas
13 Bookstore
14 National Bank of Greece
15 OTE
17 Archaeological Museum
18 Fruit Market
19 Post Office
20 Town Hall
21 Boat Tickets to
Hrysi Islet
22 Saxo Bar
23 Agios Georgios Church
24 The Figaro
25 Boats to Hrysi Islet
26 Agios Ioannis Church
30 Agios Nikolaos Church
31 Turkish Mosque
32 Turkish Fountain

LIBYAN SEA

owner also has some rooms for 3000/4000 dr with shared bathroom, and comfortable apartments for 6000 dr. The hotel is signposted just south of the port police building on the waterfront. ***Katerina Hotel*** (*☎ 28 345*) on the seafront has pleasant doubles with private bathroom for 7000 dr. To reach the hotel from the bus station, follow Patriarhou Metaxaki to the waterfront, turn right and you'll see the hotel on the right.

Four Seasons Hotel (*☎ 24 390*), on Kazantzakis is on a quiet street near the bus station and has some unusual features, since the building dates from 1866. Try to get the ground floor room with the painted wooden ceiling. Singles/doubles are 5000/7000 dr.

Hotels-Mid-Range *Cretan Villa Hotel* (*☎ 28 522, Lakerda 16*), is a lovely, well-maintained 18th-century house with traditionally furnished rooms and a peaceful courtyard. Room rates are 7000/9000 dr with private bathroom. From the bus station walk towards the town centre and take the first right, from where the hotel is signposted. *Hotel Cosmo* (*☎ 25 900, fax 26 251, Koundourou 16*), in the centre of town, has singles/doubles with balconies and TVs for

8000/10,000 dr including breakfast. Air-conditioning is an extra 2000 dr. *Hotel El Greco* (☎ 28 471, fax 28 791, Kothri 6) has rooms for the same price. It's located near the beach and some rooms have seaviews.

Hotels -Top End The best hotel in town is the B-class *Astron Hotel* (☎ 25 114, fax 25 91) at the beach end of Patriarhou Metaxaki. The rooms are comfortably furnished with satellite TV, telephone and air-conditioning. Rates are 13,000/17,500 dr, including breakfast.

A few kilometres east of Ierapetra, and on the beach, is *Petra Mare Hotel* (☎ 23 341/349, fax 23 350, Filotheou A). It's architecturally uninspiring but has indoor and outdoor pools, tennis courts, sauna, fitness centre, children's play area and a water sports centre. Rooms have air-con, TVs and telephones. Single/doubles are 25,000/30,000 dr. Prices include buffet breakfast. Their Web site is at www.forthnet.gr/internetcity/hotels/petramare/.

Places to Eat
Most of the souvlaki outlets are on Kyrba. On Saturday mornings there is a food market on Psilinaki. *Taverna Babi's*, in the old quarter, is one of the better tavernas along the waterfront. They have an excellent seafood pasta dish for 1500 dr. It's open noon to midnight daily. *Taverna Napoleon*, nearby, is the oldest taverna in Ierapetra and still manages to serve up a delicious array of Cretan specialties. Try the stuffed cabbage and the local white wine. It's open noon to midnight daily. When the locals celebrate a special occasion they often head to *Lambrakis* about a kilometre east of the town centre along the beach road. The grilled chicken (1100 dr) is tender and juicy, and it would be hard to find better stuffed tomatoes (1000 dr). It's open noon to midnight Monday to Sunday.

For light snacks *Odeion,* on Metaxaki Lasthenous, is a converted music school that serves mezedes in the basement while the 1st floor is a music bar. *Veteranos*, on Plateia Eleftherias, is a popular hang out for breakfast and light meals during the day.

Entertainment
Kyrba is Ierapetra's nightlife street with a number of choices for a casual drink. *Saxo Bar* is a good spot for Greek music and *Figaro* tends to play international music. *Waikiki* is a cafe/bar that often plays dance music. There are no discos in town but next to the Petra Mare Hotel is *SXS* that plays a combination of Greek and international dance music.

Getting There & Away
In summer, there are six buses a day to Iraklio (2½ hours, 2100 dr) via Agios Nikolaos (one hour, 750 dr), Gournia and Istron; eight to Makrigialos (30 minutes, 600 dr); six to Sitia (1½ hours, 1200 dr) via Koutsounari (for camp sites); six to Mirtos (30 minutes, 320 dr) and two a week to Ano Viannos (one hour, 800 dr).

AROUND IERAPETRA
The beaches to the east of Ierapetra tend to get crowded. For greater tranquillity, head for **Hrysi Islet**, where there are good uncrowded sandy beaches.

In summer an excursion boat (5500 dr) leaves from the quay near the town centre for the islet every morning and returns in the afternoon. There are three tavernas on the islet. Tickets are available at the ticket office on Kybra.

MIRTOS
☎ 0842 • postcode 722 00 • pop 600
Mirtos, on the coast 17km west of Ierapetra, is a sparkling village of whitewashed houses with flower-filled balconies. Despite it's popularity with independent travellers Mirtos has preserved its charm. It has a decent dark sand and pebble beach. To get to the waterfront from the bus stop, head south and take the road to the right, passing Mertiza Studios on the right. Mirtos is easily navigable as it is built on a grid system.

Orientation & Information
There is no post office, bank or OTE, but Aris Travel Agency (☎ 51 017/300) on the main street has a currency exchange.

LASSITHI

Places to Stay & Eat

Despina Rent Rooms (☎ 51 343) has pleasant but noisy doubles/triples with private bathroom for 5000/6500 dr. *Pandora Domatia* (☎ 51 589), on the main street, has prettily furnished singles/doubles for 3500/4000 dr with shared bathroom. *Hotel Panorama* (☎ 51 362) uphill from the town centre has studios with bathrooms, kitchenettes and spectacular views at 5000/7000 dr for singles/doubles. The superior C-class *Hotel Mirtos* (☎ 51 227) has large, well-kept rooms for 5000/7000 dr with private bathroom. *Big Blue* (☎ 51 094) on the western edge of town has rooms for 6000/7000 dr with bathroom and two-room apartments with two bathrooms and a kitchenette for 12,000 dr.

Mirtos Hotel Restaurant is popular with both locals and tourists. The no-frills *Kostos Taverna* nearby has good dolmades for 800 dr and *stifado* for 1500 dr. The waterfront *Karavoslasi Restaurant* is more stylish, with vegetarian dishes for 1000 dr and meat dishes for 1500 dr to 1800 dr.

Getting There & Away

There are six buses a day from Ierapetra to Mirtos (30 minutes, 320 dr). The Ano Viannos-Ierapetra bus passes through Mirtos.

Language

The Greek language is probably the oldest European language, with an oral tradition of 4000 years and a written tradition of approximately 3000 years. Its evolution over the four millennia was characterised by its strength during the golden age of Athens and the Democracy (mid-5th century BC); its use as a lingua franca throughout the Middle Eastern world, spread by Alexander the Great and his successors as far as India during the Hellenistic period (330 BC to 100 AD); its adaptation as the language of the new religion, Christianity; its use as the official language of the Eastern Roman Empire; and its eventual proclamation as the language of the Byzantine Empire (380-1453).

Greek maintained its status and prestige during the rise of the European Renaissance and was employed as the linguistic perspective for all contemporary sciences and terminologies during the period of Enlightenment. Today, Greek constitutes a large part of the vocabulary of any Indo-European language, and much of the lexicon of any scientific repertoire.

The modern Greek language is a southern Greek dialect which is now used by most Greek speakers both in Greece and abroad. It is the result of an intralinguistic influence and synthesis of the ancient vocabulary combined with words from Greek regional dialects, namely Cretan, Cypriot and Macedonian.

Those wishing to delve a little deeper into the language should get a copy of Lonely Planet's *Greek phrasebook*.

Pronunciation

All Greek words of two or more syllables have an acute accent which indicates where the stress falls. For instance, άγαλμα (statue) is pronounced *aghalma*, and αγάπη (love) is pronounced *aghapi*. In the following transliterations, bold lettering indicates where stress falls. Note also that **dh** is pronounced as 'th' in 'then'; **gh** is a softer, slightly guttural version of 'g'.

Greetings & Civilities

Hello.
| *ya**sas*** | Γειά σας. |
| *ya**su*** (informal) | Γειά σου. |

Goodbye.
| *an**dio*** | Αντίο. |

Good morning.
| *kali**mera*** | Καλημέρα. |

Good afternoon.
| *herete* | Χαίρετε. |

Good evening.
| *kalis**pera*** | Καλησπέρα. |

Good night.
| *kali**nihta*** | Καληνύχτα. |

Please.
| *paraka**lo*** | Παρακαλώ. |

Thank you.
| *efharis**to*** | Ευχαριστώ. |

Yes.
| *ne* | Ναι. |

No.
| ***ohi*** | Οχι. |

Sorry. (excuse me, forgive me)
| *sigh**nomi*** | Συγγνώμη. |

How are you?
| *ti **kanete**?* | Τι κάνετε; |
| *ti **kanis**?* (informal) | Τι κάνεις; |

I'm well, thanks.
| *kala efharis**to*** | Καλά ευχαριστώ. |

Essentials

Do you speak English?
| *mi**late** angli**ka**?* | Μιλάτε Αγγλικά; |

I understand.
| *katala**veno*** | Καταλαβαίνω. |

I don't understand.
| *dhen katala**veno*** | Δεν καταλαβαίνω. |

Where is ...?
| *pou **ine** ...?* | Πού είναι ...; |

How much?
| ***poso** kani?* | Πόσο κάνει; |

When?
| ***pote**?* | Πότε; |

LANGUAGE

The Greek Alphabet & Pronunciation

Greek	Pronunciation Guide		Example		
Α α	a	as in 'father'	αγάπη	*agha*pi	love
Β β	v	as in 'vine'	βήμα	*vi*ma	step
Γ γ	gh	like a rough 'g'	γάτα	*gha*ta	cat
	y	as in 'yes'	για	*ya*	for
Δ δ	dh	as in 'there'	δέμα	*dhe*ma	parcel
Ε ε	e	as in 'egg'	ένας	*e*nas	one (m)
Ζ ζ	z	as in 'zoo'	ζώο	*zo*o	animal
Η η	i	as in 'feet'	ήταν	*it*an	was
Θ θ	th	as in 'throw'	θέμα	*the*ma	theme
Ι ι	i	as in 'feet'	ίδιος	*i*dhyos	same
Κ κ	k	as in 'kite'	καλά	*ka*la	well
Λ λ	l	as in 'leg'	λάθος	*la*thos	mistake
Μ μ	m	as in 'man'	μαμά	*ma*ma	mother
Ν ν	n	as in 'net'	νερό	*ne*ro	water
Ξ ξ	x	as in 'ox'	ξύδι	*ksi*dhi	vinegar
Ο ο	o	as in 'hot'	όλα	*o*la	all
Π π	p	as in 'pup'	πάω	*pa*o	I go
Ρ ρ	r	as in 'road'	ρέμα	*re*ma	stream
		a slightly trilled *r*	ρόδα	*ro*dha	tyre
Σ σ, ς	s	as in 'sand'	σημάδι	*si*madhi	mark
Τ τ	t	as in 'tap'	τόπι	*to*pi	ball
Υ υ	i	as in 'feet'	ύστερα	*is*tera	after
Φ φ	f	as in 'find'	φύλλο	*fi*lo	leaf
Χ χ	h	as the *ch* in Scottish *loch*, or like a rough *h*	χάνω	*ha*no	I lose
			χέρι	*he*ri	hand
Ψ ψ	ps	as in 'lapse'	ψωμί	*psomi*	bread
Ω ω	o	as in 'hot'	ώρα	*o*ra	time

Combinations of Letters

The combinations of letters shown here are pronounced as follows:

Greek	Pronunciation Guide		Example		
ει	i	as in 'feet'	είδα	*i*dha	I saw
οι	i	as in 'feet'	οικόπεδο	*iko*pedho	land
αι	e	as in 'bet'	αίμα	*e*ma	blood
ου	u	as in 'mood'	πού	*pou*	who/what
μπ	b	as in 'beer'	μπάλα	*ba*la	ball
	mb	as in 'amber'	κάμπος	*kam*bos	forest
ντ	d	as in 'dot'	ντουλάπα	*dou*lapa	wardrobe
	nd	as in 'bend'	πέντε	*pen*de	five
γκ	g	as in 'God'	γκάζι	*ga*zi	gas
γγ	ng	as in 'angle'	αγγελία	*angeli*a	classified
γξ	ks	as in 'minks'	σφιγξ	*sfinks*	sphynx
τζ	dz	as in 'hands'	τζάκι	*dza*ki	fireplace

The pairs of vowels shown above are pronounced separately if the first has an acute accent, or the second a dieresis, as in the examples below:

γαϊδουράκι	*gaidhoura*ki	little donkey
Κάιρο	*ka*iro	Cairo

Some Greek consonant sounds have no English equivalent. The υ of the groups αυ, ευ and ηυ is generally pronounced 'v'. The Greek question mark is represented with the English equivalent of a semicolon ';'.

to 10 pm Monday to Saturday from May to October. You can check your email at Kazamias Rent-a-car (☎ 61 093, Karamanli 20).

Places to Stay & Eat

The best accommodation in town is at *Hotel Hellas (☎ 61 240)* which has singles/doubles with air-con, TV and telephone and double-glazed windows for 6000/7000 dr. It's on the right fork from the town centre. Nearby is *Itanos Rooms (☎ 61 205)* which has basic but good rooms for 5000/6000 dr.

Rooms and Apartments Nikos (☎ 61 480), near the Hotel Hellas, is on the left fork and has six-bed apartments with kitchens for 14,000 dr and double rooms for 6000 dr. *Evas Rooms (☎ 61 388)* is also a good choice with singles/doubles for 5000/6000 dr.

Two kilometres east of Palekastro on the road to Vai is *Castri Village Hotel Bungalows (☎ 61 100, fax 61 249)*, an attractively designed establishment on the slope of a hill overlooking Kouremenos Beach. Fresh modern singles/doubles cost 7000/9000 dr and there's a swimming pool.

There are not a large number of tavernas in town and most do not open until the evening. *Restaurant Elena* next to the tourist office serves good Cretan cuisine and the Hotel Hellas and Itanos Rooms also have good restaurants. ˙

Entertainment

Design is a music and dance club on the eastern end of town as you are leaving Palekastro.

Getting There & Away

There are two buses a day from Sitia that stop at Palekastro (30 minutes, 600 dr) before continuing on to Kato Zakros and three buses a day from Sitia that stop at Palekastro on their way to Vai.

AROUND PALEKASTRO

The closest beach to Palekastro is **Kouremenos**, a nearly deserted pebble beach with good swimming and excellent windsurfing. You can rent boards from Kouremenos Windsurfing (☎ 093 751 7444). There are a

few domatia. *Rooms Kouremenos Beach (☎ 61 370)*, right on the beach, has six apartments sleeping four people each that cost 12,000 dr. Also on the beach, *Apartments Grandes (☎ 61 496)*, a pretty place surrounded by a flower garden and trees, has apartments for about the same price.

There's also a Minoan **archaeological site** about a kilometre from Palekastro town. The site is still being excavated and most of it is closed to visitors but it's a pleasant walk getting there and you can still see the layout of the streets. Excavations have produced important finds such as Kamares ware, amphorae, soapstone lamps and pithoi.

MONI TOPLOU Μονή Τοπλού

The imposing Moni Toplou looks more like a fortress than a monastery – a necessity imposed by the dangers it faced at the time of its construction. The middle of the 15th century was marked by piracy, banditry and constant rebellions. The monks defended themselves with all the means at their disposal including a heavy gate, cannons (the name Toplou is Turkish for 'with a cannon'), and small holes for pouring boiling oil onto the heads of their attackers. Nevertheless, it was sacked by pirates in 1498, looted by the Knights of Malta in 1530, looted by the Turks in 1646 and captured by the Turks in 1821.

With the wealth and treasure that the monastery had accumulated, it's not surprising that it was a tempting target for looters and sackers. The star attraction is undoubtedly the icon *Lord Thou Art Great* by Koannis Kornaros. Each of the 61 small scenes painted on the icon is beautifully worked out and each is inspired by a phrase from the Orthodox prayer that begins 'Lord, Thou Art Great'. The icon is in the north aisle of the church along with 14th-century frescoes and an antique icon stand from 1770.

Moni Toplou had always been active in the cause for Cretan independence and paid a price for it. Under the Turkish occupation, its reputation for hiding rebels led to severe reprisals. During WWII many resistance leaders were sheltered in the monastery and operated an underground radio transmitter that led to the execution of Abbot Silignakis. The monastery is open from 9 am to 1 pm and 2 to 6 pm. It's a 3km walk from the Sitia-Palekastro road. Buses can drop you off at the junction.

VAI Βάι

The beach at Vai, on Crete's east coast 24km from Sitia, is famous for its palm forest. There are many stories about the origin of these palms including the theory that they sprouted from date pits spread by Roman legionaries relaxing on their way back from conquering Egypt. While these palms are closely related to the date, they are a separate species found only on Crete.

You'll need to arrive early to appreciate the setting, because the place gets packed out in July and August. It's possible to escape the worst of the ballyhoo – jet skis and all – by clambering over a rocky outcrop (to the right facing the sea) to a small secluded beach. Alternatively, there's a quiet beach over the hill in the other direction which is frequented by nudists. There are two tavernas at Vai but no accommodation.

The Vai Watersports & Scuba Centre (☎ 0843 61 070) is on the left side of the beach. You can dive for 10,000 dr including equipment or take a certification course for 100,000 dr.

If you're after more secluded beaches, head north for another 3km to the ancient Minoan site of Itanos. Although inhabited from about 1500 BC Itanos was clearly prosperous by the 7th century BC since it was an important trading post for exports to the Near East and Middle East. Its archrival was Praisos, near Ieraptera, and in 260 BC Itanos hosted a garrison of Egyptians to fortify its position against Praisos.

When Ierapetra destroyed Praisos 155 BC Itanos fought with Ierapetra as well and again received foreign help from Magnesia, a Roman city. The town was destroyed somewhere toward the end of the Byzantine era and may have been re-inhabited by the Venetians. It's difficult to discern any recognisable building in Itanos

but there are remains of two early Christian basilicas and a Hellenistic wall. The site is well-marked and next to swimming coves shaded by pine trees.

Getting There & Away
There are five buses a day to Vai from Sitia that stop at Palekastro (one hour, 600 dr).

ZAKROS Ζάκρος
☎ 0843
The village of Zakros, 45km south-east of Sitia, is the nearest permanent settlement to the east-coast Minoan site of Zakros, which is 7km away. Kato Zakros, next to the site, is a beautiful little seaside settlement that springs to life between March and October. If the weather is dry, there is a lovely two-hour walk from Zakros to Kato Zakros through a gorge, known as the Valley of the Dead due to the cave tombs dotted along the cliffs. The gorge emerges close to the Minoan site.

Places to Stay
Zakros has one hotel, the bleak C-class *Hotel Zakros* (☎ 93 379), where doubles with private bathroom are 5000 dr. Rooms in the back have great views over the gorge. Kato Zakros is a much better place to stay.

Getting There & Away
There are two buses a day to Zakros (via Palekastro) from Sitia (one hour, 1000 dr). They leave Sitia at 11 am and 2.30 pm and return at 12.30 and 4 pm. In summer, the buses continue to Kato Zakros. The Hotel Zakros offers guests free transport to Kato Zakros.

ZAKROS PALACE
A visit to Zakros Palace and Kato Zakros combines two of the best things about Crete – an intriguing archaeological site and a long stretch of under-populated beach. Although Zakros Palace was the last Minoan palace to have been discovered, the excavations proved remarkably fruitful.

The exquisite rock crystal vase and stone bull's head now in Iraklio's Archaeological Museum were found at Zakros Palace along

JON DAVISON

Looking over Agios Nikolaos towards the sea.

NEIL SETCHFIELD

Scooters for hire: a great way to get around Agios Nikolaos.

NEIL SETCHFIELD

Shopping in Agios Nikolaos

NEIL SETCHFIELD

ining along scenic Voulismeni Lake is one of the great pleasures of Agios Nikolaos.

While less ostentatious than Knossos and Phaestos, Gournia is still an important Minoan site.

Agios Georgios – an interesting little village which maintains its pastoral serenity in the mountain-fringed and tourist-friendly Lassithi Plateau.

The ancient Dorian city of Lato sprawls over two acropolises.

ZAKROS PALACE

1 Storeroom Block
2 Storerooms
3 Kitchen & Dining Room
4 Hall of Ceremonies
5 Light Well
6 Archive Room
7 Central Shrine
8 Lustral Basin
9 Treasury
10 Banquet Hall
11 King's Apartment
12 Queen's Apartment
13 Bathroom
14 Main Gate
15 Cistern Hall
16 Well Spring Chamber
17 Well
18 Work Rooms

with a treasure-trove of Minoan antiquities. Ancient Zakros, the smallest of Crete's four palatial complexes, was a major port in Minoan times, trading with Egypt, Syria, Anatolia and Cyprus. The palace consisted of royal apartments, storerooms and workshops flanking a central courtyard but the ruins are not well-preserved and water levels have risen over the years so that some parts of the palace complex are submerged.

Exploring the site

If you enter the palace complex on the south side you will first come to **workshops** for

the palace. The **King's apartment** and **Queen's apartment** are to the right of the entrance. Next to the King's apartment is the **Cistern Hall** which once had a cistern in the centre surrounded by a colonnaded balustrade. Seven steps descended to the floor of the cistern which may have been a swimming pool, an aquarium or a pool for a sacred boat. To the left of the cistern room is the **Light Well** and then the **Central Court** which was the focal point of the whole palace. Notice the altar base in the north-west corner of the court; there was a well in the south-east corner of the court at the bottom of eight steps. When the site was excavated the well contained the preserved remains of olives that had been offered to the deities. Adjacent to the central court is the **Hall of Ceremonies** in which two rhytons were found. The room to the south is the **Banquet Hall** so named for the quantity of wine vases found there. To the north of the central court is the **kitchen**. The column bases probably supported the dining room above. To the west of the central court is another **light well** and to the left of the banquet hall is the **Lustral Basin** which once contained a magnificent marble amphora. The Lustral Basin served as a washroom for those entering the nearby **Central Shrine**. You can still see a ledge and a niche in the south wall for the ceremonial idols. Below the Lustral Basin is the **Treasury** which yielded nearly a hundred jars and rhytons. Next to the treasury is the **Archive Room** which once contained Linear A record tablets. Although there were hundreds of tablets, only the ones baked by the fire that destroyed the palace were preserved. North-east of the archives room is the **bathroom** with a cesspit.

The site is open from 8.30 am to 3 pm Tuesday to Sunday. Admission is 500 dr.

KATO ZAKROS

Little more than a long stretch of pebbly beach shaded by pine trees and bordered by a string of tavernas, Kato Zakros is about the most tranquil place to stay on Crete's south coast. Although there is the *Amnesia* bar for nightlife there is little to do here but relax on the beach and poke around the archaeological site. There is no bank, post office or OTE but you can change money at the tavernas and make phone calls from a kiosk.

Places to Stay

The several domatia in Kato Zakros fill up fast. If there are no rooms available you can camp on the beach.

Make sure you bring your own supplies since there are no stores in Kato Zakros. *Athena Rooms* (π 93 458, 93 377) has doubles with private bathroom for 8000 dr.

It is jointly owned with *Poseidon Rooms* which has singles/doubles for 5000/6000 dr with shared bathroom.

Taverna Akrogiali (π 93 316) is also on the beach and has rooms for 5000/6000 dr. *George's Villas* (π 93 201/207) has spotless, beautifully furnished rooms with private bathroom and terrace for 6000/7000 dr. The villas are in a verdant setting 500m along the old road to Zakros.

Nearby is *Ameles Rooms* (π 93 020) which has singles/doubles for 5000/6500 dr.

About 2km up the road is *Faragi Rooms* (π 93 439/458), a pretty tree-shaded structure with rooms for 6000/7000 dr.

Getting There & Away

There are two buses a day to Zakros (via Palekastro) from Sitia (1 hour, 1000 dr). In summer, the buses continue to Kato Zakros.

South Coast

XEROKAMBOS

Xerokambos is an isolated idyllic spot with several kilometres of an almost deserted, wide sandy beach.

It lies at the foot of the Sitian Mountains which form a dramatic backdrop to the beach. The paved road stops several hundred metres before the beach and turns into a rocky track. There is no shade on the beach and just a few tavernas and half-finished buildings set back from the wide cove. The new road from Ziros offers a spectacular drive with many hairpin turns and the occasional goat herd ambling across the road. There are only a few places to stay.

Taverna Kastri and Rooms (π 0843-31 745) is a sleek, upmarket pension with rooms overlooking the beach. Singles/doubles cost 7000/9000 dr. *Apartments Eolos* (0843-31 792) has studios for 9000 dr on the north side of the beach.

Getting There & Away

There is no public transport to Xerokambos; the only road runs through the town of Ziros and zigzags across the mountains.

IERAPETRA Ιεράπετρα
☎ 0842 • postcode 722 00 • pop 11,000
Ierapetra is Crete's most southerly major town. It was an important city for the Dorians and the last city to fall to the Romans, who made it a major port of call in their conquest of Egypt. Despite its antiquity virtually nothing survives from the classical period.

The city languished under the Venetians, but they did build a small fortress at the western end of the harbour. In recent years agriculture has made the town wealthy enough to finance the restoration of the old town and the harbourside. The town attracts few tourists – after the tourist hype of Agios Nikolaos, the unpretentiousness of Ierapetra is refreshing.

Orientation & Information
The bus station is on Lasthenous, one street back from the beachfront north of the town centre. From the ticket office, turn right and after about 50m you'll come to a six-road intersection. There are signposts to the beach, via Patriarhou Metaxaki, and to the city centre, via the pedestrian mall section of Lasthenous.

The mall emerges after about 150m on to the central square of Plateia Eleftherias. To the north of the square is the National Bank of Greece.

The OTE is one block inland on Koraka. South of Plateia Eleftherias is Plateia Emmanual Kothri, where you'll find the post office at Stylianou Houta 3. You can check email at the cybercafe Orpheas (☎ 80 462, Kountouriotou 25).

There is no tourist office, but South Crete Tours (☎ 22 892, Lasthenous 36), opposite the bus station is a good source of information. It's open 8 am to 6 pm Monday to Friday.

There's a bookstore with English language books at Marcopoulou 71.

Things to See
Ierapetra's one-room **archaeological museum** is perfect for those with a short concentration span. It does have a good collection of headless classical statuary and a superb statue of the goddess of Demeter that dates from the 2nd century AD. Also notable is a *larnax* or clay coffin dating from around 1300 BC. The chest is decorated with 12 painted panels showing hunting scenes, an octopus and a chariot procession among others. It's at the intersection of Adrianou and Keraka.

Opening times are 8.30 am to 3 pm Tuesday to Sunday. Admission is free.

If you walk south along the waterfront from the central square you will come to the **fortress**, which was built in the early years of Venetian rule and strengthened by Francesco Morosini in 1626. It's in a pretty fragile state but you can visit it 8.30 am to 3 pm Tuesday to Sunday. Admission is free.

Inland from here is the labyrinthine old quarter, a delightful place to lose yourself for a while. Notice the **Turkish fountain**, the restored **Turkish mosque** with its minaret, and the old churches of **Agios Ioannis** and **Agios Georgios**.

Beaches Ierapetra has two beaches. The main town beach is near the harbour and the other one stretches east from the bottom of Patriarhou Metaxaki. Both have coarse, grey sand.

Special Events
Ierapetra's Kyrvia Festival runs from July through August and includes concerts, plays and art exhibits. Brochures are available in hotels and at the town hall. Some of the bands are free but tickets to top name concerts cost 1500 dr to 5000 dr. An all inclusive ticket costs about 10,000 dr

Places to Stay
Camping The nearest camp site to Ierapetra is *Koutsounari Camping (☎ 61 213)* 7km east of Ierapetra at Koutsounari. It has a restaurant, snack bar and minimarket. Ierapetra-Sitia buses pass the site.

Hotels-Budget Most of the places to stay are either near the bus station or in the old quarter. *Hotel Coral (☎ 22 846, Katzonovatsi 14)* has well-kept singles/doubles for 3000/5000 dr with private bathroom. The

LASSITHI

IERAPETRA

To Agios Nikolaos & Iraklio

Papageorgiou

To Koutsounari / Camping, SXS, Lambrakis & Sitia

Pediferiakos

Frangaki

Kazantzaki

Lakerda

Paspagou

Lambaki

Filotheou

Metaxaki

Lasthenous

Kothri

Konaki

Kiprou

Adrianou

Houta

Metaxaki

Sports Centre

Promenade

Markopoulou

Plateia Venizelou

Plateia Eleftherias

Plateia Emmanual Kothri

Medieval Port

Medieval Fortress

Medieval Wall

Port

To Arkalochori

LIBYAN SEA

To Hrysi Islet

0   100   200 m
0   100   200 yd

PLACES TO STAY
4 Four Seasons
5 Cretan Villa Hotel
8 Astron Hotel
9 Katerina Hotel
10 Hotel Cosmo
12 Hotel El Greco
27 Hotel Coral

PLACES TO EAT
6 Odeion
16 Veteranos
28 Taverna Napoleon
29 Taverna Babi's

OTHER
1 Saturday Street Market
2 South Crete Tours
3 Bus Station
7 Waikiki Cafe/Bar
11 Cafe Orpheas
13 Bookstore
14 National Bank of Greece
15 OTE
17 Archaeological Museum
18 Fruit Market
19 Post Office
20 Town Hall
21 Boat Tickets to Hrysi Islet
22 Saxo Bar
23 Agios Georgios Church
24 The Figaro
25 Boats to Hrysi Islet
26 Agios Ioannis Church
30 Agios Nikolaos Church
31 Turkish Mosque
32 Turkish Fountain

owner also has some rooms for 3000/4000 dr with shared bathroom, and comfortable apartments for 6000 dr. The hotel is signposted just south of the port police building on the waterfront. *Katerina Hotel* (☎ 28 345) on the seafront has pleasant doubles with private bathroom for 7000 dr. To reach the hotel from the bus station, follow Patriarhou Metaxaki to the waterfront, turn right and you'll see the hotel on the right.

Four Seasons Hotel (☎ 24 390), on Kazantzakis is on a quiet street near the bus station and has some unusual features, since the building dates from 1866. Try to get the ground floor room with the painted wooden ceiling. Singles/doubles are 5000/7000 dr.

Hotels-Mid-Range *Cretan Villa Hotel* (☎ 28 522, Lakerda 16), is a lovely, well-maintained 18th-century house with traditionally furnished rooms and a peaceful courtyard. Room rates are 7000/9000 dr with private bathroom. From the bus station walk towards the town centre and take the first right, from where the hotel is signposted. *Hotel Cosmo* (☎ 25 900, fax 26 251, Koundourou 16), in the centre of town, has singles/doubles with balconies and TVs for

8000/10,000 dr including breakfast. Air-conditioning is an extra 2000 dr. *Hotel El Greco* (☎ *28 471, fax 28 791, Kothri 6*) has rooms for the same price. It's located near the beach and some rooms have seaviews.

Hotels -Top End The best hotel in town is the B-class *Astron Hotel* (☎ *25 114, fax 25 91*) at the beach end of Patriarhou Metaxaki. The rooms are comfortably furnished with satellite TV, telephone and air-conditioning. Rates are 13,000/17,500 dr, including breakfast.

A few kilometres east of Ierapetra, and on the beach, is *Petra Mare Hotel* (☎ *23 341/349, fax 23 350, Filotheou A)*. It's architecturally uninspiring but has indoor and outdoor pools, tennis courts, sauna, fitness centre, children's play area and a water sports centre. Rooms have air-con, TVs and telephones. Single/doubles are 25,000/30,000 dr. Prices include buffet breakfast. Their Web site is at www.forthnet.gr/inter netcity/hotels/petramare/.

Places to Eat
Most of the souvlaki outlets are on Kyrba. On Saturday mornings there is a food market on Psilinaki. *Taverna Babi's*, in the old quarter, is one of the better tavernas along the waterfront. They have an excellent seafood pasta dish for 1500 dr. It's open noon to midnight daily. *Taverna Napoleon*, nearby, is the oldest taverna in Ierapetra and still manages to serve up a delicious array of Cretan specialties. Try the stuffed cabbage and the local white wine. It's open noon to midnight daily. When the locals celebrate a special occasion they often head to *Lambrakis* about a kilometre east of the town centre along the beach road. The grilled chicken (1100 dr) is tender and juicy, and it would be hard to find better stuffed tomatoes (1000 dr). It's open noon to midnight Monday to Sunday.

For light snacks *Odeion,* on Metaxaki Lasthenous, is a converted music school that serves mezedes in the basement while the 1st floor is a music bar. *Veteranos*, on Plateia Eleftherias, is a popular hang out for breakfast and light meals during the day.

Entertainment
Kyrba is Ierapetra's nightlife street with a number of choices for a casual drink. *Saxo Bar* is a good spot for Greek music and *Figaro* tends to play international music. *Waikiki* is a cafe/bar that often plays dance music. There are no discos in town but next to the Petra Mare Hotel is *SXS* that plays a combination of Greek and international dance music.

Getting There & Away
In summer, there are six buses a day to Iraklio (2½ hours, 2100 dr) via Agios Nikolaos (one hour, 750 dr), Gournia and Istron; eight to Makrigialos (30 minutes, 600 dr); six to Sitia (1½ hours, 1200 dr) via Koutsounari (for camp sites); six to Mirtos (30 minutes, 320 dr) and two a week to Ano Viannos (one hour, 800 dr).

AROUND IERAPETRA
The beaches to the east of Ierapetra tend to get crowded. For greater tranquillity, head for **Hrysi Islet**, where there are good uncrowded sandy beaches.

In summer an excursion boat (5500 dr) leaves from the quay near the town centre for the islet every morning and returns in the afternoon. There are three tavernas on the islet. Tickets are available at the ticket office on Kybra.

MIRTOS
☎ 0842 • postcode 722 00 • pop 600
Mirtos, on the coast 17km west of Ierapetra, is a sparkling village of whitewashed houses with flower-filled balconies. Despite it's popularity with independent travellers Mirtos has preserved its charm. It has a decent dark sand and pebble beach. To get to the waterfront from the bus stop, head south and take the road to the right, passing Mertiza Studios on the right. Mirtos is easily navigable as it is built on a grid system.

Orientation & Information
There is no post office, bank or OTE, but Aris Travel Agency (☎ 51 017/300) on the main street has a currency exchange.

Places to Stay & Eat
Despina Rent Rooms (☎ *51 343*) has pleasant but noisy doubles/triples with private bathroom for 5000/6500 dr. ***Pandora Domatia*** (☎ *51 589*), on the main street, has prettily furnished singles/doubles for 3500/4000 dr with shared bathroom. ***Hotel Panorama*** (☎ *51 362*) uphill from the town centre has studios with bathrooms, kitchenettes and spectacular views at 5000/7000 dr for singles/doubles. The superior C-class ***Hotel Mirtos*** (☎ *51 227*) has large, well-kept rooms for 5000/7000 dr with private bathroom. ***Big Blue*** (☎ *51 094*) on the western edge of town has rooms for 6000/7000 dr with bathroom and two-room apartments with two bathrooms and a kitchenette for 12,000 dr.

Mirtos Hotel Restaurant is popular with both locals and tourists. The no-frills ***Kostos Taverna*** nearby has good dolmades for 800 dr and *stifado* for 1500 dr. The waterfront ***Karavoslasi Restaurant*** is more stylish, with vegetarian dishes for 1000 dr and meat dishes for 1500 dr to 1800 dr.

Getting There & Away
There are six buses a day from Ierapetra to Mirtos (30 minutes, 320 dr). The Ano Viannos-Ierapetra bus passes through Mirtos.

Language

The Greek language is probably the oldest European language, with an oral tradition of 4000 years and a written tradition of approximately 3000 years. Its evolution over the four millennia was characterised by its strength during the golden age of Athens and the Democracy (mid-5th century BC); its use as a lingua franca throughout the Middle Eastern world, spread by Alexander the Great and his successors as far as India during the Hellenistic period (330 BC to 100 AD); its adaptation as the language of the new religion, Christianity; its use as the official language of the Eastern Roman Empire; and its eventual proclamation as the language of the Byzantine Empire (380-1453).

Greek maintained its status and prestige during the rise of the European Renaissance and was employed as the linguistic perspective for all contemporary sciences and terminologies during the period of Enlightenment. Today, Greek constitutes a large part of the vocabulary of any Indo-European language, and much of the lexicon of any scientific repertoire.

The modern Greek language is a southern Greek dialect which is now used by most Greek speakers both in Greece and abroad. It is the result of an intralinguistic influence and synthesis of the ancient vocabulary combined with words from Greek regional dialects, namely Cretan, Cypriot and Macedonian.

Those wishing to delve a little deeper into the language should get a copy of Lonely Planet's *Greek phrasebook*.

Pronunciation

All Greek words of two or more syllables have an acute accent which indicates where the stress falls. For instance, άγαλμα (statue) is pronounced **agh**alma, and αγάπη (love) is pronounced a**gh**api. In the following transliterations, bold lettering indicates where stress falls. Note also that **dh** is pronounced as 'th' in 'then'; **gh** is a softer, slightly guttural version of 'g'.

Greetings & Civilities

Hello.
   yasas   Γειά σας.
   yasu (informal) Γειά σου.
Goodbye.
   an**dio**   Αντίο.
Good morning.
   kali**mera**   Καλημέρα.
Good afternoon.
   he**rete**   Χαίρετε.
Good evening.
   kalis**pera**   Καλησπέρα.
Good night.
   kali**nihta**   Καληνύχτα.
Please.
   paraka**lo**   Παρακαλώ.
Thank you.
   efharis**to**   Ευχαριστώ.
Yes.
   ne   Ναι.
No.
   ohi   Οχι.
Sorry. (excuse me, forgive me)
   sigh**nomi**   Συγγνώμη.
How are you?
   ti **kanete?**   Τι κάνετε;
   ti **kanis?**   Τι κάνεις;
   (informal)
I'm well, thanks.
   ka**la** ef**haris**to Καλά ευχαριστώ.

Essentials

Do you speak English?
   mi**late** ang**lika?** Μιλάτε Αγγλικά;
I understand.
   katala**veno**   Καταλαβαίνω.
I don't understand.
   dhen katala**veno** Δεν καταλαβαίνω.
Where is ...?
   pou **ine** ...?   Πού είναι ...;
How much?
   poso kani?   Πόσο κάνει;
When?
   pote?   Πότε;

The Greek Alphabet & Pronunciation

Greek	Pronunciation Guide		Example		
Α α	a	as in 'father'	αγάπη	*agha*pi	love
Β β	v	as in 'vine'	βήμα	*vi*ma	step
Γ γ	gh	like a rough 'g'	γάτα	*gha*ta	cat
	y	as in 'yes'	για	*ya*	for
Δ δ	dh	as in 'there'	δέμα	*dhe*ma	parcel
Ε ε	e	as in 'egg'	ένας	*e*nas	one (m)
Ζ ζ	z	as in 'zoo'	ζώο	*zo*o	animal
Η η	i	as in 'feet'	ήταν	*it*an	was
Θ θ	th	as in 'throw'	θέμα	*the*ma	theme
Ι ι	i	as in 'feet'	ίδιος	*i*dhyos	same
Κ κ	k	as in 'kite'	καλά	*ka*la	well
Λ λ	l	as in 'leg'	λάθος	*la*thos	mistake
Μ μ	m	as in 'man'	μαμά	*ma*ma	mother
Ν ν	n	as in 'net'	νερό	*ne*ro	water
Ξ ξ	x	as in 'ox'	ξύδι	*ksi*dhi	vinegar
Ο ο	o	as in 'hot'	όλα	*o*la	all
Π π	p	as in 'pup'	πάω	*pa*o	I go
Ρ ρ	r	as in 'road'	ρέμα	*re*ma	stream
		a slightly trilled r	ρόδα	*ro*dha	tyre
Σ σ, ς	s	as in 'sand'	σημάδι	*sima*dhi	mark
Τ τ	t	as in 'tap'	τόπι	*to*pi	ball
Υ υ	i	as in 'feet'	ύστερα	*is*tera	after
Φ φ	f	as in 'find'	φύλλο	*fi*lo	leaf
Χ χ	h	as the *ch* in Scottish *loch*, or like a rough *h*	χάνω	*ha*no	I lose
			χέρι	*he*ri	hand
Ψ ψ	ps	as in 'lapse'	ψωμί	*pso*mi	bread
Ω ω	o	as in 'hot'	ώρα	*o*ra	time

Combinations of Letters

The combinations of letters shown here are pronounced as follows:

Greek	Pronunciation Guide		Example		
ει	i	as in 'feet'	είδα	*i*dha	I saw
οι	i	as in 'feet'	οικόπεδο	*iko*pedho	land
αι	e	as in 'bet'	αίμα	*e*ma	blood
ου	u	as in 'mood'	πού	*pou*	who/what
μπ	b	as in 'beer'	μπάλα	*ba*la	ball
	mb	as in 'amber'	κάμπος	*kam*bos	forest
ντ	d	as in 'dot'	ντουλάπα	*doula*pa	wardrobe
	nd	as in 'bend'	πέντε	*pen*de	five
γκ	g	as in 'God'	γκάζι	*ga*zi	gas
γγ	ng	as in 'angle'	αγγελία	*angeli*a	classified
γξ	ks	as in 'minks'	σφιγξ	*sfinks*	sphynx
τζ	dz	as in 'hands'	τζάκι	*dza*ki	fireplace

The pairs of vowels shown above are pronounced separately if the first has an acute accent, or the second a dieresis, as in the examples below:

γαϊδουράκι	*gaidhoura*ki	little donkey
Κάιρο	*ka*iro	Cairo

Some Greek consonant sounds have no English equivalent. The υ of the groups αυ, ευ and ηυ is generally pronounced 'v'. The Greek question mark is represented with the English equivalent of a semicolon ';'.

Small Talk

What's your name?
pos sas lene? Πώς σας λένε;
My name is ...
me lene ... Με λένε ...
Where are you from?
apo pou iste? Από πού είστε;

I'm from ...
ime apo ... Είμαι από ...
America
tin ameriki την Αμερική
Australia
tin afstralia την Αυστραλία
England
tin anglia την Αγγλία
Ireland
tin irlandhia την Ιρλανδία
New Zealand
ti nea zilandhia τη Νέα Ζηλανδία
Scotland
ti skotia τη Σκωτία

How old are you?
poson hronon iste? Πόσων χρονών είστε;
I'm ... years old.
ime ... hronon Είμαι ... χρονών.

Getting Around

What time does the ... leave/arrive?
ti ora fevyi/ ftani to ...? Τι ώρα φεύγει/ φτάνει το ...;

plane *aeroplano* αεροπλάνο
boat *karavi* καράβι
bus *astiko* αστικό

I'd like ...
tha ithela ... Θα ήθελα ...
a return ticket
isitirio me epistrofi εισιτήριο με επιστροφή
two tickets
dhio isitiria δυο εισιτήρια
a student's fare
fititiko isitirio φοιτητικό εισιτήριο
first class
proti thesi πρώτη θέση

Signs

ΕΙΣΟΔΟΣ	ENTRY
ΕΞΟΔΟΣ	EXIT
ΩΘΗΣΑΤΕ	PUSH
ΣΥΡΑΤΕ	PULL
ΓΥΝΑΙΚΩΝ	WOMEN (toilets)
ΑΝΔΡΩΝ	MEN (toilets)
ΝΟΣΟΚΟΜΕΙΟ	HOSPITAL
ΑΣΤΥΝΟΜΙΑ	POLICE
ΑΠΑΓΟΡΕΥΕΤΑΙ	PROHIBITED
ΕΙΣΙΤΗΡΙΑ	TICKETS

economy
touristiki thesi τουριστική θέση
timetable
dhromologio δρομολόγιο
taxi
taxi ταξί

Where can I hire a car?
pou boro na nikyaso ena aftokinito?
Πού μπορώ να νοικιάσω ένα αυτοκίνητο;

Directions

How do I get to ...?
pos tha pao sto/ sti ...? Πώς θα πάω στο/ στη ...;
Where is ...?
pou ine ...? Πού είναι...;
Is it near?
ine konda? Είναι κοντά;
Is it far?
ine makria? Είναι μακριά;

straight ahead *efthia* ευθεία
left *aristera* αριστερά
right *dexia* δεξιά
behind *piso* πίσω
far *makria* μακριά
near *konda* κοντά
opposite *apenandi* απέναντι

Can you show me on the map?
borite na mou to dhixete sto harti?
Μπορείτε να μου το δείξετε στο χάρτη;

Around Town

I'm looking for (the) ...
psahno ya ...
Ψάχνω για ...

bank	*trapeza*	τράπεζα
beach	*paralia*	παραλία
castle	*kastro*	κάστρο
church	*ekklisia*	εκκλησία
... embassy	*tin ... presvia*	την ... πρεσβεία
market	*aghora*	αγορά
museum	*musio*	μουσείο
police	*astynomia*	αστυνομία
post office	*tahydhromio*	ταχυδρομείο
ruins	*arhea*	αρχαία

I want to exchange some money.
thelo na exaryiroso lefta
Θέλω να εξαργυρώσω λεφτά.

Accommodation

Where is ...?
pou ine ...? Πού είναι ...;
I'd like ...
thelo ena ... Θέλω ένα ...

a cheap hotel
ftino xenodohio φτηνό ξενοδοχείο
a clean room
katharo dho-matio καθαρό δωμάτιο
a good hotel
kalo xenodohio καλό ξενοδοχείο
a camp site
kamping κάμπιγκ

single	*mono*	μονό
double	*dhiplo*	διπλό
room	*dhomatio*	δωμάτιο
with bathroom	*me banio*	με μπάνιο
key	*klidhi*	κλειδί

How much is it ...?
poso kani ...? Πόσο κάνει ...;
per night
ti vradhya τη βραδυά
for ... nights
ya ... vradhyez για ... βραδυές

Emergencies

Help!
voithya! Βοήθεια!
Police!
astynomia! Αστυνομία!
There's been an accident.
eyine atihima Εγινε ατύχημα.
Call a doctor!
fonaxte ena yatro! Φωνάξτε ένα ιατρό!
Call an ambulance!
tilefoniste ya asthenoforo! Τηλεφωνήστε για ασθενοφόρο!
I'm ill.
ime arostos (m) Είμαι άρρωστος
ime arosti (f) Είμαι άρρωστη
I'm lost.
eho hathi Εχω χαθεί
Thief!
klefti! Κλέφτη!
Go away!
fiye! Φύγε!
I've been raped.
me viase kapyos Με βίασε κάποιος.
I've been robbed.
meklepse kapyos Μ'έκλεψε κάποιος.
Where are the toilets?
pou ine i toualetez? Πού είναι οι τουαλέτες;

Is breakfast included?
symberilamvani ke pro-ino? Συμπεριλαμβάνει και πρωϊνό;
May I see it?
boro na to dho? Μπορώ να το δω;
Where is the bathroom?
pou ine tobanio? Πού είναι το μπάνιο;
It's expensive.
ine akrivo Είναι ακριβό.
I'm leaving today.
fevgho simera Φεύγω σήμερα.

Food

breakfast	pro-ino	πρωϊνό
lunch	mesimvrino	μεσημβρινό
dinner	vradhyno	βραδυνό
beef	vodhino	βοδινό
bread	psomi	ψωμί
beer	byra	μπύρα
cheese	tyri	τυρί
chicken	kotopoulo	κοτόπουλο
Greek coffee	ellinikos kafes	ελληνικός καφές
iced coffee	frappe	φραππέ
lamb	arni	αρνί
milk	ghala	γάλα
mineral water	metalliko nero	μεταλλικό νερό
tea	tsai	τσάι
wine	krasi	κρασί

I'm a vegetarian.
ime hortofaghos   Είμαι χορτοφάγος.

Shopping

How much is it?
poso kani?
Πόσο κάνει;
I'm just looking.
aplos kitazo
Απλώς κοιτάζω.
I'd like to buy ...
thelo n'aghoraso ...
Θέλω ν΄αγοράσω :..
Do you accept credit cards?
pernete pistotikez kartez?
Παίρνετε πιστωτικές κάρτες;
Could you lower the price?
borite na mou kanete mya kaliteri timi?
Μπορείτε να μου κάνετε μια καλύτερη τιμή;

Time & Dates

What time is it?
ti ora ine?   Τι ώρα είναι;

It's ...	ine ...	είναι ...
1 o'clock	mia i ora	μία η ώρα
2 o'clock	dhio i ora	δύο η ώρα
7.30	efta ke misi	εφτά και μισή
am	to pro-i	το πρωί
pm	to apoyevma	το απόγευμα
today	simera	σήμερα

tonight	apopse	απόψε
now	tora	τώρα
yesterday	hthes	χθες
tomorrow	avrio	αύριο

Sunday	kyriaki	Κυριακή
Monday	dheftera	Δευτέρα
Tuesday	triti	Τρίτη
Wednesday	tetarti	Τετάρτη
Thursday	pempti	Πέμπτη
Friday	paraskevi	Παρασκευή
Saturday	savato	Σάββατο

January	ianouarios	Ιανουάριος
February	fevrouarios	Φεβρουάριος
March	martios	Μάρτιος
April	aprilios	Απρίλιος
May	maïos	Μάιος
June	iounios	Ιούνιος
July	ioulios	Ιούλιος
August	avghoustos	Αύγουστος
September	septemvrios	Σεπτέμβριος
October	oktovrios	Οκτώβριος
November	noemvrios	Νοέμβριος
December	dhekemvrios	Δεκέμβριος

Health

I need a doctor.
hriazome yatro   Χρειάζομαι ιατρό.
Can you take me to hospital?
borite na me pate sto nosokomio?   Μπορείτε να με πάτε στο νοσοκομείο;
I want something for ...
thelo kati ya ...   Θέλω κάτι για ...

diarrhoea	dhiaria	διάρροια
insect bites	tsimbimata apo endoma	τσιμπήματα από έντομα
travel sickness	naftia taxidhiou	ναυτία ταξιδιού

aspirin	aspirini	ασπιρίνη
condoms	profylaktika (kapotez)	προφυλακτικά (καπότες)
contact lenses	faki epafis	φακοί επαφής
medical insurance	yatriki asfalya	ιατρική ασφάλεια

Numbers

0	*midhen*	μηδέν	20	*ikosi*	είκοσι
1	*enas*	ένας (m)	30	*trianda*	τριάντα
	mia	μία (f)	40	*saranda*	σαράντα
	ena	ένα (n)	50	*peninda*	πενήντα
2	*dhio*	δύο	60	*exinda*	εξήντα
3	*tris*	τρεις (m & f)	70	*evdhominda*	εβδομήντα
	tria	τρία (n)	80	*oghdhonda*	ογδόντα
4	*teseris*	τέσσερεις (m & f)	90	*eneninda*	ενενήντα
	tesera	τέσσερα (n)	100	*ekato*	εκατό
5	*pende*	πέντε	1000	*hilii*	χίλιοι (m)
6	*exi*	έξη		*hiliez*	χίλιες (f)
7	*epta*	επτά		*hilia*	χίλια (n)
8	*ohto*	οχτώ			
9	*enea*	εννέα			
10	*dheka*	δέκα			

one million
  ena ekatomyrio   ένα εκατομμύριο

Glossary

Achaean civilisation – see Mycenaean civilisation

acropolis – highest point of an ancient city

agia (f), **agios** (m) – saint

agora – commercial area of an ancient city; shopping precinct in modern Greece

agria – wild

amphora – large two-handled vase in which wine or oil was kept

ANEK – Anonymi Naftiliaki Eteria Kritis; main shipping line to Crete

Archaic period (800-480 BC) – also known as the Middle Age; period in which the city-states emerged from the 'dark age' and traded their way to wealth and power; the city-states were unified by a Greek alphabet and common cultural pursuits, engendering a sense of national identity

architrave – part of the entablature which rests on the columns of a temple

arhontika – 17th and 18th century AD mansions which belonged to arhons, the leading citizens of a town

askitiria – mini-chapels; places of solitary worship

Astakos – lobster

baglamas – miniature bouzouki with a tinny sound

bakaliaros – cod

barbounia – red mullet

basilica – early Christian church

bougatsa – custard-filled pastry

bouleuterion – council house

bourekaki – tiny meat pie

bouzouki – stringed lute-like instrument associated with rembetika music

bouzoukia – 'bouzoukis'; used to mean any nightclub where the bouzouki is played and low-grade blues songs are sung; see skyladika

buttress – support built against the outside of a wall

Byzantine Empire – characterised by the merging of Hellenistic culture and Christianity and named after Byzantium, the city on the Bosphorus which became the capital of the Roman Empire in 324 AD; when the Roman Empire was formally divided in 395 AD, Rome went into decline and the eastern capital, renamed Constantinople after Emperor Constantine I, flourished; the Byzantine Empire dissolved after the fall of Constantinople to the Turks in 1453

caïque – small, sturdy fishing boat

capital – top of a column

cella – room in a temple where the cult statue stood

chipura – ouzo without anise

chochliii boubouristi – snails simmered in vinegar or snails with barley

choregos – wealthy citizen who financed choral and dramatic performances

city-states – states comprising a sovereign city and its dependencies; the city-states of Athens and Sparta were famous rivals

classical Greece – period in which the Greek city-states reached the height of their wealth and power after the defeat of the Persians in the 5th century BC; ended with the decline of the city-states as a result of the Peloponnesian Wars, and the expansionist aspirations of Philip II, King of Macedon (ruled 359-336 BC and his son, Alexander the Great ruled 336-323 BC)

Corinthian – order of Greek architecture recognisable by columns with bell-shaped capitals with sculpted elaborate ornaments based on acanthus leaves

cornice – the upper part of the entablature, extending beyond the frieze

crypt – lowest part of a church, often a burial chamber

Cycladic civilisation (3000-1100 BC) – civilisation which emerged following the settlement of Phoenician colonists on the Cycladic islands

cyclopes – mythical one-eyed giants

dark age (1200-800 BC) – period in which Greece was under Dorian rule

delfini – dolphin; common name for hydro-foil

diglossy – the existence of two forms of one language within a country; has existed in Greece for most of its modern history

dimarhio – town hall

Dimotiki – Demotic Greek language; the official spoken language of Greece

dolmades – stuffed vine leaves

domatio (s), **domatia** (pl) – room; a cheap accommodation option available in most tourist areas

Dorians – Hellenic warriors who invaded Greece around 1200 BC, demolishing the city-states and destroying the Mycenaean civilisation; heralded Greece's 'dark age', when the artistic and cultural advancements of the Mycenaeans and Minoans were abandoned; the Dorians later developed into land-holding aristocrats which encouraged the resurgence of independent city-states led by wealthy aristocrats

Doric – order of Greek architecture characterised by a column which has no base, a fluted shaft and a relatively plain capital, when compared with the flourishes evident on Ionic and Corinthian capitals

ELPA – Elliniki Leshi Periigiseon & Aftokinitou; Greek motoring and touring club

ELTA – Ellinika Tahydromia; Greek post office

entablature – part of a temple between the tops of the columns and the roof

EOS – Ellinikos Orivatikos Syllogos; Greek alpine club

EOT – Ellinikos Organismos Tourismou; national tourism organisation which has offices in most major towns

Epitaphios – picture on cloth of Christ on his bier

estiatorio – restaurant serving ready-made food as well as a la carte dishes

ET – Elliniki Tileorasi; state television company

fasolia – white haricot beans

Filiki Eteria – friendly society; a group of Greeks in exile; formed during Ottoman rule to organise an uprising against the Turks

fluted – of a column having vertical indentations on the shaft

frappé – iced coffee

frieze – part of the entablature which is above the architrave

galaktopoleio (s), **galaktopoleia** (pl) – a shop which sells dairy products

garides – shrimps

Geometric period (1200-800 BC) – period characterised by pottery decorated with geometric designs; sometimes referred to as Greece's 'dark age'

GESEE – Greek trade union association

gigantes – lima beans

giouvetsi – casserole of meat and pasta

glossa – sole

glyko – sweet

gopes – similar to sardines

halva – made from semolina or sesame seeds

Hellas, Ellas or Ellada – the Greek name for Greece

Hellenistic period – prosperous, influential period of Greek civilisation ushered in by Alexander the Great's empire-building and lasting until the Roman sacking of Corinth in 146 BC

hora – main town, usually on an island

horta – cooked wild greens

iconostasis – altar screen embellished with icons

ikonostassia – miniature chapels

imeri – tame

Ionic – order of Greek architecture characterised by a column with truncated flutes and capitals with ornaments resembling scrolls

ipnakos – siesta

kafeneio (s), **kafeneia** (pl) – traditionally a male-only coffee house where cards and backgammon are played

kafeteria – upmarket kafeneio, mainly for younger people

kalamaria – squid
kalderimi – cobbled footpath
kalimera – good morning
kalispera – good evening
karabida – crayfish
karpouzi – watermelon
kasseri – mild, slightly rubbery sheep's-milk cheese
kastro – walled-in town
katafi – chopped nuts inside shredded wheat pastry or filo soaked in honey
katholikon – principal church of a monastic complex
kefi – an undefinable feeling of good spirit, without which no Greek can have a good time
keftedes – meatballs
kerasia – cherries
kilim – flat-woven rugs that were traditional dowry gifts
KKE – Kommounistiko Komma Elladas; Greek communist party
Koine – Greek language used in pre-Byzantine times; the language of the church liturgy
kokkino – homemade rosé wine
kolokythakia – deep-fried zucchini
kore – female statue of the Archaic period; see kouros
kosmoi – ruling committees of elected officials in Dorian Crete
kouros – male statue of the Archaic period, characterised by a stiff body posture and enigmatic smile
KTEL – Kino Tamio Eispraxeon Leoforion; national bus cooperative; runs all long-distance bus services

labrys – double axe symbol of Minoan civilization
lammergeier – bearded vulture
libation – in ancient Greece, wine or food which was offered to the gods
Linear A – Minoan script; so far undeciphered
Linear B – Mycenaean script; has been deciphered
loukanika – little sausages
loukoumades – puffs or fritters with honey or syrup

loukoumi – Turkish delight
lyra – small violin-like instrument, played on the knee; common in Cretan and Pontian music

maistos – light to moderate north-westerly wind which rises in the afternoon
malakas – literally 'wanker'; used as a familiar term of address, or as an insult, depending on context
mangas – 'wide boy' or 'dude'; originally a person of the underworld, now any streetwise person
mantinades – traditional Cretan songs often with improvised lyrics
marides – whitebait sometimes cloaked in onion, pepper and tomato sauce
mavromatika – black-eyed beans
mayiria – cook houses
megaron – central room of a Mycenaean palace
melitzana – deep-fried aubergine
melitzanosalata – aubergine or eggplant dip
Melizanes papoutsakia – baked eggplant stuffed with meat and tomatoes and topped with cheese, which looks, as its Greek name suggests, like a little shoe
meltemi – north-easterly wind which blows throughout much of Greece during the summer
metope – sculpted section of a Doric frieze
metrio – medium
meze (s), **mezedes** (pl) – appetiser
Middle Age – see Archaic period
Minoan civilisation (3000-1100 BC) – Bronze Age culture of Crete named after the mythical king Minos and characterised by pottery and metalwork of great beauty and artisanship
mitata – round stone shepherd's huts
moni – monastery or convent
moussaka – layers of eggplant or zucchini, minced meat and potatoes topped with cheese sauce and baked pastitsio
Mycenaean civilisation (1900-1100 BC) – first great civilisation of the Greek mainland, characterised by powerful independent city-states ruled by kings; also known as the Achaean civilisation

myzithra – soft sheep's-milk cheese

narthex – porch of a church
nave – aisle of a church
Nea Dimokratia – New Democracy; conservative political party
necropolis – literally 'city of the dead'; ancient cemetery
nefos – cloud; usually used to refer to pollution in Athens
neo kyma – 'new wave'; left-wing music of the boîtes and clubs of 1960s Athens
nomarhia – prefecture building
nomos – prefectures into which the regions and island groups of Greece are divided
nymphaeum – in ancient Greece, building containing a fountain and often dedicated to nymphs

OA – Olympiaki Aeroporia or Olympic Airways; Greece's national airline and major domestic air carrier
octopus saganaki – octopus fried with tomato and cheese
odeion – ancient Greek indoor theatre
odos – street
ohi – 'no'; what the Greeks said to Mussolini's ultimatum when he said surrender or be invaded; the Italians were subsequently repelled and the event is celebrated on October 28
ohtapodi – octopus
omphalos – sacred stone at Delphi which the ancient Greeks believed marked the centre of the world
OSE – Organismos Sidirodromon Ellados; Greek railways organisation
OTE – Organismos Tilepikinonion Ellados; Greece's major telecommunications carrier
oud – a bulbous, stringed instrument with a sharply raked-back head
ouzeri (s), **ouzeria** (pl) – place which serves ouzo and light snacks
ouzo – a distilled spirit made from grapes and flavoured with aniseed

pagoto – ice cream
Panagia – Mother of God; name frequently used for churches
Pantokrator – painting or mosaic of Christ in the centre of the dome of a Byzantine church
pantopoleio – general store
paralia – waterfront
PASOK – Panellinio Sosialistiko Komma; Greek socialist party
pasta stifado – meat stewed with onions
pediment – triangular section, often filled with sculpture above the columns, found at the front and back of a classical Greek temple
perioeci – a subject class of free men without political rights in Dorian Crete
periptero (s), **periptera** (pl) – street kiosk
peristyle – columns surrounding a building, usually a temple or courtyard
pinakotheke – picture gallery
pithos (s), **pithoi** (pl) – large Minoan storage jar
plateia – square
Politiki Anixi – Political Spring; centrist political party
portokalia – oranges
PRO-PO – Prognostiko Podosferou; Greek football pools
propylon (s), **propylaia** (pl) – elaborately built main entrance to an ancient city or sanctuary; a propylon had one gateway and a propylaia more than one
psarotaverna – taverna specialising in seafood
psistaria – restaurant serving grilled food

rembetika – blues songs commonly associated with the underworld of the 1920s
retsina – resinated white wine
rhyton – another name for a libation vessel
rizitika – traditional, patriotic songs of Crete
rizogalo – rice pudding

sacristy – room attached to a church where sacred vessels etc are kept
saganaki – fried cheese
salingaria – snails in oil with herbs
sandouits – sandwiches
sandouri – hammered dulcimer from Asia Minor
SEO – Syllogos Ellinon Orivaton; Greek mountaineers' association

sketo – without sugar
skites (s), **skiti** (pl) – hermit's dwelling
Skopia – what the Greeks call the Former Yugoslav Republic of Macedonia (FYROM)
skyladika – literally 'dog songs'; popular, but not lyrically challenging, blues songs often sung in bouzoukia nightclubs
soutzoukakia – spicy meatballs in tomato sauce
spanakopitta – spinach pie
spicy loukanika – sausage with potatoes or rice
spilia – cave
splinogardouba – spleen
stafylia – grapes
stele (s), **stelae** (pl) – grave stone which stands upright
stifado – stew
stoa – long colonnaded building, usually in an agora; used as a meeting place and shelter in ancient Greece
syka – figs
synagrida – snapper

taverna – traditional restaurant which serves food and wine
temblon – votive screen

tholos – Mycenaean tomb shaped like a beehive
toumberleki – small lap drum played with the fingers
triglyph – sections of a Doric frieze between the metopes
trireme – ancient Greek galley with three rows of oars on each side
tsikoudia – Cretan version of tsipouro
Tsingani – Gypsies or Roma
tsipouro – distilled spirit made from grapes
tyropitta – cheese pie
tzatziki – yogurt, cucumber and garlic dip

velenza – flokati rug
Vlach – traditional, semi-nomadic shepherds from northern Greece who speak a Latin-based dialect
volta – promenade; evening stroll
volute – spiral decoration on Ionic capitals

xythomyzithra – soft sheep's-milk cheese

zaharoplasteio (s), **zaharoplasteia** (pl) – patisserie; shop which sells cakes, chocolates, sweets and, sometimes, alcoholic drinks
zouridha – Cretan polecat

LONELY PLANET

Phrasebooks

Lonely Planet phrasebooks are packed with essential words and phrases to help travellers communicate with the locals. With colour tabs for quick reference, an extensive vocabulary and use of script, these handy pocket-sized language guides cover day-to-day travel situations.

- handy pocket-sized books
- easy to understand Pronunciation chapter
- clear & comprehensive Grammar chapter
- romanisation alongside script to allow ease of pronunciation
- script throughout so users can point to phrases for every situation
- full of cultural information and tips for the traveller

'... vital for a real DIY spirit and attitude in language learning'
— *Backpacker*

'the phrasebooks have good cultural backgrounders and offer solid advice for challenging situations in remote locations'
— *San Francisco Examiner*

Arabic (Egyptian) • Arabic (Moroccan) • Australian *(Australian English, Aboriginal and Torres Strait languages)* • Baltic States *(Estonian, Latvian, Lithuanian)* • Bengali • Brazilian • British • Burmese • Cantonese • Central Asia (Uyghur, Uzbek, Kyrghiz, Kazak, Pashto, Tadjik • Central Europe *(Czech, French, German, Hungarian, Italian, Slovak)* • Eastern Europe *(Bulgarian, Czech, Hungarian, Polish, Romanian, Slovak)* • Ethiopian (Amharic) • Fijian • French • German • Greek • Hebrew • Hill Tribes • Hindi & Urdu • Indonesian • Italian • Japanese • Korean • Lao • Latin American Spanish • Malay • Mandarin • Mediterranean Europe *(Albanian, Croatian, Greek, Italian, Macedonian, Maltese, Serbian, Slovene)* • Mongolian • Nepali • Pidgin • Pilipino (Tagalog) • Quechua • Russian • Scandinavian Europe *(Danish, Finnish, Icelandic, Norwegian, Swedish)* • South-East Asia *(Burmese, Indonesian, Khmer, Lao, Malay, Tagalog Pilipino, Thai, Vietnamese)* • South Pacific Languages • Spanish (Castilian) *(also includes Catalan, Galician and Basque)* • Sri Lanka • Swahili • Thai • Tibetan • Turkish • Ukrainian • USA *(US English, Vernacular, Native American languages, Hawaiian)* • Vietnamese • Western Europe *(Basque, Catalan, Dutch, French, German, Greek, Irish, Italian, Portuguese, Scottish Gaelic, Spanish (Castilian), Welsh)*

Lonely Planet Journeys

Journeys is a unique collection of travel writing – published by the company that understands travel better than anyone else. It is a series for anyone who has ever experienced – or dreamed of – the magical moment when they encountered a strange culture or saw a place for the first time. They are tales to read while you're planning a trip, while you're on the road or while you're in an armchair in front of a fire.

These outstanding titles explore our planet through the eyes of a diverse group of international writers. JOURNEYS books catch the spirit of a place, illuminate a culture, recount a crazy adventure or introduce a fascinating way of life. They always entertain, and always enrich the experience of travel.

MALI BLUES
Traveling to an African Beat
Lieve Joris (translated by Sam Garrett)
Drought, rebel uprisings, ethnic conflict: these are the predominant images of West Africa. But as Lieve Joris travels in Senegal, Mauritania and Mali, she meets survivors, fascinating individuals charting new ways of living between tradition and modernity. With her remarkable gift for drawing out people's stories, Joris brilliantly captures the rhythms of a world that refuses to give in.

THE GATES OF DAMASCUS
Lieve Joris (translated by Sam Garrett)
This best-selling book is a beautifully drawn portrait of day-to-day life in modern Syria. Through her intimate contact with local people, Lieve Joris draws us into the fascinating world that lies behind the gates of Damascus. Hala's husband is a political prisoner, jailed for his opposition to the Assad regime; through the author's friendship with Hala we see how Syrian politics impacts on the lives of ordinary people.

THE OLIVE GROVE
Travels in Greece
Katherine Kizilos
Katherine Kizilos travels to fabled islands, troubled border zones and her family's village deep in the mountains. She vividly evokes breathtaking landscapes, generous people and passionate politics, capturing the complexities of a country she loves.

'beautifully captures the real tensions of Greece' – *Sunday Times*

KINGDOM OF THE FILM STARS
Journey into Jordan
Annie Caulfield
Kingdom of the Film Stars is a travel book and a love story. With honesty and humour, Annie Caulfield writes of travelling in Jordan and falling in love with a Bedouin with film-star looks.

She offers fascinating insights into the country – from the tent life of traditional women to the hustle of downtown Amman – and unpicks tight-woven western myths about the Arab world.

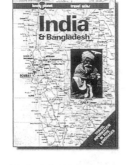

LONELY PLANET

Lonely Planet Online

W hether you've just begun planning your next trip, or you're chasing down specific info on currency regulations or visa requirements, check out Lonely Planet Online for up-to-the-minute travel information.

As well as miniguides to more than 250 destinations, you'll find maps, photos, travel news, health and visa updates, travel advisories and discussion of the ecological and political issues you need to be aware of as you travel. You'll also find timely upgrades to popular guidebooks that you can print out and stick in the back of your book.

There's an online travellers' forum (The Thorn Tree) where you can share your experience of life on the road, meet travel companions and ask other travellers for their recommendations and advice.

There's also a complete and up-to-date list of all Lonely Planet travel products including travel guides, diving and snorkeling guides, phrasebooks, atlases, travel literature and videos, and a simple online ordering facility if you can't find the book you want elsewhere.

Lonely Planet Diving & Snorkeling Guides

B eautifully illustrated with full-colour photos throughout, Lonely Planet's Pisces books explore the world's best diving and snorkeling areas and prepare divers for what to expect when they get there, both topside and underwater.

Dive sites are described in detail with specifics on depths, visibility, level of difficulty, special conditions, underwater photography tips and common and unusual marine life present. You'll also find practical logistical information and coverage on topside activities and attractions, sections on diving health and safety, plus listings for diving services, live-aboards, dive resorts and tourist offices.

LONELY PLANET

Guides by Region

L onely Planet is known worldwide for publishing practical, reliable and no-nonsense travel information in our guides and on our Web site. The Lonely Planet list covers just about every accessible part of the world. Currently there are thirteen series: travel guides, shoestring guides, walking guides, city guides, phrasebooks, audio packs, city maps, travel atlases, diving & snorkeling guides, restaurant guides, first-time travel guides, healthy travel and travel literature.

AFRICA Africa on a shoestring ● Africa – the South ● Arabic (Egyptian) phrasebook ● Arabic (Moroccan) phrasebook ● Cairo ● Cape Town ● Cape Town city map● Central Africa ● East Africa ● Egypt ● Egypt travel atlas ● Ethiopian (Amharic) phrasebook ● The Gambia & Senegal ● Healthy Travel Africa ● Kenya ● Kenya travel atlas ● Malawi, Mozambique & Zambia ● Morocco ● North Africa ● South Africa, Lesotho & Swaziland ● South Africa, Lesotho & Swaziland travel atlas ● Swahili phrasebook ● Tanzania, Zanzibar & Pemba ● Trekking in East Africa ● Tunisia ● West Africa ● Zimbabwe, Botswana & Namibia ● Zimbabwe, Botswana & Namibia travel atlas
Travel Literature: The Rainbird: A Central African Journey ● Songs to an African Sunset: A Zimbabwean Story ● Mali Blues: Traveling to an African Beat

AUSTRALIA & THE PACIFIC Auckland ● Australia ● Australian phrasebook ● Bushwalking in Australia ● Bushwalking in Papua New Guinea ● Fiji ● Fijian phrasebook ● Healthy Travel Australia, NZ and the Pacific ● Islands of Australia's Great Barrier Reef ● Melbourne ● Melbourne city map ● Micronesia ● New Caledonia ● New South Wales & the ACT ● New Zealand ● Northern Territory ● Outback Australia ● Out To Eat – Melbourne ● Out to Eat – Sydney ● Papua New Guinea ● Pidgin phrasebook ● Queensland ● Rarotonga & the Cook Islands ● Samoa ● Solomon Islands ● South Australia ● South Pacific Languages phrasebook ● Sydney ● Sydney city map ● Sydney Condensed ● Tahiti & French Polynesia ● Tasmania ● Tonga ● Tramping in New Zealand ● Vanuatu ● Victoria ● Western Australia
Travel Literature: Islands in the Clouds ● Kiwi Tracks: A New Zealand Journey ● Sean & David's Long Drive

CENTRAL AMERICA & THE CARIBBEAN Bahamas, Turks & Caicos ● Bermuda ● Central America on a shoestring ● Costa Rica ● Cuba ● Dominican Republic & Haiti ● Eastern Caribbean ● Guatemala, Belize & Yucatán: La Ruta Maya ● Jamaica ● Mexico ● Mexico City ● Panama ● Puerto Rico
Travel Literature: Green Dreams: Travels in Central America

EUROPE Amsterdam ● Amsterdam city map ● Andalucía ● Austria ● Baltic States phrasebook ● Barcelona ● Berlin ● Berlin city map ● Britain ● British phrasebook ● Brussels, Bruges & Antwerp ● Budapest city map ● Canary Islands ● Central Europe ● Central Europe phrasebook ● Corsica ● Croatia ● Czech & Slovak Republics ● Denmark ● Dublin ● Eastern Europe ● Eastern Europe phrasebook ● Edinburgh ● Estonia, Latvia & Lithuania ● Europe on a shoestring ● Finland ● France ● French phrasebook ● Germany ● German phrasebook ● Greece ● Greek Islands ● Greek phrasebook ● Hungary ● Iceland, Greenland & the Faroe Islands ● Ireland ● Italian phrasebook ● Italy ● Krakow ● Lisbon ● London ● London city map ● London Condensed ● Mediterranean Europe ● Mediterranean Europe phrasebook ● Norway ● Paris ● Paris city map ● Poland ● Portugal ● Portugal travel atlas ● Prague ● Prague city map ● Provence & the Côte d'Azur ● Romania & Moldova ● Rome ● Russia, Ukraine & Belarus ● Russian phrasebook ● Scandinavian & Baltic Europe ● Scandinavian Europe phrasebook ● Scotland ● Slovenia ● Spain ● Spanish phrasebook ● St Petersburg ● Switzerland ● Trekking in Spain ● Ukrainian phrasebook ● Vienna ● Walking in Britain ● Walking in Ireland ● Walking in Italy ● Walking in Spain ● Walking in Switzerland ● Western Europe ● Western Europe phrasebook
Travel Literature: The Olive Grove: Travels in Greece

INDIAN SUBCONTINENT Bangladesh ● Bengali phrasebook ● Bhutan ● Delhi ● Goa ● Hindi & Urdu phrasebook ● India ● India & Bangladesh travel atlas ● Indian Himalaya ● Karakoram Highway ● Kerala ● Mumbai (Bombay) ● Nepal ● Nepali phrasebook ● Pakistan ● Rajasthan ● Read This First: Asia & India ● South India ● Sri Lanka ● Sri Lanka phrasebook ● Trekking in the Indian Himalaya ● Trekking in the Karakoram & Hindukush ● Trekking in the Nepal Himalaya
Travel Literature: In Rajasthan ● Shopping for Buddhas

LONELY PLANET

Mail Order

Lonely Planet products are distributed worldwide. They are also available by mail order from Lonely Planet, so if you have difficulty finding a title please write to us. North and South American residents should write to 150 Linden St, Oakland, CA 94607, USA; European and African residents should write to 10a Spring Place, London NW5 3BH, UK; and residents of other countries to PO Box 617, Hawthorn, Victoria 3122, Australia.

ISLANDS OF THE INDIAN OCEAN Madagascar & Comoros • Maldives • Mauritius, Réunion & Seychelles

MIDDLE EAST & CENTRAL ASIA Arab Gulf States • Central Asia • Central Asia phrasebook • Hebrew phrasebook • Iran • Israel & the Palestinian Territories • Israel & the Palestinian Territories travel atlas • Istanbul • Istanbul to Cairo • Jerusalem • Jordan & Syria • Jordan, Syria & Lebanon travel atlas • Lebanon • Middle East on a shoestring • Syria • Turkey • Turkey travel atlas • Turkish phrasebook • Yemen
Travel Literature: The Gates of Damascus • Kingdom of the Film Stars: Journey into Jordan

NORTH AMERICA Alaska • Backpacking in Alaska • Baja California • California & Nevada • Canada • Chicago • Chicago city map • Deep South • Florida • Hawaii • Honolulu • Las Vegas • Los Angeles • Miami • New England • New Orleans • New York City • New York city map • New York, New Jersey & Pennsylvania • Pacific Northwest USA • Puerto Rico • Rocky Mountain • San Francisco • San Francisco city map • Seattle • Southwest USA • Texas • USA • USA phrasebook • Vancouver • Washington, DC & the Capital Region • Washington DC city map
Travel Literature: Drive Thru America

NORTH-EAST ASIA Beijing • Cantonese phrasebook • China • Hong Kong • Hong Kong city map • Hong Kong, Macau & Guangzhou • Japan • Japanese phrasebook • Japanese audio pack • Korea • Korean phrasebook • Kyoto • Mandarin phrasebook • Mongolia • Mongolian phrasebook • North-East Asia on a shoestring • Seoul • South-West China • Taiwan • Tibet • Tibetan phrasebook • Tokyo
Travel Literature: Lost Japan

SOUTH AMERICA Argentina, Uruguay & Paraguay • Bolivia • Brazil • Brazilian phrasebook • Buenos Aires • Chile & Easter Island • Chile & Easter Island travel atlas • Colombia • Ecuador & the Galapagos Islands • Healthy Travel Central & South America • Latin American Spanish phrasebook • Peru • Quechua phrasebook • Rio de Janeiro • Rio de Janeiro city map • South America on a shoestring • Trekking in the Patagonian Andes • Venezuela
Travel Literature: Full Circle: A South American Journey

SOUTH-EAST ASIA Bali & Lombok • Bangkok • Bangkok city map • Burmese phrasebook • Cambodia • Hanoi • Healthy Travel Asia & India • Hill Tribes phrasebook • Ho Chi Minh City • Indonesia • Indonesia's Eastern Islands • Indonesian phrasebook • Indonesian audio pack • Jakarta • Java • Laos • Lao phrasebook • Laos travel atlas • Malay phrasebook • Malaysia, Singapore & Brunei • Myanmar (Burma) • Philippines • Pilipino (Tagalog) phrasebook • Singapore • South-East Asia on a shoestring • South-East Asia phrasebook • Thailand • Thailand's Islands & Beaches • Thailand travel atlas • Thai phrasebook • Thai audio pack • Vietnam • Vietnamese phrasebook • Vietnam travel atlas

ALSO AVAILABLE: Antarctica • The Arctic • Brief Encounters: Stories of Love, Sex & Travel • Chasing Rickshaws • Lonely Planet Unpacked • Not the Only Planet: Travel Stories from Science Fiction • Sacred India • Travel with Children • Traveller's Tales

FREE Lonely Planet Newsletters

We love hearing from you and think you'd like to hear from us.

Planet Talk

Our FREE quarterly printed newsletter is full of tips from travellers and anecdotes from Lonely Planet guidebook authors. Every issue is packed with up-to-date travel news and advice, and includes:

- a postcard from Lonely Planet co-founder Tony Wheeler
- a swag of mail from travellers
- a look at life on the road through the eyes of a Lonely Planet author
- topical health advice
- prizes for the best travel yarn
- news about forthcoming Lonely Planet events
- a complete list of Lonely Planet books and other titles

To join our mailing list, residents of the UK, Europe and Africa can email us at go@lonelyplanet.co.uk; residents of North and South America can email us at info@lonelyplanet.com; the rest of the world can email us at talk2us@lonelyplanet.com.au, or contact any Lonely Planet office.

Comet

Our FREE monthly email newsletter brings you all the latest travel news, features, interviews, competitions, destination ideas, travellers' tips & tales, Q&As, raging debates and related links. Find out what's new on the Lonely Planet Web site and which books are about to hit the shelves.

Subscribe from your desktop: www.lonelyplanet.com/comet

Index

Text

Boxed Text

MAP LEGEND

CITY ROUTES

≡Freeway≡ .... Freeway	==== .... Unsealed Road
⁻Highway⁻ .... Primary Road	━⇒━ .... One Way Street
⁻Road⁻ ...... Secondary Road	═══ .... Pedestrian Street
⁻Street⁻ .... Street	⊓⊓⊓⊓⊓ .... Stepped Street
⁻Lane⁻ .... Lane	⇒══ .... Tunnel
═══ .... On/Off Ramp	═══ .... Footbridge

REGIONAL ROUTES

.... Tollway, Freeway
.... Primary Road
.... Secondary Road
.... Minor Road

BOUNDARIES

━·━·━ .... International
━━━ .... State
━ ━ ━ .... Disputed
◆━━ .... Fortified Wall

HYDROGRAPHY

～～ .... River, Creek	⬭ ⬭ .. Dry Lake; Salt Lake
━·━·━ .... Canal	⊙ ～ .... Spring; Rapids
⬭ .... Lake	◉ ┿⚟ .... Waterfalls

TRANSPORT ROUTES & STATIONS

┝━O ....Train	----🗗 .... Ferry
┝+++-. Underground Train	------ .... Walking Trail
━M━ ....Metro	········ .... Walking Tour
━━━━━ ....Tramway	▨▨ .... Path
┝━┈┈━ .. Cable Car, Chairlift	━━━ .... Pier or Jetty

AREA FEATURES

▬▬ ....Building	▨ .... Market	🦶 .... Beach	▨ .... Campus
❀ ....Park, Gardens	⬭ .... Sports Ground	+++ .... Cemetery	⌐_L .... Plaza

POPULATION SYMBOLS

✪ **CAPITAL** .... National Capital	● **CITY** .... City	● Village .... Village	▨ .... Urban Area
◉ **CAPITAL** .... State Capital	○ **Town** .... Town		

MAP SYMBOLS

♠ .... Place to Stay	▼ .... Place to Eat	● .... Point of Interest

✈	.... Airport	⛴	.... Ferry	☪	.... Mosque	✉	.... Post Office
⬛	.. Archaeological Site	🏰	.... Fort	▲	.... Mountain	▣	.... Pub or Bar
❸	.... Bank	⚓	.... Fountain	⌒	... Mountain Range	⬛	... Shopping Centre
▣	.... Bus Terminal	⊕	...... Hospital	⬚	.... Museum	☎	.... Telephone
⌂	.... Cave	ⓐ	.. Internet Cafe	🦜	... National Park	❶	.. Tourist Information
▬ ✝	.... Church	✳	...... Lookout	P	.... Parking		
▤	.... Cinema	▲	.... Monument	✚	.... Police Station		

Note: not all symbols displayed above appear in this book

LONELY PLANET OFFICES

Australia
PO Box 617, Hawthorn, Victoria 3122
☎ 03 9819 1877 fax 03 9819 6459
email: talk2us@lonelyplanet.com.au

UK
10a Spring Place, London NW5 3BH
☎ 020 7428 4800 fax 020 7428 4828
email: go@lonelyplanet.co.uk

USA
150 Linden St, Oakland, CA 94607
☎ 510 893 8555 TOLL FREE: 800 275 8555
fax 510 893 8572
email: info@lonelyplanet.com

France
1 rue du Dahomey, 75011 Paris
☎ 01 55 25 33 00 fax 01 55 25 33 01
email: bip@lonelyplanet.fr
www.lonelyplanet.fr

World Wide Web: www.lonelyplanet.com *or* AOL keyword: lp
Lonely Planet Images: lpi@lonelyplanet.com.au